The Politics of Fear

THE
POLITICS
OF FEAR

Joseph R. McCarthy and the Senate

Second edition, with a new introduction

ROBERT GRIFFITH

The University of Massachusetts Press

Amherst, 1987

Copyright © 1970 by Robert Griffith
Introduction to the Second Edition © 1987 by Robert Griffith
All rights reserved
Printed in the United States of America

Library of Congress Cataloging-in-Publication Data

Griffith, Robert, 1940–
The politics of fear.

Bibliography: p.
Includes index.
1. McCarthy, Joseph, 1908–1957. 2. Legislators—United States—Biography.
3. United States. Congress. Senate—Biography. 4. Anti-communist move-
ments—United States—Biography. 5. United States—Politics and govern-
ment—1945–1953.
I. Title.
E748.M143G7 1987   973.918'092'4   87-13766
ISBN 0-87023-554-0 (alk. paper)
ISBN 0-87023-555-9 (pbk. : alk. paper)

British Library Cataloguing in Publication Data are available

For Barbara

CONTENTS

INTRODUCTION TO THE
SECOND EDITION

Two Decades of Scholarship on the
Politics of Anti-Communism

I completed the first draft of *The Politics of Fear* twenty years ago as a doctoral dissertation at the University of Wisconsin, Madison. At the time, Americans were in the midst of a great debate, not just over Vietnam and the Cold War, but over the very character of American politics and society as well. One important part of that debate, though I did not then fully understand it, was the attempt by historians like myself to rethink the postwar politics of anti-communism—to reexamine the rise of the Cold War, the emergence of Joe McCarthy, and the impact of what came to be called "McCarthyism" on American politics and culture. The world, of course, has changed a lot since then; certainly I have. I know, or at least hope I know, a great deal more than I did then. Nevertheless, I have resisted the temptation to rewrite the book or tailor it to current intellectual fashions. In part, this is because of the immodest notion that, two decades later, it still stands up fairly well. In part, too, it is because like other artifacts of the past it possesses a sort of integrity that ought to be respected, even by its author. What I would like to do instead is to discuss some of the many books on the politics of anti-communism that have appeared *since* 1967, and to suggest how they have affected my own thinking about McCarthy and McCarthyism.

In 1967, most accounts of McCarthy and McCarthyism were

dominated by two themes: the portrayal of anti-communism as a mass movement of the new "radical right" and the depiction of McCarthy as its charismatic leader. The first of these concepts, popularized by Daniel Bell and other contributors to *The New American Right* (1955), described McCarthyism as the forerunner of an American "totalitarianism," a populistic, "pseudo-conservative" revolt against modernization and the nation's modern, elite-managed institutions.[1] The second, and corollary, concept was that McCarthy himself was an extraordinary demagogue with a unique talent for probing "the dark reaches of the American mind" and galvanizing the masses into action outside the boundaries of conventional social and political institutions.[2] Both of these themes were in turn part of a larger orthodox historiography that depicted Harry Truman and other liberals as embattled defenders of a "vital center," struggling even-handedly with the menace of the Soviet Union abroad and the rising tide of McCarthyism at home.

The more I read and studied the politics of McCarthy's sudden rise, however, the more I began to question these interpretations. What struck me most forcefully about McCarthy was not the extra-

---

[1] See Daniel Bell, ed., *The New American Right* (New York: Criterion Books, 1955), and its revised edition, *The Radical Right* (Garden City, N.Y.: Doubleday, 1963). Contributors to the original edition included Bell, Richard Hofstadter, David Riesman, Nathan Glazer, Peter Viereck, Talcott Parsons, and Seymour Martin Lipset. See also their individual publications, especially Hofstadter, *The Paranoid Style in American Politics and Other Essays* (New York: Knopf, 1965); Bell, *The End of Ideology: On the Exhaustion of Political Ideas in the Fifties* (New York: Free Press, 1962); and Peter Viereck, *Shame and Glory of the Intellectuals: Babbitt Jr. vs the Rediscovery of Values* (Boston: Beacon Press, 1953). Shaken by the rise of fascism and communism and deeply disillusioned by what they thought were the consequences of popular democracy, these "cold war" intellectuals distrusted popular rule and hoped that America's conservative, elite-managed institutions would serve as a bulwark against the dangers of popular passion.

[2] For the portrait of McCarthy as a charismatic leader, see especially Richard Rovere's deftly written *New Yorker* profile, subsequently published as *Senator Joe McCarthy* (New York: Harcourt, Brace and Co., 1959). McCarthy, Rovere later wrote, was "the most gifted demagogue in American history." The image of McCarthy as a charismatic leader, moreover, has continued to shape most popular accounts of the senator's life. See, for example, Fred Cook, *The Nightmare Decade: The Life and Times of Joe McCarthy* (New York: Random House, 1971), and Lately Thomas, *When Even Angels Wept: The Senator Joe McCarthy Affair—A Story Without a Hero* (New York: William Morrow, 1973).

ordinary nature of his character and talents, but the very ordinary circumstances of his ascendancy. Distrusting most "great men" theories, I saw in Joe McCarthy the creature of America's postwar politics, not its creator. Nor, hard as I searched, could I discover much evidence for a new, mass politics of the radical right. Indeed, the more I studied the sources of McCarthy's power, the more I found a thoroughly conventional politics rooted in political parties and interest groups.

My own thinking on these issues was deeply influenced by Michael Paul Rogin's work, *The Intellectuals and McCarthy: The Radical Specter,* which appeared after I had completed my dissertation but before it was published.[3] Rogin argued that McCarthyism, unlike populism to which it had been frequently compared, was never really a mass movement. It neither split apart existing coalitions nor created a new mass basis for politics. Instead, it was the product of the actions and inactions of conservative and liberal elites—indeed of precisely those groups to whom Bell and the radical right theorists had turned for the defense of liberty and order.

The Intellectuals and McCarthy provided an important theoretical context for my work on McCarthy and the Senate, which first appeared in 1970. In it I sought to show how a fairly conventional politics, operating through conventional partisan alignments and established political institutions, helped to create and sustain McCarthy's power and notoriety. In particular, I emphasized the conservative and mostly Republican sources of postwar anti-communism, McCarthy's relatively late emergence on the scene, and the failure of political leaders, both Republican and Democratic, to restrain him.[4]

[3] Rogin, *The Intellectuals and McCarthy: The Radical Specter* (Cambridge: MIT Press, 1967). Rogin's book was itself part of a broad challenge to modern "pluralism," the liberal political theory that dominated the study of American politics in the 1950s and 1960s. Pluralism, in Rogin's view, offered both a descriptive and *prescriptive* view of American politics that centered on elite-managed interest groups. Politics, in this analysis, was the process through which various elites sought to advance the interests of their groups, a process that required an atmosphere of compromise and civility made possible in part by the insularity of leaders from their constituents. Mass politics, in the pluralist view, threatened the orderly operation of politics through the introduction of emotionalism, inflexibility, and unreasonableness.

[4] Nelson Polsby stressed the Republican origins of McCarthyism in his early

Conventional conservative politics, however, was but part of the dynamic that produced McCarthyism, as Athan Theoharis soon made clear in *Seeds of Repression: Harry S. Truman and the Origin of McCarthyism* (1971). Strongly influenced by the new revisionist historiography of the Cold War, Theoharis argued that McCarthyism was not only "a logical extension of traditional conservative politics," but was also a function of the Cold War and of the rhetoric used to sustain it. The success of conservatives, and in particular the Republican right, was made possible by the dramatic changes that took place in the climate of American politics between 1945 and 1950—changes that Theoharis argued were in large measure the product of the Truman Administration. Truman's militantly anti-Communist rhetoric, with its stress on American innocence, Soviet depravity, and the need for confrontation with communism, Theoharis insisted, contributed to a new political environment that narrowed the arena of legitimate political debate and sharply reduced the flexibility of American foreign policy. The administration's conservative critics, he concluded, were faithful to Truman's own assumptions when they denounced the Yalta Conference, blamed the administration for "losing" China, and demanded total victory in Korea. In a similar manner, the Truman Administration legitimized red-baiting at home by the institution of a federal loyalty–security program, which applied sweeping standards to all government employees, not just those in sensitive positions, and by the promulgation of the attorney general's list, which, based on the concept of guilt by association, rapidly became the most widely used litmus for "subversive tendencies."[5]

---

and provocative critique of the radical right thesis, "Toward an Explanation of McCarthyism," *Political Studies* (October 1960). See also Earl Latham, *The Communist Controversy in Washington: From the New Deal to McCarthy* (Cambridge: Harvard University Press, 1966).

[5] Theoharis, *Seeds of Repression: Harry S. Truman and the Origins of McCarthyism* (New York: Quadrangle, 1971); see also his *Yalta Myths: An Issue in U.S. Politics, 1945–1955* (Columbia: University of Missouri Press, 1970). Richard Freeland reached very similar conclusions in *The Truman Doctrine and the Origins of McCarthyism: Foreign Policy, Domestic Politics, and Internal Security, 1946–1948* (New York: Knopf, 1972). Theoharis's and Freeland's work contrasted sharply with Alan Harper's earlier book, *The Politics of Loyalty: The White House and the Communist Issue, 1946–1952* (Westport, Conn: Greenwood Press, 1969), which continued to depict Truman as an embattled champion of civil liberties.

The relationship between foreign policy and domestic politics, of course, was complex and multidimensional. Neither Truman nor his advisers were free actors, nor was it the Truman Administration alone that shaped the new cold war political culture. The Cold War itself, real conflicts of interest exacerbated by decades of distrust and misunderstanding, produced a mirrored dynamic in which hostile act begat hostile act. Escalating international conflict, moreover, reinforced and in turn was reinforced by the rhythms of American politics. Both the Truman Administration's articulation of goals and its choice of diplomatic tactics were thus dictated at least in part by the growing power of conservatives, including important conservative figures within the administration itself. Indeed, it is easy to forget that in 1946, even as Truman and his advisers laid the foundations for the new diplomacy of confrontation with Russia, Republican critics were attacking the administration for being "soft on communism." The relationship between Truman and his adversaries, and in a larger sense between Democrats and Republican conservatives, was thus reciprocal. If Clark Clifford could boast in 1947 that the administration had "adroitly stolen" the anti-Communist issue from the G.O.P., by 1950, following the fall of China, the detonation of the Russian A-bomb, and the conviction of Alger Hiss, the Republicans were once again on the offensive. The emergence of Joe McCarthy, as I had sought to show in *The Politics of Fear*, was the natural result of this reciprocity. The work of Theoharis and other revisionists, however, exerted a strong influence on my own thinking which would be reflected in my subsequent writings on McCarthyism and the Cold War.[6]

By the early 1970s, many other historians had also begun to investigate the politics of postwar anti-communism, and in 1974 Athan Theoharis and I edited a collection of the new scholarship entitled *The Specter: Original Essays on the Cold War and the Origins of McCarthyism*.[7] Although the contributors to *The Specter* shared no single or uniform interpretive standard, most of their

[6] See especially Griffith, "The Politics of Anti-Communism: A Review Article," *Wisconsin Magazine of History* 54 (Summer 1971): 299–308; "Truman and the Historians: The Reconstruction of Postwar American History," ibid. 59 (Autumn 1975): 20–50; and "American Politics and the Origins of McCarthyism," in *The Specter: Original Essays on the Cold War and the Origins of McCarthyism*, ed. Griffith and Theoharis (New York: Franklin Watts, 1974), pp. 2-17.

[7] Griffith and Theoharis, *The Specter.*

essays nevertheless reinforced our critical analysis of McCarthyism as a product of the politics of national elites and interest
groups, and of the reciprocal dynamics of postwar conservatism
and the Cold War. These essays also served to identify many of the
major themes that would shape scholarship on the McCarthy era in
the next decade, during which historians, including many of the
original contributors to *The Specter,* would produce a rich and detailed literature on the politics of anti-communism.

Some of these studies, most notably Richard Fried's *Men Against
McCarthy,* continued to explore the ways in which Congress pro-
vided an institutional context for McCarthy and McCarthyism.[8]
Far more scholars focused on the executive branch, however, and
especially on the "national security bureaucracy," that constellation
of agencies that originated or expanded with the Cold War—the
FBI, the CIA, the NSA, the military intelligence branches. In *Cold
War Political Justice,* for example, Michael Belknap explored the
Justice Department's prosecution of American Communist leaders,[9]
while Athan Theoharis, in *Spying on Americans,* showed how J.
Edgar Hoover and the FBI had manipulated successive presidents in
efforts to both shape and control the politics of anti-communism.[10]

Still other scholars focused on what might be called the "infrastructure" of McCarthyism, the network of politicians, government officials, businessmen, lobbyists, and others who created and

[8] Richard Fried, *Men Against McCarthy* (New York: Columbia University
Press, 1976). See also William Tanner and Robert Griffith, "Legislative Politics
and 'McCarthyism': The Internal Security Act of 1950," in *The Specter,* pp.
172–89; Richard Fried, "Electoral Politics and McCarthyism: The 1950
Campaign," in ibid, pp. 190–223; and Mary S. McAuliffe, "Liberals and the
Communist Control Act of 1954," *Journal of American History* 63 (September
1976): 351–67.

[9] Belknap, *Cold War Political Justice: The Smith Act, the Communist Party
and American Civil Liberties* (Westport, Conn: Greenwood Press, 1977).
Peter L. Steinberg retraces much of the same ground in *The Great "Red
Menace": United States Prosecution of American Communists, 1947–1952*
(Westport, Conn.: Greenwood Press, 1984).

[10] Theoharis, *Spying on Americans: Political Surveillance from Hoover to
the Huston Plan* (Philadelphia: Temple University Press, 1978). Also see
Frank J. Donner, *The Age of Surveillance: The Aims and Methods of
America's Political Intelligence System* (New York: Knopf, 1981). The Theoharis and Donner books were among a large number of critical studies published in the wake of Watergate and the Church Committee's investigation of
illegal intelligence activities by the FBI, the CIA, and other national security
agencies.

sustained the new politics of anti-communism. Peter Irons, for example, showed in *The Specter* how the anti-labor, anti–New Deal crusade of the United States Chamber of Commerce contributed to the rise of domestic anti-communism. Indeed, the Chamber's activities were but part of a much larger effort by business organizations to refashion the political climate of postwar America, an effort that made an important contribution to the rise of McCarthyism.[11] Similarly, Donald Crosby explored the response of Catholic Church leaders to McCarthy.[12] Still others sought to examine the impact of McCarthyism at state and local levels, exploring ways in which state politics both reflected and shaped the new politics of the Cold War era.[13] There has been surprisingly

[11] Irons, "American Business and the Origins of McCarthyism," *The Specter*, pp. 72–89. Although I have touched briefly on this in "The Selling of America: The Advertising Council and American Politics, 1942–1960," *Business History Review* 57 (Autumn 1983), and in "Forging America's Postwar Order: Domestic Politics and Political Economy in the Age of Truman" (forthcoming in the Proceedings of the Harry S. Truman Centennial Symposium, Woodrow Wilson International Center for Scholars, Smithsonian Institution), much, much more work needs to be done on this important topic.

[12] Crosby, "The Politics of Religion," *The Specter*, pp. 18–39; *God, Church, and Flag: Senator Joseph R. McCarthy and the Catholic Church* (Chapel Hill: University of North Carolina Press, 1978). Crosby did not fully explore the broader issue of Catholic anti-communism, however, or the ways in which church leaders may have contributed to "McCarthyism" if not always to McCarthy. See also, Douglas P. Seaton et al., *Catholics and Radicals: The Association of Catholic Trade Unionists and the American Labor Movement* (Lewisburg, Pa.: Bucknell University Press, 1981).

[13] On California, for example, see Edward R. Long, "Earl Warren and the Politics of Anti-Communism," *Pacific Historical Review* 51 (1982): 51–70; and "Loyalty Oaths in California, 1947–1952: The Politics of Anti-Communism" (Ph.D. diss., University of California, San Diego, 1981); Ingrid Winther Scobie, "Jack B. Tenney: Molder of Anti-Communist Legislation in California, 1940–1949" (Ph.D. diss., University of Wisconsin, 1970); and Michael J. Heale, "Red Scare Politics: California's Campaign Against Un-American Activities, 1940–1970," *Journal of American Studies* 20 (1986): 5–32. On the Middle West, see especially James Truett Selcraig, *The Red Scare in the Midwest, 1945–1951: A State and Local Study* (Ann Arbor: University of Michigan Research Press, 1982); Michael O'Brien, *McCarthy and McCarthyism in Wisconsin* (Columbia: University of Missouri Press, 1980); Dale R. Sorenson, "The Anticommunist Consensus in Indiana, 1945–1968" (Ph.D. diss., University of Indiana, 1980); and Ronald W. Johnson, "The Communist Issue in Missouri, 1946–1956" (Ph.D. diss., University of Missouri, 1973); Gary Paul Henrickson, "Minnesota in the 'McCarthy' Period: 1946–1954" (Ph.D. diss., University of Minnesota, 1981). See also Thomas M. Holmes, "The Specter of

little study on the American Legion or the right-wing press, though both played important roles in generating the new anti-communism. Nor has much been written on the "little" Red Scare of the late 1930s, a prologue to McCarthyism which produced both the Smith Act and the House Un-American Activities Committee.[14]

Most studies of the Truman Administration have tended, perhaps unsurprisingly, to stress the initiatory role of the president and other executive leaders in fashioning the new politics. By contrast, most studies of the McCarthyite infrastructure have tended to emphasize the broader, often more conservative, interest-group origins of McCarthyism. One of the very best of the recent studies, Kenneth O'Reilly's *Hoover and the Un-Americans*, does both, skillfully exploring the relationship between Hoover and the FBI, on the one hand, and HUAC, the American Legion, the Chamber of Commerce, and other groups on the other.[15] The result is a persuasive account of the complex interaction of executive agency, congressional committee, and interest groups, what political scientists would call an "iron triangle," in creating and sustaining McCarthyism.

The resurgence of postwar conservatism has been traced in several broad accounts, including *The Republican Right Since 1945* by David Reinhard and *The Odyssey of the American Right* by Michael Miles.[16] Ronald Radosh's *Prophets on the Right* and Justus Doenecke's *Not To the Swift* are important studies of conservative foreign policy, though in their attempts to emphasize the Ameri-

---

Communism in Hawaii, 1947–1953" (Ph.D. diss., University of Hawaii, 1975); and, on Texas, Don E. Carleton, "A Crisis of Rapid Change: The Red Scare in Houston, 1945–1955" (Ph.D. diss., University of Houston, 1978).

[14] There is no modern study of the origins of HUAC. Most students still begin with August R. Ogden's badly dated *The Dies Committee* (Washington: Catholic University Press, 1945), and Walter Goodman's highly journalistic *The Committee: The Extraordinary Career of the House Committee on Un-American Activities* (New York: Farrar, Straus and Giroux, 1968). Nor have historians paid much attention to the prewar politics of anti-communism at the state level. An exception is Marvin E. Gettleman, "Rehearsal for McCarthyism: The New York State Rapp–Coudert Committee and Academic Freedom, 1940–41," a paper delivered at the annual meeting of the American Historical Association, 1982. A more thorough examination of prewar and wartime anti-communism, I believe, would reinforce the predominantly conservative sources of postwar politics.

[15] O'Reilly, *Hoover and the Un-Americans: The FBI, HUAC, and the Red Menace* (Philadelphia: Temple University Press, 1983).

can right's early opposition to cold war internationalism both authors tend to very badly underestimate its subsequent contributions to global interventionism.[17] John P. Diggins, *Up from Communism*, George Nash, *The Conservative Intellectual Movement in America Since 1945* (1976), and Ronald Lora, *Conservative Minds in America*, explore conservative thought in the postwar era.[18] While McCarthyism was thus obviously a product of the Cold War and of a new cold war politics shaped by both liberal and conservative elites, it was also, and this needs to be stressed, a politics firmly rooted in the powerful, conservative reaction to the New Deal, which began during the late 1930s and which, though partially adjourned during World War II, resumed in force after the war's end. Indeed, to underestimate this fact is to risk misunderstanding both McCarthyism and the Cold War.

If the resurgence of conservatism defined one aspect of the new postwar politics, the collapse of New Deal liberalism marked another. Older New Deal and popular front liberals were highly critical of the new diplomacy of containment and believed it possible to make common cause with Communists and other radicals at home. Newer "cold war" liberals supported both the new diplomacy and the purge of Communists from government, unions, and other voluntary associations. The overwhelming defeat of Henry Wallace in 1948 and the emergence of Americans for

[16] Reinhard, *The Republican Right Since 1945* (Lexington: University Press of Kentucky, 1983), and Miles, *The Odyssey of the American Right* (New York: Oxford University Press, 1980). The latter is one of the few accounts that attempt to trace continuities between anti–New Deal conservatism, McCarthyism, and the contemporary New Right. See also Robert Justin Goldstein, *Political Repression in Modern America* (Cambridge, Mass.: Schenkman, 1978), especially chap. 8. One of the very best biographies on early postwar conservatism is James T. Patterson's *Mr. Republican: A Biography of Robert A. Taft* (Boston: Houghton Mifflin, 1972). On the far right see Leo Ribuffo's recent *The Old Christian Right: The Protestant Far Right from the Great Depression to the Cold War* (Philadelphia: Temple University Press, 1983).

[17] Radosh, *Prophets on the Right: Profiles of Conservative Critics of American Globalism* (New York: Simon and Schuster, 1975), and Doenecke, *Not To the Swift: The Old Isolationists in the Cold War Era* (Lewisburg, Pa.: Bucknell University Press, 1979).

[18] Diggins, *Up from Communism: Conservative Odysseys in American Intellectual History* (New York: Harper and Row, 1975); Nash, *The Conservative Intellectual Movement in America Since 1945* (New York: Basic Books, 1976); Lora, *Conservative Minds in America* (Chicago: Rand McNally, 1971).

Democratic Action (ADA) marked the triumph of the new liberalism and the beginning of an era in which the difference between liberalism and conservatism steadily narrowed.[19] The same civil war erupted within the ranks of American labor, eventually leading to the expulsion from the CIO of eleven Communist-led unions and to a significantly weakened and more politically conservative labor movement.[20] American Communists, too, found themselves deeply divided by the Cold War and by the increasingly repressive poli-

[19] In *The Rise and Fall of the People's Century: Henry A. Wallace and American Liberalism* (New York: Free Press, 1973), Norman Markowitz critically traced the postwar collapse of popular front liberalism and the emergence of the new, cold war liberalism best epitomized by Americans for Democratic Action. Alonzo Hamby, in *Beyond the New Deal: Harry S. Truman and American Liberalism* (New York: Columbia University Press, 1973) defended both the Truman Administration and the new cold war liberalism as necessary and realistic responses to developments both at home and abroad. The best study of this topic, however, is Mary Sperling McAuliffe's *Crisis on the Left: Cold War Politics and American Liberals, 1947–1954* (Amherst: University of Massachusetts Press, 1978). See also Richard J. Walton, *Henry Wallace, Harry Truman, and the Cold War* (New York: Viking Press, 1976); Alan Yarnell, *Democrats and Progressives: The 1948 Presidential Election as a Test of Postwar Liberalism* (Berkeley: University of California Press, 1974); and F. Ross Peterson, *Prophet Without Honor: Glenn H. Taylor and the Fight for American Liberalism* (Lexington: University Press of Kentucky, 1974).

[20] Early accounts of labor and communism were highly polemical. See, for example, David J. Saposs, *Communism in American Unions* (New York: McGraw-Hill, 1959); and Max M. Kampelman, *The Communist Party vs. the C.I.O.: A Study in Power Politics* (New York: Praeger, 1957). More recent studies, on the other hand, have been far more balanced although by no means uniformly uncritical. See Harvey Levenstein, *Communism, Anti-Communism, and the C.I.O.* (Westport, Conn.: Greenwood Press, 1981); Roger Keeran, *The Communist Party and the United Auto Workers Unions* (Bloomington: University of Indiana Press, 1980); and Burt Cochran, *Labor and Communism: The Conflict that Shaped American Unions* (Princeton: Princeton University Press, 1977). See also Ronald Schatz's fine study, *The Electrical Workers: A History of Labor at General Electric and Westinghouse, 1923–1960* (Urbana: University of Illinois Press, 1983). For the response of labor unions to McCarthy himself, see David M. Oshinsky, *Senator Joseph McCarthy and the American Labor Movement* (Columbia: University of Missouri Press, 1976). For an especially valuable study which treats the anti-Communist purge only briefly, but which places it within the important context of postwar industrial relations, see Howell John Harris, *The Right to Manage: Industrial Relations Policies of American Business in the 1940s* (Madison: University of Wisconsin Press, 1982).

tics of the United States government. Unsure what the role of a
radical party in the United States should be and unable in the end
to detach themselves from the foreign policies of the Soviet Union,
they were abandoned by many of their former liberal allies who,
though ready to defend liberals *falsely* accused of being Communist, were increasingly unwilling to defend the rights of Communists themselves.[21] What is clear from all of this, of course, is that
the broad liberal coalition of the New Deal era was one of the first
and principal casualties of the new politics of anti-communism,
and that with its destruction the center of American politics and
political debate shifted decisively toward the right.

One of the most important consequences of the new anti-communism, of course, was the purge of thousands of government employees, educators, labor leaders, journalists, scientists, writers, and
entertainers and, perhaps more important, the intimidation of
hundreds of thousands more. It was a process in which, ironically,
McCarthy himself was for the most part only indirectly involved.
It began well before his sudden rise to notoriety and continued
well after his equally sudden demise. It included the institution

[21] Recent histories of American communism, while not uncritical, are far
more sympathetic and nuanced than the earlier, highly polemical accounts
published during the early cold war era. Among recent scholarly accounts see
especially Harvey E. Klehr, *The Heyday of American Communism* (New
York: Basic Books, 1984); Mark Naison, *Communists in Harlem During the
Depression* (Urbana: University of Illinois Press, 1983); Maurice Isserman,
*Which Side Were You On?: The American Communist Party During the
Second World War* (Middletown, Conn.: Wesleyan University Press, 1982);
and Paul Lyons, *Philadelphia Communists, 1936–1956* (Philadelphia: Temple
University Press, 1982). See also Joseph R. Starobin, *American Communism
in Crisis, 1943–1957* (Cambridge: Harvard University Press, 1972), a scholar-
ly account written by a former leader of the American CP. Among the volum-
inous memoir literature, see especially Vivian Gornick, *The Romance of
American Communism* (New York: Basic Books, 1977), as well as George
Charney, *A Long Journey* (Chicago: Quadrangle, 1968); John Williamson,
Dangerous Scot: The Life and Work of an American "Undesirable" (New
York: International Publishers, 1969); Al Richmond, *A Long View from the
Left: Memoirs of an American Revolutionary* (New York: Delta, 1972);
Jessica Mitford, *A Fine Old Conflict* (New York: Knopf, 1977); Peggy
Dennis, *The Autobiography of an American Communist: A Personal View of
a Political Life* (Westport, Conn.: Lawrence, Hill and Co., 1978); Harry
Haywood, *Black Bolshevik: Autobiography of an Afro-American Communist*
(Chicago: Liberator Press, 1978); Nell Painter, *The Narrative of Hosea Hud-
son: His Life as a Negro Communist in the South* (Cambridge: Harvard Uni-

of increasingly restrictive loyalty and security programs by the Truman and Eisenhower administrations, the spread of the black-list in Hollywood and New York, the dismissal of teachers for re-fusing to sign loyalty oaths or testify before congressional com-mittees, the expulsion of left-wing trade unionists, and the denial of security clearance to scientists, the most prominent of whom was J. Robert Oppenheimer.

There is a huge and still-growing literature on the purge, in-cluding many of the volumes already cited. There are literally dozens of books and memoirs, for example, on the impact of anti-communism on Hollywood, the best of which include Larry Ceplair and Steven Englund's *Inquisition in Hollywood* and Victor S. Navasky's *Naming Names*.[22] Edwin R. Bayley's *Joe McCarthy and the Press* is a fine account by a reporter who in his youth covered McCarthy for the *Milwaukee Journal*, though it is somewhat limited by its narrow focus on McCarthy alone and should be supplemented with James Aronson's lively if polemical *The Press and the Cold War*.[23] *Scoundrel Time*, Lillian Hellman's acid and controversial memoir on the impact of McCarthyism on arts and letters, re-fueled the literary wars of the McCarthy era, showing, I suppose, that, like the Bourbon monarchs, writers neither forget nor for-give.[24] The very best of the recent studies, Ellen Schrecker's *No*

versity Press, 1979); and Steve Nelson et al. *Steve Nelson: American Radical* (Pittsburg: University of Pittsburg Press, 1981).

[22] Ceplair and Englund, *The Inquisition in Hollywood: Politics in the Film Community, 1930–1960* (Garden City, N.Y.: Doubleday, 1980); Navasky, *Naming Names* (New York: Viking, 1980).

[23] Bayley, *Joe McCarthy and the Press* (New York: Pantheon, 1981); Aronson, *The Press and the Cold War* (Indianapolis: Bobbs-Merrill, 1970). See also David Halberstam's massive chronicle, *The Powers That Be* (New York: Knopf, 1979). Erik Barnouw, *A History of Broadcasting in the United States*, Vol. 3: *The Image Empire* (New York: Oxford University Press, 1970) and Barnouw, *Tube of Plenty: The Evolution of Television* (New York: Oxford University Press) remain the standard, if inadequate, references for television and the Cold War. Quite a bit has been written on Edward R. Murrow's cele-brated confrontation with McCarthy, most of which exaggerates the signifi-cance of the encounter. See, for example, Alexander Kendrick, *Prime Time: The Life of Edward R. Murrow* (Boston: Little, Brown, 1969) and Halber-stam, *The Powers That Be*. Unfortunately, John Coagley's very badly dated *Report on Blacklisting*, Vol. 2: *Radio-Television* (New York: Fund for the Republic, 1954), remains the best single source on the impact of McCarthyism on the broadcasting industry.

[24] Hellman, *Scoundrel Time* (Boston: Little, Brown, 1976).

Ivory Tower, explores the impact of McCarthyism on a handful of America's most prestigious universities. What is clear from Schrecker's account, and indeed this is the pattern revealed by almost every study of institutional response to McCarthyism, is that the faculty and administrations of America's best universities consistently placed institutional interests above academic freedom and collaborated, however reluctantly, with the new anti-Communist politics emanating from Washington.[25] Here, as elsewhere, the pluralist institutions that were supposed to protect civil liberty from popular hysteria served instead as instruments for repression. The broadest and most comprehensive study of the purge is David Caute's encyclopedic *The Great Fear,* which covers, as does no other single account, the great sweep of the purge and its impact on the lives of thousands of Americans.[26] Certainly no one who reads this and other recent studies can doubt the profound effect of the purge on American politics and culture.

Few issues of the McCarthy era continue to arouse more intense controversy than the celebrated case of Alger Hiss. At the time, conservatives, for whom Hiss embodied all that they abhorred, found it easy to credit charges that he was a Communist spy. Leftists who still identified with the radicalism of the thirties and the wartime policy of cooperation with Russia, on the other hand, insisted on his innocence. Opinion among the new cold war liberals was divided. Some, sensing that the attack on Hiss was an attack on themselves and the Truman Administration, at first dismissed the charges; others, however, soon embraced his guilt as part of their own transition to the new liberalism of the vital center. It is a testament to the continuity of our political passions that even today these divisions continue to shape responses to the case. Thus

[25] Schrecker, *No Ivory Tower: McCarthyism and the Universities* (New York: Oxford University Press, 1986). See also Jane Sanders, *Cold War on the Campus: Academic Freedom at the University of Washington, 1946–1964* (Seattle: University of Washington Press, 1979). Although it focuses on a private foundation and not an educational institution, Thomas C. Reeves, *Freedom and the Foundation: The Fund for the Republic in the Era of Mc-Carthyism* (New York: Knopf, 1969), remains a classic account of the limits of liberalism and dissent in the cold war era.

[26] Caute, *The Great Fear: The Anti-Communist Purge under Truman and Eisenhower* (New York: Simon and Schuster, 1978). See also Stanley Kutler, *The American Inquisition: Justice and Injustice in the Cold War* (New York: Hill and Wang, 1982). For the recent memoir of an individual inadvertently (and unknowingly) caught up in the toils of the federal loyalty–security pro-

when Allen Weinstein reopened the debate in 1978 with a long, densely detailed account that concluded that Chambers had told the truth, that Hiss had lied, and that the jury in the second trial "made no mistake in finding Alger Hiss guilty as charged," reactions followed predictable lines. Conservatives and some cold war liberals (many now calling themselves "neoconservatives") quickly and uncritically embraced Weinstein's conclusions; most of those on the left denounced them.[27] Although Weinstein's book was, I thought, tendentious and meanly argued, the case against Hiss was fairly damaging—not so much because of the new evidence, the significance of which I thought Weinstein greatly exaggerated, but because of the old evidence, especially the typewriter, that led to the 1950 conviction. Yet if the old evidence remained, so did the old nagging doubts concerning the credibility of Whittaker Chambers and the secret role played by the FBI. In the end, I remained unconvinced of Hiss's guilt *or* innocence.[28]

A very similar reaction followed the 1983 publication of *The Rosenberg File: A Search for the Truth* by Ronald Radosh and Joyce Milton. Though highly critical of the government's prosecution and of the double death sentence, Radosh and Milton nevertheless concluded that Julius Rosenberg managed an extensive espionage operation and that Ethel probably knew of and supported his actions.[29] Their conclusions, unsurprisingly, were hailed

---

gram, see Penn Kimball, *The File* (New York: Harcourt Brace Jovanovich, 1983).

[27] Weinstein, *Perjury: The Hiss-Chambers Case* (New York: Knopf, 1978). John Cabot Smith, *Alger Hiss: The True Story* (New York: Holt, Rinehart and Winston, 1976), reargued the case for Hiss's innocence, but offered little in the way of new or persuasive evidence. Tony Hiss, *Laughing Last* (Boston: Houghton, Mifflin, 1977), gave an intimate view of the Hiss family, but offered only oblique insights into the question of Hiss's guilt or innocence. For reaction to Weinstein's book, see especially Victor Navasky, "Weinstein, Hiss, and the Transformation of Historical Ambiguity into Cold War Verity"; Athan G. Theoharis, "Unanswered Questions: Chambers, Nixon, the FBI, and the Hiss Case"; and Kenneth O'Reilly, "Liberal Values, the Cold War, and American Intellectuals: The Trauma of the Alger Hiss Case, 1950–1978," all in *Beyond the Hiss Case: The FBI, Congress, and the Cold War*, ed. Athan Theoharis (Philadelphia: Temple University Press, 1982).

[28] See my "Perjury?" *Civil Liberties Review* (July/August, 1978): 64-71.

[29] Radosh and Milton, *The Rosenberg File: A Search for the Truth* (New York: Holt, Rinehart and Winston, 1983). For a moving account by the Rosenbergs' children, see Robert and Michael Meeropol, *We Are Your Sons:*

by conservatives and cold war liberals and denounced by leftists and the Rosenbergs' children. Here, too, I remained something of an agnostic. What puzzled me, I suppose, was the way in which both sides to the debate seemed to share the unstated assumption that somehow the legitimacy of McCarthyism turned on issues of guilt or innocence, thus reinforcing a political symbolism that was itself one of the principal products of the cold war era. McCarthyism, in my view, was a terribly, terribly destructive phenomenon, quite independent of whether Hiss or the Rosenbergs were guilty or innocent.

The most destructive consequences of the McCarthy era, however, were not individual, but collective, and must be measured less by the pain inflicted on individuals and their families in the 1950s than by the collective costs assessed to future generations. A product of the Cold War and the new global diplomacy, McCarthyism in turn reinforced the worst aspects of the new diplomacy. Nowhere was this better illustrated than by the course of United States policy in Asia, where the onslaughts of McCarthy, Nevada Senator Pat McCarran, and the China lobby virtually destroyed the Asia desk of the State Department and contributed not only to the new Cold War in the Pacific, but also to the hot wars in Korea and, later, Vietnam.[30] Indeed, one need but reflect on the recent history of the Reagan Administration to appreciate the degree to which the assumptions of the 1950s still shape our lives.

Joe McCarthy himself remains a somewhat elusive figure in much of the recent literature. From the outset he had been the creature of legends, spun by friends and foes alike, as well as of

---

The Legacy of Ethel and Julius Rosenberg, 2nd ed. (Urbana: University of Illinois Press, 1986); and, for the memoir of their co-defendant, Morton Sobell, On Doing Time (New York: Charles Scribner's Sons, 1974).

[30] E. J. Kahn, Jr., The China Hands: America's Foreign Service Officers and What Befell Them (New York: Viking, 1975). See also Gary May, China Scapegoat: The Diplomatic Ordeal of John Carter Vincent (Washington: New Republic Books, 1979); Lewis McCarroll Purifoy, Harry Truman's China Policy: McCarthyism and the Diplomacy of Hysteria, 1947-1951 (New York: Franklin Watts, 1976); John N. Thomas, The Institute of Pacific Relations: Asia Scholars and American Politics (Seattle: University of Washington Press, 1974); and Stanley D. Backrack, The Committee of One Million: "China Lobby" Politics, 1953–1971 (New York: Columbia University Press, 1976). Among the many memoirs by old China hands, see especially O. Edmund Clubb, The Witness and I (New York: Columbia University Press, 1974).

his own unique talent for self-invention. Like Jay Gatsby, he sprang from a "Platonic conception of himself." Until recently, moreover, most biographers simply repeated the assertions, both accurate and not, of contemporary accounts such as Jack Anderson and Ronald May's *McCarthy: The Man, The Senator, The "Ism."*[31] Most cold war scholars, on the other hand, intent on locating the sources of his sudden fame and notoriety in the larger dynamics of cold war politics, have been relatively uninterested in McCarthy himself. Indeed, in most of these accounts McCarthy fades into the background, his name occasionally invoked as a symbol of the era's discordant politics, but otherwise largely ignored. Two recent and very important exceptions to this tendency, however, are the full-length biographies written by Thomas C. Reeves and David M. Oshinsky.[32] Both books serve to clear away many of the rumors, exaggerations, and legends that surround McCarthy, and, in the absence of important new sources, they are likely to remain the definitive accounts of his life. If neither author fully disentangles the enigma of McCarthy's character—the reckless gambling, the repeated lying, the alcoholism, the vulnerability to injury and illness; if neither fully succeeds in linking McCarthy to his era—there is more life than times in both accounts—Reeves and Oshinsky have made, nevertheless, important contributions to our understanding of Joe McCarthy.

Two decades have thus produced an exhaustively researched, densely detailed, and finely nuanced account of the postwar politics of anti-communism. Although some sources remain closed to historians—McCarthy's own papers, for example, as well as still-classified files of the Federal Bureau of Investigation—most are now open. Although some topics remain to be more fully explored—the "little" Red Scare of the late 1930s, for example—most have attracted at least some attention. Although not all questions have been resolved—the guilt or innocence of Alger Hiss, the relative contributions to McCarthyism of the Truman administration and its conservative opponents—the main outlines of the era seem neverthe-

---

[31] Anderson and May, *McCarthy: The Man, The Senator, The "Ism"* (Boston: Beacon Press, 1952).

[32] Reeves, *The Life and Times of Joe McCarthy: A Biography* (New York: Stein and Day, 1982); and Oshinsky, *A Conspiracy So Immense: The World of Joe McCarthy* (New York: Free Press, 1983).

less well defined. The rise of McCarthy and of what came to be called McCarthyism were products of both the older rhythms of American politics and the newer dynamics of the Cold War. They were the products not of a mass politics of the radical right, but of a fairly conventional politics of politicians and interest groups. And their effects were amplified, not restrained, by the pluralist organization of American culture and society.

The limits of this literature are the limits common to most of our recent political history—conceptual orthodoxy, isolation from other subdisciplines, the tyranny of the "presidential synthesis," the tendency of graduate students (and not just graduate students) to explore narrow, seemingly discrete episodes and to ignore broader issues of synthesis and significance.[33] The challenge to future historians of the McCarthy era, I believe, is to explore more fully and systematically the relationship of the politics of anti-communism to the broader themes of American politics, diplomacy, political economy, and culture. How did the new anti-Communist politics connect, as both cause and effect, to the struggle over the character and direction of the New Deal state, the rise of the Cold War and its bureaucratic penumbra, the forging of a new political economy, the campaign to win American hearts and minds for the new diplomacy of protracted conflict, and the maintenance of a domestic order riven by divisions of class, race, and gender? When we have begun to answer these questions we also will have begun to understand more fully the politics of anti-communism and their role in the reconstruction of postwar America.

ROBERT GRIFFITH
Amherst, Massachusetts
March 1987

[33] Alan Brinkley, "Writing the History of Contemporary America: Dilemmas and Challenges," *Daedalus* 113 (Summer 1984). See also Thomas Bender, "Wholes and Parts: The Need for Synthesis in American History," *Journal of American History* 73 (June 1986), and William E. Leuchtenberg, "The Pertinence of Political History: Reflections on the Significance of the State in America," ibid. (December 1986).

PREFACE

It is now more than twenty years since Joe McCarthy's famous speech at Wheeling, West Virginia, nearly fifteen years since his censure by the United States Senate; yet many of the most important questions raised by that era of turmoil and controversy remain unanswered. How did McCarthy come to power? What was the source and nature of the influence he wielded over the nation's most powerful legislative assembly? Why did the members of that body acquiesce, for nearly five years, in his continued abuse of the democratic process? Beyond this, were the McCarthy years aberrational? Did they represent some malfunction in our political machinery, or were they the natural and inevitable byproduct of that system itself?

Joe McCarthy did not win national notoriety simply because of some chance remarks made at Wheeling, West Virginia, nor because of the conviction of Alger Hiss, nor even because of the cold war. He rose to power because of a political dynamic created during the late 1940s by a band of Republican partisans as they scrapped and clawed their way toward power. The broad issue of American policy toward Communist nations and the more specific issue of "communism in government" were, to be sure, made viable by the cold war, but they were made dynamic by these partisans for whom they represented success or a means to success. McCarthy's real triumph, both in 1950 and afterwards, lay in making himself a personal symbol of these issues. Once he had accomplished this, the task of dislodging or even restraining him became most complicated. He held a privileged position in American politics, and he was bold enough, audacious enough, perhaps even desperate enough, to exploit this privilege for five long years.

Because the United States Senate was the stage upon which Joe McCarthy performed, and because it was the focus of those political forces which ensured his continued success, it deserves special consideration. It did not serve this country well during those years. The conservative institutions of prerogative and precedent which should have protected the Senate from factiousness and turbulence became the instruments of McCarthy's worst abuses. Trapped by issues of its own creation and procedures of its own contrivance, the Senate failed to exercise those restraints necessary to halt McCarthy's excesses. This book is an attempt to describe that failure and to explain the individual and collective paralysis which overtook the American Senate in the first years of the mid-century.

Every endeavor of this sort is a collective enterprise. I am deeply indebted to the many journalists, scholars, librarians, and archivists without whose help this volume would not have been possible; and I regret that this debt can be repaid only in the depreciated currency of these acknowledgments. I do wish to thank the librarians and archivists of the following institutions: the Library of Congress, Columbia University and the New York Public Library, the University of Michigan, Syracuse University, the University of Maryland, the University of Tennessee, the University of Kentucky, the University of Nebraska, the University of Missouri, the State Historical Society of Nebraska, and the Ohio Historical Society. I should like particularly to thank Philip C. Brooks, Philip D. Lagerquist, and the staff of the Harry S. Truman Library; John E. Wickman and the staff of the Dwight D. Eisenhower Library; and Josephine L. Harper and the staff of the Manuscripts Division, State Historical Society of Wisconsin. I am grateful to Senator Arthur V. Watkins, who allowed me to see his private papers, and to Maurice Rosenblatt, who made available the voluminous files of the National Committee for an Effective Congress. I am also pleased to acknowledge the assistance of the American Philosophical Society.

I owe special debts of gratitude to the following: to E. David Cronon, who was a sympathetic adviser; to Charles C. Alexander, who was a good critic; to Vivian Ward and June Huff, who patiently typed the entire manuscript; to David P. Thelen, whose friendship and encouragement I dearly appreciate; to David Golden, for his kind and learned advice; and finally to my wife, Barbara, for so many reasons.

1

THE JUNIOR
SENATOR
FROM
WISCONSIN

AS SENATOR-ELECT JOSEPH R. McCarthy stepped down from the train at Union Station a cold, penetrating, December rain was falling on Washington. The capital was quieter than usual. The election was past, and it would be a month before the Republican Eightieth Congress convened. In the executive offices downtown there was considerable concern over the coal strike which John L. Lewis had called against the government-operated mines. Beyond this immediate crisis there seemed to be little thought or direction. For most of official Washington late 1946 was a time of confusion and uncertainty during which events, both here and abroad, were tending toward a future the main outlines of which were not yet visible.

The new senator from Wisconsin seemed to share few of these uncertainties. As soon as he had settled into his downtown hotel, he telephoned the White House and asked to see the president. His request was politely declined, with the suggestion that perhaps the senator might see President Truman when the new Congress met the following month.[1] Hesitating only momentarily, the senator then called a press conference to give his views on the coal strike. The way to settle the strike was to draft Lewis and his mine workers into the armed forces, he declared. Then, if the miners still refused to work, they could be court-martialed. "In wartime courts-martial," he added, "penalties range up to and including the death sentence."[2]

The proposal was radical, dramatic, probably unconstitutional, but hardly original. President Truman had suggested a similar solution for a railroad strike the previous spring and had been damned by liberals and conservatives alike. The newsmen were not impressed by the proposal as it was now being rehashed by the Senate's newest and youngest member, but they were struck by his audacity. "You're a new man here," declared one of them. "Why did you call a press conference?"[3]

If the junior senator from Wisconsin seemed just a little brash to these veteran newsmen, it was understandable. Joe McCarthy had come far and he had come fast, and boldness and audacity had been his helpmates. He had begun running early this race against himself, and in a special sense he would never stop.

BEGINNINGS

Joe McCarthy was born in 1908 on a small farm in northeastern Wisconsin. His father, Timothy, was a dour, hard-working Irish-American; his mother, Bridget, was a comfortable and kindly farm wife. His childhood was unexceptional—the rudiments of an elementary education in a small, one-room country school, hard work on his father's farm, Sunday Mass at St. Mary's in nearby Appleton. By most accounts he was a withdrawn and insecure child who shunned strangers and clung fearfully to his mother, and it was

[1] "Requests To See the President," Dec. 3, 1946, OF 3371, Harry S. Truman Papers, Truman Library, Independence, Mo.

[2] *Washington Post,* Dec. 4, 1946; *New York Times,* Dec. 6, 1946, p. 4.

[3] Jack Alexander, "The Senate's Remarkable Upstart," *Saturday Evening Post* 220 (Aug. 9, 1947): 57.

not without difficulty that he gradually adjusted to the great world which lay beyond the boundaries of the family farm.[4]

For a few years McCarthy worked around the farm. Then in the summer of 1929 he left home to manage a grocery store in nearby Manawa. This was a special year for McCarthy, and insofar as lives have precise turning points, this was probably his. He returned to school that autumn, and with the help of an obliging principal he rushed through the normal high school curriculum in one short year. In the meantime he matured from a shy, almost painfully awkward boy into a loud, amiable, and boisterously aggressive man. If there were still occasional glimmers of the old fear and insecurity, they were now masked by the fierce intensity and energy which he brought to every undertaking. He did nothing by half-measures. Both his work and play were marked by a relentless though sometimes misdirected competitiveness. There was even a forced quality in his demanding conviviality. "I never saw him when he seemed to be taking it easy," recalled one friend.[5]

In 1930 he entered Marquette University, a Jesuit-operated school in Milwaukee. He began in the school of engineering but soon switched to law. He graduated in 1935, was admitted to the Wisconsin bar, and began practice in Waupaca, another of the small country towns surrounding Appleton and Lake Winnebago. After a brief and unsuccessful apprenticeship, he was offered a position with Mike G. Eberlein, a prominent lawyer from nearby Shawano.

The association with Eberlein gave McCarthy security and a place in the community, but the older lawyer was strict and domineering and McCarthy was soon searching for new outlets for his great energy.[6] In August 1936 he was elected president of

[4] There is no authoritative study of McCarthy's early life. I have relied upon Jack Anderson and Ronald May, McCarthy: The Man, the Senator, the "Ism" (Boston, 1952), and upon Oliver Pilat and William V. Shannon, "Smear, Inc.: The One-Man Mob of Joe McCarthy," New York Post, Sept. 4–23, 1951. Of special help were the files of the National Committee for an Effective Congress, Washington, D. C. (hereafter cited as NCEC files).

[5] James M. Auer and Clark Kalvelage, "Joe McCarthy's School Days" (unpublished typescript, c. 1953), in the Manuscripts Division, State Historical Society of Wisconsin. Interview with George Kelley, Anderson and May notes, NCEC files.

[6] William T. Flarity, "Recollections of Joe McCarthy" (unpublished typescript, 1966), pp. 3-4, in possession of the author.

the district's Young Democratic Clubs, and that autumn he ran for district attorney on the Democratic ticket. His campaign was forceful and aggressive, and although his vote fell far short of the winning Progressive candidate's, he did manage to edge out the Republican nominee for second place.[7]

For the next few years McCarthy remained an obscure, small-town lawyer. Then in late 1938 he announced his candidacy for judge of the tenth circuit court. The incumbent was a veteran of twenty-four years on the bench, and although dissatisfaction with his court had been growing among lawyers in the area, no one foresaw his defeat, least of all by Joe McCarthy. But they had not reckoned with McCarthy's relentless energy and will power. Back and forth across the three-county area he drove in a battered white automobile, sometimes making speeches but more often talking to people. He supplemented these personal contacts with an extensive mailing campaign—first letters explaining his candidacy and then, just before the election, a deluge of postcards. Each card bore McCarthy's campaign slogan: "Justice Is Truth in Action." He won by more than 4,000 votes.[8]

McCarthy brought to the circuit court the same driving energy and the same casual disregard for established rules and precedents that by now characterized all his actions. Within a matter of months he disposed of a backlog of nearly 250 cases, a pace he maintained throughout his stay on the bench. Unhappily, his court was not as judicial as it was swift. In one famous case McCarthy voided an injunction on the grounds that the law on which the injunction was based would expire in six months. Then, when the state Supreme Court demanded the trial records for a review of the case, McCarthy replied that he had ordered parts of the transcript destroyed as "immaterial." The Wisconsin Supreme Court addressed itself to both points. On the first, it declared that when a court undertook to say that a law should not be enforced

[7] *Shawano County Journal,* Nov. 5, 1936.

[8] Ibid., Dec. 28, 1938, April 6, 1939; *Antigo Daily Journal,* April 5, 1939. Judge Werner's supporters later charged McCarthy with misrepresenting the judge's age and with violating the state corrupt-practices act, but their petition was dismissed. The age controversy probably originated with an error in the *Martindale-Hubbel Law Director.* See Sharon Coady, "The Wisconsin Press and Joseph McCarthy: A Case Study" (M.A. thesis, University of Wisconsin, 1965), pp. 26–32. The campaign is said to have been heavily financed by a close personal friend of McCarthy's. Confidential source.

it was usurping the legislative function. On the second point, it charged McCarthy with "highly improper" behavior in ordering the destruction of the trial notes. Later, McCarthy would also be accused of granting "quickie divorces" to his political supporters.[9] In 1942 McCarthy volunteered for the armed services. Waiving his judicial deferment, he applied for a commission in the Marine Corps and was sworn in on August 4, 1942.[10] In the summer of 1943 he joined American forces in the Pacific. Even here, however, his chief preoccupation seemed to be politics, and he quickly won a reputation among fellow officers as an "operator" and a "promoter." On one occasion he sat in the rear of a grounded dive bomber and fired off 4,700 rounds of ammunition, a publicity stunt which made the Associated Press wire. On another occasion he circulated the story that he had been wounded in action, a fiction his hometown newspaper solemnly printed.[11]

By early 1944 McCarthy had decided to run for Wisconsin's Republican senatorial nomination. At Bougainville, where he was serving as an air intelligence officer, he placarded trucks and jeeps with large signs reading "McCarthy for Senator," while back in Wisconsin his supporters began to lay the groundwork for a primary fight against Republican incumbent Alexander Wiley.[12] In July McCarthy secured a leave from the Marine Corps and came home to campaign. He stumped the state in his characteristically vigorous fashion, skirting a military regulation which forbade servicemen from speaking on political issues ("If I weren't in uniform, I would say. . . .") and ignoring an article in the Wisconsin constitution which prohibited members of the state

[9] State ex rel. Department of Agriculture v. McCarthy, 232 Wis. 258. Interview with Gordon Lappley, Anderson and May notes, NCEC files. Capital Times (Madison), Sept. 26, Oct. 29, 1946; Milwaukee Journal, Sept. 27, 28, 29, 1946.

[10] McCarthy to Major Saxon Holt, June 2, 1942, photostat in NCEC files.

[11] Captain Jack Caanan (USMC) to William T. Evjue, Dec. 1949, NCEC files; Appleton Post-Crescent, Nov. 15, 1943. McCarthy was injured; he hurt his leg during a "shellback" initiation as his ship crossed the equator. He was even decorated for it, which probably says more about the Marine Corps than it does about McCarthy. See Robert H. Fleming, Evening Star (Washington), June 13, 1952; Oliver Pilat and William V. Shannon, New York Post, Sept. 7, 1951; Anderson and May, McCarthy, pp. 60–63.

[12] Captain Jack Caanan (USMC) to William T. Evjue, Dec. 1949, NCEC files. Walter Melchior to Alexander Wiley, March 13, 1944, and R. H. Gehrke to Alexander Wiley, May 12, 1944, both in Personal Correspondence, box 16, Alexander Wiley Papers, State Historical Society of Wisconsin.

judiciary from holding any other public office during the term for which they were elected.[13] To McCarthy these were legal niceties —to be used when convenient, to be discarded when not. As some of Senator Wiley's supporters had predicted, McCarthy flooded the mails with campaign literature. He traded heavily on his rather brief military career (suddenly he was a "tail gunner" who had enlisted as a "buck private" and then risen from the ranks), and he worked hard to identify himself with his new party.[14]

Just when McCarthy became a Republican it is impossible to say. In 1936, when he ran for district attorney, he ran as a Democrat; and as a candidate for the circuit court he had needed to make no party declaration—the Wisconsin judiciary is at least nominally nonpartisan. His shift in party allegiance may have predated his decision to run for the Senate, but many regular Republicans remained suspicious. "This fellow was never active in the political activities of this county," complained one party chieftain, "and he has generally been considered a New Dealer." During the campaign McCarthy promised "job security for every man and woman" and "lasting peace throughout the world"—a tall order for any candidate, but an appeal couched nevertheless in the Rooseveltian fashion. "His support came from a good many Democrats and New Dealers who will not support you," wrote one of McCarthy's lieutenants to Wiley following the election. "They voted for him personally because they felt he is more of a Roosevelt supporter than otherwise."[15]

If the timing of McCarthy's political switch remains indeterminable, the reasons behind it seem somewhat more obvious. Wisconsin had always been a strongly Republican state, and as McCarthy later told reporters, it was an advantage being "a Republican with a Democratic name." And given this, the results of the primary must have pleased him. Although Wiley was easily

[13] Pilat and Shannon, New York Post, Sept. 7, 1951; Anderson and May, McCarthy, pp. 67–70.

[14] R. H. Gehrke to Wiley, May 12, 1944, Personal Correspondence, box 16; Judge Oscar J. Schmiege to Wiley, Aug. 9, 1944, Personal Correspondence, box 17, both in the Wiley Papers.

[15] Walter Melchior to Alexander Wiley, March 13, 1944, Personal Correspondence, box 16; Elmer R. Honkamp to Wiley, Sept. 15, 1944, Personal Correspondence, box 17, both in the Wiley Papers.

renominated, McCarthy won nearly 80,000 votes and a growing reputation among Wisconsin Republicans.[16] McCarthy returned to duty at the Marine Corps Air Station in El Centro, California, on August 20, 1944. A few months later, pleading the press of judicial duties, he applied for another leave. When this new request was turned down, he decided to resign and was relieved from active duty in February 1945. While the last months of bitter fighting continued in the Pacific, Joe McCarthy came home to accept the tribute due a returning hero. Not the least of this was overwhelming reelection to the circuit court. One suspects, though, that the affairs of that bench held little appeal for McCarthy. He was far too ambitious to be satisfied with a parochial judgeship. His goal was still the United States Senate, and toward this end he now turned all his tremendous energies.

ELECTION

In 1946 Wisconsin's senior senator was Robert M. La Follette, Jr., a veteran of more than twenty years in the upper house and the bearer of his state's most distinguished political name. He was first elected to the Senate in 1925, following the death of his father, "Fighting Bob" La Follette, and in the years that followed he proved himself to be a dedicated and capable public servant. He was also, at least by appearances, a formidable opponent. Yet there were at play beneath the surface of Wisconsin politics forces which would make him a vulnerable target.

Young La Follette was the Hamlet of Wisconsin politics. He had neither his father's charismatic appeal nor his talent for careful political organization. He was quiet and moody. He disliked the hurley-burley of campaigning, and he resisted the exigencies of political leadership. His visits to Wisconsin were brief and infrequent, and in his absence the political organization which had for so long ensured his success slipped into bad disrepair.[17] The Progressive party of Wisconsin was the heir to both the

---

[16] Pilat and Shannon, *New York Post*, Sept. 5, 1951; *Wisconsin Blue Book, 1946* (Madison, Wis., 1946), p. 595.

[17] See Roger T. Johnson, *Robert M. La Follette, Jr., and the Decline of the Progressive Party in Wisconsin* (Madison, Wis., 1964).

insurgent Republicanism of the elder La Follette and the search for new political modes which characterized much of the Midwest during the depression thirties. First, organized in 1934, it had served largely as a personal vehicle for the La Follettes. (His brother, Philip F. La Follette was elected governor on the Republican ticket in 1930 and defeated in the G.O.P. primary in 1932. He was reelected as a Progressive in 1934 and 1936 before losing again in 1938. Robert La Follette, Jr., was first elected to the Senate as a Republican in 1925 and 1928, then as a Progressive in 1934 and again in 1940.) In early 1946 La Follette formally disbanded the Progressive party and tried to lead his followers back into the G.O.P. Not only was this move unwelcome among the conservatives who now controlled the Republican organization, but it also alienated Milwaukee labor leaders who had hoped La Follette would join the Democrats, and old Progressives who would have preferred in any case to maintain their own organization. The result of all this was a fluid political situation subject to many variables and unknowns.

Joe McCarthy meanwhile had launched an all-out campaign to capture the support of the Republican organization. Throughout 1945 he crisscrossed the state, building up a personal following, especially among Wisconsin's long-dormant Young Republicans. His objective was to win the endorsement of the Republican Voluntary Committee, an inner-council of party leaders organized for the purpose of skirting the intent, if not the letter, of the state direct primary law which forbade party endorsement of candidates before the primary election. The Voluntary Committee, meeting in convention during election years, operated as a shadow party by endorsing its own candidates for the primary election. Under the leadership of "Boss" Thomas E. Coleman, a Madison industrialist, the committee had become a powerful and conservative force in Wisconsin politics.

The Republican leadership would have preferred a more established political figure, perhaps former Governor Julius P. Heil or Walter J. Kohler, Jr., but McCarthy gave them little choice. He outhustled the plodding Heil and backed Kohler into a corner by threatening to make his recent divorce a front page issue. Finally, he warned the Republican leaders that if necessary he would run without endorsement, a move which would probably have assured La Follette a victory in the primary by dividing the conservative vote. Faced with this bleak alternative, the Voluntary Committee endorsed McCarthy and made him the conservative's only hope for defeating La Follette.[18]

With the convention endorsement secured, McCarthy began one of the most energetic campaigns in Wisconsin history. Leaning once more on his war record, he urged Wisconsin voters to put a "tail gunner" in Congress. He attacked the New Deal for its "bureaucracy" and he sharply criticized wartime price controls. He fired off a scattering of personal charges at La Follette, ranging from "war profiteering" (through ownership of a Milwaukee radio station) to neglect of his Wisconsin constituency. He was indefatigable—driving from one small country town to another, making speeches, shaking hands, asking the plain folks to vote for "Joe." And behind him the Voluntary Committee mounted a large, well-financed, and smoothly operated campaign, replete with mass mailings and large newspaper advertisements.[19] La Follette, by contrast, did not campaign at all, but remained in Washington until early August, only a week before the election.

The outcome of the election, however, turned neither on McCarthy's vigor, nor on La Follette's ineptitude, but rather upon the failure of organized labor to follow La Follette into the Republican primary. The election was decided in the heavily populated industrial areas of Milwaukee, Kenosha, and Racine, which had formerly provided La Follette with his margin of victory. In 1946 La Follette lost these critical areas, not so much because workers supported McCarthy, but because they entered the Democratic primary in support of Howard McMurray. Running unopposed, McMurray won almost as many votes as La Follette in Milwaukee and Racine, and more than either La Follette or McCarthy in Kenosha.[20] The Milwaukee vote tipped the balance against La Follette, and Joe McCarthy won the Republican nomination for United States Senator by only 3,000 votes.

McCarthy's general election campaign against Democrat Howard

[18] Pilat and Shannon, *New York Post*, Sept. 9, 1951; Anderson and May, *McCarthy*, p. 83. The most detailed treatment of the 1946 campaign is John P. Steinke, "The Rise of McCarthyism" (M.A. thesis, University of Wisconsin, 1960).

[19] McCarthy's campaign expenditures were in excess of $50,000. La Follette spent less than $4,000. Anderson and May, *McCarthy*, p. 101.

[20] Johnson, *Robert M. La Follette, Jr.*, pp. 157–58; *Wisconsin Blue Book, 1948* (Madison, Wis., 1948), p. 604.

McMurray has been pictured, retrospectively, as a dark prophecy of his later career. Jack Anderson and Ronald May saw in Mc-Carthy's use of the "Communist issue" and in the support given his candidacy by *Chicago Tribune* publisher Robert R. McCormick a "preview of charges to come." An enthusiastic graduate student called the campaign "a nightmare in red."[21] Yet the most remarkable thing about the 1946 campaign was not its uniqueness, but its typicality.

To be sure, McCarthy had been cultivating the support of the untraconservative *Tribune* for some time. As early as 1944 he had been aided by John M. Murphy, the *Tribune's* Milwaukee correspondent. Murphy, declared McCarthy, was "the only man whom I know who can actually deliver votes."[22] In September 1946 McCarthy met with Colonel McCormick in Chicago and soon won the support of American Action, Inc., a McCormick-controlled rightist group built on the foundations of the old America First committee. This group sponsored several advertisements in Wisconsin newspapers supporting McCarthy as part of their nationwide campaign to defeat "radical and Communist" candidates for Congress.[23]

It would be wrong, however, to attach much significance to McCormick's help. The Chicago publisher was accustomed to contributing to a wide variety of conservative causes and candidates, and he was probably more interested in defeating Mc-Murray than in electing McCarthy. In any case, McCormick apparently had little influence on McCarthy's voting record in the years immediately following his election. McCarthy remained throughout this period a moderate internationalist in foreign affairs, much closer ideologically to Republicans like Arthur H. Vandenberg than to hard-core isolationists like Colonel Mc-Cormick. Indeed, as late as December 1949, McCormick columnist Walter Trohan was gleefully lumping the Wisconsin senator in the "me too" ranks of the "Eastern Seaboard internationalists."[24] It was the events which followed that speech at Wheeling, not

[21] Anderson and May, *McCarthy*, pp. 106–10; Steinke, "The Rise of Mc-Carthyism."

[22] Joe McCarthy to Alexander Wiley, Sept. 28, 1944, Personal Correspondence, box 17, Wiley Papers.

[23] *Capital Times* (Madison), Sept. 30, 1946; *Milwaukee Journal,* Oct. 7, 1946.

[24] *Washington Times-Herald,* Dec. 19, 1949.

those which preceded it, which made Joe McCarthy the darling
of the right.

As for the "Communist issue," McCarthy did use it against
Democrat Howard McMurray. He told one audience that Mc-
Murray was "communistically inclined," and another that he was
a "megaphone being used by the Communist-controlled P.A.C."[25]
But this was not a major theme of his campaign. He concentrated
instead on broad and generalized attacks on the New Deal and
upon the Truman administration. He came out against farm price
controls, the Murray-Wagner-Dingell health insurance bill, and
New Deal "bureaucracy." He equivocated on foreign affairs, and
as in the primary he played heavily upon his inflated military
record.[26]

When McCarthy did use the "Communist issue," moreover, he
was in step with party leaders across the country. Senator Robert
A. Taft, the G.O.P.'s leading conservative spokesman, had charged
in May that the Democratic legislative requests "bordered on
Communism." House Minority Leader Joseph W. Martin called
for the election of a Republican Congress to sweep the Communists
and fellow travelers from office, while Republican National Chairman B. Carroll Reece accused the Democrats of adopting the
precepts of Karl Marx. Even supposedly liberal leaders such as
New York Governor Thomas E. Dewey declared that the Democrats were subject to "adventurers" who owed their allegiance to
a foreign ideology, a polite way of saying what the governor's
conservative colleagues were putting more bluntly.[27] The fre-
quency and shrillness of these charges would increase in the years
which followed, but by 1946 they were already a staple of Republican platform oratory. In helping himself to this potent
political commodity, Joe McCarthy was doing little more than his
better-known party cohorts all across the nation.

[25] *Milwaukee Journal*, Oct. 17, 25, 1946; *Capital Times* (Madison), Oct. 23,
1946. The Political Action Committee (PAC) was the political arm of the
Congress of Industrial Organizations (CIO).

[26] *Milwaukee Journal*, Oct. 2, 23, 1946; *Eau Claire Leader*, Oct. 16, 17,
1946; *Appleton Post-Crescent*, Oct. 9, 1946.

[27] *New York Times*, May 11, 1946, p. 5; July 17, 1946, p. 15; Aug. 13, 1946,
p. 18; Sept. 5, 1946, p. 1; Sept. 22, 1946, p. 53. In Montana, where Republican Zales M. Ecton was fighting for office, the campaign was framed as "a
battle of people of Montana against outside interests of communistic people
of America." J. W. Morrow, Jr., chairman, Ecton for Senator Club, to Kenneth
S. Wherry, Aug. 25, 1946, Kenneth S. Wherry Papers, University of Nebraska.

Joe McCarthy's senatorial campaign was distinguished neither by his use of the Communist issue nor by the support of Robert McCormick. The plain fact was that he was a Republican candidate in a Republican year. In 1946 Republicans all over the country were asking voters if they had "Had Enough?" of Democratic rule, and the G.O.P. was heading toward its first national victory since 1928. McCarthy knew this, and he knew that he had "every reason to be confident."[28] He rode in on the crest of this Republican wave and was elected by an overwhelming majority.

A REMARKABLE UPSTART

The United States Senate lies at the very crossroads of the American political system. It is a pivot of power subject to all the great and conflicting pressures of our society. It does not have the relative isolation which the president achieves because of the sheer size and anonymity of his constituency or which the Constitution grants to our courts. It is smaller and more personal than the House of Representatives, and its proceedings have a specificity often lacking in the Lower Chamber. It has been called with some justification the greatest deliberative body in the world. How would McCarthy acquit himself here?

In many ways the new senator from Wisconsin appeared unexceptional. He was a country boy by birth and a lawyer by profession, characteristics which could be applied to most of the members. Like most, he had held prior public office, although his rural judgeship compared rather poorly with the distinguished early careers of many of the Senate professionals. There were some significant differences. McCarthy's class origin was lower than most, a fact he himself seemed to realize, and his rise to the Senate had been more rapid.[29] At thirty-eight he was ten years younger than the average incumbent and more than twenty-five years junior to the average committee chairman.

In an interview shortly after his election, McCarthy intimated that he would follow the liberal Republicanism of former Governor Harold E. Stassen of Minnesota rather than the conservatism of Senator Robert A. Taft of Ohio.[30] Once in the Senate, however,

[28] Joe McCarthy to Kenneth S. Wherry, Oct. 11, 1946, Wherry Papers.
[29] Alexander, "The Senate's Remarkable Upstart," p. 58.
[30] *Milwaukee Journal*, Nov. 10, 1946.

McCarthy followed an erratic course, supporting Taft and the conservatives on domestic policy, but following the lead of Senator Arthur H. Vandenberg and the Republican internationalists in foreign affairs.[31] As one of the "meat shortage boys," as the class of 1946 was irreverently called, he voted against price, rent, and credit controls, and in favor of speedy tax reductions. He was a strong supporter of the Taft-Hartley labor legislation, and an opponent of public housing and federal aid to education. In 1947 he supported the Greek-Turkish aid bill, which implemented the "Truman Doctrine," and in later years he supported both the Marshall Plan and the North Atlantic Treaty Organization.

McCarthy also busied himself with a dozen or so matters of concern to specific interest groups in Wisconsin and a smattering of measures relating to veterans' affairs. His major legislative interests, however, grew quite naturally from his committee assignments. As a freshman, McCarthy was placed on one major committee, the moderately prestigious Committee on Banking and Currency, then chaired by liberal Republican Charles W. Tobey of New Hampshire. He was also assigned a seat on the Committee on Expenditures in the Executive Departments, the potential importance of which neither he nor his colleagues then realized.

What was remarkable about McCarthy's Senate apprenticeship was not policy positions—liberal or conservative, internationalist or isolationist—but rather his continual violation of the rules, customs, and procedures under which the Senate operates. Because it is the preserve of ambitious men and parties, often locked in fierce political combat, the Senate has developed self-protective rules and customs. In many ways these folkways favor entrenched groups within the Senate. But these unwritten laws of seniority, apprenticeship, reciprocity, courtesy, and so forth, also provide the framework for the resolution of charged political issues. Without such rules, the divisive forces of partisanship and ambition would cripple the legislative process and make such resolution impossible.[32]

The observance of Senate folkways requires patience, restraint, and moderation, however; these were qualities which the junior

---

[31] The best brief summary of McCarthy's Senate career appears in *Congressional Quarterly*, April 30, 1954, pp. 525–36.

[32] The definitive study of the postwar Senate is Donald R. Matthews, *U. S. Senators and Their World* (New York, 1960).

senator from Wisconsin singularly lacked. Instead, he brought to the Upper Chamber a restless and compulsive energy, a hunger for power and public notice, and a casual disregard for custom and authority. It was not surprising then that he should soon be called the Senate's "remarkable upstart."

His opponents described him as an opportunist and a consummate cynic, but this only suggests more questions. The answers lie perhaps among those demons of fear and self-hatred which pursued him on his short race through life. Wanting power, yet unable to forgo yearnings for love and esteem, he was divided against himself. There was "Joe" the good-fellow-well-met, and "McCarthy" the public extremist, and only a shadow in the recesses of his fears of the quiet, shy boy he had once been.[33]

The division of public and private self ran like a thread throughout his career. "He can be the most affable man in the world," recalled a fellow senator, "and suddenly he will run the knife into you—particularly if the public is going to see it—and he will do it for no particular reason."[34] McCarthy seemed to recognize this division himself, for he often referred to himself in the third person ("no matter how much McCarthy bleeds . . ."; ". . . nevertheless, you say McCarthy lied because McCarthy said. . ."; an attempt to "discredit and smear McCarthy").

McCarthy's public statements were almost without exception delivered with a breathless hyperbole. Events were "fantastic," "incredible," and "unbelievable." One suspects that this very quality of disproportion arose from McCarthy's inner sense of doubt and insecurity. There was, moreover, a surface mien to his public performances which seemed to belie the very words he spoke. His speeches, even the most violent, were delivered in a

[33] Richard H. Rovere's *Senator Joe McCarthy* (New York, 1959) remains the best and most perceptive study of McCarthy's character. Of particular value are two psychiatric studies of McCarthy referred to by Rovere and available to the interested student in the Americans for Democratic Action Papers (hereafter cited as ADA papers), Manuscripts Division, State Historical Society of Wisconsin, Legislative File, box 39, and Public Relations File, box 81, respectively. Long-distance analysis is at best a dubious practice, yet both studies strike at what appears to me to be the heart of McCarthy's problem. "The key to understanding McCarthy," reads one, "is a recognition of his basic *insecurity, self-doubt* and *self-contempt.*" Public criticism, added the other report, helped him to reaffirm this identity, the existence of which was drawn into question by the very intensity of his inner doubts and insecurities.

[34] Quoted by William S. White in the *New York Times*, Aug. 15, 1954, sec. 4, p. 3.

flat, unemotional tone. "His voice seldom conveys anger, contempt, or scorn," wrote Douglass Cater. "He utters even the most virulent phrases unfeelingly." He was, recalled James A. Wechsler, "one of the least passionate demagogues I have ever encountered." Even McCarthy's onetime ally and confidant, Frederick Woltman, remembered that the senator "sometimes appeared to be playing a game."[35]

It was this disassociation of public and private roles which allowed McCarthy to distort, misrepresent, even lie, and yet through it all retain what Richard Rovere has called his essential innocence.[36] The lies, the violent accusations, the disregard for law and custom, all took place on the periphery of his personality. They never touched "Joe," the genial and charming Irishman who wanted nothing more than to love and be loved. They were all attributes of "McCarthy," the public figure he had conjured up from some bizarre notion of himself.

From the beginning there was about him a sense of desperation, as though he never quite believed that the charade could last and lived in perpetual fear that at any moment it might come tumbling down about him. Out of this inner desperation came a recklessness and daring which never failed to confound his enemies. He could never admit defeat, for to do so would be to admit he was living a lie. "One should play poker with him to really know him," recalled a Wisconsin friend, "but in case that you do it would be my advice to play table stakes or get some big bank to back you. He raises on the poor hands and always comes out the winner."[37] And so this strangely driven young man embarked upon a career in the nation's greatest deliberative body.

THE JUNIOR SENATOR FROM WISCONSIN

McCarthy's first sally into the legislative arena was an attempt to defeat a bill extending wartime sugar controls for an additional year. The debate arrayed senators from sugar-consuming states, led by Republicans Charles W. Tobey of New Hampshire and

[35] Douglass Cater, "Is McCarthy Slipping," *Reporter* 5 (Sept. 18, 1951): 26; James A. Wechsler, *The Age of Suspicion* (New York, 1953), p. 286; *Washington News*, July 12, 1954.

[36] Rovere, *Senator Joe McCarthy*, p. 60.

[37] Bradley R. Taylor to Elaine Kretchman, June 3, 1954, box 5, Bradley Taylor Papers, Manuscripts Division, State Historical Society of Wisconsin.

Ralph E. Flanders of Vermont, against senators from the sugar-producing states of Louisiana and the Midwest and a miscellany of various lobbies. The leadership of this latter group was seized by McCarthy, whose intimate association with sugar lobbyists soon earned for him the title of "Pepsi-Cola Kid."[38] McCarthy had more immediate reasons for championing decontrol than the support of Washington lobbyists. As one of the "meat shortage boys" he had campaigned in general opposition to price controls and other wartime regulations. Even more importantly, Wisconsin's beet sugar producers were clamoring for decontrol, and the Wisconsin legislature had already memorialized Congress to end control at once.[39] McCarthy's position, thus, followed quite naturally from the legitimate—if not quite public-spirited—interests of his own constituency. The significance of this debate did not lie in McCarthy's advocacy of decontrol, or even in the possible breach of public trust which his associations with lobbyists may have involved. What was important, and prophetic, was the manner in which he conducted himself, and the level to which he lowered the entire debate.

The senator from Wisconsin demonstrated a ready willingness to disregard truth and to manipulate evidence to "prove" his case. Bent on showing that there was enough sugar available to make controls unnecessary, he produced a meaningless assortment of figures and statistics. When Senator Flanders sought to correct the record, McCarthy first refused to yield the floor, then accused the elderly Vermonter of attempting to make a speech. He attributed to Secretary of Agriculture Clinton Anderson a remark which the secretary had never made, and when Senator Tobey called him to book on this point, he simply retorted that he "did not give a tinker's dam" (the phrase was already a McCarthy favorite) what the secretary had said about the measure.[40]

This same disregard for truth and accuracy characterized Mc-

---

[38] When McCarthy found himself in a tight financial squeeze in late 1947, Russell M. Arundel, a wealthy sugar lobbyist for the Pepsi-Cola interests, endorsed a $20,000 note for deposit with McCarthy's Appleton Bank. About this same time McCarthy appeared at a Senate Appropriations hearing to attack the sugar control program. Matthew Shuh to McCarthy, Dec. 4, 1946; McCarthy to Shuh, Dec. 9, 1947, photostats of both in the NCEC files. These two letters are reprinted in Anderson and May, *McCarthy*, p. 134. *New York Times*, Dec. 10, 1947, p. 3.

[39] *Congressional Record*, 80th Cong., 1st sess., March 12, 1947, pp. 1933–34.

[40] Ibid., March 27, 1947, pp. 2698–2700.

Carthy's statements before a Senate Appropriations Committee in December 1947. In reply to a suggestion that the Commodity Credit Corporation point out any inaccuracies in his remarks on sugar supplies, the associate director of the agency wrote McCarthy that "an examination of the record discloses a number of errors so fundamental to the entire discussion that the transcript could not be corrected by minor revisions." There followed six single-spaced typewritten pages spelling out some thirteen major errors of fact or interpretation.[41]

During the debate, McCarthy was by turn rude and provocative. He would refuse to yield the floor for unfriendly questions, or would turn upon an interrogator with some personal charge or accusation. In a matter of minutes he turned a staid and dignified Senate debate into an angry brawl. He tended to reduce all issues to personal terms and to attack men rather than ideas. The way to discredit an issue was to discredit its advocate, so McCarthy lashed out at Tobey and Flanders, charging that they had told him personally that they intended to introduce a "fictitious amendment" which was designed to "deceive the housewife." Both men rose to points of personal privilege, and the excitable Tobey, red-faced and shouting, accused McCarthy of lying, misrepresenting the truth, and attempting to confuse the Senate.[42]

The sugar control bill eventually passed the Senate, although not until McCarthy had weakened it by an amendment to lift controls five months earlier than originally provided, and not until Tobey had taken the floor to denounce "a group in my own party . . . who have been trying to sabotage this measure at every possible opportunity."[43]

McCarthy's next adventure was in the field of housing. In 1946 the United States was faced with a critical housing shortage due to the return of servicemen and to the lack of new home construction during the depression and war years. There was a widespread demand for public housing, and even such a conservative as Robert A. Taft of Ohio joined with Democrats Robert F. Wagner of New York and Allen J. Ellender of Louisiana in sponsoring an omnibus housing bill which included a public housing provision.

[41] Lawrence Myers to McCarthy, Dec. 19, 1947, photostat in the NCEC files.
[42] Congressional Record, 80th Cong., 1st sess., March 27, 1947, pp. 2696–2702; New York Times, March 28, 1947, p. 19.
[43] Congressional Record, 80th Cong., 1st sess., March 27, 1947, pp. 2728, 2732.

Opposition to public housing centered among homebuilders and real estate groups, and it was for these interests that McCarthy spoke in the Senate. Instead of public housing, he urged that greater emphasis be placed upon the mass production of pre-fabricated homes, a position warmly applauded by the various homebuilders with whom McCarthy associated.[44] As with the sugar debate, it was not McCarthy's position on substantive issues which attracted attention, but rather his unwonted methods and manners.

In the summer of 1947, Congress established a Joint Committee on Housing, made up of members of the Senate and House Banking and Currency Committees, for the purpose of investigating the housing shortage. The committee, which held its first organizational meeting on August 19, 1947, was almost immediately entangled in controversy. By right of seniority, the chairmanship of the Joint Committee should have gone to Senator Tobey, the chairman of the Senate Banking and Currency Committee. But McCarthy took advantage of a discrepancy between Senate rules, which allow the use of proxies, and House rules, which do not, and moved that no vote by proxy be accepted. Tobey, who held the proxies of four absent members, was outraged, but there was little he could do. McCarthy had the votes and the motion was carried, after which the committee elected Republican Congressman Ralph A. Gamble of New York as chairman and McCarthy as vice-chairman. By a shrewd parliamentary coup, the freshman senator from Wisconsin had overturned one of the Senate's most cherished traditions, the right of seniority. "I frankly didn't want Tobey to be chairman," McCarthy told reporters. "He thinks the sole answer to the problem is public housing."[45]

The Joint Committee spent the remainder of 1947 and early 1948 traveling across the country, listening to any and every citizen who wished to testify on the subject of housing. The result was some six thousand pages of undigested testimony and a short,

---

[44] McCarthy had close connections with a number of actual or prospective prefabricated home builders, including Walter Harnischfeger, a Milwaukee industrialist, William J. Levitt, the New York builder of the "Levitt House," and the ill-fated Lustron Corporation of Columbus, Ohio. Anderson and May, *McCarthy*, p. 141; *New York Times*, Sept. 5, 1947, p. 28. For a thorough discussion of the housing controversy see Richard O. Davies, *Housing Reform during the Truman Administration* (Columbia, Mo., 1966).

[45] *New York Times*, Aug. 20, 1949, p. 8.

apparently unrelated report prepared by the committee staff. In the introduction of the report, Congressman Gamble warned that any further use of federal funds in the field of housing would be "unwarranted, unwise, and may lead to further and more extensive refusal of private capital and enterprise to enter the field of housing."[46]

At this point Tobey and a majority on the Joint Committee on Housing finally regained control of the proceedings and drafted a new report to meet their own specifications. Presented in the name of the full committee, this final study contradicted the Gamble report and urged support of measures embodied in the Taft-Ellender-Wagner bill.[47]

The Taft-Ellender-Wagner bill passed the Senate on April 22, 1948, but was bottled up by the House leadership, which refused to go along with the public housing provision. During the summer of 1948, Taft finally surrendered and allowed the passage of a McCarthy substitute which eliminated the section on public housing. The embittered Tobey charged McCarthy with having proposed a measure "that will benefit the builders and those wealthy and moderately well-to-do who can afford to buy their own homes."[48]

By the time the Eightieth Congress adjourned in the late summer of 1948, the junior senator from Wisconsin had established a reputation for trouble. He had no respect for the spirit of senatorial courtesy or for the rules of seniority, and he was perfectly willing to make personal attacks on fellow senators. The normal social pressures through which the Senate imposes conformity on its members seemed to have little effect on McCarthy, in part, perhaps, because of the peculiar disconnectedness between his public and private behavior. In public he was harsh, brutal, and often extreme.

[46] U. S., Congress, House, 80th Cong., 2d sess., Joint Committee on Housing, *Housing in America: Its Present Status and Future Implications* (Washington, D. C., 1948), pp. 5–6. According to Anderson and May, the report was prepared by the public relations firm of Bell, Jones and Taylor, whose clients included the country's most powerful real estate groups. Anderson and May, *McCarthy,* pp. 143–44.

[47] U. S., Congress, House, 80th Cong., 2d sess., *Housing Study and Investigation. Final Majority Report of the Joint Committee on Housing* (Washington, D. C., 1948).

[48] *New York Times,* Aug. 7, 1948, p. 1. For a brief discussion of the entire housing controversy, see *Congressional Quarterly Almanac, 1948* (Washington, D. C., 1948), 4:138–42.

In private he was friendly and gregarious, and many of the senators enjoyed his hearty and robust conviviality.

A less subtle type of pressure was applied when the Democrats organized the newly elected Eighty-first Congress. Senator Burnet R. Maybank, the aristocratic and conservative South Carolinian who became chairman of the Senate Banking and Currency Committee, insisted on "bumping" McCarthy from his committee. "He's a troublemaker, that's why I don't want him," declared Maybank, who told Democratic Majority Leader Scott Lucas that he simply would not serve on the committee if McCarthy remained. McCarthy's Republican colleagues relegated him to the Committee on the District of Columbia, the lowliest among the hierarchy of Senate committees.[49]

Without a major committee assignment, and with the Democrats in control of the Senate, McCarthy's legislative effectiveness dropped sharply. During the Republican Eightieth Congress he had played an active, if controversial, role. As 1949 wore on, his amendments to pending bills were summarily rejected almost without exception. It was perhaps natural, then, that the junior senator from Wisconsin should turn from legislation to investigation. In the legislative process a newcomer might be stifled by the weight of formal rules, by the silent force of entrenched authority, or by the combined will of many others. In the investigative process the rules were more ambiguous and a senator more his own man. The political dividends were not recorded in the statute books, but in the headlines. If not power, why not public notice? Thus McCarthy began the third great adventure of his early Senate career, an investigation into the "Malmedy massacre."

In December 1944 the Germans had launched their last great offensive of the war, thrusting deep into Allied lines in Luxembourg and Belgium. During the battle hundreds of unarmed American prisoners and Belgian civilians were slaughtered by the German First SS Panzer Division. Most of these murders took place in and about the crossroads of the small Belgian village of Malmedy. At the crossroads themselves, some 150 captured GIs

---

[49] Maybank is quoted in the *New York Post*, Sept. 4, 1951. Also see Kirkley Coulter to Hugh A. Butler, Nov. 24, 1948, and Butler to Joe McCarthy, Jan. 8, 1949, in box 120, the Hugh A. Butler Papers, Nebraska State Historical Society.

were marched into a wheatfield and then shot down with machine guns.

After the war, some seventy-three SS troopers were convicted of participation in the "Malmedy massacre" by an American war crimes court, and forty-three of them were sentenced to death. The cases were subsequently reviewed by the War Crimes Review Board and by the office of the Judge Advocate, and a number of the sentences were reduced or disapproved.[50]

In early 1948 the German defendants petitioned the United States Supreme Court to overturn the convictions. In a series of affidavits presented for the first time by their lawyer, they charged that the American prosecution had used torture and other means of intimidation to extract confessions, and that the entire proceeding had been in gross violation of accepted standards of due process.[51]

The Supreme Court refused the petition on the grounds that it had no jurisdiction in the matter, but the attendant publicity occasioned two additional investigations. One of these was conducted by the office of the Judge Advocate, the other by a panel headed by Judge Gordon Simpson of the Texas Supreme Court and including Judge Edward L. Van Roden of the Orphans' Court of Delaware County, Pennsylvania. The two boards found ample evidence of a wide variety of psychological ruses and stratagems which were used in the interrogation process, including a small number of "mock trials," which certainly exceeded the bounds of propriety. They found no evidence of the general or systematic use of physical force, however, and they concluded that the trials were, in the words of the Simpson report, "essentially fair." In view of the procedural irregularities the Simpson panel did recommend that the twelve remaining death sentences originating with the Malmedy prosecution be commuted to life imprisonment.[52]

Neither review succeeded in ending the controversy. Judge Van Roden, whose sympathies seem to have been very strongly pro-German, returned to America to make a number of sweeping and unsubstantiated allegations as to the conduct of the American

---

[50] U.S., Congress, Senate, 81st Cong., 1st sess., Committee on Armed Services, *Malmedy Massacre Investigation*, pt. 1 (Washington, D. C., 1949), pp. 586–89 (hereafter cited as *Malmedy Hearings*).

[51] The petition is printed in *Malmedy Hearings*, pp. 1181–90.

[52] *Malmedy Hearings*, pp. 1196-1205; *New York Times*, Jan. 7, 1949, p. 1.

prosecution. He also allowed the publication of a magazine article, ostensibly written by him, which made similarly unfounded charges and which he later repudiated point by point before a Senate committee.[53]

By early 1949 the Malmedy case was beginning to stir interest on Capitol Hill. Senator William Langer, the eccentric and unpredictable North Dakota isolationist, introduced a resolution calling for an investigation by the Senate Judiciary Committee, of which he was the ranking Republican member. McCarthy hinted that the Committee on Expenditures in the Executive Departments was also interested in the matter. The investigation fell to the Senate Armed Services Committee, however, through a resolution introduced by Senator Raymond E. Baldwin, a Connecticut Republican.[54]

It is sometimes difficult to assess the motives which lie behind senatorial behavior, but it seems fair to say that McCarthy and Baldwin had quite different purposes in mind. The Armed Services Committee on which Baldwin served maintained a proprietary interest in the military establishment and was generally disposed to protect its good name. Baldwin told the Senate, in introducing his resolution, that he especially wanted to allow the American prosecutors, who had not been questioned by the Simpson panel, an opportunity to present their side of the case.[55] One of these prosecutors, moreover, was a member of Baldwin's Bridgeport law firm, a fact which was to have unfortunate consequences in view of Baldwin's decision to accept the chairmanship of the investigation.

McCarthy's interest in the Malmedy affair is less easily explained. Like Langer, he was probably influenced to some degree by his state's large German population. The senator from Wisconsin had especially close ties with Walter Harnischfeger, a pro-German

[53] Edward L. Van Roden, "American Atrocities in Germany," *Progressive* 13 (Feb. 1949): 21–22. The article was written by the executive secretary of a pacifist organization which was seeking to overturn the convictions. *Malmedy Hearings*, p. 1304. Judge Van Roden had earlier endorsed for "all Americans," a book by Ludwig Adolphus Fritch, *The Crime of Our Age*, which set forth the thesis that "the Jews and the Anglo-Saxons succeeded in unifying the nations of the world into an unholy alliance in order to destroy Germandom." The "one Holy Reich," the author said, was "the defender, guardian, and protector of Christianity and the white race." *New York Post*, May 31, 1949.
[54] *Congressional Record*, 81st Cong., 1st sess., Jan. 27, 1949, pp. 598–99.
[55] Ibid.

Milwaukee industrialist to whom he had earlier turned for financial help. Tom Korb, a lawyer for the Harnischfeger Corporation and an old school friend of McCarthy's, was loaned to the senator during the course of the investigation.[56] Beyond this, the senator was perhaps lured on by the prospect of headlines and by his own inner sense of combativeness. While Baldwin and the Armed Services Committee would seek to defend the army and its proceedings in the Malmedy case, McCarthy's intention was precisely the opposite.

The entire investigation was shot with irony and prophecy. Elected to the Senate in 'large part because of his war record, McCarthy was now challenging the military establishment. A fellow Republican, Raymond Baldwin, was to bear the brunt of his animus. And although he would later become notorious as a foe of civil liberties and a scourge of unpopular causes, McCarthy now cast himself as defender of the rights of a most unpopular group. Most prophetic, however, was the manner in which McCarthy bullied and intimidated the entire investigating committee, its staff, and the witnesses who appeared before it.

The Malmedy investigation was conducted by a subcommittee of three, chaired by Baldwin and including Democrats Estes Kefauver of Tennessee and Lester C. Hunt of Wyoming. McCarthy, who had threatened an investigation by his own Committee on Expenditures in the Executive Departments, was permitted to sit in on the hearings, and it was McCarthy who soon dominated the entire proceedings. The junior senator from Wisconsin instinctively grasped the basic weakness of the committee and exploited it to his own ends. Part of this weakness was a result of the committee's personnel. Kefauver was seldom present at the hearings; the mild and inoffensive Hunt attended, but said very little. But the key factor behind the committee's impotence was the compromised position of its chairman. At the very outset of the hearings, Baldwin's impartiality was challenged because a member of his law firm had been involved in the prosecution of the Malmedy cases. Although Baldwin offered to resign, Senator Millard Tydings and the other members of the Armed Services Committee assured

---

[56] McCarthy to Matthew Shuh, May 9, 1947, in the NCEC files; *Milwaukee Journal*, May 1, 1949. Korb is said to have been the author of McCarthy's intemperate Senate speech of July 26, 1949, on the Malmedy case. Anderson and May, *McCarthy*, p. 164.

him of their confidence in him and urged him to remain. Baldwin was undoubtedly the most knowledgeable and informed senator on the Malmedy case, but because of the delicacy of his position he was unable to bring this knowledge to bear forcefully in rebuttal to McCarthy's allegations.

The junior senator from Wisconsin labored under no such liabilities. From the very outset it was McCarthy the prosecutor, McCarthy the grand inquisitor. In retrospect, his techniques seem almost too familiar. There were the elaborate hypothetical questions. McCarthy knew that the way a question is framed determines the way it is answered, and that hypothetical questions allow the interrogator to manipulate the elements of the inquiry so as to structure the response.[57] There was also the inflated and extreme language. The attitude of the secretary of the army was "fantastic." A statement by the judge advocate general was "the most phenomenal I ever heard." The American military judges were "morons." There were sudden, personal attacks. "I have been a judge so long . . . that it makes me rather sick down inside to hear you testify what you think is proper or improper." Or, "I think you are lying."[58] There were diversions and attempts to lead the investigation far afield from the original scope of the inquiry. And there was the constant misrepresentation of facts which on occasion would send the committee members scurrying to the transcript for corrections, but which at other times would pass unchallenged.[59] Most importantly, it was the senator from Wisconsin who dominated the press. "McCarthy Scores Brutality!" "McCarthy Charges Whitewash!" "McCarthy Challenges Testimony!" He had discovered, it would appear, the quickest and surest avenue to notoriety.[60]

After nearly a month of hearings, McCarthy suddenly demanded that the American interrogation and prosecution team be given a lie detector test. When the full Armed Services Committee

[57] See, for example, *Malmedy Hearings*, pp. 20–22, 42–44, 681–82.

[58] Ibid., pp. 23, 27, 46, 224, 631.

[59] Although most of the SS men were veterans, a few were relatively young. One, who was mentioned in the transcript, was only eighteen years old. McCarthy would characteristically knock a few years off the defendant's age each time he discussed the case, speaking of boys of "17 and 18," then "16 or 17," and finally "15 or 16." Ibid., p. 200.

[60] *New York Times*, April 19, 1949, p. 1; April 21, 1949, p. 5; April 23, 1949, p. 4.

rejected this proposal, as McCarthy undoubtedly knew they would, he dramatically marched out of the hearing. He repeated his list of specific charges against the American prosecutors and accused the committee of attempting to "whitewash a shameful episode."[61] Two months later he took the Senate floor to denounce the committee and to attack Baldwin personally. He accused Baldwin of whitewashing the case in order to protect his law partner, and he charged that the mild-mannered Connecticut Republican was "criminally responsible" for a miscarriage of justice. Mc-Carthy's old nemesis, Senator Tobey, was on his feet shouting that McCarthy had violated the Senate rule against personal attacks on fellow senators. Hunt and Kefauver defended the investigation, and Baldwin lashed back at McCarthy. The senator from Wisconsin had once again displayed his genius for creating division and turmoil.[62]

Following McCarthy's savage attack, the full membership of the Senate Armed Forces Committee felt compelled to pass a resolution of confidence in Baldwin's conduct of the investigation. "We, his colleagues," the accompanying message read, "take this unusual step in issuing this statement because of the most unusual, unfair and utterly undeserved comments" which have been made about Senator Baldwin.[63]

The Malmedy hearings were completed during the autumn of 1949, and the subcommittee's report was unanimously adopted by the Armed Services Committee on October 13, 1949. The committee found, reported Baldwin, that although there had been some cases of improper procedure, the trials on a whole had been conducted fairly and the defendants allowed ample opportunity for review and redress.[64]

For Baldwin, the Malmedy hearings were the end of his Senate career. The entire proceeding had been hard on him and on his family, and when the governor of Connecticut offered him an

---

[61] *Malmedy Hearings*, pp. 630–31, 837–43; *New York Times*, May 14, 1949, p. 5; May 21, 1949, p. 3. Only a few weeks earlier, McCarthy had expressed his complete confidence in Baldwin's fairness and impartiality. See McCarthy to Raymond E. Baldwin, April 21, 1949, *Malmedy Hearings*, p. 98.

[62] *Congressional Record*, 81st Cong., 1st sess., July 26, 1949, pp. 10160–75; *New York Times*, July 27, 1949, p. 10.

[63] Millard Tydings *et al.* to Raymond E. Baldwin, Aug. 16, 1949, photostat in the NCEC files.

[64] *Congressional Record*, 81st Cong., 1st sess., Oct. 14, 1949, pp. 14512–34.

appointment to the state Supreme Court he reluctantly accepted, resigning from the Senate in December 1949. The McCarthy brawl, he later told reporters, was the last straw in his decision to leave politics.[65] For McCarthy, the Malmedy investigation was even more important. The hearings confirmed the direction in which he was heading—away from the law-making process, with its attention to tedious detail and its dependency upon others, and toward the investigative process, where the obstacles to notice and notoriety were fewer and more easily hurdled. The hearings also deepened the estrangement between McCarthy and the Senate leadership of both parties. The resolution passed by the Armed Services Committee was a direct rebuke to the senator from Wisconsin, and it carried the signatures of some of the Chamber's most powerful men—Democrats such as Richard Russell, Millard Tydings, and Lyndon Johnson, and Republicans such as Styles Bridges, Leverett Saltonstall, and William Knowland. McCarthy was not an "establishment senator," nor would he ever become one. If he hoped for power or acclaim, he would be obliged to seek it outside the closed corporation represented by these Senate leaders.

[65] *New York Times,* Dec. 14, 1949, p. 39; Anderson and May, *McCarthy,* p. 163.

2

THE LONG ROAD TO WHEELING

NINETEEN FORTY-NINE WAS NOT a good year for the junior senator from Wisconsin. He had lost his only major committee assignment and incurred the displeasure of powerful senators on both sides of the Chamber. In Wisconsin it was even worse. His annual quarrels with the state Department of Taxation were attracting wide publicity, and on top of this he came very close to being disbarred. In 1948 Miles McMillin of the *Capital Times* (Madison) had complained to the State Board of Bar Commissioners that McCarthy had violated the canons of judicial ethics of the American Bar Association by running for the Senate while still holding a judicial office.[1] In December 1948, after some additional prodding by the *Capital Times*, the commissioners petitioned the Wisconsin Supreme Court to take disciplinary action against the state's delinquent senator. The commissioners charged McCarthy with having willfully defied "the rules of ethical conduct prescribed by the constitution, the laws of the state of Wisconsin, and the members of the profession, in order to gain selfish personal advantage."[2]

The justices acknowledged that in accepting the office of senator, McCarthy "did so in violation of the terms of the constitution and laws of Wisconsin, and [in] so doing violated his oath as a circuit judge and as an attorney-at-law." Nevertheless, they concluded that the case was "one in a class by itself which is not likely to be repeated," and therefore dismissed the petition. As McCarthy himself later summarized it, the court said "it was illegal—Joe was a naughty boy, but we don't think he'll do it again."[3]

DINNER AT THE COLONY

As the year drew to an end McCarthy was increasingly uneasy over his prospects for reelection in 1952. The fleeting notoriety which he had gleaned from the Malmedy hearings was no substitute for a solid legislative record, and McCarthy had little chance of achieving one. Wisconsin had ended up in the Democratic column in 1948, as indeed it had in four of the last five presidential elections. The state's long-torpid Democratic organization was beginning to stir to life, and there were even rumblings of opposition to McCarthy's candidacy from within his own party.

Still, the year had been instructive. McCarthy had discovered certain truths about the institution of which he was a member. He had learned quite pragmatically that power gravitates toward those who are strong enough to seize it, and that the Senate con-

[1] Miles McMillin to Arthur McLeod, Secretary of the State Board of Bar Commissioners, July 7, 1948, in the Edward J. Dempsey Papers, Manuscripts Division, State Historical Society of Wisconsin. *Capital Times* (Madison), July 8, 1948. In 1946 Fred Felix Wettengel, an eccentric Appleton, Wis., insurance man, attempted to remove McCarthy's name from the ballot because he had violated the state constitution by not resigning his judgeship. The Supreme Court declined to intervene, however, on the grounds that it had no jurisdiction over the qualifications of candidates for national office. *State ex rel. Wettengel* v. *Zimmerman et al.*, 249 Wis. 206 (1946).

[2] For a copy of the commission's brief, see Harlan B. Rogers to Members of the Board, Nov. 11, 1948, in the Dempsey Papers.

[3] *State* v. *McCarthy*, 255 Wis. 234 (1949). McCarthy quite typically denounced the commissioners as "a disgrace to every honest, decent lawyer in the State of Wisconsin." *Milwaukee Journal*, July 13, 1949; W. Wade Boardman to Harlan B. Rogers, July 13, 1949, in the Dempsey Papers; Jay H. Cerf to Ronald May, Jan. 7, 1952, in the NCEC files.

tained a goodly number of men who could not withstand a ruthless and determined onslaught. If certain avenues of advancement had been closed to McCarthy there remained yet other channels for his incessant drive. If nothing else, he had begun to realize the insatiable hunger of the press for drama and sensationalism.

As 1950 opened, it remained for McCarthy to join his driving energy and style of senatorial politics to the issue which was to make his name a byword. History does not always allow us to plot the point at which the trajectory of an individual life is intercepted by some great national movement. McCarthy's championship of the "Communists-in-government" issue, however, may be traced to a now-famous dinner at Washington's Colony Restaurant. The meeting had been arranged by Charles Kraus, a member of McCarthy's staff and an instructor of political science at Washington's Georgetown University. The guests were Father Edmund A. Walsh, dean of the Georgetown School of Foreign Service, and "Colonel" William A. Roberts, a Washington attorney. The subject was Joe McCarthy's political future.

The senator quickly confessed to his guests that he desperately needed an issue on which to build a record for 1952. "How about pushing harder for the St. Lawrence seaway," suggested Roberts. Not enough sex, replied McCarthy, who then suggested his own idea, a Townsend-type pension plan for the elderly. The others quickly rejected this suggestion and the conversation drifted aimlessly on. Finally, Father Walsh asked, "How about communism as an issue?" McCarthy pounced upon the suggestion. "The government is full of Communists," he declared. "The thing to do is hammer at them."[4] A month later the senator was aboard a plane bound for Wheeling, West Virginia. Tucked away in a briefcase beside him were the notes for a hastily assembled speech on "Communists in government."

The Communist issue was not exactly new to McCarthy. In 1946 he had characterized his Democratic opponent as "communistically inclined." In 1947 he sponsored an amendment to the Taft-Hartley bill which would have given employers the authority to dismiss workers previously expelled from unions because of membership in the Communist party or because of Communist "sympathies." North Dakota Republican William

---

[4] *Capital Times* (Madison), Sept. 28, 1951; Jack Anderson and Ronald May, *McCarthy: The Man, the Senator, the "Ism"* (Boston, 1952), pp. 172–73.

Langer attacked the proposal as a violation of basic constitutional rights, and Senator Taft himself brushed it aside as unnecessary and irrelevant. That same year McCarthy dropped in to pay his respects at an open hearing of the House Committee on Un-American Activities. "I just came over to watch the very excellent job that you gentlemen are doing," he told the committee.[5]

Again, the significance of these encounters was not their uniqueness but their typicality. They heralded not the rise of Joe McCarthy, but rather the rise of the Communist issue in American politics. When Joe McCarthy stepped down from his plane and out before the Republican ladies of Wheeling, he entered a full-dress debate in which the sides were already chosen, the issues drawn, and the slogans manufactured. The crusade (if it may be called that) of which he was about to assume leadership had been nearly ten years in the making.

THE ANTI-COMMUNIST PERSUASION &
THE GROWTH OF A POLITICAL ISSUE

"McCarthyism" has been dismissed by some as a passing aberration, a chimera of mid-century politics. It was not. It was a natural expression of America's political culture and a logical though extreme product of its political machinery. What came to be called "McCarthyism" was grounded in a set of attitudes, assumptions, and judgments with deep roots in American history. There has long been a popular fear of radicalism in this country. Its effluvia are scattered throughout the past—the Alien and Sedition acts, immigration restriction, the Haymarket affair, anti-syndicalist laws, the Palmer raids, Sacco and Vanzetti. Since the Bolshevik Revolution these fears and suspicions have been generally identified with the Soviet Union, making of Russia and the Communist experiment a "menace" and a "threat" to American institutions. The United States did not recognize the new government of Russia until sixteen years after the revolution, and then only grudgingly. At home, even during the New Deal, most Americans favored denying freedom of speech, press, and assembly

---

[5] *Milwaukee Journal*, Oct. 17, 1946. *Congressional Record*, 80th Cong., 1st sess., May 9, 1947, pp. 4879–84. McCarthy is quoted in Walter Goodman, *The Committee: The Extraordinary Career of the House Committee on Un-American Activities* (New York, 1968), p. 199.

to native Communists.[6] The mobilization and political articulation of these fears is the anti-Communist "persuasion."[7] As such it has informed and in some instances dominated American politics for more than fifty years.

In domestic affairs the anti-Communist persuasion often found expression in the mindless identification of all social change with communism. Conservative critics accused New Dealers and Fair Dealers of "leading the country down the road" to collectivism; the latter, captives themselves of the persuasion, spent much of their time trying to free their own programs from any taint of suspicion. In foreign affairs the anti-Communist persuasion crystallized about the postwar debate over American policy toward the Soviet Union, replacing the old and threadbare quarrels between isolationists and internationalists with an entirely new set of emotionally charged issues and slogans. Republicans accused the Democrats of "selling out" Eastern Europe and China and "appeasing" the Russians; the Democrats insisted, somewhat less successfully, that they were as "hard" on communism as anyone. Although this issue was blunted initially by the triumph within the Truman administration of the "hard line" symbolized by Secretary of State James F. Byrnes and by the bipartisan consensus in Congress represented by Republican Senator Arthur Vandenberg, it finally surfaced during the angry postmortem over United States policy in China and during the acrimonious debate which followed the dismissal of General Douglas A. MacArthur.

A third expression of the anti-Communist persuasion, extreme and yet characteristic, was the charge of "Communists-in-government" and treason in high places. After 1950 this came to be identified with Joe McCarthy. Yet to call it "McCarthyism" is to

---

[6] See, for example, James Morton Smith, *Freedom's Fetters: The Alien and Sedition Laws and American Civil Liberties* (Ithaca, N. Y., 1956); John Higham, *Strangers in the Land: Patterns of American Nativism, 1860–1925* (New Brunswick, N. J., 1955); William Preston, Jr., *Aliens and Dissenters: Federal Suppression of Radicals, 1903–1933* (New York, 1966); Robert K. Murray, *Red Scare: A Study of National Hysteria* (Minneapolis, Minn., 1955). For popular attitudes toward native Communists see Hadley Cantril, *Public Opinion, 1933–1946* (Princeton, N. J., 1951), pp. 130, 164, 244.

[7] Marvin Meyers has defined a persuasion as "a matched set of attitudes, beliefs, projected actions: a half-formulated moral perspective involving emotional commitment. The community shares many values; at a given social moment some of these acquire compelling importance. The political expression given to such values forms a persuasion." Marvin Meyers, *The Jacksonian Persuasion* (New York, 1960), p. 10.

obscure the fundamental fact that it had been in the works for more than a decade before the Wisconsin senator made his national debut. The "Communists-in-government" issue went back at least to the late 1930s, when the conservative Texas Democrat Martin Dies and his Special House Committee on Un-American Activities turned it upon the Roosevelt administration.

Created in 1938, the Dies Committee pioneered the whole spectrum of slogans, techniques, and political mythologies that would later be called "McCarthyism."[8] It was the Dies Committee, for example, that popularized in the United States the technique of "guilt by association," through which a person is considered suspect because of the organizations to which he belongs or the friends whose company he keeps. This technique was perhaps an inevitable result of the Popular Front, during which Communists and non-Communist leftists joined to support a wide range of causes, thus creating great difficulty in proving a given individual's party membership. It also allowed the committee to let loose broadsides at a wide variety of liberals, socialists, and fellow travelers, all of whom appeared to Dies as only slightly less sinister than Communists. The committee also established the value of ex-Communist witnesses, and it carefully cultivated a growing body of these disillusioned extremists. Former Communists such as Benjamin Gitlow, the party's 1924 nominee for vice president, became star performers before the committee. Even the committee's staff director, J. B. Matthews, was a former "fellow traveler" who had bounced in and out of a dozen left-wing organizations during the 1930s.

The Dies Committee "named names" with a vengeance—563 federal employees were on the mailing list of the American League for Peace and Democracy; 1,121 government workers were "sympathetic with totalitarian ideology," 72 New Deal officials had ties to the cio's Political Action Committee. Martin Dies named more names in one single year than Joe McCarthy did in a lifetime. The membership of the Dies Committee perfected all the gambits that McCarthy would later use: "I have reliable evidence which I am not at liberty to disclose at the present time." Or, if the Justice Department will only investigate, it will "have

---

[8] The earliest study of the Dies Committee is August R. Ogden, *The Dies Committee* (Washington, D. C., 1945). A more recent and more lively account may be found in Walter Goodman, *The Committee*.

no difficulty getting the facts." Even the rhetoric of the "Communist issue" took hold. The Roosevelt administration was guilty of "coddling" Communists and being "soft" on Red Russia; its critics were dedicated to "ferreting out" disloyalty. More than one congressman began a discourse on subversion, as did Eugene E. Cox of Georgia, with the declaration, "I hold in my hand."[9]

The Dies Committee became a rallying point, not only for disillusioned ex-Communists and right-wing crusaders, but also for a host of conservative newspapermen. The Hearst and McCormick papers, as well as individual columnists such as George Sokolsky, Westbrook Pegler, and Fulton Lewis, Jr., all took a proprietary interest in the committee's activities.[10] These same journalists later helped to guide McCarthy through his first weeks and months of national fame.

Martin Dies and his supporters showed that the "Communist issue" appealed strongly to the American people. Despite, or perhaps because of, the obstreperous behavior of Chairman Dies, the committee continued to draw wide support throughout the late thirties and early forties. The Gallup polls showed a uniformly high rating for the committee, and Congress voted overwhelmingly each year to extend the committee's life and to increase its appropriation. Such was the depth of the liberal terror that one early critic of the committee, John M. Coffee of Washington, campaigned in 1940 under the slogan "The Dies Committee endorses John Coffee's reelection."[11]

During World War II the Dies Committee attracted much less public attention. Dies himself retired from Congress in 1944 rather than face a tough campaign for reelection. The committee staff, however, continued to collect, file, and index clippings from the *Daily Worker,* names of sponsors from the letterheads and programs of evanescent "front" organizations, and miscellaneous other memorabilia of the 1930s. In 1944 the committee published a set of nine appendixes containing a distillation of these labors, and including a seven-volume "Appendix Nine" listing the names of some 22,000 alleged "fellow travelers." Although this last volume was called back and suppressed by the full committee, Appendix

---

[9] Ogden, *The Dies Committee,* p. 60; Goodman, *The Committee,* pp. 71, 130–35, 140–59.
[10] Goodman, *The Committee,* pp. 85, 128, 159, 232.
[11] Ibid., p. 116.

Nine, together with the voluminous files of the committee itself, remained a prime source for those who would later seek to make political careers from exposing "Communists" in government.[12]

It was not until the end of World War II that the issue of communism-in-government began to gather momentum. The attendant causes were no doubt the anxiety and frustration of the cold war and revelations of Russian espionage in Canada, Great Britain, and the United States. The generating force behind its emergence as a political issue, however, was neither the cold war nor Soviet spies, but rather the fight back toward power of a group of Republican and Democratic partisans denied influence over national affairs for nearly two decades. As the Seventy-ninth Congress opened in early 1945, a coalition of Republicans and southern Democrats prophetically joined forces to establish the House Committee on Un-American Activities as a standing committee. This same group would help to make the Communist issue a staple of American politics during the years which followed.

The charge of communism-in-government was a broad one, covering a wide variety of allegations ranging all the way from espionage (a concrete and specific act), to the mere presence of Communists or "fellow travelers" in government agencies (It was not until 1939 that an amendment to the Hatch Act specifically forbade federal employment to members of organizations advocating the overthrow of the government.), to vague and often unsubstantiated charges of Communist "influence" or Communist "thinking." Throughout the late 1940s there was a steady accumulation of such charges and accusations, and each charge, each "case" so-called, provided new ammunition for the administration's critics.

In some few instances the issues appeared to be clear. Carl Marzani, a member of the Office of Strategic Services and later of the State Department, was convicted for having denied under oath his membership in the Communist party. George Shaw Wheeler, an economist who was removed from government in 1947 through a routine "reduction in force," later fled behind the iron curtain. H. Julian Wadleigh, who was accused of espionage by

---

[12] Robert K. Carr, *The House Committee on Un-American Activities, 1945–50* (Ithaca, N. Y., 1952), pp. 338–39. By 1949 HUAC had an index of 470,000 card references on the activities and affiliations of various individuals. U. S., Congress, House, 80th Cong., 1st sess., *Annual Report of the Committee on Un-American Activities for the year 1949* (Washington, D. C., 1950), p. 19.

Whittaker Chambers in the summer of 1948, later admitted that he had indeed supplied information to Soviet agents.[13] More often than not, however, the "cases" twisted back through a gray area of fact and fantasy, of judgment, opinion, and prejudice. Seen through the distorting lens of political partisanship and sensational journalism, they sometimes appeared to have a life and logic of their own.

One of the earliest and most durable of these incidents involved the magazine *Amerasia*, a small, bimonthly publication specializing in Far Eastern political and economic affairs. Although its editor, Philip J. Jaffe, was an ardent left-wing activist, the magazine had a fairly good reputation among Far Eastern specialists.

The *Amerasia* "case" began in early 1945, when a research analyst for the Office of Strategic Services (oss) discovered that an article appearing in the January 26, 1945, issue of *Amerasia* was an almost verbatim reproduction of a classified oss report.[14] The oss assigned a security officer, Frank Brooks Bielaski, to investigate the case. In company with a handful of fellow agents, Bielaski forced his way into the *Amerasia* offices late one evening and discovered a large number of classified government documents. The case was immediately turned over to the Federal Bureau of Investigation, which placed the magazine's staff under intensive surveillance. The FBI investigators also made surreptitious entries into the *Amerasia* offices and into the homes of its staff members and their friends. They confirmed the presence of large numbers of government documents in the magazine's offices, and singled out Emmanuel Larsen, a member of the State Department's Far Eastern division with whom Jaffe was in frequent contact, as a prime suspect. The FBI was prepared to turn the case over to the Justice Department for prosecution on April 18, 1945, but the navy and the State Department both urged that the investigation be continued in order to learn whether others might be involved.[15] On May 31 the FBI forwarded the case to the Justice

---

[13] Earl Latham, *The Communist Controversy in Washington: From the New Deal to McCarthy* (Cambridge, Mass., 1966), pp. 94, 195. Hornell Hart, *McCarthy versus the State Department* (Durham, N. C., 1952), pp. 14–15.

[14] The following is based largely upon testimony before the Tydings Committee in 1950. See U. S., Congress, Senate, 81st Cong., 2d sess., Committee on Foreign Relations, *State Department Loyalty Investigation* (Washington, D. C., 1950), pp. 923–1453 (hereafter cited as *Tydings Committee Hearings*).

[15] A chance casualty of this decision was John Stewart Service, a foreign service officer who had just returned from the Far East. Service held a number

Department's criminal division for prosecution. After another brief delay at the request of Secretary of the Navy James V. Forrestal, the FBI arrested Larsen, Jaffe, and four others on charges of espionage. In addition to Jaffe and Larsen, they included Kate Mitchell, a co-editor of the magazine, Lt. Andrew Roth, an officer in the Office of Naval Intelligence, Mark Gayn, a freelance journalist, and John Stewart Service, a foreign service officer.

The Justice Department began its presentation to the grand jury in the summer of 1945, charging the six with conspiracy to steal government documents.[16] During the course of the testimony before the grand jury, it soon became evident that Jaffe and Larsen were the main culprits, and in August indictments were returned against them and against Roth. The jurors found no evidence to warrant indictment of Service, Mitchell, or Gayn.

At this point, what remained of the case began to fall apart. Larsen learned from his landlord of the illegal searches which had been conducted by the FBI and filed a motion to quash the case against him.[17] The Justice Department realized that as soon as Jaffe learned of Larsen's action he would file a similar motion, so they hurriedly arranged a conference at which Jaffe agreed to plead guilty in return for a light sentence. Jaffe pleaded guilty and was fined $2,500. Larsen was ultimately allowed to plead *nolo contendere* and was fined $500.[18]

---

of routine debriefings with newsmen and other Far Eastern specialists, including Jaffe, to whom he gave personal copies of reports he had prepared on conditions in China. Although Service was completely exonerated from any complicity in the *Amerasia* case, this was doubtless a factor in his eventual dismissal from the department in 1951. Ibid., pp. 1257–1453; *New York Times*, Dec. 14, 1951, p. 1.

[16] The original warrants against the six had charged them with conspiracy to improperly receive, obtain, or communicate information relating to the national defense (e.g., espionage). Critics later interpreted the shift in charges as part of a sinister whitewash of the case. The decision rested upon three simple facts: The penalty for conspiracy in either case was the same; the great mass of documents found did *not* appear to relate to the national defense; to have proceeded on the original count would have forced upon the prosecution the added burden of proving that the documents did relate to the national defense. *Tydings Committee Hearings*, p. 1044.

[17] The Supreme Court has held that evidence obtained through illegal entry and evidence derived from leads or clues arising from illegal entry are inadmissible. See *Silverthorne Lumber Co. v. United States*, 251 U. S. 385 and *Nardone v. United States*, 308 U. S. 338. Also see Robert L. Heald and Lyon L. Tyler, "The Principle behind the Amerasia Case," *Georgetown Law Journal* 39 (1951): 181–215.

[18] *Tydings Committee Hearings*, pp. 1020–24. The evidence against Roth,

The issues involved in the *Amerasia* case are complex and difficult to assess. The transmission of the documents by Larsen to Jaffe clearly constituted a breach of security. The defendants, however claimed that they were merely following the general practice among newsmen in seeking to obtain government information and that any excesses were but the result of journalistic zeal. The documents found in the *Amerasia* offices related almost without exception to Far Eastern affairs, the magazine's legitimate concern. There was no known attempt to conceal the documents nor to transmit them clandestinely to any third party. It is difficult to imagine the conspirators of an espionage organization printing the fruits of their labor in a magazine, as in the case of the report which led to the opening of the *Amerasia* case. Although later critics of the Justice Department sought to magnify the importance of the documents involved, they were for the most part harmless and overclassified.

Still, the case disturbed many who believed that the government had failed to prosecute a clear case of espionage, and these doubts and suspicions fired a political controversy which would flare up intermittently for the next ten years. It was a "whitewash," charged Michigan Congressman George Dondero, an "open invitation to sabotage" rigged by the "left-wing crowd" in government.[19]

At the instigation of Dondero and other Republicans, the House of Representatives authorized an investigation of the *Amerasia* case in the spring of 1946 under the chairmanship of Congressman Samuel F. Hobbs, a shrewd Alabama Democrat. At the request of Dondero, the hearings were held in closed session and there was no published transcript. A long list of witnesses were called, including Emmanuel Larsen. Larsen had approached Dondero sometime during 1945 or 1946 and had given the congressman an elaborate and fanciful version of the *Amerasia* case in which he tried to shift the burden of guilt onto anyone and everyone but himself. Larsen appeared before the Hobbs Committee and repeated his story, replete with sinister innuendos about the role of various State Department officials. Nevertheless, the testimony

---

who had already been dismissed from the navy, was insubstantial, and the Justice Department declined to prosecute the case further. Ibid., p. 1011.

[19] *Congressional Record*, 79th Cong., 2d sess., Oct. 10, 1945, pp. 9552–53. For similar attacks see ibid, Nov. 1, 1945, p. 10310, and Nov. 28, 1945, pp. 1150–51.

of officials from the oss, FBI, and Justice Department convinced the committee that while there was evidence of lax security methods and faulty classification, there was nothing to justify adverse criticism of "either grand jury, any prosecuting attorney, FBI, judicial, or other official."[20]

Despite the Hobbs Committee report, the *Amerasia* case continued to receive widespread publicity throughout the late 1940s, especially among the Hearst and Scripps-Howard newspapers. Reporters for both chains helped to keep this issue alive in the years that followed. Other "cases" would be set alongside it, and in time it would provide ammunition for a major political issue.

Following close upon the heels of the *Amerasia* case came the report of the Canadian Royal Commission, made public in the summer of 1946, which disclosed widespread Russian espionage in Canada, and by inference the United States as well. The significance of the report was lost on neither Truman nor the Congress. To forestall precipitous congressional legislation, Truman first named a study commission in the fall of 1946, and then in March 1947 followed the commission's recommendation by establishing a federal loyalty program.[21]

But the Communist issue continued to grow. The Republicans had made it an important part of their successful congressional campaign in 1946, and as the new Eightieth Congress convened they were determined to capitalize on it. Speaker Joseph W. Martin, Jr., the short, drab, little man who led the House Republicans, pledged that the new Congress would "ferret out" (the phrase was already popular) all those who sought to destroy the "American way of life."[22]

Other congressmen were more specific. Representative Alvin E. O'Konski of Wisconsin made a vehement attack on Gustavo

[20] U. S., Congress, House, 79th Cong., 2d sess., *Report of Subcommittee IV of the Committee on the Judiciary in Pursuance of H. Res. 430* (Washington, D. C., 1946), p. 8. Larsen repeated a highly colored version of his story in the October 1946 issue of *Plain Talk,* a right-wing magazine edited by Ralph de Toledano. In subsequent testimony before the Tydings Committee, Larsen repudiated both the article and his testimony before the Hobbs Committee. *Tydings Committee Hearings,* pp. 1118–29. Also see excerpts from the State Department Loyalty Board hearings in the case of John Stewart Service in ibid., pp. 2202–25.

[21] *New York Times,* March 23, 1947, p. 1; Eleanor Bontecou, *The Federal Loyalty-Security Program* (Ithaca, N. Y., 1953), pp. 21–30.

[22] *New York Times,* Feb. 4, 1947, p. 18.

Duran, a naturalized American of Spanish ancestry who had been an assistant of Spruille Braden, onetime ambassador to Argentina and later assistant secretary of state. O'Konski charged that Duran, who had served in the Republican Army during the Spanish Civil War, was "one of the most notorious international Communists the world ever knew." He was, according to the Wisconsin Republican, part of an evil conspiracy (the State Department, Moscow, and the CIO) to wreck American relations in the southern hemisphere.[23]

An even wilder set of accusations were made by Illinois Congressman Fred Buseby in an attack on Assistant Secretary of State William Benton and the Office of International Information and Cultural Affairs (OIC). Buseby accused some half-dozen OIC employees of Communist sympathies or affiliations. He attacked William T. Stone because Stone had served on the editorial board of *Amerasia* from 1937 to 1941. It made little difference to the congressman that the magazine had been a reputable scholarly publication during these years, or that the *Amerasia* case did not begin until 1945. It was enough that Stone's name had once appeared upon its masthead. He charged a second official, Haldore E. Hanson, with Communist sympathies because of a book which Hanson had written about the Sino-Japanese war during the 1930s. Although Hanson had been a war correspondent for the Associated Press, the congressman attached grave and sinister implications to the fact that he had traveled briefly behind Chinese Communist lines.

Buseby also attacked Esther Caulkin Brunauer, a distinguished career officer who had been active in the establishment of UNESCO, by misquoting and distorting a speech which Mrs. Brunauer had recently delivered over the radio. Who was responsible, he next asked, for the appointment of Harlow Shapley, a Harvard astronomer and a veteran left-wing activist, to the United States Na-

[23] At the time of O'Konski's attack, Duran was working for the United Nations where, again according to the congressman, he was "now screening refugees" as a representative to the United Nations Refugee Committee. *Congressional Record*, 80th Cong., 1st sess., March 13, 1947, pp. 2045–47, A1010–14. Senator Kenneth S. Wherry (R-Nebr.) had urged Duran's dismissal in 1946, but Duran had been cleared by the State Department's Security Committee. Wherry to James F. Byrnes, Aug. 2, 1946; Donald Russell to Wherry, Sept. 14, 1946, both letters in the *Tydings Committee Hearings*, pp. 1544–45.

tional Commission of UNESCO? Shapley was in fact nominated by the American Association for the Advancement of Science, but Buseby apparently did not scruple over such details.[24]

Throughout 1947 and 1948, attacks like those of O'Konski and Buseby were increasing. They had a certain self-perpetuating and self-reinforcing quality, so that a series of such half-truths, repeated long enough and often enough, seemed to take on a sense of credibility.

It was Congress' many investigating committees, however, that labored most diligently to raise the Communist issue. After sixteen years out of power, the Republicans of the Eightieth Congress were determined to investigate nearly every phase of the Democratic administration. Within less than a month there were thirty-five projected investigations, and none of these offered more bountiful political dividends than did those investigations into the field of loyalty and security.[25]

A concerted effort to probe the State Department centered about a House Appropriations subcommittee chaired by Congressman Karl Stefan of Nebraska. Under heavy congressional pressure, the State Department allowed a team of committee investigators headed by Robert E. Lee to examine departmental loyalty files. The result of this investigation was a list of data on some 108 past, present, and prospective employees.[26] The security files themselves were made up of material gathered by the FBI, the Civil Service Commission, and various other department agencies. They included all data collected by these investigators, even false or unconfirmed statements and allegations.[27] The files tended to reflect the biases and prejudices of the security investigators. In one file, for example, the American Civil Liberties Union was listed as a Communist front. In another, the testimony of an employer about a former employee who had led a strike was uncritically accepted.[28] There was some evidence, moreover, that the House investigators compounded these distortions by their

[24] *Congressional Record*, 80th Cong., 1st sess., May 14, 1947, pp. 5296–5300. For an effective reply to the Buseby charges, see William Benton to Congressman James P. Richards (D-S. C.), July 25, 1947, in ibid., July 26, 1947, pp. A4012–13.

[25] *New York Times*, Jan. 26, 1947, sec. 4, p. 10.

[26] The "Lee list" is printed in the *Tydings Committee Hearings*, pp. 1771–1813.

[27] Testimony of J. Edgar Hoover, ibid., pp. 328–29.

[28] Ibid., pp. 1775–76, 1785.

own tendency to pick out for summary only the most alarming material they could find.

The "Lee list" was first used during Appropriations Committee hearings in early 1948. Chairman Stefan read a number of the individual case summaries into the record during the course of questioning State Department officials on the loyalty program.[29] From the Appropriations Committee, the Lee list then made its way to the House Committee on Expenditures in the Executive Departments, where it again became the basis for the questioning of State Department officials. The department supplied this committee with a statistical summary showing that of the 108 "cases" on the Lee list, only some 57 were then employed by the department.[30]

The Lee list also went to the Senate Committee on Expenditures in the Executive Departments, which under the rather inept leadership of Homer Ferguson was searching for disloyal employees in the Commerce Department. After 1948 the list was returned to the committee files, where it collected dust for the next few years. From time to time an enterprising right-wing journalist would refer to its contents, but otherwise it attracted little public notice.[31]

Other congressional committees tried to cash in on the Communist issue. The House Committee on Education and Labor conducted extensive hearings into Communist infiltration of trade unions. The House Judiciary Committee held hearings on a subversive activities control bill. But the center of attention in this, as in preceding Congresses, was the House Committee on Un-American Activities (HUAC). As usual, the committee covered a wide field of inquiry. It heard testimony from Communists, who generally appeared unwillingly and said little, and it listened to ex-Communists, who came gladly and talked at length. It held hearings on internal security bills introduced by committee members Karl E. Mundt of South Dakota and Richard M. Nixon of

[29] U. S., Congress, House, 80th Cong., 2d sess., Committee on Appropriations, *Department of State Appropriation Bill for 1949* (Washington, D. C., 1948), pp. 173–91.

[30] U. S., Congress, House, 80th Cong., 2d sess., Committee on Expenditures in the Executive Departments, *State Department* (Washington, D. C., 1948), p. 23. Of the 57 who remained, 26 had been approved and 31 were in security channels as of March 1948.

[31] See, for example, Willard Edwards in the *Chicago Daily Tribune*, Feb. 14, 1950.

California. It investigated communism in labor unions and communism in Hollywood. Sooner or later it was inevitable that it should investigate "communism in government."

One of the prime objectives of the House Committee was to gain access to the confidential loyalty files of government employees. The Truman administration was already beginning to regret having allowed the House Appropriations Committee to use these files when, in 1948, HUAC demanded the records of Edward U. Condon. Condon was a distinguished scientist and director of the National Bureau of Standards. He had been a target of the committee for some time, and although both the Commerce Department and the Atomic Energy Commission had cleared him, the committee charged that he was "one of the weakest links in our atomic security." Although Condon urged that his records be opened, the president decided that an issue of executive privilege was at stake, and on March 13, 1948, he issued a directive to all government officers ordering that loyalty files be maintained in strictest confidence and that any subpoena, demand, or request for them be respectfully declined.[32]

The result was a standoff. Congress was unwilling to admit any limitations upon its power of investigation, and on April 22, the House passed a bill introduced by Congressman Clare E. Hoffman (R-Mich.) which would have opened all investigative files to the Congress.[33] The president was equally determined. He ignored the House resolution and threatened the Hoffman bill (which never left the Senate) with veto. He reaffirmed his position at a press conference in August 1948, stating that "no information of any sort relating to the employee's loyalty . . . shall be included in the material submitted to a congressional committee."[34] The controversy over executive files would remain at the heart of many subsequent investigations. This 1948 confrontation had resolved

[32] *Public Papers of the Presidents of the United States, 1946* (Washington, D. C., 1964), pp. 181–82; *New York Times*, March 16, 1948, p. 1.

[33] *New York Times*, April 23, 1948, p. 1; May 13, 1948, p. 1; May 14, 1948, p. 15.

[34] *Public Papers, 1946*, pp. 432–33. At the same time, Attorney General Tom C. Clark restated the administration position in a letter to Senator Homer Ferguson explaining why the Commerce Department could not turn over the files of William Remington, then under investigation by Ferguson's Investigations Subcommittee. Tom C. Clark to Homer Ferguson, Aug. 5, 1948, U. S., Congress, Senate, 80th Cong., 2d sess., Committee on Expenditures in the Executive Departments, *Export Policy and Loyalty* (Washington, D. C., 1948), pp. 383–84.

no question of executive or congressional prerogative, but had added yet another element to the growing debate over "communism in government."

The great watershed in the growth of the Communist issue in American politics came in the summer of 1948 when Elizabeth Bentley and Whittaker Chambers testified before the House Committee on Un-American Activities. Miss Bentley appeared before the committee on July 31, 1948, and told how for five years she had served as a courier for a Soviet spy ring. She accused some thirty former government employees of membership in this "apparatus," including Lauchlin Currie, a wartime assistant to President Roosevelt, and Harry Dexter White, a former assistant secretary of the treasury.[35] Three days later, the committee heard former Communist Whittaker Chambers, then a senior editor for *Time* magazine, accuse nine former government officials of party membership. The most notable of these was Alger Hiss, former director of special political affairs in the State Department and then head of the Carnegie Endowment for International Peace.[36]

The testimony which the two witnesses related was not entirely new. Miss Bentley had given her story to the FBI in 1945, and had appeared before the grand jury of the Southern District of New York in 1947. Chambers had first told his story to Undersecretary of State Adolph A. Berle in 1939, and had later been visited, in piecemeal fashion, by agents of the FBI, the Civil Service Commission, the Office of Naval Intelligence, and the State Department.[37]

What was new was the drama and publicity which the hearings

[35] Miss Bentley had earlier appeared before the New York Grand Jury investigating communism. She had also testified before Senator Homer Ferguson's Investigations Subcommittee on July 30, 1948. *New York Times,* July 31, 1948, p. 1.

[36] Ibid., Aug. 4, 1948, p. 1. This and subsequent testimony relating to the Bentley-Chambers charges may be found in U. S., Congress, House, 80th Cong., 2d sess., Committee on Un-American Activities, *Hearings Regarding Communist Espionage in the United States Government,* 2 pts. (Washington, D. C., 1948-1949).

[37] Whittaker Chambers, *Witness* (New York, 1952), pp. 463–70, 486, 491–92, 509–11. Miss Bentley has published her story in *Out of Bondage* (New York, 1951). Almost all those named in the 1948 hearings were no longer in government. Some had left well before Miss Bentley's celebrated break with the party in the mid-1940s. Some were doubtless removed through routine "reductions in force" during the postwar consolidation of government agencies. Still others probably resigned rather than face loyalty proceedings arising from reports by the FBI and other security agencies.

focused upon these disclosures. Here at last was meat and substance for the Republican charge of communism in government. Here was confirmation of their worst suspicions and their fondest hopes. Here was proof positive of treason in high places and perfidy at the vitals of government. The controversy which surrounded these charges will probably never be fully resolved. There were no disinterested parties to this dispute. Although much of what Bentley and Chambers told the committee was contradictory and ambiguous, many of their accusations were never disproved.

The two sets of charges followed widely differing courses. The impact of the Bentley testimony was diffuse. It reappeared only in scattered bits and pieces during the Congresses which immediately followed, and it was not until 1953 that it was exhaustively exploited by Senator William E. Jenner's Subcommittee on Internal Security.[38] By contrast the case of Alger Hiss had all the clean, straight lines of a classical drama unfolding toward its predestined conclusion.[39]

For the conservatives who gave voice to the anti-Communist persuasion, Hiss was a symbol for all that they abhorred. He represented the liberalism of the early New Deal, he was associated with the wartime conference at Yalta, and he now stood accused of espionage. For most liberals the innocence of Alger Hiss was an article of faith, partially because of the liberalism and internationalism for which they believed he stood, and partly because of a reaction justifiably conditioned by the previous performances of the House Committee on Un-American Activities. Alger Hiss may not have been the symbol of a generation, but the long and emotional debate between these two groups went far toward making him this.

Hiss had graduated from Johns Hopkins and Harvard Law School with high honors, going on to serve as law clerk to the great Oliver Wendell Holmes. He had entered government in the early 1930s, first in the Agricultural Adjustment Administration,

---

[38] See especially U. S., Congress, Senate, 83d Cong., 1st sess., Committee on the Judiciary, *Interlocking Subversion in Government Departments* (Washington, D. C., 1953).

[39] Whittaker Chambers's autobiographical account of the Hiss case, *Witness*, has become a minor classic in the literature of American communism. Alger Hiss has presented his own case with *In the Court of Public Opinion* (New York, 1957). The best contemporary account of the trials is Alistair Cooke, *A Generation on Trial* (New York, 1950).

then as counsel for a Senate committee, later in the solicitor general's office, and finally in the State Department. He served as an adviser to the Yalta conference and was secretary of the Dumbarton Oaks conference which first drafted the charter for the United Nations. His character witnesses included two Supreme Court justices and half a dozen high-ranking State Department officials. President Truman dismissed the entire proceedings as a "red herring" dragged out to distract the public's attention from the legislative failures of the Eightieth "do nothing" Congress.

On August 5, 1948, Hiss testified that he had never been affiliated with any Communist organization. At a subsequent hearing he dared Chambers to repeat his story outside the privileged floor of the committee room. Chambers reiterated his charges August 27 on "Meet the Press," and after some initial hesitation, Hiss filed suit for libel. The case took a more serious turn at a November pretrial hearing, when Chambers produced sixty secret State Department documents which he charged Hiss had given him. It was no longer a question of membership in the Communist party, but a question of espionage. When the House Committee on Un-American Activities issued subpoenas for any further documents, Chambers led committee investigators to a pumpkin on his farm where he had secreted microfilms he declared he had received from Hiss during the late 1930s. On December 15, 1948, Hiss was indicted for perjury. (The statute of limitations prevented a charge of espionage.) The first trial ended with a hung jury. The second resulted in Hiss's conviction.

While the trial of Alger Hiss wound slowly through the courts, the pressure behind the "Communist issue" continued to mount. For some politicians it was a convenient camouflage for their true purposes. For example, "natural gas" senators such as Edwin C. Johnson of Colorado and Lyndon Baines Johnson of Texas blocked the reappointment of Leland Olds to the Federal Power Commission by charging that he was an "egotistical chameleon whose predominant color is pink" and that he traveled with "those who proposed the Marxian answer."[40] Nevada Democrat Pat McCarran used an investigation of communism among aliens and nationality groups as part of his xenophobic campaign for more

[40] Rowland Evans and Robert Novak, *Lyndon B. Johnson: The Exercise of Power* (New York, 1968), pp. 45–49. The first quotation is from Edwin Johnson, the second from Lyndon Johnson.

restrictive immigration controls. Even Democratic liberals such as Hubert H. Humphrey took to baiting third-party candidate Henry Wallace and his followers in an effort to strengthen their own position as sober, industrious, and 100 percent American reformers.[41]

Under the leadership of Georgia Democrat John S. Wood, the House Committee on Un-American Activities proceeded less sensationally, but more or less along the same lines laid out during the previous Congress. The committee investigated communism in labor unions, communism among minority groups, and communism in the District of Columbia. It conducted a number of probes into charges of Russian espionage.[42]

The driving force behind the Communist issue, however, continued to be the Republican party. Harold E. Stassen, campaigning for the G.O.P. presidential nomination, called for a purge of Communists from American society and for a ban on the Communist party itself. Prominent Republican leaders Joseph W. Martin, Jr., Leonard W. Hall, and Hugh D. Scott, Jr., all charged that Truman was soft on communism. So did the keynote speaker at the Republican National Convention in 1948. During the campaign itself Thomas E. Dewey declared that the Democrats had abetted Communist inroads in government. His running mate, California Governor Earl Warren, was even blunter, accusing the administration of "coddling" Communists. These attacks continued after the 1948 election, so that by June 1949 President Truman was already comparing the anti-Communist hysteria to the era of the Alien and Sedition Acts.[43]

Other events were deepening the apprehensions of the American public. In August 1949 the State Department issued its White Paper on the failure of American policy in China. On September 23 President Truman announced to hastily assembled reporters that the Soviet Union had exploded its first nuclear bomb. In

[41] *New York Times,* Jan. 14, 1949, p. 8.

[42] Carr, *The House Committee on Un-American Activities;* Goodman, *The Committee,* chapt. 9.

[43] *New York Times,* Feb. 20, 1948, p. 3; March 19, 1948, p. 4; April 3, 1948, p. 13; April 17, 1948, p. 8; April 18, 1948, p. 33; April 23, 1948, p. 26; June 22, 1948, p. 1; Sept. 22, 1948, p. 19; Sept. 25, 1948, p. 1; Sept. 26, 1948, p. 60. Alben Barkley replied for the Democrats by charging that a Republican victory would be the quickest way to bring on communism. Ibid., Oct. 2, 1948, p. 8. For Truman's statement on the Alien and Sedition acts see ibid., June 17, 1949, p. 1.

December the defeated remnants of Chiang Kai-shek's Nationalist government fled to the island of Formosa. To many, the menace of communism never seemed greater than in that winter of 1949–1950. On October 14, 1949, eleven leaders of the American Communist party were convicted for conspiracy to advocate the overthrow of the government by force and violence. In early 1950 Justice Department aide Judith Coplon and Russian United Nations attaché Valentin Gubitchev were brought to trial on charges of spying for the Soviet Union.[44] On February 3 British physicist Klaus Fuchs, who at one time had worked at Los Alamos, was arrested on charges of atomic espionage, and a week later the scientist gave authorities a detailed confession.[45] His arrest led to the eventual capture in the United States of Harry Gold, David Greenglass, Morton Sobel, and Julius and Ethel Rosenberg, all of whom were later convicted of conspiracy to commit espionage.

The conviction of Alger Hiss on January 21, 1950, released a torrent of abuse upon the Truman administration. It was a vindication for Republicans such as Richard M. Nixon and Karl E. Mundt, and they wasted no time in pressing their advantage. Mundt demanded that Truman should now help to "ferret out" those government employees "whose Soviet leanings have contributed so greatly to the deplorable mess of our foreign policy." Harold H. Velde of Illinois charged that Russian espionage agents were running loose all over the country, and Robert F. Rich of Pennsylvania suggested that Dean Acheson was working for Stalin.[46]

While McCarthy was preparing his famous speech for the ladies of Wheeling, West Virginia, other Republicans were taking much the same approach. According to a platform adopted on February 6, 1950, the Republicans deplored "the dangerous degree to which Communists and their fellow travelers have been employed in important Government posts," and they denounced the "soft attitude of this Administration toward Government employees and officials who hold or support Communist attitudes."[47] And in Lincoln Day speeches across the nation, Republicans such as

[44] Miss Coplon had been convicted on two previous counts stemming from a separate indictment in July 1949. This highly publicized trial ended in conviction on March 7, 1950. *New York Times,* March 8, 1950, p. 1. The conviction was later reversed on the basis of procedural irregularities.

[45] Ibid., Feb. 4, 1950, p. 1; Feb. 11, 1950, p. 1.

[46] Ibid., Jan. 24, 1950, p. 22; Jan. 27, 1950, p. 13.

[47] Ibid., Feb. 7, 1950, p. 1.

Congressman William S. Hill of Colorado were telling receptive audiences that "we found them [the Communists] heavily infiltrated into high policy-making positions . . . . We were fully vindicated." The Hiss case, declared Richard Nixon, was only "a small part of the whole shocking story of Communist espionage in the United States."[48]

WHEELING

The speech McCarthy delivered in Wheeling, West Virginia, was part and parcel of this rising Republican issue. Few realized, however, just how great the senator's debt was to those who had preceded him. The "rough draft" which McCarthy handed reporters as he stepped from the plane in Wheeling was a scissors-and-paste job made up of disparate fragments from a wide variety of Republican charges. There was a long section on Alger Hiss drawn from a speech Richard Nixon had delivered in the House of Representatives on January 26, 1950. Nixon had told the House, for example, "The great lesson which should be learned from the Alger Hiss case is that we are not just dealing with espionage agents· who get 30 pieces of silver to obtain the blueprint of a new weapon . . . but this is a far more sinister type of activity, because it permits the enemy to guide and shape our policy." McCarthy, at Wheeling, declared, "One thing to remember in discussing the Communists in our Government is that we are not dealing with spies who get 30 pieces of silver to steal the blueprint of a new weapon. We are dealing with a far more sinister type of activity because it permits the enemy to guide and shape our policy."[49] There were three short paragraphs on alleged Com-

[48] *Denver Post*, Feb. 10, 1950; *Deseret News* (Salt Lake City), Feb. 10, 1950.

[49] *Congressional Record*, 81st Cong., 2d sess., Jan. 26, 1950, pp. 1002–1008. A transcript of McCarthy's "rough draft" appears in the appendix of the *Tydings Committee Hearings*, pp. 1759–63. It was typical of McCarthy's inventiveness that he should inflate even Nixon's remarks. Nixon had told the House that in 1944 there had been 180,000,000 people in the Soviet orbit, and 1,625,000,000 on the "anti-totalitarian side." Today, he declared, there were 540,000,000 on "our side," 600,000,000 neutrals, and 800,000,000 on the Soviet side. The odds had changed from 9-1 in our favor to 5-3 against us. McCarthy correctly cited the first figures, but then declared that today there were 80,000,000,000 people "under the absolute domination of Soviet Russia" (The world population in 1950 was approximately 2,490,000,000.) while on "our side" the figure had shrunk to around 500,000 (about the population of

munists in the State Department, neatly clipped from a story by Willard Edwards in the *Chicago Tribune*.[50] Then there was a section on John Stewart Service from the *Washington Times-Herald* which McCarthy had read into the *Congressional Record* in early January.[51] Finally, McCarthy read an excerpt from testimony taken by the Senate Judiciary Committee which he represented as proving that the State Department was covering up espionage and preventing the prosecution of spies.[52]

But all the names which the senator had mentioned were rather shopworn. Even the alleged crimes of Alger Hiss had taken place ten years earlier during the late 1930s. What was lacking was the fire of immediacy and drama, and this McCarthy could supply. His precise words that evening will probably never be known. According to the radio and newspaper men who followed his rough draft the senator waived aloft a sheaf of paper and shouted, "I have here in my hand a list of 205—a list of names that were made known to the Secretary of State as being members of the Communist Party and who nevertheless are still working and shaping policy in the State Department."[53]

Columbus, Ohio). *Tydings Committee Hearings*, p. 1760. McCarthy corrected these and other exaggerations in the version of the Wheeling speech which he read into the *Congressional Record* on Feb. 20, 1950.

[50] *Chicago Daily Tribune*, Feb. 2, 1950. Edwards had been among the first to whom McCarthy had turned in his search for material on communism in government. Author's interview with Willard Edwards, May 26, 1966.

[51] *Congressional Record*, 81st Cong., 2d sess., Jan. 5, 1950, p. 86. McCarthy told his Wheeling audience that while on duty in the Far East, Service had sent back reports "stating *in unqualified terms (and I quote)* that 'Communism was the only hope of China.'" When he presented the speech to the Senate, ten days later, he declared that Service had sent back reports "stating, *in effect, that* communism was the best hope of China." *Tydings Committee Hearings*, p. 1760. *Congressional Record*, 81st Cong., 2d sess., Feb. 20, 1950, p. 1956. My emphasis.

[52] *Tydings Committee Hearings*, pp. 1761–62; U. S., Congress, Senate, 80th Cong., 1st sess., Committee on the Judiciary, *Communist Activities among Aliens and National Groups* (Washington, D. C., 1949), pp. 813–16.

[53] *Wheeling Intelligencer*, Feb. 10, 1950. Affidavits of Paul A. Meyers and James K. Whittaker (WWVA), *Tydings Committee Hearings*, pp. 1758–68. McCarthy would later claim that he had declared that he held a list of *fifty-seven* names. An intensive investigation by Senate investigators concluded that precisely what McCarthy said that night "is still shrouded in doubt." "Report of Preliminary Investigation of Senator William Benton's Charges against Senator Joseph R. McCarthy Relating to Senate Resolution 187," a report made by the staff of the Privileges and Elections Subcommittee of the Senate Committee on Rules and Administration, in the Robert C. Hendrickson Papers, box 18, Syracuse University.

McCarthy, of course, had no list at all. What he did have was a letter from Secretary of State James F. Byrnes to Congressman Adolph J. Sabath of Illinois, dated July 26, 1946, which had appeared in the *Congressional Record.* In this letter Secretary Byrnes explained that a preliminary screening of some 3,000 federal employees transferred into the State Department from wartime agencies had resulted in recommendations against the permanent employment of 285. Of these 285, the employment of 79 had already been terminated as of July 1946; 285 minus 79 leaves—if your arithmetic and logic are none too scrupulous—205 "Communists" in the State Department.[54]

It had been the kind of speech one gives to a Republican Women's Club in Wheeling, West Virginia. No one, least of all the senator from Wisconsin, anticipated the results. That night the Associated Press wire service carried the story across the country. Most big metropolitan dailies, including the *New York Times,* ignored the dispatch, writing it off for what it was, a typical piece of Lincoln Day enthusiasm. The *Chicago Tribune* briefly noted the speech on an inner sheet. The *Denver Post* carried it on page one.[55]

McCarthy was startled by the excitement which attended his flight to Salt Lake City for a second speaking engagement. When he changed planes in Denver he was surrounded by reporters clamoring for the list of "Communists" in the State Department. He offered to show them the list, but then "discovered he had left it in his baggage on the plane." There was an engaging picture of the senator peering into his briefcase for the elusive list.[56]

By the time McCarthy reached Salt Lake City, he had recovered enough to begin a series of dissimulations. There were, or so it now appeared, two lists. The first was a list of 205 "bad risks" still working in the State Department. In addition, and more ominously, there was fifty-seven "card-carrying Communists" in the State Department.[57] By the time McCarthy reached Reno, the following day, the number 205 had been neatly scratched from the rough draft which the senator had for newsmen, the number

---

[54] *Congressional Record,* 79th Cong., 2d sess., July 26, 1946, p. A4892. The preliminary recommendations against employment, of course, were based on a variety of reasons, of which security considerations were only one.

[55] *Chicago Daily Tribune,* Feb. 10, 1950; *Denver Post,* Feb. 10, 1950.

[56] *Denver Post,* Feb. 11, 1950.

[57] Ibid., Feb. 11, 1950; *Deseret News* (Salt Lake City), Feb. 11, 1950.

fifty-seven written in its place.[58] The origin of the number fifty-seven was as bizarre as that of the 205. In late 1947 a group of investigators for a House Appropriation Subcommittee had compiled a list of 108 case summaries of past, present, and prospective State Department employees about whom questions of loyalty and security had been raised. When a representative of the department was questioned about this list in March 1948, he declared that *only fifty-seven* of those listed were then employed by the department.[59]

As in the case of the "205," McCarthy in all probability did not have this list either. That would only come later. So too would the senator's assertion that in his original speech at Wheeling he had held in his hand "57 cases of individuals who would appear to be either card-carrying members or certainly loyal to the Communist Party." The senator's words were lost to history that evening when the radio operator of WWVA in Wheeling reversed his tape and erased the speech. Did the senator follow the rough draft and claim to "hold in his hand" a list of 205 "Communists" in the State Department? Or was it fifty-seven? Were they "card-carrying Communists," as he declared in Denver and Salt Lake City? Or were they "loyal to the Communist Party," as he told the Senate? Or were they only innocent employees caught up in the machinery of the government's loyalty program and singled out for public attack by their inclusion on a two-year-old list?

These and other questions went unanswered in those early weeks of 1950. McCarthy, the Senate rowdy, had taken up the issue of communism in government, but not even the most prescient observer could foretell where this unique juncture of personality and politics would lead.

---

[58] *Nevada State Journal* (Reno), Feb. 12, 1950.
[59] See above, p. 41. U. S., Congress, House, 80th Cong., 2d sess., Committee on Expenditures in the Executive Departments, *State Department* (Washington, D. C., 1948), p. 23. My emphasis.

3

THE RISE OF JOE McCARTHY

THE RISE OF JOE MC CARTHY took only a few short months. In February he was an undistinguished and indistinguishable midwestern senator. By July he had become a symbol of Republican extremism and a political force of major proportions. What follows is an attempt to describe and to understand that meteoric rise.

It should be clear by now that the "Communist issue" was a staple of postwar Republican campaign oratory, and that McCarthy had said little more than his party colleagues across the nation. It is easy to see that the anti-Communist crusade demanded a leader of McCarthy's temerity. It has been somewhat less evident that even more important was the quiet, cautious, and yet continuous support the senator received from his own party. "Communism-in-government" was a Republican issue, and one the

G.O.P. could ill afford to lose in its battle against the Democrats. McCarthy's support among Republicans grew proportionately with his increasing identification with this issue, and this in turn contributed to his rising power and influence.

McCarthy's true significance lay in the fact that he brought to this thoroughly conventional political issue his own thoroughly unconventional personal qualities—a flair for self-dramatization, a superb sense of press-agentry, and a stubborn unwillingness to back down. He would later recall that Republicans had been yelling "treason" for some time, but that their notices had been buried in the want ads. The way to get action, he declared, was to change "treason" to "traitors."[1] From Wheeling, McCarthy had headed West for a speaking engagement in Salt Lake City. By the time he reached Denver, reporters had in hand a State Department denial of his first charges. McCarthy scoffed at the statement and told reporters he had "a complete list of 207 [sic] 'bad risks' still working in the State Department." When he arrived in Salt Lake City a few hours later, he told the newsmen that he would be glad to furnish the names to the State Department if only the department would open the loyalty files of the "fifty-seven" who were "card-carrying Communists."[2]

By February 11, when McCarthy reached Reno, Nevada, the pressure was building. He was met by a telegram from Deputy Undersecretary of State John E. Peurifoy demanding any information McCarthy might have. Another senator might have drawn back, allowed the issue to cloud, and then sought out a strategic retreat. But not McCarthy. ("He raises on the poor hands and always comes out the winner.") From Reno he telegraphed the president that in spite of the "blackout" on loyalty files he had been able to compile "the names of 57 Communists" in the State Department. He demanded that Truman revoke the directive closing the files to Congress and charged that "failure on your part

---

[1] Jay H. Cerf to Ronald May, Jan. 7, 1952, NCEC files.
[2] *Denver Post*, Feb. 11, 1950. The *Post* carried two articles on the incident, one from the Associated Press wires and another by a staff member. Both appear to have been filed from Salt Lake City. The reporters were confused as to the exact number of names (57? 205? 207?) which McCarthy claimed to have, and it is likely that McCarthy himself had not decided on the number in question until he reached Salt Lake City, where he first appears to have distinguished between the 205 who were "bad risks" and the 57 who were "card-carrying Communists."

will label the Democratic Party of being the bedfellow of international communism."[3]

While Deputy Undersecretary of State Peurifoy denied the McCarthy accusations one by one, the senator, not visibly perturbed, left Reno for a dinner speech in Huron, North Dakota, and there the issue hung for the next week.[4]

THE ANATOMY OF A SPEECH

> *I have given Senators the fullest, most complete, fairest resume of the files that I possibly could.*
>
> Joe McCarthy

Early on the evening of February 20 McCarthy appeared on the floor of the Senate clutching a bulging and battered tan briefcase. In it were photostatic copies of some 100-odd individual dossiers prepared in 1947 from the State Department loyalty files by a team of investigators from the House Appropriations Committee.[5] The list included past and present employees of the department as well as a large number of applicants. Of the original 108 singled out by the House investigators, only about forty remained with the department, and all of these had received full field investigations by the FBI. The "derogatory information" in most, but not all, of these cases pertained to alleged Communist or left-wing activity. Several involved alleged instances of homosexuality; one was the case of a Bible student from Ohio Wesleyan University whom the investigators believed had been *too thoroughly investigated;* and another concerned an elderly Russian emigré who had been refused employment.

McCarthy probably did not have these dossiers when he made his first speeches in Wheeling and Salt Lake City—at least he made no references to the material contained in them. He may have received the list from Robert E. Lee, the House investigator

---

[3] McCarthy to Truman, Feb. 11, 1950, OF 3371, Truman Papers. Also in *Congressional Record,* 81st Cong., 2d sess., Feb. 20, 1950, p. 1953. *Milwaukee Journal,* Feb. 12, 1950. McCarthy also declared that he knew of "approximately 300" employees certified for dismissal "because of communism" of whom only 80 had been discharged. "I understand that this was done after lengthy consultation with the now-convicted traitor, Alger Hiss," he declared.

[4] *New York Times,* Feb. 14, 1950, p. 16.

[5] See above, pp. 40–41.

and a friend of McCarthy's, but this would hardly have been necessary. There were many copies of the "Lee list" scattered around Capitol Hill, including a copy in the files of Senator McCarthy's own Committee on Expenditures in the Executive Departments. The list then was hardly new, nor was it entirely accurate. The individual case summaries contained a goodly number of unconfirmed and unsubstantiated allegations. They reflected both the professional bias of the State Department's security force and the political bias of the House investigators digging out material for the Republican Eightieth Congress. Whatever the faults of the "Lee list," it was a godsend for McCarthy, and he turned upon it with his exceptional talent for compounding distortion upon distortion. At no point did he admit that he was reading to the Senate from a badly outdated committee file. Instead, he told his colleagues that he had pierced the "iron curtain" of State Department secrecy and with the aid of "some good, loyal Americans in the State Department" had compiled an alarming picture of espionage and treason. He read to the Senate "81" of these cases. Well, not quite 81. He skipped 15, 27, and 59; 7 and 99 were the same; and in cases 21 through 26 he merely repeated himself.[6]

He also changed the numbers which the House investigators had assigned to the cases (they were not identified by name), a fact which caused some slight consternation to Senator Homer Ferguson, who was apparently following McCarthy's speech from his own copy of the Lee list.[7] McCarthy recounted a number of fetching "conversations" he had held with security officers and with "good, loyal Americans." He told the Senate that "I learned"

[6] McCarthy's speech appears in the *Congressional Record*, 81st Cong., 2d sess., Feb. 20, 1950, pp. 1953–80. The "Lee list" is reprinted in *Tydings Committee Hearings*, pp. 1771–1813. Secretary of State Dean Acheson hinted at the origins of the McCarthy speech at a press conference on Feb. 24, 1950, and Congressman Frank M. Karsten made it the subject of a House speech on May 1. *New York Times*, Feb. 25, 1950, p. 6; May 2, 1950, p. 9. The most comprehensive contemporary analysis of the speech was Alfred Friendly, "The Noble Crusade of Senator McCarthy," *Harper's* 20 (Aug. 1950): 34–42.

[7] "Mr. Ferguson. I wondered why the Senator had taken them out of order . . . .
Mr. McCarthy. I did take them in order. I get the impression that the Senator may have a file of his own."
Congressional Record, 81st Cong., 2d sess., Feb. 20, 1950, p. 1980.

this or "I was told" that. The results were sometimes unusual. The Lee investigators had reported, for example, that a memorandum was missing from the files of a certain employee. McCarthy told the Senate: "Upon contact with the keeper of the records, he stated that, to the best of his knowledge, the major portion of the file had been removed."[8]

But these misrepresentations were minor compared to the manner in which he twisted and distorted each individual case to wring from it the most sinister and sensational implications. Sometimes he would only omit a line or two. Thus in "case no. one" he neglected to mention that a full field investigation had developed "nothing derogatory." In "case no. six" he omitted the sentence: "On January 7, 1947, a memorandum summarizing the investigation stated that nothing had been developed tending to affect adversely the subject's loyalty." In "case no. 46" he cited a State Department report of March 22, 1947, raising questions as to the individual's loyalty, but left out a subsequent memorandum of June 18, 1947, in which the security officer concluded: "It is not believed by this office that the information at hand raises a reasonable doubt as to (subject's) loyalty to the United States and, accordingly, security clearance is recommended."[9]

In other cases, McCarthy would reverse the operation and add a telling phrase or two. This or that person, for example, had "top secret clearance" or was "a very close associate of active Soviet agents." It was not without its comic side. One job applicant, never hired by the State Department, had "top secret clearance" while another was "still in the Department as of today."[10]

At times the exaggeration was subtle. A "subject" on the Lee list became "an important subject" on the McCarthy list. Three people "with Russian names" became "three Russians." A "high official" became "high officials," "agent" became "agents," and a "soviet espionage subject" became a "soviet espionage agent." Words like "reportedly" and "allegedly" disappeared for more positive modifiers, and "may be" and "may have been" gave way to "is" and "was." Of a person reportedly "inclined toward communism," McCarthy declared "he was a Communist." "Con-

---

[8] McCarthy case no. 2; Lee case no. 52.

[9] See McCarthy's case nos. 4, 11, 20, 41, 51, 55, 57, 60, 61, 66, 67, 68, 69, 75, and 79 for comparable omissions.

[10] See McCarthy case nos. 6, 7, 10, 14, 20, 22, 62, 64, 67, 68, 71, and 79.

siderable derogatory information" became "conclusive evidence
of . . . Communist activity." A "liberal" on the Lee list became
"communistically inclined" in McCarthy's speech, while an "active
fellow traveler" became an "active Communist."[11]
At other points, the enormity of his lie was staggering. Compare,
for example, the following (Lee case no. 40):

> This employee is with the Office of Information and Educational Ex-
> change in New York City.
> His application is very sketchy. There has been no investigation.
> (C-8) is a reference. Though he is 43 years of age, his file reflects no
> history prior to June 1941.

McCarthy case no. 36:

> This individual is 43 years of age. He is with the Office of Information
> and Education. According to the file, he is a known Communist. I
> might say that when I refer to someone as being a known Communist,
> I am not evaluating the information myself. I am merely giving what
> is in the file. This individual also found his way into the Voice of
> America broadcast. Apparently the easiest way to get in is to be a
> Communist.[12]

McCarthy could not even keep his "facts" straight in the case
of a man whom he cited as an example of "a good, loyal American"
who had been refused employment with the Voice of America.
This proved, he declared, that "unless one has a communist background one cannot qualify for a position with the Voice of
America." Neither the senator nor the House investigators found
it significant that the gentleman in question was nearly seventy
years old, and perhaps a little elderly to be starting out in the
civil service.[13]

In short, the speech was a lie; it demanded, especially of those
Republican partisans who, like Senator Ferguson, must have
realized the enormity of McCarthy's fraud, a willing suspension
of disbelief.

[11] In order, McCarthy case nos. 58, 56, 13, 16, 50, 57, 6, 78, 70, 74, 4,
5, 63, 73.
[12] *Tydings Committee Hearings,* p. 1784; *Congressional Record,* 81st Cong.,
2d sess., Feb. 20, 1950, pp. 1971–72.
[13] McCarthy case no. 72; Lee case no. 90.

SENATE RESOLUTION 231

> The atmosphere of the Senate all
> day was one of awareness on both
> sides that a partisan issue might be
> developing.
>
> William S. White

The McCarthy speech was fantasy, but the political byplay which surrounded it was very real. Behind the facade of Senate decorum stormed a potentially explosive party debate.[14] Majority Leader Scott Lucas and the Democrats did their best to harry McCarthy. Lucas tried to pin him down: Was it "205" Communists as he had declared in Wheeling? Or only "57" as he now told the Senate? And if there were "57 card-carrying Communists" in the State Department, who were they? But McCarthy eluded his pursuers, first offering, then refusing to turn over any names to his Democratic interrogators.[15] Lucas then told the Senate that there would be no vote on the cotton bill, the pending question when McCarthy rose to speak, and as he had anticipated, the Chamber quickly emptied.

Minority Leader Kenneth Wherry and the Republicans labored hard on McCarthy's behalf. They vigorously protested the absence of many senators, and McCarthy himself finally called for a quorum. When the necessary number failed to answer the bells, Lucas then moved for a recess, but was defeated 16-18 on a straight party-line vote. Lucas had no alternative but to send out the sergeant at-arms to compel attendance, the first time in five years that this expedient had been necessary.

During the "friendly questioning" the Republican professionals of the "Communist issue" took McCarthy in hand. Homer Ferguson helped him stumble over difficult matters of internal security procedures, and Ferguson, Owen Brewster, and others drew out the controversial files issue and the argument over Congress's right to papers originating in the Executive Department. Karl Mundt contributed the thought that the State Department policy of allow-

---

[14] *Congressional Record*, 81st Cong., 2d sess., Feb. 20, 1950, pp. 1953–80.

[15] This was, of course, quite beside the point. McCarthy did not have the names. On February 20 all he had was a list of numbered cases, the Lee list. Not until sometime in March did he obtain the "key" to the Lee list in which the numbers were matched with the names of the individuals involved.

ing "Communists" to resign enabled them to infiltrate other government agencies.

Most of the burden of backstopping McCarthy fell to Minority Leader Wherry, who threw Republican support behind a suggestion that "an appropriate committee of the Senate make a thorough investigation" of McCarthy's charges. The Nebraska senator even suggested that the inquiry be assigned to the Appropriations Committee, whose chairman, the ultraconservative Democrat Kenneth B. McKellar of Tennessee, would have given substantial aid to the Republicans.[16]

McCarthy's performance and the Republican support it received were enough to trigger the investigation. The Democratic leadership met in caucus the following morning, and when the Senate convened, Majority Leader Lucas introduced Senate Resolution 231, authorizing an investigation of McCarthy's charges. Sensing that the demands for an investigation would be irresistible, the Democrats stole a march on their opposition. The Lucas resolution, moreover, gave jurisdiction of the investigation to the moderate Foreign Relations Committee rather than to the conservative-led Appropriations Committee.

The Republicans were prepared with a counterstrategy. They first sought to broaden the inquiry. Homer Ferguson, who had investigated the Commerce Department during the Eightieth Congress, demanded that the investigation include "any other agency of the Government concerned with the intercourse of the United States with other nations." Although Lucas rejected this proposal, he compromised by expanding the investigation to include persons who "are, or have been, employed by the State Department," and by agreeing to delete specific references to McCarthy's charges.[17]

A more difficult problem was raised by Republican demands that the resolution explicitly include the authority to subpoena executive records. Truman's March 13, 1948, directive closing all loyalty files to congressional investigation still rankled most senators, and the issue was one not only of partisan politics but also of congressional prerogative.[18] McCarthy declared that if the committee failed to get the files, then the investigation would be "a complete

---

[16] *Congressional Record*, 81st Cong., 2d sess., Feb. 20, 1950, p. 1971.
[17] Ibid., Feb. 22, 1950, pp. 2140–41; *New York Times*, Feb. 22, 1950, p. 9; Feb. 23, 1950, p. 4.
[18] See above, pp. 42–43.

farce and nothing but a whitewash." He was supported by a phalanx of Republicans (Wherry, Brewster, Ferguson, Knowland) who were prepared to echo this cry of "whitewash" if the Democratic leadership did not accede to their demands. Lucas finally gave in, and the resolution incorporated an amendment by Ferguson directing the committee to "procure by subpoena" the loyalty records of all government employees against whom charges were heard.[19]

Wayne Morse of Oregon insisted that the hearings be conducted in public so that any person accused of disloyalty might have the right to confront his accusers. Even Morse, however, conceded that the committee might take preliminary evidence and testimony in executive session, and he finally agreed to a rather vague amendment proffered by Massachusetts Republican Leverett Saltonstall, which was duly incorporated by Lucas into the resolution.[20]

The final Senate resolution authorized "a full and complete study and investigation as to whether persons who are disloyal to the United States are, or have been employed by the Department of State."[21]

THE McCARTHY LOBBY

> *Congress cannot function today without lobbyists.*
>
> Senator Estes Kefauver

McCarthy had joined the Communist issue, but it remained for him to exploit the materials which nearly five years of Republican attacks had produced. In the interim between the passage of Senate Resolution 231 and the beginning of the hearings on March 8, he had to develop a major indictment of the State Department and the Democratic administration. The "cases" which he had read to the Senate on February 20 were a poor start. Some had never been employed by the department and others were long gone. His preposterous exaggerations would show up rather badly under close examination, and it would be especially embarrassing

---

[19] *Congressional Record*, 81st Cong., 2d sess., Feb. 21, 1950, pp. 2063–66; Feb. 22, 1950, pp. 2142–50; *New York Times*, Feb. 22, 1950, p. 9; Feb. 23, 1950, p. 4.

[20] *Congressional Record*, 81st Cong., 2d sess., Feb. 22, 1950, pp. 2129–37.

[21] *Tydings Committee Hearings*, p. 1.

if he could not produce the names which he had "held in his hand."

He reserved a room at the Library of Congress and set his staff members to digging into old congressional investigations. He badgered fellow congressmen for documents and materials on the Communist issue, and some, including Congressman Richard M. Nixon, allowed him to use their files.[22] He even added to his staff a former FBI man, Donald Surine, who had been cashiered from the service.[23] McCarthy also sought the aid of a heterogeneous collection of individuals and groups which might be described as Washington's "anti-Communist lobby."

Most senators are faced with a staggering load of legislative and political responsibilities, and their professional staffs are notoriously overworked. Any senator who would play a large role in the affairs of state must almost of necessity depend upon lobbies of one sort or another for the technical aid which they offer.[24] From a friendly lobby a senator might receive a variety of assistance ranging all the way from research and speechwriting to press relations. A lobby will very often line up witnesses for a congressional hearing and sometimes even coach them on what they will say. While the American public has traditionally frowned upon the existence of lobbies, they are probably indispensable, given the present structure of congressional government.

On the traditional issues of American politics, mostly economic, organizations representing the interested parties, whether they be business, farm, or labor, have provided all of these services. A senator might, for example, save hours of tedious research on the right-to-work law by simply telephoning the "legislative director" of either (depending on his politics) the Congress of Industrial Organizations (CIO) or the National Association of Manufacturers (NAM). But the Communist issue was a new issue,

[22] Earl Mazo, *Richard Nixon: A Political and Personal Portrait*, rev. ed. (New York, 1959), p. 127. Jack Anderson and Ronald May, *McCarthy: The Man, the Senator, the "Ism"* (Boston, 1952), pp. 187, 191. *Minneapolis Tribune*, April 15, 1950; *New York Times*, March 6, 1950, p. 10. Congressman Alvin O'Konski to author, Nov. 9, 1966.

[23] For the lurid particulars see Affidavit of Raymond F. Weber, May 9, 1951; Affidavit of Doris Jo Perry, April 4, 1951; J. Edgar Hoover to Donald A. Surine, March 6, 1950; Hoover to Senator A. S. "Mike" Monroney, April 3, 1951—all photostatic copies in box 5, William Benton Papers, Manuscripts Division, State Historical Society of Wisconsin.

[24] For an excellent discussion of senators and lobbyists, see Donald R. Matthews, *U. S. Senators and Their World* (New York, 1960), pp. 176–96.

largely noneconomic, and certainly not based on traditional interest-group politics. There were no regularly constituted lobbies to push and plead their causes or provide the requisite "technical" assistance.

For Senator McCarthy this vacuum was filled by a loose coalition of right-wing journalists and zealots. They were not a "lobby" at all in the strictest sense of that word. They did not register as such with the secretary of the Senate, nor did they have the organizational coherence which usually characterizes a modern lobby. Nor were they really "McCarthy's." They existed well before the senator made his sudden appearance as a national figure, and they continued to exist well after his equally sudden demise. Nevertheless, they provided for McCarthy all the essential services which lobbies have at their disposal and, as in the case of traditional lobbies, the relationship proved mutually beneficial.

In the forefront of the "McCarthy lobby" was a large group of right-wing newspapermen. It would later be said that "during the McCarthy exposures a whole new group of reporters arose who worked closely with him and his staff."[25] In fact these newsmen were active long before the senator from Wisconsin discovered communism as an issue. They were the closest thing that Washington had to "experts" on the Communist issue, and they provided McCarthy with quick leads and elementary research. Willard Edwards, a veteran correspondent of the *Chicago Tribune,* supplied the senator with material for his very first speech in Wheeling, West Virginia. George Waters, a reporter for the McCormick-owned *Washington Times-Herald* and a sometime member of McCarthy's staff, probably wrote the speech or, to be more accurate, pasted it together.[26] Reporters served as informal liaison between McCarthy and other Republican congressmen, and in some instances they were conduits for information leaked from federal bureaus and agencies.[27] There is ample evidence that reporters played an active role in procuring and coaching witnesses. During the Tydings Committee hearings Lawrence Kerley, a reporter for the *New York Journal-American* (Hearst), tried to bring before the senators a camera-shy informant whose testimony had been prepared at a meeting with Hearst employees George

[25] Ibid., p. 202.
[26] Author's interview with Willard Edwards, May 26, 1966.
[27] Ibid.; author's interview with Walter Trohan, May 26, 1966.

Sokolsky and J. B. Matthews. Hearst reporters Ray Richards, Howard Rushmore, and Ken Hunter were involved with other prospective witnesses before the committee.[28] Frederick Woltman, a columnist for the Scripps-Howard newspapers, was specifically assigned to stimulate a reinvestigation of the *Amerasia* case, and worked closely with McCarthy's staff.[29] Because of their privileged position astride the lines of communication, these reporters were able to assure McCarthy of excellent press coverage, both in their own papers and—through competition—in other papers.

McCarthy already had connections with Colonel Robert R. McCormick,[30] and in the weeks and months which followed his speech at Wheeling this relationship became ever closer. In addition to Edwards and Walters, McCarthy was aided by Walter Trohan, an important columnist for the McCormick papers, by most of the staff of the *Washington Times-Herald,* and by a host of commentators and analysts on the McCormick-owned Mutual radio network.

Even more important was the support of William Randolph Hearst, Jr., and his large publishing empire. Like the McCarthy-McCormick alliance, the relationship between the newspaper heir and the senator was one of mutual expedience. McCarthy desperately needed the semblance of proof to support his charges, and the Hearst people wanted a forum for their own rare view of current events. Columnists such as George Sokolsky, Westbrook Pegler, and especially Fulton Lewis, Jr. (who also broadcast for the Mutual network), all worked intimately with the Wisconsin senator, turning up leads, "hot tips," and that peculiar brand of pseudoevidence on which the Communist controversy thrived. Other Hearst employees, including Ken Hunter, Howard Rushmore, Lawrence Kerley, and Ray Richards, also did footwork for the senator.

The most valuable appendage of the Hearst organization was J. B. Matthews, whom the publisher had snatched up after his sojourn as staff director for the Dies Committee and now employed as a "researcher." It was from Matthews's private files (especially his personal copy of "Appendix Nine" of the Dies Committee) that

---

[28] *Tydings Committee Hearings,* pp. 660–62, 1480–83, 1099, 1144, 2229.

[29] Frederick Woltman, *Washington Daily News,* July 12, 1954; *Tydings Committee Hearings,* p. 1200.

[30] See above, pp. 10–12

McCarthy collected the material he first took before the Senate subcommitte.[31]

A third major figure in the "McCarthy lobby" was the mysterious yet ubiquitous Alfred Kohlberg. For thirty years an importer of Chinese textiles, Kohlberg became a prodigiously energetic anti-Communist zealot during the mid-forties and the most persistent exponent of the thesis that China had been betrayed to the Communists by a sinister cabal of State Department officials. In 1945 he had attempted unsuccessfully to seize control of the Institute of Pacific Relations, charging that its directors followed the "Communist line." He subsequently founded the China Policy Association to support Chiang Kai-shek. He maintained very close contacts with representatives of the Nationalist government in this country and he was the titular leader of what sometimes was called the "China lobby." Although his main concern was American policy in China, his interests spanned a broad range of extremist causes. He was the financial "angel" behind *Plain Talk,* a periodical whose contributors fancied themselves as the "intellectual right." He also financed the magazine's successor, *The Freeman,* and was indirectly involved in the organization of *Counter-attack,* a newsletter edited by three former FBI agents.[32] The research and editorial staffs of all these Kohlberg-subsidized publications were apparently placed at McCarthy's disposal.

Kohlberg supplied McCarthy with voluminous "documents" to support his (and McCarthy's) thesis of conspiracy in high places. Much of this material was from Kohlberg's profuse writings on the China controversy, but the lace merchant also had access to the files of the Chinese Nationalist secret police, and—through the good offices of a government clerk—to the files and minutes of the Civil Service Commission's Loyalty Review Board. He also

[31] Author's interview with Willard Edwards, May 26, 1966. In addition to the McCormick and Hearst chains, McCarthy was also warmly supported by the Scripps-Howard and Gannett newspapers. The ardor of the former cooled considerably when the senator began attacking Republicans instead of Democrats.

[32] In a strict sense the "China lobby" was a myth. Like the "McCarthy lobby," it was not a cohesive, well-organized group, but a coalition including representatives of the Nationalist government seeking arms and aid, true believers in the cause of Chiang Kai-shek as against the Communists, and a bevy of Republican politicians. See Max Ascoli, Philip Horton, and Charles Wertenbaker, "The China Lobby," *Reporter* 6 (April 15, 1952): 2–24; (April 29, 1952): 5–24. For a more sympathetic treatment of Kohlberg's activities, see Joseph Keeley, *The China Lobby Man* (New Rochelle, N. Y., 1969).

provided McCarthy with entrée to the strange and haunted world of the far right. He helped the senator line up important witnesses for the hearings, and one suspects that on more than one occasion he also helped provide the script.

There were others; the senator's tipsters were probably legion. However, the McCormick, Hearst, and Kohlberg organizations were his main source of "technical" assistance, affording McCarthy all the services he might expect from a well-financed and smoothly operating lobby. It is doubtful that he could ever have maintained himself without them.

THE TYDINGS COMMITTEE

Chairman Tom Connally of the Senate Foreign Relations Committee impaneled a tough and aggressive subcommittee to hear the McCarthy charges. As chairman he appointed Senator Millard E. Tydings of Maryland. First elected to the Senate in 1926 and now chairman of the powerful Armed Services Committee, the aristocratic Tydings had the self-assurance that comes from birth and station. A conservative who had survived the Roosevelt purge of 1938, he was a master of invective and a shrewd political operator.

The second Democrat on the committee was Brien McMahon of Connecticut. Like McCarthy, McMahon was a thick-set man of solid Irish stock. Elected to the Senate in 1944, he had sponsored the legislation creating the Atomic Energy Commission and had pushed it through Congress in the face of those who believed that the military should have control of atomic energy. He became chairman of the Joint Committee on Atomic Energy in 1949. Like Tydings, he was a powerful adversary.

The third Democrat on the committee was Theodore Francis Green, the remarkable Senate octogenarian from Rhode Island. Well-born and well-educated, he was a "Yankee Democrat" who had pioneered the New Deal as governor of Rhode Island and turned that state into a tiny Democratic barony. He had an extraordinarily shrewd and active mind and was one of the few Senate liberals accepted among the Upper Chamber's "inner club." He was the one Democratic member on the committee whom McCarthy never dared to attack.

The Republicans on the committee were Henry Cabot Lodge of Massachusetts and Bourke B. Hickenlooper of Iowa. Lodge, the grandson of one of the Senate's most famous leaders, was an intelligent and open-minded conservative, who because of a peculiar quirk in the American political lexicon was known as a Republican "liberal." Although his "liberalism" had little in common with the progressivism of earlier Republicans such as George Norris and Robert M. La Follette, it usually led him into opposition to his own party's leadership. He supported bipartisanship in foreign affairs and had no particular desire to demolish the New Deal. His position on the subcommittee was ambivalent, for while he refused to sign the final report prepared by the Democrats, neither did he endorse any of McCarthy's wild charges.

Hickenlooper was the only member of the subcommittee sympathetic to McCarthy. In 1949 he had dipped into the Communist issue himself, accusing the chairman of the Atomic Energy Commission, David E. Lilienthal, of being "soft on communism." But McCarthy could gather little comfort from Hickenlooper's appointment, for the Iowa Republican was an inveterate bumbler whose occasional antics had given currency to the phrase "to pull a Hickenlooper."

The Tydings Committee was indeed one to inspire confidence among Democrats and supporters of the administration. If they had hoped for a smooth and decorous investigation, however, their expectations were quickly shattered. The hearings opened on March 8 amid a scene of bewildering confusion and tumult. Tydings immediately demanded that McCarthy produce the name of "case 14" and identify the "high State Department official" whom McCarthy charged had shielded the man. The question was designed to embarrass McCarthy and put an end to his efforts at dissimulation. McCarthy's "case 14" compared to "case 10" on the Lee list and concerned not charges of communism but of homosexuality and pro-Nazi sympathies during World War II. The State Department official whom the Lee investigators (and hence McCarthy) had accused of clearing him was J. Anthony Panuch, a security officer who ironically had become something of a minor hero to the political right. After his dismissal from the State Department in 1947, Panuch had become a contributor to *Plain Talk*. McCarthy had warmly praised him in his speech at Salt Lake City and again in his Senate speech of February 20.[33] Now

---

[33] *Congressional Record*, 81st Cong., 2d sess., Feb. 20, 1950, pp. 1961, 1976; *Tydings Committee Hearings*, pp. 1777–78; *Deseret News* (Salt Lake City), Feb. 11, 1950.

Tydings placed McCarthy in the position of charging Panuch with covering up for traitors.

McCarthy would not give the committee the name of "case 14," probably because he did not have it, nor would he give them the name of Panuch, who after all was on his side! It was a draw. Tydings would demand to know who "case 14" was and McCarthy would reply that he had not brought the material on "case 57" [sic], but that he would get to it eventually. He bobbed, weaved, and evaded the persistent Tydings until finally Senator Lodge broke in to demand that McCarthy be allowed to present his charges in his own way and in his own order.[34]

McCarthy and the committee then went a second round over whether the hearings should proceed in open or closed session. The subcommittee had earlier rejected the idea of closed hearings, and the committee room was jammed with photographers and newsmen. Still, Tydings suggested that if McCarthy desired, the committee could go into executive session for his testimony. McCarthy squirmed, hedged, and then finally admitted that he had already given the text of his remarks, names and all, to the press.[35]

For the first few weeks McCarthy was scraping rock bottom; only his unique and overblown sense of drama, together with the sensational coverage given his charges in the press, saved his act from complete collapse. The first "case" he pulled out was that of Dorothy Kenyon, a distinguished and liberal lawyer from New York City. Miss Kenyon had not been among those mentioned by McCarthy in his Wheeling speech, nor was she on his list of "81" cases presented to the Senate. She was not even in the State Department, though she had served from 1947 to 1949 as a United States delegate to the United Nations Commission on the Status of Women. She had belonged to a large number of liberal left-wing, and in some instances "front" organizations, and the famous "Appendix Nine" of the Dies Committee had listed twenty-eight such groups behind her name. McCarthy began his presentation: "This lady has been affiliated with 28 Communist front organiza-

---

[34] *Tydings Committee Hearings*, pp. 2–7. It was not until McCarthy had checked into Washington police records (the Lee list indicated an arrest in the District of Columbia for "disorderly conduct") that he was able to give the committee the name of "case 14." A few weeks later Senator Wherry announced that the individual in question had resigned from the agency in which he was then employed. Ibid., pp. 128–30; *New York Times*, April 26, 1950, p. 3.

[35] *Tydings Committee Hearings*, pp. 15–18.

tions."[36] McCarthy named eighteen of these organizations in two days of testimony. Senator Hickenlooper added six more a few days later.

It is difficult to recapture the enormity of McCarthy's performance. One begins with his sources. Appendix Nine listed some twenty-eight organizations with which Miss Kenyon had been "affiliated," and McCarthy produced from the files of J. B. Matthews a number of photostats "documenting" these connections. Of the twenty-eight, only a half-dozen had ever been "cited" by the attorney general as "Communist fronts," and in no instance did Miss Kenyon's "affiliation" postdate this listing. Others were variously cited by the Dies Committee, the House Committee on Un-American Activities, and the California Committee on Un-American Activities, all of whose judgment has tended to be less than reassuring. One organization was "cited" by the New York City Council Committee investigating the Municipal Civil Service Commission. In most instances, Miss Kenyon's connection with these groups had been fleeting or nonexistent.

All this McCarthy ignored, and as was so very characteristic of him, the weaker his case, the more inflated his rhetoric. Thus while most observers would conclude that the dates of Miss Kenyon's alleged affiliations were a little dusty with age, McCarthy found in this evidence that her "Communist activities" were not only deep-rooted "but extend back through the years." A 1938 letterhead, he triumphantly proclaimed, showed an affiliation "going back 12 years." If her name appeared in a grouping, McCarthy would declare: "In signing this statement Miss Kenyon collaborated [an especially charged and sinister word] with such well-known Communists as. . . ." He studiously avoided mentioning any of the non-Communist liberals, radicals, and conservatives whose names appeared. The lists he cited almost always included many names of well-known and unimpeachably safe citizens—Republican senators, Wall Street lawyers, eminent clergymen—and Tydings took to reading the entire lists of names, over the loud protests of Lodge and Hickenlooper.[37]

The attack on Dorothy Kenyon was symptomatic of McCarthy's desperation and audacity. No one then nor since has been able to suggest that Miss Kenyon was anything but a generous and

[36] Ibid., p. 18.
[37] Ibid., pp. 20–23, 31–32.

liberal citizen. She called McCarthy "an unmitigated liar," and the senator never proved the contrary. McCarthy also took an offhand swing at United States Ambassador at Large Philip C. Jessup, accusing the diplomat of "an unusual affinity" for Communist causes. Jessup had been under fire for some time from right-wing Republicans because he had testified as a character witness for Alger Hiss and because he was identified with the administration's Far Eastern policy. Richard Nixon had recently dubbed him "the architect of our far-eastern policy," a title McCarthy would later bestow upon others.[38] Unlike Miss Kenyon, Jessup was a very real and high-ranking American diplomat. But McCarthy's "case" against the ambassador, as developed by Senator Hickenlooper during a committee session on March 20 and elaborated by McCarthy in a Senate speech on March 30, was pathetic. They accused Jessup of membership in six "Communist fronts." Of the six, Jessup had not been affiliated with two, and two more were not fronts at all. As for the remaining pair, he had been briefly connected with each, well before they were "cited" as Communist fronts, and in the company of many other distinguished citizens. Only one of these, the American Russian Institute, had been listed by the attorney general and Jessup had not even been a member; he had been among the sponsors of a dinner the group held in 1944.[39]

In his Senate speech of March 30, McCarthy also repeated a number of charges originally made against Jessup by Alfred Kohlberg. In 1949 Kohlberg had charged Jessup with being "the initiator of the smear campaign against Nationalist China and Chiang Kai-shek, and the originator of the myth of the 'democratic' Chinese Communists."[40] In the Senate, with no more substantiation than had Kohlberg, McCarthy declared that Jessup had "pioneered the smear campaign against Chiang Kai-shek and the idea that the Communists in China were merely agrarian re-

[38] Ibid., p. 28. For Nixon's remarks see *Congressional Record*, 81st Cong., 2d sess., Jan. 26, 1950, p. 1006. For attacks on Jessup by Styles Bridges and Karl Mundt see ibid., Jan. 24, 1950, p. 816, and Jan. 25, 1950, p. 905. Although McCarthy made only brief reference to Jessup in his first appearance before the subcommittee, Colonel McCormick's *Washington Times-Herald* ran an eight-column headline reading "Jessup Pal of Reds—McCarthy." See James Reston, *New York Times*, March 9, 1950, p. 2.

[39] *Tydings Committee Hearings*, pp. 216–60.

[40] Kohlberg, "Open Letter to Mr. Allen," *China Monthly* 10 (Aug. 1949): 167–68.

formers and really not Communists at all." He charged that Jessup was "the originator of the myth of the 'democratic' Chinese Communists."[41] Against these accusations, Jessup placed his record as a distinguished diplomat, together with warmly commendatory letters from former Secretary of State George C. Marshall and General Dwight D. Eisenhower.[42]

McCarthy showed no more originality when the subcommittee reconvened on March 13. Drawing on an attack which Congressman Fred Buseby had made on the State Department in 1947, and probably again on materials supplied by Kohlberg, he charged that Haldore Hanson, an administrator in the newly created Point Four program, was a man with "a mission to communize the world."[43] The burden of McCarthy's charges rested on a series of quotes (and misquotes) from a book Hanson had written while an Associated Press war correspondent in China.[44] Publishers and readers alike were doubtless surprised by McCarthy's description of the volume as "a book which sets forth his pro-Communist answer to the problems of Asia as clearly as Hitler's *Mein Kampf* set forth his solutions for the problems of Europe." On examination by the committee, McCarthy admitted that he did not know the name of the book, but he promised that he would look it up immediately.[45]

McCarthy next turned to Esther Caulkin Brunauer, who had served for seventeen years on the staff of the American Association of University Women, later joining the State Department, where she was a liaison officer between the department and UNESCO. Her husband was Hungarian-born and had belonged to the Young Workers' League for a brief time during the mid-1920s. He was a chemist, a commander in the Naval Reserve, and an ordnance specialist who had been decorated for his wartime services.[46]. The Brunauers had been discussed by a Senate committee in 1941, by the House Committee on Un-American Activities in 1947, and by Congressman Buseby in his attack on the State Department. Both Esther Brunauer and her husband had been processed by

[41] *Congressional Record,* 81st Cong., 2d sess., March 30, 1950, p. 4402.
[42] *Tydings Committee Hearings,* p. 271.
[43] Ibid., p. 82.
[44] Haldore Hanson, *Humane Endeavor: The Story of the China War* (New York, 1939).
[45] *Tydings Committee Hearings,* pp. 76, 83.
[46] Ibid., pp. 293–306.

security officers and cleared. Their names, however, had been gathered up by the Lee investigators. Of McCarthy's "nine public cases," she was the only one who also appeared on the list of "81" cases which he had read in the Senate.[47]

McCarthy also gave the committee the name of Owen Lattimore, a Far Eastern scholar who was then director of the Walter Hines Page School of International Relations at Johns Hopkins University. Although Lattimore had served only briefly in the State Department, he had been one of the main targets in Alfred Kohlberg's battle over the Institute of Pacific Relations and had been frequently attacked by Kohlberg in the years which followed. Lattimore would later become the center of controversy, but in this first presentation, McCarthy said little that was not already public knowledge.[48]

On the fourth and final day of his testimony before the Tydings Committee, McCarthy produced four more names, three of which he had mentioned in his Wheeling and Reno speeches. One of these was Gustavo Duran, a former State Department employee then working for the United Nations. Like the others, Duran had been the subject of previous attacks.[49] McCarthy gathered together the files of other congressmen and, typically, embroidered on their allegations. Wisconsin Congressman Alvin O'Konski had charged in 1947 that Duran was "a notorious international Communist." McCarthy told the Tydings Committee that "our own intelligence files" had so labeled Duran.[50]

McCarthy also attacked Harlow Shapley, the director of the Harvard Observatory, and Frederick L. Schuman, a professor at Williams College. Both men were ardent left-wing activists, but they were scarcely subversive in any recognized meaning of that term. Moreover, they had only the most tenuous of relations with the State Department. Shapley had served from 1947 to 1950 as a representative of the United States National Commission for

---

[47] *Congressional Record*, 81st Cong., 2d sess., Feb. 20, 1950, pp. 1976–77; *Tydings Committee Hearings*, pp. 1789–90.

[48] *Tydings Committee Hearings*, pp. 92–104.

[49] See above, pp. 38–39.

[50] *Tydings Committee Hearings*, pp. 110–24, 1865–70. Congressman Alvin O'Konski to author, Nov. 9, 1966. A major portion of the attack on Duran, who had served in the Spanish Loyalist Army, stemmed from a scurrilous article in *Arriba*, a Madrid newspaper of the Falangist party, which was in turn cabled to Washington *verbatim* by military intelligence channels.

UNESCO. Schuman's only contact had been a 1946 lecture to Foreign Service officers during an orientation program. Both men had been the target for HUAC, CUAC, and other congressional critics, and McCarthy now followed suit by listing the various "front" affiliations of each.[51]

Finally, McCarthy turned to John Stewart Service, who like Owen Lattimore would later figure as a protagonist in the hearings. The charges against Service were a rehash of all the old accusations: Patrick Hurley's declaration before a Senate Foreign Relations Committee in 1945 that Service had worked to undermine American policy in Asia, the *Amerasia* case, and so forth. McCarthy drew at great length from an article by Emmanuel Larsen in *Plain Talk,* and he noted that the Civil Service Commission had only recently ordered another loyalty hearing for Service.[52]

The sum of McCarthy's "nine public cases" was not impressive. Of the nine, only four were in the State Department, and all four had been carefully checked by the department's security force. Each of them, moreover, offered strong and persuasive rebuttal to McCarthy's charges.[53]

This first phase of the Tydings investigation ended amid increasingly sharp Democratic attacks on McCarthy and a growing uneasiness among "liberal" Republicans over the senator's failure to prove his charges. Henry L. Stimson, who had served as secretary of state under Herbert Hoover and later as secretary of war under Franklin Roosevelt, wrote a long and eloquent letter to the *New York Times* expressing the concern of many over the extreme partisanship exhibited by McCarthy and other Republicans in their attacks on the Department of State. "The man who seeks to gain political advantage from personal attacks on a Secretary of State," declared Stimson, "is a man who seeks political advantage from damage to his country."[54] With the exceptions which one might anticipate, the nation's press was generally cool to the McCarthy

[51] *Tydings Committee Hearings,* pp. 125–28, 142–70.

[52] Ibid., pp. 130, 135. McCarthy learned of the Civil Service Commission's action even before the State Department was informed, thanks to an elderly spinster who was forwarding Civil Service Commission documents to Alfred Kohlberg. *New York Times,* March 16, 1950, p. 1.

[53] *Tydings Committee Hearings,* pp. 176–214, 215–75, 293–313, 341–71.

[54] *New York Times,* March 27, 1950, p. 22. For other "liberal" Republican reactions see ibid., March 24, 1950, p. 3; March 25, 1950, p. 2; March 29, 1950, p. 27.

performance, and even such veteran redbaiters as Eugene Lyons discounted the senator's claims.[55]

Still, the Wisconsin senator had not fared altogether badly. The Republican leadership had naturally been cautious. They had been taken by surprise by his original accusations, and they still feared that the charges might somehow boomerang and destroy a good political issue. The Republican caucus had explicitly declined to make the charges a party issue, but McCarthy received growing support from his colleagues as the hearings proceeded. Within the subcommittee both Hickenlooper and Lodge worked to give him the advantage. Senator Owen Brewster of Maine quickly charged the Democrats on the committee with attempting to "whitewash" the State Department, while other Republican leaders trained their fire on the administration. Senator Wherry charged that Dean Acheson was a "bad security risk," and Republican National Chairman Guy Gabrielson declared that the Republicans were exposing the fact that "spies, emissaries, agents and members of the Communist Party . . . infest the Government of the United States."[56] Republican Senate Leader Robert A. Taft gave McCarthy his personal endorsement and told him that "if one case didn't work, to bring up another."[57]

Even more important was the growing publicity which McCarthy was attracting. There is a maxim to the effect that a politician should never worry about what the papers are saying, but only when they are not saying anything. If this is true, then McCarthy had good cause for rejoicing. The bitter wrangling of the committee hearings, their thinly veiled adversary character, the drama of McCarthy's accusations and in turn the attacks which were leveled at him, all created an irresistible news source. Even such staid and conservative journals as the *New York Herald Tribune* and the *New York Times* gave the hearings extensive front page coverage.

A Wisconsin friend wrote enthusiastically of the "great amount of damn good publicity that you are getting in your battle against

[55] Ibid., March 19, 1950, sec. 4, p. 6; Richard H. Rovere, *Senator Joe McCarthy* (New York, 1959), p. 135.

[56] *New York Times*, March 13, 1950, p. 11; March 20, 1950, p. 6. For other Republican attacks see ibid., March 18, 1950, p. 7; March 23, 1950, p. 1; March 25, 1950, p. 3.

[57] Ibid., March 23, 1950, p. 1. Taft later disavowed this statement, but the consensus among the newsmen was that he had indeed made it.

the subversives in public positions of trust." Wisconsin legionnaires and young Republicans rallied to his defense, and the Marine Corps League announced that he had won its "national American-ism award" for his heroic actions in "rousing the nation to the menace of bad security risks in our government." The senator's office was deluged by letters and postcards.[58] In short, Joe Mc-Carthy was already becoming a symbol of the anti-Communist persuasion. For a man who loved the roar of public acclaim, the consequences were far from discouraging.

AGENTS AND ARCHITECTS

> *I believe you can ask almost any school child who the architect of our far eastern policy is, and he will say, 'Owen Lattimore.'*
>
> Joe McCarthy

The second phase of the Tydings investigation was precipitated by McCarthy's sensational charges against Owen Lattimore and took place amidst an increasingly bitter debate over American policy in China. The Communist victory in China had shocked many Americans, and some who still nurtured the illusion of American omnipotence abroad sought to blame this "catastrophe" upon those who made and executed United States foreign policy. For Republicans such as Senator William F. Knowland of Cali-fornia and Congressman Walter H. Judd of Minnesota, the "China issue" became the lever for breaking up the bipartisan consensus which had shaped national policy since the end of World War II. And as the restraining influence of Arthur Vandenberg declined, the tempo of partisan debate steadily increased.[59]

[58] Bradley R. Taylor to McCarthy, March 25, 1950, box 5, Taylor Papers. *New York Times*, March 12, 1950, p. 36; March 21, 1950, p. 25; March 25, 1950, p. 2.

[59] Vandenberg's correspondence for 1949 and 1950 reveals the Michigan senator's strong though unsuccessful attempts to bridle the Republican right. See Vandenberg to David Lawrence, Nov. 15, 1949; Vandenberg to John Foster Dulles, Nov. 19, 1949; Vandenberg to Senator Henry Cabot Lodge, Nov. 19, 1949; Vandenberg to Senator Arthur V.. Watkins, Dec. 28, 1949; Vandenberg to Jack Bell, April 5, 1950; Vandenberg to Senator Homer Ferguson, May 31, 1950, all in the Arthur Vandenberg Papers, W. L. Clements Library, University of Michigan. For examples of Republican use of the "China issue" see remarks by William F. Knowland, *Congressional Record*, 81st Cong., 2d sess., Jan. 5, 1950, pp. 79–99; and by H. Styles Bridges, ibid., Jan. 23, 1950, p. 816.

President Truman was enraged by McCarthy's charges and by the continuing Republican attacks on the Department of State. When Senator Styles Bridges confided to reporters that he and other Republicans planned to "go after" Acheson, the president wrote a long letter to the New Hampshire Republican, appealing as an "old-time personal friend and Senate colleague" for the senator to weigh carefully "this unwarranted attack on bipartisan foreign policy." By the time Bridges received the letter he had already launched a major attack on the secretary of state. Two days later, at a press conference, reporters coaxed the angry president into charging that the partisan attempt "to sabotage bipartisan foreign policy" by Bridges, Wherry, and McCarthy was the Kremlin's "greatest asset."[60]

Whatever else the president may have intended, the immediate result of his remarks was further to inflame his congressional critics and to force McCarthy more firmly than ever upon the Republican leadership. Taft denounced the attack as "bitter and prejudiced" and praised McCarthy as "a fighting marine" who had been "slandered" by the president.[61]

On the same day that Truman lashed out at the Republicans from his vacation White House in Palm Beach, McCarthy made his second major speech on "communism-in-government," concentrating exclusively this time on the Far East and charging that China had been "betrayed" by a State Department "more loyal to the ideals and designs of communism than to those of the free, God-fearing half of the world."[62] The speech reflected the strong influence of Alfred Kohlberg and Walter Judd, both of whom were supplying McCarthy with material on the "China issue."[63] In it McCarthy repeated his earlier charges against John Stewart

[60] *New York Times,* March 26, 1950, p. 1; March 28, 1950, p. 1. Truman to Styles Bridges, March 26, 1950; Bridges to Truman, March 29, 1950, OF 419-K, Truman Papers. *Public Papers, 1950,* pp. 235–36; *New York Times,* March 31, 1950, p. 1. "The approach of several senators to the foreign policy program, in an effort to find an issue for the coming campaign this fall, is unfortunate," Truman complained to Arthur Vandenberg. "I am sorry that they can't find a domestic issue on which to carry on the campaign." Truman to Vandenberg, March 27, 1950, Vandenberg Papers.

[61] *New York Times,* April 1, 1950, pp. 1, 6.

[62] *Congressional Record,* 81st Cong., 2d sess., March 30, 1950, pp. 4378–98.

[63] *New York Times,* April 8, 1950, p. 14; *Minneapolis Tribune,* April 15, 1950. Philip Horton, "The China Lobby," *Reporter* 6 (April 29, 1952): 2. Congressman Judd apparently had some misgivings. After giving McCarthy material on the China question, he then spent several hours vainly trying to talk McCarthy out of making certain charges.

Service, Philip C. Jessup, and Haldore Hanson. His main target this time, however, was Owen Lattimore.

Lattimore had never been a regular member of the State Department in the strictest sense, though he had held several government posts and was a respected authority on Far Eastern affairs. During the early 1940s he had served briefly as an adviser to Chiang Kai-shek. During the war he had ·worked for the Office of War Information (owi), and in this capacity he had accompanied Henry Wallace on his 1944 trip to China. He had been an adviser to the Pauley Reparations Mission to Japan in 1946. In June 1949 he had given a lecture to State Department officers on Japanese problems, and in October 1949 he had participated in a two-day symposium on Chinese affairs. As a specialist in Far Eastern studies he had been active in the Institute of Pacific Relations and at one time edited its magazine, *Pacific Affairs.* He had been on the editorial board of *Amerasia* from 1937 to 1941, though he was never active in its management.[64]

Although Lattimore had originally been a warm supporter of Chiang Kai-shek, he became increasingly critical of the Nationalist leader during the mid-1940s and increasingly sympathetic toward the Generalissimo's Communist opposition. This earned for him the wrath of Chiang's highly vocal supporters in this country, and in particular that of Alfred Kohlberg and the "China lobby." Kohlberg charged, by implication and innuendo, that Lattimore was a Communist and a traitor; and these charges were repeated intermittently throughout the late 1940s by right-wing journalists and politicians.[65] In 1949 Lattimore argued that the United States should withdraw from South Korea, a position which prompted William F. Knowland to attack him on the floor of the Senate for advocating "a policy of appeasement."[66]

[64] *Tydings Committee Hearings,* pp. 421–22.

[65] See Alfred Kohlberg, "Owen Lattimore: Expert's Expert," *China Monthly* 6 (Oct. 1945): 10–13, 26; William R. Johnson, "The United States Sells China down the Amur," ibid. 8 (Dec. 1947); 412–15, 525–27; Chia-You Chen, "The Confusion and Ignorance of the Self-Proclaimed China Expert," ibid. 10 (Feb. 1949): 133–34. Also see speech by Congressman William E. Hess (R-Ohio) in *Congressional Record,* 79th Cong., 2d sess., Jan. 18, 1946, pp. A116–17, and by Congressman George Dondero (R-Mich.) in ibid., June 7, 1946, p. A3297.

[66] *Congressional Record,* 81st Cong., 2d sess., March 2, 1950, p. 2642. Criticism of Lattimore was not limited to conservative Republicans. In a sharp attack on American policy in China, John F. Kennedy, then a young congressman from Massachusetts, denounced the advice given by "the Lattimores and the Fairbanks." "What our young men had saved," declared

McCarthy had not mentioned Lattimore in his Wheeling or Reno speeches, nor had Lattimore been among the "81" cases he had given the Senate on February 20. On March 13 Lattimore became one of McCarthy's "nine public cases." He described Lattimore as "one of the principal architects of our far eastern policy" and accused him of pro-Communist leanings. His evidence consisted of an editorial from the *Washington Times-Herald*, a magazine article by James F. Kearney, S.J., a few references to books and articles by former Communists Louis Budenz and Freda Utley, and a miscellany of charges against the Institute of Pacific Relations. He also accused Lattimore of membership in several Communist fronts.[67]

Then on March 21 the senator told eager reporters that he was prepared to name the "top Russian espionage agent" in the United States. Tydings immediately called an emergency session of the subcommittee, which met behind closed doors to hear the senator's charge. It was a farce, except for the seriousness which the committee was forced to accord McCarthy. He had absolutely nothing new. "There is nothing mysterious about this one," he declared. "This has all been put in the record, already, plus some exhibits." The senator's description of the case, however, was something else again. Lattimore was "definitely an espionage agent," he said. It was "explosive." "If you crack this case," he declared, "it will be the biggest espionage case in the history of this country." Pressed for facts to support these allegations, he replied that while he could not give the committee any additional evidence, all they had to do was to look at the loyalty and security files and they would find all the proof they needed. The following day he told reporters, "I am willing to stand or fall on this one."[68]

Kennedy, "our diplomats and our President have frittered away." Ibid., 81st Cong., 1st sess., Jan. 25, 1949, pp. 532–33, and Feb. 21, 1949, p. A993.

[67] *Tydings Committee Hearings*, pp. 92–104. McCarthy was drawing upon Kohlberg-inspired material as early as March 13, his third day before the Tydings Committee. For a comparison of Kohlberg's and McCarthy's charges see ibid., pp. 1641–46. Father Kearney admitted to FBI investigators that the information contained in the article which McCarthy cited had been supplied by Kohlberg. Peyton Ford to Millard Tydings, June 22, 1950, ibid., p. 1876. According to Joseph Keeley, Kohlberg's friendly biographer, Kohlberg did not meet McCarthy personally until the two dined together at the Mayflower Hotel on March 23. Keeley, *The China Lobby Man*, pp. 1–3, 98–99.

[68] *Tydings Committee Hearings*, pp. 277–92; *New York Times*, March 24, 1950, p. 1.

On March 24 Attorney General J. Howard McGrath showed the Lattimore file to four of the subcommittee members (Hickenlooper was absent). Subsequently, Senator Lodge declared that "none of the charges has been proven," and a few days later Tydings announced that "it was the universal opinion of all the members of the committee present" that there was nothing in the file to show that Lattimore was or ever had been a Communist.[69] By now, however, the press of partisan politics had become too strong for such a statement to go unchallenged. Hickenlooper, once he had seen the files, charged that the chairman's conclusion was "unwarranted" and that he "completely disagreed" with him. Lodge rather belatedly disassociated himself from the Tydings statement, declaring that he had "reached no final conclusions" and that when he did he would announce them for himself.[70]

Meanwhile, the Lattimore case became public. Following the closed hearing of March 21 at which McCarthy had accused Lattimore of being a spy, the professor's name was bruited about Washington by McCarthy and by several members of the subcommittee. A few days later, McCarthy gave Jack Anderson permission to publish Lattimore's name, and Drew Pearson broke the story on Sunday evening, March 26.[71]

By the time McCarthy made his Senate speech of March 30, he was already backing away from his sensational spy charges of a few days before. ("I fear in the case of Lattimore, I have perhaps placed too much stress on the question of whether or not he has been an espionage agent.") Drawing on material supplied by Alfred Kohlberg, he now returned to his earlier charge that Lattimore was "the principal architect of our far-eastern policy" and as such had subverted both American and Chinese interests. He presented to the Senate the affidavit of a former Communist (later identified as Louis Budenz) whom he declared would testify that Lattimore had belonged to the party. He read a statement by another unidentified ex-Communist (Freda Utley) which asserted that Lattimore was "very obviously receiving instructions

[69] New York Times, March 25, 1950, p. 1; April 4, 1950, p. 1; April 7, 1950, p. 1; Tydings Committee Hearings, p. 484. "All that we can learn so far shows that none of the current charges have been proven," declared Lodge. Baltimore Sun, April 6, 1950.
[70] New York Times, April 8, 1950, p. 1; April 11, 1950, p. 1.
[71] Anderson and May, McCarthy, p. 213; Owen Lattimore, Ordeal by Slander (Boston, 1950), p. 35; New York Times, March 27, 1950, p. 1. Jack Anderson was Drew Pearson's aide and collaborator.

from the Soviet Union" when he visited Moscow in 1936. He read portions of a letter Lattimore had written in 1943,[72] purportedly showing Lattimore's "pro-Communist" inclinations, but when other senators pressed him to place the entire letter in the *Record,* he refused, replying that it was still "classified." It was an angry session. Democratic Senators Herbert H. Lehman, Dennis Chavez, Hubert H. Humphrey, Clinton P. Anderson, and Brien McMahon were all on their feet at one point or another, and the easily aroused New Hampshire Republican Charles Tobey nearly exploded when McCarthy refused to place the Lattimore letter in the *Record.* The galleries were crowded and noisy, and at one point McCarthy was applauded in defiance of Senate rules.[73]

By the time Lattimore first testified before the subcommittee, the drama of his appearance had already been intensified by the increasingly vehement Republican attacks upon the administration's foreign policy in China. If Alger Hiss could be made the symbol of the New Deal generation, perhaps Lattimore might serve as a scapegoat in the China debate. The day before Lattimore testified, Senator William F. Knowland attacked him in a major Senate speech comparing the professor's many books and articles to the Communist party "line."[74]

The subcommittee convened on April 6 in the large, marble-pillared Senate caucus room. Newsmen reported the largest crowd since Wendell Willkie had packed that same room when testifying in favor of lend-lease shortly before World War II. Lattimore, a bespectacled, slightly balding man with a sharp professorial air, denounced McCarthy's charges as "base and contemptible lies." He accused the Wisconsin senator of serving as the willing tool of the "China lobby." He defended himself against each of McCarthy's specific accusations and introduced into the record letters from Chiang Kai-shek and Madame Chiang warmly praising his services. At the end of the hearing, Tydings announced that four

[72] The letter in question had probably come from Alfred Kohlberg, although how Kohlberg came into its possession remains a mystery. It is quite possible that he received it from the Nationalist Chinese. For an early reference to the letter see Kohlberg, "He Knew What They Wanted," *China Monthly* 10 (June 1949): 133–34.

[73] *Congressional Record,* 81st Cong., 2d sess., March 30, 1950, pp. 4375–93; *New York Times,* March 31, 1950, p. 1. McCarthy subsequently refused to submit his "evidence" to the Tydings Committee, but turned it over instead to the FBI. For a summary, see Peyton Ford to Millard Tydings, n.d. [but June 1950], *Tydings Committee Hearings,* pp. 1895–96.

[74] *Congressional Record,* 81st Cong., 2d sess., April 5, 1950, pp. 4804–4806.

of the committee members had examined Lattimore's loyalty file and found no evidence indicating that he was or ever had been a Communist.[75] Lattimore was loudly applauded at the end of the hearing. Obviously, he had won this round, but the fight was far from over.[76]

The fact that Louis F. Budenz would testify in the Lattimore case had been an open secret in Washington for some time. In his speech of March 30, McCarthy had promised he would produce a witness who would testify that Lattimore was a Communist, and as early as April 1, Lattimore had telegraphed Budenz, asking him to disavow the statements which were being attributed to him.[77] Following Lattimore's emphatic testimony, the press continued to buzz with rumors that Budenz would come forth to "identify" Lattimore, and on April 11 McCarthy confirmed that subpoenas had been served on the onetime editor of the *Daily Worker*. The growing intensity of the party debate, together with the careful press agentry which preceded Budenz's appearance, created a mood of tense expectancy and apprehension. The demand for seats was almost unprecedented, and veteran political observers declared that the testimony would play an important role in the future of Senator McCarthy and the Communist issue with which he was increasingly identified.[78]

Louis Budenz was another of that strange breed of embittered extremists who came to public attention during the late 1940s and early 1950s. He had been born in 1891 in Indianapolis, Indiana, and was reared in the parochial schools of that city. He received the rudiments of a legal education and worked at the bar for a few years before joining the labor movement in 1913. He moved thereafter through a succession of radical organizations.

---

[75] *Tydings Committee Hearings*, pp. 417–84; *New York Times*, April 7, 1950, pp. 1, 7. The letters caused a great deal of consternation among the Nationalist agents who were working with the Republicans in an effort to discredit Acheson and the administration. Congressman Walter Judd even considered making a personal telephone call to Madame Chiang in an effort to "debunk" Lattimore. Chen Chih-mai to Chiang Kai-shek, April 7, 1950, among the many cables placed in the *Congressional Record* by Oregon's indomitable Wayne Morse. *Congressional Record*, 82d Cong., 2d sess., April 10, 1952, pp. 3970–72.

[76] Lattimore, *Ordeal by Slander*, pp. 108–09.

[77] *Congressional Record*, 81st Cong., 2d sess., March 30, 1950, p. 4375; *New York Times*, April 2, 1950, p. 1.

[78] *New York Times*, April 16, 1950, sec. 4, p. 3; April 20, 1950, p. 3. Budenz's appearance was arranged by Republican Congressman Walter Judd. See *Minneapolis Tribune*, April 15, 1950.

During the 1920s he edited *Labor Age*, a socialist publication. From there he went to the Conference for Progressive Labor Action, then to the American Workers party, then to the "Mustites," a factional group named for their leader, A. J. Muste. He joined the Communist party in 1935, staying with it throughout the vicissitudes occasioned by the Moscow trials and the Nazi-Soviet Pact. In 1941 he became managing editor of the *Daily Worker*, a position he held until he left the party in 1945. In that year he returned to the Roman Catholic Church under the tutelage of Fulton J. Sheen and was subsequently employed by the University of Notre Dame and later by Fordham University. He was interrogated at great length by the FBI, and he later became a star witness at a whole series of trials and investigations.[79]

Budenz appeared before the Tydings Committee on April 20, 1950. The hearing resembled a scene by Nathanael West. The caucus room was choked with spectators, nearly 700 in a space designed to hold less than half that number. There were senators and congressmen, high administration officials, and other less distinguished onlookers. The giant klieg lights blazed away, making the room insufferably hot. The television and newsreel cameras whirred constantly, and there were flurries of popping explosions as the photographers rushed about. Occasionally a microphone would shriek out of control, adding to the noise and confusion.

Budenz began in a quiet, ordinary voice. His remarks were long, discursive, and at some points incoherent, but there emerged from his testimony at least four specific accusations. He declared that Lattimore was a member of a Communist cell within the Institute of Pacific Relations; that in 1943 he had been told by party headquarters that the "line" on Chiang Kai-shek had been changed to opposition and hostility; that at the time of Henry Wallace's trip to China in 1944, Budenz was told "to consider Owen Lattimore as a Communist"; and finally that he, Budenz, had been informed that Lattimore had "been of service" in the *Amerasia* case.[80]

Senate Republicans eagerly grasped the Budenz testimony, declaring that it went far toward proving their charges and that

[79] Herbert L. Packer, *Ex-Communist Witnesses: Four Studies in Fact Finding* (Stanford, Calif., 1962), pp. 121–24; *Tydings Committee Hearings*, p. 488.

[80] *Tydings Committee Hearings*, pp. 487–98.

the Lattimore case "looks like another Alger Hiss case." Even such a moderate as Ralph Flanders got up in the Senate to note that the investigation had "taken a more serious turn." William S. White solemnly repeated that Budenz had been "officially informed" that Lattimore was a Red, and Arthur Krock declared that "many fair-minded persons" were beginning to change their minds. The Democrats were just as conspicuous by their silence. What is surprising, and indeed not a little alarming, is how little convincing so many people needed.[81]

To begin with, the "official reports" on which Budenz based his charges were oral. He was told this, or told that; or, as he put it, he was "officially informed." When the committee pressed him for corroboration, he suggested that they subpoena Earl Browder and other Communist leaders, although he admitted that they would be "inclined to lie."[82] He next suggested that the typewritten "onionskin" communications which he claimed passed through party headquarters (Lattimore was identified in them as "X" or "LX," he said) would prove his story, though he had none of these himself and declared that "we had strict instructions to destroy them all." He presented Father Kearney's article from *Columbia*, the Knights of Columbus magazine, and two other pieces used previously by Kohlberg and McCarthy "in corroboration of my story." He helpfully offered to work up whatever additional "evidence" the committee needed in just two weeks.[83]

The senators wondered whether the fact that Lattimore had been an active supporter of "Aid to Finland" in 1940 when the Russians invaded that country might indicate that he was not a Communist agent, but Budenz assured them that he was not, that the party granted "exemptions" in such cases. He declared that Lattimore was no doubt similarly excused for his support of the Communist-opposed Marshall Plan. When questioned about a critical review of one of Lattimore's books which had appeared in the *Daily Worker*, he declared that "we had the policy in protecting people who are out beyond the party proper, to criticize

---

[81] William S. White, *New York Times*, April 21, 1950, p. 1; April 22, 1950, p. 5; April 23, 1950, sec. 4, p. 1; Arthur Krock, April 23, 1950, sec. 4, p. 3.

[82] *Tydings Committee Hearings*, pp. 497–98, 528. At a later hearing he suggested that Manning Johnson, an ex-Communist who was (by coincidence!) employed by Alfred Kohlberg, would support his story. Ibid., pp. 571–72.

[83] Ibid., pp. 495–96, 516.

them with faint praise—that is to say, that is, to damn them with faint praise—rather, to praise them with faint damns, is the way I want to put it."[84]

With the aid of Lattimore's attorneys, Abe Fortas and Paul Porter, the senators pressed Budenz on several other weaknesses in his story. Budenz had spent, by his own admission, many long and grueling hours with the FBI between 1946 and 1950. He had also testified at great length before congressional committees, grand juries, and trial courts. Yet never once in his voluminous testimony had he mentioned Owen Lattimore. In 1947 he had specifically told a State Department security officer that he knew nothing which would indicate that Lattimore was a member of the party. In early 1949 he had suggested in the rough draft of an article for *Colliers* that Lattimore might be a fellow traveler, but specifically denied that he was a Communist.[85] When subcommittee counsel Edward P. Morgan pointed out that there were no charges made against Lattimore in Budenz's newest book, then at the publishers, the ex-Communist hopefully volunteered that "in another book which I am writing Mr. Lattimore is very prominent."[86]

Budenz had been in frequent contact with Alfred Kohlberg for some years, and only recently had conferred with him about the Lattimore case. It is more than probable that all of Budenz's charges concerning the China question (including the 1949 article for *Colliers*) sprang not at all from the ex-Communist's facile memory, but rather from the fertile imagination of the China merchant. Budenz merely served to legitimize these accusations and give them an aura of authority. And though Budenz was very vague and evasive, it also turned out that he had conferred with Robert Morris, a right-winger hired at the instigation of the Republicans on the subcommittee as assistant counsel, and

[84] Ibid., pp. 523–26.

[85] "Q. You're not saying that they [Lattimore and Joseph Barnes] acted as Communist agents in any way?

A. No.

Q. That ought to be quite clear.

A. Oh yes."

The transcript of Budenz's conversation with the *Colliers* editor, which was quite revealing in many ways, was introduced into the record by Lattimore's lawyers. Ibid., pp. 512–16.

[86] Ibid., p. 519.

with Charles J. Kersten, a former Wisconsin congressman who was working for McCarthy.[87] Budenz's background, moreover, was such as to raise very serious questions as to his reliability as a witness, even though he told the subcommittee that because of the Catholic sacrament he was able to gain redemption for the sins of his past and was therefore "a different man than 5 years ago."[88]

After Budenz had concluded, Abe Fortas asked that Brigadier General Elliott R. Thorpe, a retired army intelligence officer who had served on the staff of General Douglas MacArthur during World War II, be allowed to testify. Fortas argued, with very good reason, that it was not fair to allow Budenz's uncontradicted testimony to monopolize the headlines until the subcommittee reconvened the following week. Tydings overruled the strenuous protests of Lodge and Hickenlooper and allowed the general to testify. Thorpe was a stern, professional army man who had encountered Lattimore on three occasions in his professional capacity as an intelligence officer in the Far East. He told the committee that it was his "strong conviction, based on careful examination, that Owen Lattimore is a loyal American citizen and is in no way an agent of the Communist Party nor of the U.S.S.R."[89]

On April 25 Budenz appeared again before the subcommittee, this time in executive session. He expanded on the Kohlberg thesis that the Institute of Pacific Relations (IPR) was infiltrated by Communists, and he named a list of contributors to IPR publications whom he "knew" to be Communists. The only important innovation was his declaration that he knew "from official reports" that Haldore Hanson was a member of the Communist

---

[87] Ibid., pp. 534–36, 619–25. Although Budenz remembered with striking clarity conversations about Lattimore in 1938 and 1943, he had, strange to say, only the vaguest recollections of these meetings of two weeks prior.

[88] Ibid., p. 629. For particulars see, "In the Matter of Desideriu Hammer, Alias John Santo, Respondent in Deportation Proceedings File No. a-6002660," a transcript from which is printed in ibid., pp. 1691–1725. This material was used as the basis for a violent attack on Budenz by Senator Dennis Chavez, himself a Catholic, who accused the former Communist of "using the Cross as a club." *Congressional Record*, 81st Cong., 2d sess., May 11, 1950, pp. 6969–75.

[89] *Tydings Committee Hearings*, p. 559. Abe Fortas to Theodore F. Green, April 7, 1950, box 1108, Theodore F. Green Papers, Library of Congress. Fortas was unsuccessful in a further maneuver to place in the Committee Record the affidavit of a former Communist contradicting Budenz, but released it to newsmen after the hearing had recessed. *New York Times*, April 21, 1950, p. 1.

party.[90] McCarthy, who was excluded from the closed session, told reporters that Budenz had testified that a "very important" official of the State Department was a "very valuable member of the Communist Party."[91] None of the reporters seemed interested in how McCarthy knew what Budenz said, what right he had to disclose it, or whether he had accurately represented the witness's remarks. Three days later, McCarthy declared on the floor of the Senate that Budenz had named Hanson as "an active member of the Communist Party."[92]

After Budenz came a whole series of Communists and ex-Communists. First was Bella V. Dodd, a graduate of Hunter College and New York University and a left-wing activist since the 1930s. She had joined the Communist party in 1943 and had been elected to the National Committee (Politburo) in 1945. She became disillusioned with the Communists during the late 1940s and was expelled from the party in 1949. Miss Dodd's contribution was largely to ridicule the picture Budenz had drawn of the Communist party. She had never heard Lattimore referred to as a Communist or fellow traveler, nor had she even seen any "onionskin" documents. She described Budenz's testimony as laughable.[93]

Dr. Dodd was followed by a comic episode featuring a *New York Journal-American* reporter, Lawrence E. Kerley, and a mysterious vanishing witness. It had been a typical McCarthy maneuver which had ingloriously collapsed at the last moment. The testimony had been arranged by assistant counsel Robert Morris, un-

[90] *Tydings Committee Hearings*, p. 591.

[91] *New York Times*, April 26, 1950, p. 1. McCarthy also told the newsmen that the individual named was one of his "public cases."

[92] Ibid., April 28, 1950, p. 1. The case of Haldore Hanson is perhaps typical of what was happening throughout the government during these years. Hanson was a bright and knowledgeable career officer with a great deal of experience in Far Eastern affairs. Outside of Budenz's unsubstantiated accusations there was not a jot of evidence against him. The Civil Service Loyalty Review Board subsequently verified his loyalty. Nevertheless, during the Tydings investigation both he and his family suffered all sorts of harassment, and when Harold Stassen took over the Technical Cooperation Administration in 1953, Hanson was summarily dismissed. He subsequently had some difficulty finding new employment, for, as one company president explained, "Big corporations are timid." John Howe to John B. Oakes (of the *New York Times*), Oct. 26, 1953, box 5; Howe to Robert M. Hutchins, Aug. 11, 1954, box 4; Howe to William Benton, Sept. 10, 1954, box 5, all in the Benton Papers.

[93] *Tydings Committee Hearings*, pp. 631–43; *New York Times*, April 26, 1950, p. 2.

known to the Democratic members of the committee, at a meeting which included two Hearst employees, J. B. Matthews and George Sokolsky. The witness was John Huber, who had served as an informant for the FBI during the early 1940s. Huber would presumably testify that Lattimore was a Communist. Kerley, who had been an FBI agent during the war, was to testify first in order to establish Huber's credentials as a secret informer. Kerley arrived in Washington with Huber in tow, but the prospective witness took one look at the giant klieg lights, blanched, and disappeared, leaving Kerley and Morris holding the bag.[94]

The committee then spent two fruitless days listening to ex-Communist party chairman Earl Browder and to Frederick Vanderbilt Field. Both denied that Lattimore was a Communist or fellow traveler, but they refused to answer most other questions put to them by the committee.[95]

Next came Freda Utley, a shrill and excitable ex-Communist who testified that although Lattimore was not a spy, he had been a "Judas Cow" who had led other innocents to the slaughter. Miss Utley had been a member of the British Communist party during the late 1920s, later moving to the Soviet Union, where she married a Russian. She left during the mid-1930s, when her husband was caught up in the Stalinist purges, and came to this country. She soon drifted into the extreme right-wing politics of the America First committee. She was a member of Alfred Kohlberg's China Policy Association and a contributor to the Kohlberg-subsidized journal, *Plain Talk*.[96] She told the committee that "the Communist cancer must be cut out if we are to survive as a free nation. Perhaps in this operation some healthy tissues on the fringe will be destroyed." She never specified whether Lattimore was "on the fringe" or not, but like Budenz she offered no corroboration of any sort. At one point the exasperated Tydings declared: "We

[94] *Tydings Committee Hearings*, pp. 660–62, 1480–82; *New York Times*, April 26, 1950, p. 2; April 27, 1950, p. 26. Kerley and Huber had both testified in 1949 before a Senate Judiciary subcommittee chaired by Pat McCarran. *New York Times*, Sept. 16, 1949, p. 15; Dec. 21, 1949, p. 3.

[95] *Tydings Committee Hearings*, pp. 669–706, ·709–33; *New York Times*, April 28, 1950, p. 1; April 29, 1950, p. 1. Field was a well-known and well-to-do left-winger who had bankrolled a number of radical causes. He was especially active in Far Eastern affairs and had served on the editorial board of *Amerasia*. Although he never admitted to party membership, he was a close and active supporter of the party in this country.

[96] *Tydings Committee Hearings*, pp. 773–79.

don't want opinion evidence here. We want facts, f-a-c-t-s. We are getting few of them."[97]

Lattimore appeared for a second time before the committee. As before, the caucus room was crowded, though on this occasion the crowd was not nearly so partial toward Lattimore. The professor denied each of the specific accusations made by Budenz and Utley, and he attacked the credibility of both.[98]

Senator McCarthy had produced no evidence to support his contention that Lattimore was the "top Russian espionage agent" in America. Even Budenz and Utley had denied this. Nor had he been able to prove his second thesis, that Lattimore was the "architect of our far eastern policy."[99] Excepting the very dubious and unsubstantiated testimony of Budenz and Utley, there was nothing to show that Lattimore was a Communist at all. At the very worst, the sharp-tongued little professor was a "fellow traveler," although McCarthy had not even proved this.[100]

Nevertheless, McCarthy emerged from the Lattimore hearings stronger than before. Whatever the probative value of the Budenz testimony, it was greedily seized upon by Republican partisans as proof of G.O.P. charges of long standing, and by the end of April close observers discerned a steady growth of support for McCarthy from within his party.[101] His charges had become inextricably caught up in the acrimonious debate over America's "failure" in China, and hardly a day passed without an attack on the Department of State. The "Communist issue," moreover, appeared to be gaining momentum all across the country. In

[97] Ibid., p. 767.

[98] Ibid., pp. 799–914; *New York Times*, May 3, 1950, p. 1; Lattimore *Ordeal by Slander*, pp. 146–99.

[99] Toward the end of April Senator Tydings released letters from four secretaries of state, Cordell Hull, James Byrnes, George Marshall, and Dean Acheson, all denying as emphatically as possible that Lattimore was the "architect of our far-eastern policy." *New York Times*, April 30, 1950, p. 1.

[100] The McCarran investigation of the Institute of Pacific Affairs in 1951–1952 would further discredit Lattimore, but even this notoriously biased body was unable to prove its charge that Lattimore had acted as "a conscious agent of the Communist conspiracy." Senator McCarran successfully pressured the Justice Department into indicting Lattimore for perjury, but the indictments were later dismissed. U. S., Congress, Senate, 82d Cong., 2d sess., Committee on Judiciary, Report no. 2050 Pursuant to Senate Res. 366, *Institute of Pacific Relations* (McCarran Committee Report); Thurman Arnold, *Fair Fights and Foul: A Dissenting Lawyer's Life* (New York, 1965), pp. 215–16.

[101] William S. White, *New York Times*, April 30, 1950, sec. 4, p. 7.

Florida, Congressman George A. Smathers defeated the veteran Democratic Senator Claude Pepper in a scurrilous primary campaign based on charges that Pepper was too friendly with Communists and Negroes. Willis Smith followed suit in his successful attempt to unseat North Carolina Senator Frank P. Graham, and both Democrat Manchester Boddy and Republican Richard M. Nixon used the Communist issue in their campaign against Helen Gahagan Douglas in California.[102]

In the middle of April the administration rallied its forces for a counteroffensive against the Republican right in general and McCarthy in particular. Vice President Alben Barkley denounced all those who would "abridge our freedom" and "sow rumors and suspicions among us." Senate Majority Leader Scott Lucas pleaded for an end to the "angry wrangling" over foreign policy. Even the aging Tom Connally was drawn out by the attacks on United States foreign policy and shouted across the Senate that the Republican charges against the Department of State were "base slander."[103] Secretary of State Acheson compared McCarthy to the Mad Slayer of Camden, New Jersey, and called for an end to the 'filthy business" which was destroying public confidence in the State Department. The president himself denounced the Wisconsin senator before a dinner gathering of the Federal Bar Association, and other administration supporters echoed his charges.[104]

In the House, Congressman Frank M. Karsten of Missouri denounced McCarthy for using old and disproved charges in his February 20 speech to the Senate, and for misrepresenting the source of his information. Two days later the Senate was thrown into a turmoil when Majority Leader Lucas presented the affidavits of two Wheeling, West Virginia, radio employees and charged that McCarthy had not given the Senate a true version of his Lincoln Day speech. West Virginia Democrats Harley M. Kilgore and Matthew Neely offered clippings from Wheeling newspapers which also cast doubt on the senator's veracity. The Democrats pressed McCarthy on the discrepancy between the "205" figure

---

[102] *New York Times*, May 3, 1950, p. 1; May 24, 1950, p. 4; May 30, 1950, p. 32. Richard Nixon carefully studied Smather's campaign and adopted some of the Florida Democrat's tactics as his own. Earl Mazo, *Richard Nixon*, p. 74.

[103] *New York Times*, April 14, 1950, p. 1; April 16, 1950, pp. 1, 29.

[104] Ibid., April 23, 1950, p. 1; April 24, 1950, p. 4; April 25, 1950, p. 1; April 28, 1950, pp. 16, 19; April 30, 1950, sec. 4, p. 1.

he had reportedly used at Wheeling and the "57" which he used in his Senate speech of February 20. Minority Leader Wherry was on his feet, shouting that Lucas had broken Senate Rule XXIX by implying that McCarthy was a liar, and Tydings shouted back that "any honest man" would answer categorically the questions they pressed upon McCarthy.[105]

It was clear that the confidence with which Tydings had begun the investigation had evaporated in the face of McCarthy's growing support. In early March he had sarcastically told McCarthy that as the "man who occasioned this hearing" he, McCarthy, would get one of the most thorough investigations in the history of the Republic. He had patronizingly referred to the senator as "this boy" in executive session. Now he was worried and apprehensive. At a meeting in the office of the Senate secretary, Leslie Biffle, on May 8, 1950, he appealed to fellow senators to "go after McCarthy."[106] Senator William Benton, a freshman Democrat from Connecticut, took the floor on the following day to denounce McCarthy as a "hit-and-run propagandist of the Kremlin model." A few days later, the veteran New Mexico lawmaker, Dennis Chavez, made a vehement attack on Louis Budenz. Speaking as a Roman Catholic, Chavez accused Budenz of "using the Cross as a club" and hiding behind it to conduct a campaign of smear and vilification.[107]

McCarthy thrived upon such attacks and the publicity which they brought him, and he turned upon his adversaries his own unparalleled skills at vituperation. He denounced all the "egg-sucking phony liberals" whose "pitiful squealing . . . would hold sacrosanct those Communists and queers" who had sold China into "atheistic slavery," and he pledged himself to the task of driving out the "prancing mimics of the Moscow party line in the State Department." He charged that Lucas and Chavez were "dupes" of the Kremlin and were spewing "its malignant smear." He accused Tydings and McMahon of conducting "Operation Whitewash." He railed at Acheson and Jessup as "dilettante diplomats" who "whined" and "whimpered" and "cringed" in the

[105] Ibid., May 2, 1950, p. 9; May 4, 1950, p. 1; Memorandum for Mr. [Donald] Dawson, "Subject: Continuing the Counter-Offensive against McCarthy," May 8, 1950, OF 419-K, Truman Papers.

[106] William Benton to John Howe, Feb. 21, 1955, box 4, Benton Papers.

[107] Ibid., Congressional Record, 81st Cong., 2d sess., May 9, 1950, p. 6696; May 11, 1950, pp. 6969-75.

face of communism. He declared that former Secretary of State George C. Marshall was "a pathetic thing" who was "completely unfit" for high office.[108]

THE FILES CONTROVERSY

The Tydings Committee, meanwhile, had reached an impasse. Before they could proceed further in their investigation, they had to reach an agreement with the president over the thorny issue of the Executive Department's loyalty and security files. The controversy stemmed from Truman's 1948 presidential directive ordering the files closed to congressional committees.[109] The question was one of executive privilege versus legislative prerogative and involved not only the substantive issue of "communism-in-government" but also the procedural question of Congress's right to information originating in the executive branch. The issue had been given wide currency during the late forties by repeated Republican demands for the "loyalty files" of this or that government employee, and it was a dispute in which the Republicans could win strong support among Democratic legislators who were loath to accept Truman's broad interpretation of executive privilege.

McCarthy demanded that the files be opened in his telegram to the president on February 11, and again in his Senate speech of February 20. He was strongly supported by Senate Republicans during the debate over Senate Resolution 231, and the Democrats reluctantly agreed to an amendment providing that "in the conduct of this study and investigation, the committee is directed to procure by subpoena and examine the complete loyalty and employment files and records of all the Government employees against whom charges have been heard."[110]

The Wisconsin senator was one of the first to convert the inability of Congress to gain access to the files into a positive asset. Time and time again he declared that the files would

---

[108] Address to the Midwest Council of Young Republicans, *Congressional Record*, 81st Cong., 2d sess., May 9, 1950, pp. A3426–28; Address to the Sons of the American Revolution, ibid., May 19, 1950, pp. A3786–89; Speech to the American Society of Newspaper Editors, ibid., pp. A4159–62; *New York Times*, April 21, 1950, p. 3; April 29, 1950, p. 32; May 1, 1950, p. 5.

[109] See above, pp. 42–43.

[110] See above, pp. 59–60.

prove his charges. He could not give the Tydings Committee evidence that, say, Owen Lattimore was the "top Russian espionage agent" in America, but he assured the senators they would find all the proof they needed in the files. He also covered himself against the real possibility that the files might *not* support his charges by suggesting, as early as March 9, that the State Department's files were being "rifled."[111]

The Republicans hammered at the files issue throughout the first two months of the investigation. They argued that the menace of Communist subversion was so great that Congress must be allowed to examine the files, and that indeed the Congress had the right to do so. They warned that failure to open the files would be interpreted as "covering up."[112]

The administration replied that opening the files would only jeopardize the security program by disclosing confidential procedures and informants; that because the files were full of hearsay and unconfirmed statements their disclosure would be unfairly damaging to the individuals involved; and that the decision as to what might or might not be disclosed to congressional committees was a matter of executive prerogative.[113]

Senator Tydings was caught in the middle. He was a good party man who would support the president, but he was not prepared to surrender on the procedural question of Congress's right to know. He was determined to prevent a Republican "fishing expedition" into the files, but he did not relish being accused of covering up for the administration. The issue was one of those conflicts which are built into the American political system and which probably never can be permanently decided. Such conflicts depend for resolution upon the judgment and integrity of leaders in both branches of government. The Tydings Committee did finally reach an accord with the president, but not until the issue had generated several months of confused wrangling and controversy.

The president's immediate reaction to the Republican-sponsored

---

[111] *Tydings Committee Hearings*, pp. 9, 34–35, 42, 45, 104, 277–87.

[112] *New York Times*, Feb. 24, 1950, p. 4; March 3, 1950, p. 9; March 29, 1950, p. 3; March 30, 1950, p. 1.

[113] Especially see the testimony of Attorney General J. Howard McGrath and FBI Director J. Edgar Hoover, *Tydings Committee Hearings*, pp. 315–39. McGrath to Donald Dawson, March 22, 1950, OF 419-K, Truman Papers; *New York Times*, March 14, 1950, p. 4; March 26, 1950, sec. 4, p. 7.

amendment to Senate Resolution 231 had been a strong declaration in support of executive privilege. He repeated the remark attributed to Andrew Jackson after the Supreme Court decision in *Cherokee Nation* v. *Georgia* ("John Marshall has made his decision; now let him enforce it."), and he implied that Congress might well heed the analogy.[114]

Still, there were indications that an agreement might be worked out between the committee and the chief executive. The State Department was willing, and Senator Tydings worked hard on an arrangement whereby the files would be made available to the committee in a special room at the White House.[115] The Justice Department objected to opening the files at all, however, and when Tydings addressed formal letters of request to the president and other executive officers, the attorney general urged that the request be refused. Both Attorney General J. Howard McGrath and FBI Director J. Edgar Hoover appeared before the Tydings Committee, and both made strong arguments against opening the files.[116]

The day after Hoover and McGrath's appearance, the president released the text of his reply to Tydings, publicly reaffirming his decision not to release the loyalty records. The senator accordingly served subpoenas upon Acheson, McGrath, and the chairman of the Civil Service Commission, but on the order of the president the subpoenas were ignored.[117]

The committee and the president were back at the same point at which they had begun nearly a month earlier, and Tydings once again appealed to the president to release the files. Citing the damage which the inquiry had already occasioned, he urged Truman to take a "bold, forthright and courageous action" so that "the present Communist inquiry be not allowed to worsen." Part

[114] *New York Times*, Feb. 24, 1950, p. 4.

[115] Adrian Fisher, State Department, "Suggested Message to the President," March 15, 1950, Disclosure of Loyalty Information, in the Stephen J. Spingarn Papers, Truman Library. *New York Times*, March 3, 1950, p. 9; March 16, 1950, p. 1.

[116] *Tydings Committee Hearings*, pp. 315–39; Howard McGrath to Donald Dawson, March 22, 1950, OF 419-K, Truman Papers. Even McGrath made an exception in the case of Owen Lattimore, whose file he showed the senators three days after McCarthy's "spy" charges. *New York Times*, March 25, 1950, p. 1.

[117] *New York Times*, March 29, 1950, p. 1; March 30, 1950, p. 3. Charles S. Murphy to Stephen J. Spingarn, April 1, 1950, Disclosure of Loyalty Information, Spingarn Papers.

of such a program, he declared, would be to make available to the committee, at the White House, the files of all those accused by McCarthy.[118]

On May 4 the president finally agreed to open the files under the procedures worked out in early March. The senators would examine the files at the White House, but they would be allowed to take no notes on the materials nor would the committee staff be allowed to participate. The examination of the files began in early May and continued into late June. For all the sound and fury which had surrounded the controversy, there was no noticeable effect on the investigation or on the terms of partisan debate. McCarthy announced in advance that the files were "not tamper proof," and Owen Brewster and other Senate Republicans supported him. Hickenlooper declared before the examination had even begun that no matter what was found, "a great deal" would remain to be done.[119]

The Democrats on the Tydings Committee found nothing in the files to support McCarthy's charges. Lodge did not contest this conclusion in his dissenting report, but argued that the files alone were inadequate to support a final verdict. McCarthy announced that the files had been "raped."[120] The examination of the files had not ended the controversy. Indeed, it had not even greatly contributed to the committee's credibility. The genesis of the controversy was not factual, and facts alone would not lead to its resolution.

AMERASIA REDIVIVUS

The third and last phase of the Tydings Committee Hearings was yet another investigation of the *Amerasia* affair. The incident had been hopefully buried by the Democrats following the Hobbs Committee investigation in 1946, but it contained far too many exploitable elements to be left at peace. At stake were Republican

118 Millard Tydings, "Memorandum for the President," April 12, 1950, OF 419-K, Truman Papers.

119 *New York Times*, May 7, 1950, pp. 34, 35; May 8, 1950, pp. 1, 3; May 12, 1950, p. 12.

120 U. S., Congress, Senate, 81st Cong., 2d sess., Committee on Foreign Relations, Report No. 2108 Pursuant to S. Res. 231, *State Department Employee Loyalty Investigation*, pp. 9–12; Individual Views of Senator Lodge, pp. 19–21 (hereafter cited as *Tydings Committee Report*); *New York Times*, July 18, 1950, p. 1.

charges of long standing that the administration had attempted to whitewash a case involving espionage and treason. So too was involved the Republican attack on the administration's policies in China. *Amerasia* had specialized in Far Eastern affairs, and a number of State Department officials and consultants had been associated with the magazine at one time or another. Owen Lattimore had served on the magazine's editorial board from 1939 to 1941, as had William T. Stone, the subject of one of the numbered cases which McCarthy had read to the Senate. It appeared especially sinister to some that two of the defendants in the *Amerasia* case had visited in Lattimore's home only a few days before their arrest.

The brunt of the Republican attack was directed against John Stewart Service, a career officer still with the State Department. Although Service had been completely exonerated in the *Amerasia* episode, he was a particularly vulnerable target for critics of American policy in China. Stationed in China during the early 1940s, Service had reported candidly and realistically on the growing strength of the Chinese Communists. He had been too optimistic, however (at least in retrospect), about the prospects for American accommodation with the Communists. When the unpredictable Patrick Hurley resigned as ambassador to China in 1945, he blamed the failure of his mission on State Department career officers, including Service, who had "sided with the Chinese Communist armed party and the imperialist bloc of nations." He repeated these charges before a special session of the Senate Foreign Relations Committee in December 1945, although it was not apparent until later that they would become the source of heated controversy.[121]

Attacks on Service stemming from both the *Amerasia* incident and the Hurley charges continued throughout the late 1940s, increasing as the China debate itself intensified. In 1948 Isaac Don Levine, the editor of *Plain Talk,* alleged before the House Committee on Un-American Activities that Service had been a member of an espionage ring stealing secret, vital documents and "surreptitiously passing them on to Moscow."[122] In 1949 Con-

---

[121] Department of State, *United States Relations with China* (Washington, D. C., 1949), p. 582; *New York Times,* Dec. 6, 1945, p. 1.

[122] Committee on Un-American Activities, 81st Cong., 2d sess., *Hearings regarding Communist Espionage in the United States Government, Pt. 2* (Washington, D. C., 1948), pp. 1417–18.

gressman Walter Judd made Service the principal in one of his not infrequent attacks on the administration's China policy.[123]

Senator McCarthy first mentioned Service and the *Amerasia* case on January 5, 1950, when he discussed a brief news item which had appeared in the *Washington Times-Herald.* Later he incorporated this clipping into his speech at Wheeling. He made no additional references to Service during his speech to the Senate on February 20, but discussed the case at length in his testimony before the Tydings Committee. Quoting from an article by Emmanuel Larsen, one of the defendants in the case, the senator declared that "behind the now famous State Department espionage case . . . is the story of a highly organized campaign to switch American policy in the Far East from its long-established course to the Soviet line." As in the Lattimore case, McCarthy moved easily from the specific charge of espionage to the less easily proved (or disproved) charge of pro-Communist "influence."[124] McCarthy repeated these charges against Service in his March 30 speech to the Senate, declaring (falsely) that "a number of the members of the grand jury" voted to indict Service and that (again falsely) FBI Director J. Edgar Hoover had declared that the *Amerasia* affair was "a 100-percent airtight case" of espionage and treason.[125] The Republicans quickly picked up McCarthy's cry and demanded yet another investigation.[126]

The Tydings Committee began its hearings in early May and conscientiously retraced the entire episode, beginning with the OSS officer who had begun the investigation, proceeding with the FBI, then the Justice Department, and finally the defendants themselves. They explored all the many charges which had been raised by various congressional and journalistic critics—the nature of the documents found in the magazine's office, the several delays before the final arrests, the presentation to two successive grand juries, and the final collapse of the department's case. They confirmed the findings of the Hobbs Committee and if anything strengthened the administration's position. But the circumstances

---

[123] *Congressional Record,* 81st Cong., 1st sess., Oct. 19, 1959, p. 15283.

[124] *Tydings Committee Hearings,* pp. 130–35.

[125] *Congressional Record,* 81st Cong., 2d sess., March 30, 1950, pp. 4374–78. The grand jury vote was 20-0 *against* indictment. *Tydings Committee Hearings,* p. 974. Hoover explicitly denied the remarks McCarthy attributed to him. Hoover to John Service, April 18, 1950; Peyton Ford to John E. Peurifoy, May 8, 1950, ibid., pp. 2308–10.

[126] *New York Times,* April 23, 1950, p. 46.

surrounding the hearings—the heated partisanship, the various political maneuvers, a whole series of charges and accusations—all contributed to a vague uneasiness which served not the committee's ends but McCarthy's.

The appearance before the subcommittee of Frank Brooks Bielaski was a good example of McCarthy's talent for political subterfuge. Bielaski, the oss officer who made the initial raid on the *Amerasia* offices, appeared in executive session on May 4, 1950. He repeated the testimony he had given the Hobbs Committee in 1946, but with one startling exception. In 1946 he had told the House investigators that he had no recollection of any atomic secrets involved. ("I had never heard of it. . . . It would not have meant anything to me if it had.")[127] Now he remembered that one of the documents was marked "A" bomb, and his implication was clear that the case had involved atomic espionage. While he was still testifying, the early edition of the *Washington Star* was brought into the committee room. McCarthy, it appeared had released *his* version of Bielaski's remarks to the press before the witness had even finished his testimony. The senator explained that he "felt compelled to give the American people" an account of the testimony which showed, or so he declared, "that six months before the atomic bomb was dropped on Hiroshima, the people who operated *Amerasia*, with the assistance of State Department personnel, were collecting and transmitting to Soviet Russia the secrets of the atomic bomb."[128]

Pressed hard by the committee, Bielaski admitted that he had not mentioned the "A" bomb to the Hobbs Committee. "I didn't know of the atomic bomb for a long time," he explained. He also admitted that none of the other oss officers who had accompanied him on the raid supported this recollection. The FBI had discovered no such document, and Senator McMahon later pointed out that the phrase "A bomb" had not been coined until *after* the attack on Hiroshima.[129]

[127] Transcript of Hobbs Committee Hearings, *Congressional Record*, 81st Cong., 2d sess., May 22, 1950, pp. 7428–68; or *Tydings Committee Hearings*, pp. 2502–2505 at p. 2504.

[128] *New York Times*, May 5, 1950, pp. 1, 3. *Tydings Committee Hearings*, p. 956.

[129] *Tydings Committee Hearings*, pp. 952–54, 1071. Bielaski was a private investigator who had been retained on several occasions by Republican politicians. In Rhode Island he had placed a phone tap on the state's attorney general. In Pennsylvania he was accused of hiring women to entrap Demo-

It was McCarthy's version of this highly dubious testimony which dominated the headlines, however, and even intelligent observers such as *New York Times* columnist Arthur Krock added to the hue and cry over "the newly revealed possibility that the transmission of atomic secrets to Russia in 1945 is involved."[130]

By contrast, the testimony of Emmanuel S. Larsen before the Tydings Committee went relatively unnoticed. Larsen was one of the three men originally indicted in the *Amerasia* affair. He had apparently been one of the chief culprits in the case, and he had pleaded *nolo contendere* to the charges brought against him by the Justice Department. Shortly afterwards he had turned up in the office of Michigan Congressman George A. Dondero, one of the administration's most vocal and persistent critics. A few months later in March 1946, Larsen appeared before an informal session of the Hobbs Committee and gave a version of the *Amerasia* incident which dovetailed neatly with Dondero's charges of white-wash and conspiracy. He repeated these and other accusations in a sensational and overwrought article in *Plain Talk* the following autumn.[131] This was the article that McCarthy read before the Tydings Committee on March 14 and again before the Senate on March 30.

During the spring of 1950 Larsen was approached by McCarthy and Don Surine, by Dondero and a reporter for the *New York Journal-American*, by Assistant Subcommittee Counsel Robert Morris, and by Republican Senators Wherry and Ferguson. All were interested in building up a strong case against the administration. "Oh Mac has gone out on a limb and made a fool of himself," Wherry was quoted as saying, "and we have to back him up now."[132] Unhappily for them, the unpredictable Larsen had

---

cratic legislators with a variant of the old "badger game." In an undelivered speech, Senator Theodore Francis Green denounced him as "a snooper and a spy" who was "deeply suspect." See E. J. Higgins to Green, May 1, 1950, box 1106; draft of undelivered speech by Green, box 1106; Jack A. Hayes to E. J. Higgins, Aug. 29, 1950, box 1110, all in the Green Papers.

130 *New York Times*, May 5, 1950, p. 20. Bielaski later admitted that McCarthy's release was an "enlargement" on his testimony. Ibid., May 7, 1950, sec. 4, pp. 1, 2. Again no one seemed particularly concerned as to how McCarthy got his information or what right he had to release it. For additional press reaction to the Bielaski testimony see *New York Herald Tribune*, June 1, 1950; *Wall Street Journal*, June 1, 1950; *Detroit Free Press*, June 13, 1950.

131 *Tydings Committee Hearings*, pp. 1116–28, 1144–48, 2206.

132 Ibid., pp. 1099–1112, 2227–30. Memorandum to John E. Peurifoy, April 11, 1950, box 1108, Green Papers.

switched sides. When he had appeared before the Hobbs Committee in 1946, he had not been under oath. Now, in sworn testimony before the Tydings Committee, he made a point-by-point retraction of both his earlier testimony and the article from *Plain Talk*. His statements before the Hobbs Committee, he now admitted, were "based on a great deal of talk on the part of people who interviewed me and who insisted that I had been the goat in the case." The *Plain Talk* article, he told the senators, had been completely rewritten by the magazine's editors in order to satisfy Alfred Kohlberg.[133] In one blow the main prop behind McCarthy's case had been demolished, yet the crescendo of charges and accusations continued without abatement.

The Tydings Committee examined the *Amerasia* episode exhaustively in more than five hundred pages of testimony and exhibits. A New York federal grand jury conducted a simultaneous probe of the Justice Department's disposition of the case, and the State Department Loyalty Board held hearings concerning John Stewart Service. The Tydings Committee concluded that "no agency in our Government was derelict in any way in the handling of the *Amerasia* case." The grand jury, in its presentment of June 15, 1950, found no evidence of official misconduct and declared that "the American people have been poorly served by the compounding of confusion through disclosures of half-truths [and] contradictory statements." The State Department Loyalty Board cleared Service for continued employment by the department.[134]

It was not, however, the voluminous testimony taken behind

[133] Larsen told the committee that he had been visited by two former FBI agents working for *Plain Talk* in the summer of 1946 (one was Theodore C. Kirkpatrick, later an editor of *Counter-Attack*), and had agreed to write an article based on his experiences during the *Amerasia* case. He claimed that his original draft had been disappointing to Kohlberg and the editors of the magazine, who had consequently rewritten it from their own "files." "It would be fair to say that it is not my article," he declared. *Tydings Committee Hearings*, pp. 1116–28. For a comparison of what Larsen claimed was his "original draft" and the article which appeared in *Plain Talk*, see ibid., pp. 1739–53, 2492–2501.

Plain Talk editors Isaac Don Levine and Ralph de Toledano protested strongly over Larsen's testimony and the conclusions which the Tydings Committee drew from it. See de Toledano to Tydings, July 16, 1950, box 1108, and Levine to Green, Aug. 12, 1950, box 1105, both in the Green Papers; de Toledano, Letter to the Editor, *Reporter* 6 (June 10, 1952): 3; *Congressional Record*, 81st Cong., 2d sess., Aug. 31, 1950, pp. 13925–26.

[134] *Tydings Committee Report*, pp. 144, 136–37; *New York Times*, June 16, 1950, p. 1; June 28, 1950, p. 22.

the closed doors of the committee room which determined the course of events, but the political crossfire which erupted outside. As the partisan clamor intensified, so did the spiral of charges and countercharges which McCarthy never failed to inspire. On June 2, the day after seven of his Republican colleagues had denounced him in a "Declaration of Conscience," McCarthy read to the Senate a telegram from Archibald Van Buren, a former oss officer, which charged that investigators for the Tydings Committee were only interested in attempting to discredit the senator's charges. The telegram had been rigged by McCarthy and assistant committee counsel Robert Morris, who unknown to the committee had conferred with Van Buren. McCarthy used the telegram to denounce the conduct of the committee staff as "fantastic" and "unheard of," and to write the entire investigation off as a whitewash.[135]

A few days later he was again on the floor, this time charging that an "FBI chart" revealed that at least three "Communist agents" were still employed by the State Department. There was no "FBI chart," nor were there three "Communist agents" holding high offices in the State Department. What McCarthy waved before the Senate was a report filed by a State Department security officer in 1946 containing statements which FBI Director J. Edgar Hoover quickly branded as "completely erroneous." Still, the photostats that McCarthy passed out to senators and reporters *looked* important, and many senators, such as Irving Ives who had only a few days before signed Senator Margaret Chase Smith's "Declaration of Conscience," now rushed over to congratulate McCarthy on his presentation.[136]

On June 15 the senator accused Deputy Undersecretary of State John E. Peurifoy of offering *Amerasia* witness Emmanuel Larsen a "pay off" in the form of free legal advice, in return for his testimony before the Tydings Committee. A few weeks later he drew Tydings, the State Department, the Justice Department, and

[135] *Congressional Record*, 81st Cong., 2d sess., June 2, 1950, p. 8114; *Tydings Committee Hearings*, pp. 1196–1206; *New York Times*, June 3, 1950, p. 1. Called before the Tydings Committee, Van Buren backed down and refused to endorse his own telegram.

[136] *New York Times*, June 7, 1950, p. 20; J. Edgar Hoover to James E. Webb, June 14, 1950, *Tydings Committee Hearings*, pp. 1252–53. The security officer who had prepared the report, Samuel Klaus, was one of a number of former government employees who for some time had "cooperated" with the Republicans. See the *New York Times*, Aug. 6, 1948, p. 3.

eventually even the FBI into an angry squabble over whether or not, in McCarthy's words, the loyalty files had been "raped."[137]

Each of McCarthy's charges was fraudulent, and each was duly exposed. Yet taken together they greatly increased his personal notoriety and contributed to his mounting campaign to discredit the Tydings Committee.

THE TYDINGS COMMITTEE REPORT

By late June the Democrats on the Tydings Committee were pressing hard for an end to the hearings. The sudden invasion of South Korea by the Communists on June 25 had swept McCarthy from the front page, and it was probably with a certain sense of relief that the senators turned their attention to this new crisis. Still, the Opposition was not to be denied. The Republicans wanted the investigation continued and expanded, the closer to the fall elections the better; Senator Robert A. Taft was already attacking the proceedings as a "farce" and a "whitewash."[138]

On June 28 the committee met in a special closed session and the Democrats pressed a motion to have a staff report prepared. Lodge and Hickenlooper immediately protested. The Massachusetts senator declared that he had a whole series of unanswered questions (e.g., Who was responsible for hiring "sexual perverts" in the State Department?) any one of which, he said, "would be good for 6, 7 or 8 months." The committee finally voted along straight party lines to have a report of its findings submitted by the staff.[139]

On July 14 the committee issued a majority report denouncing McCarthy in terms of harshness rarely used toward fellow senators. They accused him of perpetrating "a fraud and a hoax" upon the Senate and the American people. They denied his many accusations and charged him with deliberate and willful falsehood.

[137] New York Times, June 16, 1950, p. 4; Congressional Record, 81st Cong., 2d sess., July 12, 1950, pp. 9985–88; New York Times, July 13, 1950, p. 12.

[138] New York Times, June 16, 1950, p. 3; June 22, 1950, p. 5. See Millard Tydings to Theodore F. Green, June 14, 1950, box 1104; and memorandum, Robert Morris to Senators Henry Cabot Lodge and Bourke B. Hickenlooper, June 1950, box 1106, both in the Green Papers.

[139] Tydings Committee Hearings, pp. 1471–84, 2511–25. Either by accident or intent, most of the transcript of this session was omitted from the hearings as originally printed, and was published only after Senator Homer Ferguson had read it into the Record. Congressional Record, 81st Cong., 2d sess., July 24, 1950, pp. 10815–19.

Lodge issued his own "Individual Views," declaring that the investigation had been "superficial and inconclusive" and that "the fact that many charges have been made which have not been proved" did not relieve the committee of the responsibility for a thorough investigation. McCarthy denounced the report as "a green light to the Red fifth column in the United States" and "a signal to the traitors, Communists, and fellow travelers in our Government that they need have no fear of exposure."[140]

The Foreign Relations Committee received the report, but transmitted it to the Senate only after a bitter two-hour session in which Republicans insisted upon the removal of two paragraphs chiding Lodge and Hickenlooper for absenteeism. The Senate debate was bitter. Jenner accused Tydings of conducting "the most scandalous and brazen whitewash of treasonable conspiracy in our history." Homer Ferguson charged that the committee had used the "techniques of Goebbels and Vishinsky" to silence criticism. Tydings angrily defended the report. At one point he stormed across the floor and shook his fist in the direction of Jenner, shouting, "I do not start fights, but I do not run away from them." The report was adopted on a straight party line vote. The Tydings Committee had ended in an even more bitterly partisan atmosphere than that in which it had begun. The result of the investigation had not been the restoration of confidence in the administration, but rather the rise of Joe McCarthy as a symbol of the Republican issue of "communism-in-government."[141]

THE RISE OF JOE McCARTHY: WHY?

> It all comes down to this: are
> we going to try to win an election
> or aren't we.
>
> Tom Coleman

How to explain the rise of Joe McCarthy? The answer is necessarily complicated. There has always been a fear of radicalism in this country and what I have called the "anti-Communist persuasion." Following World War II America found itself in a world increasingly polarized between East and West, and hung upon a pre-

---

[140] *New York Times*, July 18, 1950, pp. 1, 16.
[141] *Congressional Record*, July 20, 1950, pp. 10686–10717; *New York Times*, July 20, 1950, p. 1; July 21, 1950, p. 8; July 22, 1950, p. 1; July 23, 1950, sec. 4, p. 2; July 25, 1950, p. 1.

carious "balance of terror." Joe McCarthy made his appearance at a singularly propitious moment in this postwar devolution, when events both at home and abroad (the conviction of Alger Hiss, the fall of Nationalist China) provided interested partisans with ready issues. Nor was it possible to gainsay the senator's own unique contributions—his overblown sense of drama, his talent for political invective, his willingness to "raise on the poor hands." And he seemed to have touched a popular nerve with his appeal to rid the government of "Communists and queers."

More important was the Communist issue itself, with its ready-made style and slogans, even with its own "lobby." McCarthy's real triumph in these first months was in identifying himself with this issue. The phrase "McCarthyism"—first coined by the senator's opponents—assisted in this process. For most liberals, "McCarthyism" meant reckless attacks on individuals from the privileged sanctuary of the Senate. For extremists such as Fulton Lewis, Jr., "McCarthyism" was "Americanism," a phrase faintly reminiscent of something Earl Browder once said.[142] In fact, "McCarthyism" was shorthand for the issue of "communism-in-government,"[143] a preeminently Republican issue which served as the cutting edge of the party's drive for power. And as the public, press, and politicians all came to identify McCarthy with this issue, the senator won steadily increasing support from his party.

From the very outset McCarthy had the backing of a small but strategically located group of conservative Republicans to whom the Communist issue had long been important. This group included Kenneth S. Wherry, the Republican floor leader, Bourke B. Hickenlooper, who aided McCarthy from within the Tydings Committee, Karl E. Mundt, Homer Ferguson, Owen Brewster, William E. Jenner, and others. As McCarthy began to concentrate his attacks on American policy in China, he also won over the support of hard-line "Asia Firsters" such as William F.

---

[142] "Communism is the Americanism of the twentieth century." Or, as it is more usually quoted, "Communism is twentieth century Americanism." Earl Browder, *What Is Communism* (New York, 1936), p. 19.

[143] "In my part of the country," McCarthy told columnist Arthur Krock, "it means fighting communism; it means getting tough with the subversives in Government and outside, and with those who for any reason seek to protect them to escape the consequences of their own negligence or worse. That's what 'McCarthyism' seems to mean when you get out of Washington and enter the United States." *New York Times*, Dec. 28, 1950, p. 30.

Knowland and Styles Bridges, as well as isolationists such as George W. Malone.

From the beginning the McCarthy charges had represented a potentially powerful Republican campaign issue, and although the Senate Republicans never made these charges party policy, Republican leader Robert Taft urged McCarthy to press on with the attack. Truman's blast at the Republican right on March 30 seemed to confirm this movement and reporters saw in Taft's reply ("The only way to get rid of Communists in the State Department is to change the head of government.") the emerging G.O.P. battlelines for 1952.

By May, McCarthy was a hot Republican commodity. "It seems to me that the Republicans . . . will be missing a good bet if they fail to back McCarthy, actively and wholeheartedly," wrote Stanford Goltz, a political columnist for the *Wisconsin State Journal.* "This is aside from any moral or patriotic obligations." Wisconsin's Republican "Boss," Tom Coleman, put the matter more bluntly: "The issue is fairly simple, and it was made by the newspapers. It is now a political issue, and somebody is going to gain or lose politically before it's over. It all comes down to this: are we going to try to win an election or aren't we."[144]

All Republicans, of course, did not share this idea of party strategy. From time to time senators such as Ralph E. Flanders of Vermont, H. Alexander Smith of New Jersey, and Leverett Saltonstall of Massachusetts would exhibit some uneasiness over the senator's "bare-knuckle" tactics. Republican governors James H. Duff of Pennsylvania, Alfred E. Driscoll of New Jersey, and Earl Warren of California strongly criticized the senator, and the president of Columbia University, Dwight D. Eisenhower, warned that calling names was a "behind-the-iron-curtain trick" and that Americans should not be suckered into calling anyone a Communist "who may be just a little bit brighter than ourselves."[145] The most spirited Republican dissent was the celebrated "Declaration of Conscience" made by Senator Margaret Chase Smith and six other Republican senators. Senator Smith charged that the Senate had been "debased to the level of a forum of hate and character assassination sheltered by the shield of Congressional

---

[144] Quoted by James Reston in ibid., May 19, 1950, p. 12.
[145] *New York Times,* June 8, 1950, p. 35; June 19, 1950, p. 1; June 20, 1950, p. 3.

immunity" and she declared that she did not want to see the Republican party ride to victory on "the Four Horsemen of Calumny—Fear, Ignorance, Bigotry and Smear."[146]

But the tide of party politics was running heavily against the moderates. Senators Taft, Wherry, Brewster, and Bridges spoke for the Republican majority when they praised McCarthy and urged him to continue his attacks; even such moderate Republicans as H. Alexander Smith and Alexander Wiley were unwilling to follow the lead of Margaret Chase Smith and the small group which signed the "Declaration of Conscience." The New Jersey senator later recalled that the Declaration "raised the issue pretty severely," and that while he felt it was a "beautiful job" he still intended to "try and convert McCarthy rather than get him reprimanded publicly." Alexander Wiley confided to his son that McCarthy's techniques were "rather vicious," but publicly he issued a press release calling on the Truman administration to stop trying to "smear McCarthy."[147] The strength of the Communist issue seemed to be confirmed by the spring and summer primaries in Florida, North Carolina, Idaho, and California, and the bitter debate over the Tydings Committee Report tended to draw all Republican factions together. The Republican Senate Policy Committee denounced the report as political and insulting and announced its own plans for opposition. McCarthy had become a party issue, and all good men came to his aid. The resulting division robbed the report of its most important political function and allowed the Republican right and its journalistic camp followers to cry "whitewash."[148]

The response of the Democrats to McCarthy was more com-

146 Ibid., June 2, 1950, pp. 1, 11. The other senators were George Aiken of Vermont, Wayne Morse of Oregon, Edward J. Thye of Minnesota, Irving Ives of New York, Charles Tobey of New Hampshire, and Robert C. Hendrickson of New Jersey.

147 New York Times, June 19, 1950, p. 15; June 22, 1950, p. 5; June 25, 1950, p. 55. H. Alexander Smith Reminiscences, Columbia Oral History Collection (COHC), pp. 202, 247. Alexander Wiley to Marshall A. Wiley, April 6, 1950, Personal Correspondence—Marshall Wiley, box 2, Wiley Papers. New York Times, April 2, 1950, p. 9. H. Alexander Smith had praised the Declaration, and Alexander Wiley had been one of the first men on the floor to congratulate Senator Smith on her presentation.

148 For a sampling of extreme reactions to the Tydings Committee Report see Washington Times-Herald, July 19, 1950; Appleton Post-Crescent, July 22, 1950; Shreveport Times, July 19, 1950; Dallas Morning News, July 19, 1950; Cincinnati Enquirer, July 21, 1950; Illinois State Journal, July 21, 1950.

plicated, but they too contributed to his growing power and influence. It was not that McCarthy lacked vocal enemies—he did not, at least during the spring and summer of 1950. But most of these opponents were members of the Truman administration. In the Senate, only twelve Democrats spoke out against McCarthy.

Senators Tydings, Green, and McMahon were drawn into the McCarthy opposition primarily because they were members of the Tydings Committee, Scott Lucas because he was majority leader, and a few stalwarts such as Dennis Chavez of New Mexico because of the call by Tydings and others to rally behind the party banner. The remainder were members of the rather small and as yet ineffectual liberal bloc—Herbert H. Lehman of New York, William Benton of Connecticut, Harley M. Kilgore and Matthew M. Neely of West Virginia, Clinton P. Anderson of New Mexico, Hubert H. Humphrey of Minnesota, and Paul H. Douglas of Illinois.[149]

The rest of the Senate was silent. In the aftermath of the Hiss case and the China debacle, both Dean Acheson and the State Department were exposed to all manner of partisan attack; and many Democrats, especially the Southern conservatives, were unwilling to defend them. Some of this reluctance was ideological, some of it was political, some of it was even personal—they didn't *like* Dean Acheson.[150] In July the Senate Democrats did rally for a party line vote on the Tydings Committee Report, but this was the last display of Democratic unity on the McCarthy issue until

[149] Of the seven liberals, all but one were freshmen senators elected in 1948 and 1949. Several of them were strongly disliked by the Senate's Democratic establishment. Asked how the southern and western Democrats felt about Herbert Lehman, Scott Lucas replied, "They loathe him." Hubert Humphrey was *persona non grata* among the Democratic leadership because of his recent attack on one of the Upper Chamber's most powerful southern patriarchs, Harry F. Byrd of Virginia. See Allan Nevins, *Herbert H. Lehman and His Era* (New York, 1963), p. 354; Winthrop Griffith, *Humphrey: A Candid Biography* (New York, 1965), pp. 187–94.

[150] *New York Times*, March 5, 1950, sec. 4, p. 3; March 19, 1950, sec. 4, p. 3; March 31, 1950, p. 1; April 2, 1950, sec. 4, p. 3. The desire to be rid of Acheson was by no means limited to Southern conservatives. Former Secretary of the Interior Harold L. Ickes confided that "sooner or later Acheson will have to go if Truman and the Democratic Party are to have any chance to survive in 1952." The following year Senator Paul Douglas declared that Acheson had become a "political liability" and urged his resignation. Ickes to Theodore Francis Green, Sept. 2, 1950, box 1105, Green Papers; *New York Times*, May 27, 1951, p. 1.

December 1954. Confronted by the issues and emotions symbolized by Joe McCarthy, most Democrats preferred to acquiesce.

THE RISE OF JOE McCARTHY: WAS THERE AN ALTERNATIVE?

President Truman and the Democratic leaders of the Senate contributed to the rise of Joe McCarthy through lack of political skill. There was little that either the president or the Tydings Committee could have done to preclude the conservative drive for power which had generated the issue of "communism-in-government." Nor for that matter could they effect a change in the undisciplined and capricious nature of the junior senator from Wisconsin. They might, however, have prevented the juncture of these two forces to which we have given the name "McCarthyism."

The president, for example, might have attempted to contain and resolve the McCarthy challenge within the Executive Department alone. He might have demanded at the outset that McCarthy turn over his list of names (if indeed the senator had such a list) to the FBI, and then ordered the Departments of State and Justice quickly to evaluate FBI findings.[151] But McCarthy scarcely seemed threatening in early February, and the Senate's precipitate action following his speech of February 20 foreclosed any exclusive executive response.[152]

Even after this, McCarthy remained in part the creature of his adversaries, thriving on the steady flow of charges and countercharges emanating from the Executive Department. The senator had a special talent for coaxing the maximum publicity from every accusation, and he made administrators across all of Washington his unwilling dupes. Each "startling disclosure" would set in motion a chain of denials, countercharges, corrections, and explanations. Seldom has a politician received so much free advertisement as McCarthy. The State Department, for example, took to answering each of his public pronouncements with a long

---

[151] Such a procedure was suggested by Frederick Woltman, a onetime McCarthy partisan, in the *Washington Daily News*, July 13, 1954.

[152] For initial executive reaction to the McCarthy charges see Stephen J. Spingarn, Memorandum for Mr. Murphy, Feb. 15, 1950, Federal Loyalty Program, Spingarn Papers.

and detailed analysis of each lie and distortion. At one point the department, understandably sensitive over McCarthy's attacks on "dilettante diplomats," manfully announced that American envoys had been imprisoned in China, fired upon in Greece and Palestine, and forced to carry firearms in Southeast Asia.[153]

The members of the Tydings Committee also contributed to McCarthy's sudden success. They seriously underestimated the senator's talent for mischief, and in their overconfidence they failed to establish strong and deliberate procedures which might have restrained his excesses. The decision to hold public hearings is a good example. They assumed that McCarthy could be fought more easily in the open and that the absurdity of his charges would be exposed and the senator himself demolished by sheer publicity. McCarthy was indeed exposed and his charges roundly denounced, but far from being demolished, he emerged stronger than before. He was able to exploit the committee, first as a forum for his accusations, then later as a foil to play off a whole series of challenges and allegations of foul conduct. The committee procedure, moreover, provided the press and public with all the color and action of high drama. The mass media have been criticized, and with good reason, for their sensational coverage of the entire McCarthy controversy. Yet a less flamboyant investigation would have denied these media the very source of their excitations.[154]

The identification of McCarthy with the Communist issue was further intensified by the scope and nature of the hearings themselves. Despite Republican attempts to broaden and generalize the investigation, the Democrats interpreted their mandate in narrow terms. Their task was simply to prove or disprove the charges made by McCarthy. The original resolution which Senator Lucas had introduced specifically mentioned these charges; although this clause was later omitted from the motion, it was this spirit which governed the hearings throughout. Each charge was

153 *New York Times,* June 18, 1950, p. 4.

154 "I do feel, perhaps in hindsight, that a great deal more could have been accomplished by the Committee if its initial proceedings had been in private and its revelations and conclusions then made public." Senator Homer Ferguson to Adolph Germer, May 12, 1950, box 12, Adolph Germer Papers, Manuscript Division, State Historical Society of Wisconsin. Also see statement by Ralph Flanders in the *New York Times,* May 9, 1950, p. 18.

met head on, and each specifically refuted. Yet the refutation itself seemed to work in McCarthy's favor, and the currency given the phrase "McCarthy's charges" only further inflated his public image.

It is possible that the Tydings Committee might have proceeded differently? Two later congressional hearings would seem to provide preferable models. The first of these was the Joint Senate hearings conducted by Senator Richard Russell of Georgia following the dismissal from command of General Douglas A. MacArthur. The MacArthur hearings were handled with such consummate dexterity that no one even seemed to notice that the committee filed no final report. The violent emotional reaction which followed the dismissal was diffused, and the serious talk of MacArthur as a possible presidential candidate quickly disappeared.

A second, and perhaps more relevant example of committee procedure was that used by the Senate Subcommittee on Internal Security in its investigation of the Institute of Pacific Relations. This investigation was notorious for its bias and for its unfair treatment of witnesses, yet its procedure was essentially sound. The "McCarran Committee" was authorized to investigate the IPR by a Senate Resolution in December 1950. It thereafter spent more than six months in careful study and preparation, not taking its first public testimony until July 1950. Had the Tydings Committee adopted such a procedure, it might have denied McCarthy an all-important channel of publicity. But in 1950 the autumn elections were too near and the pressure for a strong, exculpatory report too great.

To a considerable extent the problem faced by the Tydings Committee was not one of political judgment but rather of institutional weakness. The fault lay not with the individual members of the Tydings Committee, but rather with the committee itself as an institution for resolving intense party conflict. Although congressional hearings are theoretically nonadversary, any powerful issue deeply agitating the two parties must almost inevitably find expression through the majority and minority members. The "Communist issue" placed an overload upon the committee which it was simply incapable of resolving. Because of this partisan composition, McCarthy was always assured a voice within the committee, and the majority-minority "ear-marking" of staff members allowed him further to undermine the committee through Assistant Counsel Robert Morris, who time and again acted without the knowledge or consent of the full subcommittee. There is the further question as to whether any committee, no matter how well constituted and how deliberate its procedures, could have withstood McCarthy's manifold capacity for subversion and sensationalism. What was needed, then, was not a better committee, but not a committee at all. For many of those who were dismayed and disgusted by the uproar which accompanied the hearings, the most realistic and politically viable alternative to the Tydings Committee was an investigation conducted by a nonpartisan commission of distinguished citizens modeled on the British Royal Commission or Tribunal of Inquiry.

The advantages which such a commission offered seemed obvious. Proceeding in closed session, it would deny McCarthy the public stage on which he performed. As an authoritative body, "above politics," it would rob the senator of an adversary. There would be no ready sounding board for his charges. A nonpartisan commission could more easily withstand McCarthy's subversive tactics, and by studying his charges within the larger scope of internal security and individual liberties, would help to diffuse them. Such a commission could obviate the bitter conflict over the executive files. It could, with the aid of a trained staff, conduct a thorough investigation and present its findings dispassionately and with a minimum of public excitement. Such an investigation could have deflated the Communist issue as an immediate source of partisan controversy, and possibly would have restored public confidence in the institutions of government.[155]

The idea of such a commission to examine the questions of security and individual liberties antedated the rise of McCarthy by some years. It was originally discussed as a result of protests from those who feared that the loyalty and security program initiated by Truman's executive order of March 1947 posed serious threats to traditional American concepts of freedom and liberty. On February 1, 1950, only a week before McCarthy's speech at

[155] Irving M. Ives, "In Place of Congressional 'Circuses,' " *New York Times Magazine*, Aug. 27, 1950, p. 20; Alan Barth, *Government by Investigation* (New York, 1955), pp. 211–15; Telford Taylor, *Grand Inquest* (New York, 1955), pp. 285–95; Herbert Packer, *Ex-Communist Witnesses*, pp. 235–47. Also see Herbert Finer, "The British System" and Lindsay Rogers, "The Problem and Its Solution," both in *The University of Chicago Law Review* 18 (Spring 1951).

Wheeling, presidential aide Charles S. Murphy sent a memorandum to the president urging the establishment of just such a commission.[156]

There is no evidence that anyone, either among the Senate leadership or in the administration, seriously considered the idea of a nonpartisan commission during the very first days of the Tydings investigation. The committee members were confident that they had the Wisconsin senator on a very long limb and were busily calculating just how and where to saw it off. Ironically, it was Congressman Richard M. Nixon who on March 22 first suggested that such a commission might be preferable to the haggling and wrangling of the Tydings Committee hearings. A few days later, Senator H. Alexander Smith, a moderate Republican from New Jersey, also argued that the public interest might be better served by a less publicized and less partisan investigation. Then on April 3 Henry Cabot Lodge introduced a bill which would have placed the entire investigation in the hands of a bipartisan commission of twelve private citizens who would take charge of the inquiry and conduct it behind closed doors. There was still a need for an investigation, he declared, but McCarthy had proved none of his charges and the net effect of the hearings had been to inflict mounting damage to our position abroad and to "besmirch the character of innocent persons."[157]

Reaction to the Lodge proposal was mixed. McCarthy, who would have probably welcomed an opportunity to squirm off the hook as late as April, told reporters he "wholeheartedly" supported the idea. Taft and Hickenlooper gave the proposal tepid support, but the Democratic leadership demurred. Majority Leader Lucas and chairman of the Foreign Relations Committee Tom Connally both opposed any change in the venue of the investigation. They said that such a procedure would deny those accused in public the right to reply in public, but they were

[156] Stephen J. Spingarn, Memorandum for Mr. Clifford, May 5, 1949; Charles S. Murphy, Memorandum for the President, Feb. 1, 1950; both in Federal Loyalty Program, Spingarn Papers. Nancy Blaine to Rep. Sydney R. Yates, Jan. 25, 1950, Legislative file, box 38, Americans for Democratic Action Papers, State Historical Society of Wisconsin.

[157] New York Times, March 23, 1950, p. 1; March 28, 1950, p. 1; April 4, 1950, p. 1; Congressional Record, 81st Cong., 2d sess., March 27, 1950, pp. 4098–4107; April 3, 1950, pp. 4571–72.

more likely moved by fear that the Republicans would interpret this as an admission of guilt or as "covering up."[158] Despite these misgivings on the part of the Democratic leadership, the Lodge proposal began to win broad bipartisan support. Both the *New York Times* and the *Washington Post* endorsed the plan, while *Newsweek* columnist Ernest K. Lindley wrote that "the whole matter is too deeply entangled in politics to be extricated by five politicians, three of whom are candidates for reelection to the Senate."[159] In the Senate Hubert Humphrey called for the establishment of a "National Security Commission" to handle the inquiry, the Republican Irving M. Ives of New York and Democrat Elbert D. Thomas of Utah introduced an even broader resolution under which Congress would delegate its authority to "congressional investigating Commissions."[160]

By the middle of May both Tydings and McMahon were convinced that some type of nonpartisan investigation was desirable. Tydings initially had in mind a rather narrowly conceived commission which would assist the senators in evaluating the eighty-one loyalty files opened to the subcommittee by President Truman. Discussion within the administration, however, included proposals for a much broader commission. Presidential aides Charles S. Murphy and Stephen J. Spingarn urged the president to set up a presidential "Commission on Internal Security and Individual Rights" which would conduct a broad survey of the federal loyalty and security program. The commission's jurisdiction would be broad enough to include not only the charges made by McCarthy and other right-wing Republicans, but also the various internal security bills then pending before Congress.[161]

The president and the Democratic leadership in Congress did not take up the commission proposal until June 1950. By this

[158] *New York Times*, April 4, 1950, p. 1.
[159] *New York Times*, May 6, 1950, p. 14; *Washington Post*, May 22, 1950; *Newsweek* 35 (June 5, 1950): 26.
[160] *Congressional Record*, 81st Cong., 2d sess., May 22, 1950, pp. 7404–7406; June 15, 1950, p. 8620.
[161] Tydings, Green, and McMahon to Truman, May 19, 1950 (draft), box 1110; Tydings to Green, box 1104, both in the Green Papers. Charles S. Murphy and Stephen J. Spingarn, Memorandum for the President, May 24, 1950, OF 252-K (1950), Truman Papers. Spingarn to Donald Dawson, May 20, 1950; and Spingarn, Memorandum, May 22, 1950, both in National Defense—Internal Security and Individual Rights, vol. 1, Spingarn Papers.

time, of course, McCarthy had already become a major political figure and had established a strong nucleus of support both inside and out of Congress. Still, Truman's advisers were able to marshal strong arguments in favor of a commission. Only such a body as this, they declared, could withstand the hysteria fanned by McCarthy and "restore reason and perspective" to the public consideration of the troublesome problem of internal security. The Tydings Committee Report, they argued, would "not end the McCarthy business." McCarthy was only the symptom of a strong partisan drive; had he never existed the Republicans "would probably had to have invented him." The commission proposal, they believed, might win the backing of Henry Cabot Lodge and wean Republican moderates away from their support of McCarthy. Even without Lodge's aid the commission would at least partially neutralize the issue of communism in government and take McCarthy and McCarthyism off the front page.[162]

There were also many difficulties and risks involved in the commission proposal. Who would establish it? Would it be legislative or presidential; or would it be modeled on the joint commission which studied governmental reorganization under former President Herbert Hoover? Who would appoint its members? What powers would it be delegated? All these were serious and complicated questions. Even more pressing were the political problems involved. Would a presidential commission command the necessary respect and authority? Would Congress establish a legislative or joint commission? How willingly would the Congress delegate its investigatory powers? Would the Republicans amend such a proposal out of recognition?[163]

The president met with Democratic leaders at Blair House on the evening of June 22 to discuss the possibility of some type of nonpartisan commission. His advisers and aides were almost unanimous in their support for the plan, but it drew heavy criticism from the congressional leaders. Of those present, only Tydings and McMahon were strongly in favor of a commission, and both of them felt it should be created by the president rather than by

---

[162] Stephen Spingarn, "Memorandum of Pros and Cons on the Proposal To Establish a Commission on Internal Security and Individual Rights," June 26, 1950, in National Defense—Internal Security and Individual Rights, Spingarn Papers.
[163] Ibid.

Congress. House Leader John W. McCormack and Senator Theodore F. Green were strongly opposed to a commission. Vice President Alben Barkley and Speaker Sam Rayburn were both inclined against it and favored delay. The attorney general was strongly opposed to the commission, which he felt might somehow interfere with the Justice Department's prosecution of Communist party leaders under the Smith Act. In the face of this very substantial opposition, the president finally concluded that he would take no action at that time.[164]

Whether the establishment of a bipartisan commission would have prevented the rise of McCarthy, or helped to dissipate his influence, must at very best remain problematical. It could hardly have done worse than the Tydings Committee. After his defeat in November 1950 Millard Tydings thought back to that meeting at Blair House the previous June. "If . . . we had appointed a commission and turned this matter over," he told Democratic National Chairman William E. Boyle, "it not only would have made a difference to me in my campaign but would have helped others who suffered in some degree from the same tactics."[165] Instead, the fear of innovation, together with short-term bureaucratic and partisan considerations won out. The Tydings Committee denounced the Wisconsin senator in terms his richly

[164] Stephen Spingarn, "Blair House Meeting," June 23, 1950, and "Memorandum of Pros and Cons on the Proposal To Establish a Commission on Internal Security and Individual Rights," June 26, 1950, both in National Defense–Internal Security and Individual Rights, Spingarn Papers. Although not present at the Blair House meeting, the commission was violently opposed by Seth Richardson, the chairman of the Civil Service Commission's Loyalty Review Board, who seemed to interpret the proposal as a personal criticism of himself and the board. "Any step taken now in the hope of allaying hostile criticism would, in my opinion, only make a bad matter worse," he declared. Richardson to Donald Dawson, June 26, 1950, OF 419-K, Truman Papers.

[165] The commission was discussed again during the summer of 1950 in the face of growing support for internal security legislation, but it was not until 1951 that a presidential commission (under retired Admiral Chester W. Nimitz) was finally established. By then the opportunity had passed, and Senator Pat McCarran, jealous of any threats to his recently enacted Internal Security Act, successfully undermined this last effort. See Charles S. Murphy, George Elsey, and Stephen J. Spingarn, Memorandum for the President, July 11, 1950, in National Defense–Internal Security and Individual Rights, vol. 1, Spingarn Papers. For the Nimitz Commission, see Records of the President's Commission on Internal Security and Individual Rights, Truman Library. For an excellent study, see Alan D. Harper, "The Nimitz Commission," unpublished manuscript in the Truman Library.

deserved, but it also forged the final link in the rise of Joe McCarthy.[166]

Although institutional weaknesses and errors of judgment thus contributed to McCarthy's rise, they did not cause it. McCarthy's growing power and influence was not just procedural, but also substantive. It sprang not so much from the institutions of the Senate, as from the political dynamics of the Communist issue.

[166] Millard Tydings to William E. Boyle, Nov. 16, 1950, in the Millard E. Tydings Papers, University of Maryland.

4

THE
FEAR OF
HONORABLE
MEN

AMERICA AT MID - CENTURY
seemed a land of demagogues, and its politics were full of sound
and fury. The beginning of the Korean War intensified the popular
agitation over communism, precipitating what some have called
America's second great Red scare. The 1950 midterm elections
were the most bitter and factious in recent history, and apparently
no one was immune from attack. Senate Minority Leader Kenneth
Wherry charged that the secretary of state was stained with "the
blood of our boys in Korea"; Kansas Republican Andrew F.
Schoeppel accused the secretary of the interior of pro-Communist
leanings; and Indiana's William E. Jenner called General of the
Army and then Secretary of Defense George C. Marshall "a
living lie," "a front man for traitors," and "either an unsuspecting
stooge or an actual co-conspirator with the most treasonable array

of political cutthroats ever turned loose in the Executive Branch of Government."[1] The junior senator from Wisconsin rode this tide of irresponsibility, exploited its license, and turned it to his own aggrandizement. It was his element—the shouted phrase, the unreasoning accusation, the great simplification.

Yet demagoguery is the inevitable price a democracy pays for its free institutions. What needs explanation is not the existence of demagogues during those troubled years, but why their excesses were tolerated and even encouraged. And beyond this, what circumstances allowed Joe McCarthy, until early 1950 an inconspicuous midwestern senator, to capture this movement as his own?

The hysteria and confusion of the early 1950s reflected the inefficacy and limitations of all American institutions—economic, educational, and religious. But the most vivid and dramatic failure was that of the nation's political institutions and leadership. "McCarthy" and "McCarthyism" did not spring alone and unaided from the fertile imagination of the junior senator from Wisconsin. They were instead the symptoms of a malfunctioning of the entire political system.

McCarthy's own power and influence rested upon the twin issues of "communism-in-government" and American policy in the Far East. These were the two interrelated themes of the Republican attack of the late forties, the weapons given the Grand Old Party by circumstance and choice in its battle against the Democratic administration. The one rested on a myth of conspiracy in high places, the other on an illusion of American omnipotence. Together they provided the powerful symbols and slogans for a partisan drive for power, and McCarthy proved himself a daring and consummate manipulator of this entire body of political mythology.

The Republicans could not and would not disavow the excesses generated by these issues; the administration proved unable to

[1] *New York Times*, Aug. 17, 1950, p. 1; Sept. 8, 1950, p. 12; Sept. 16, 1950, p. 1. Nevada Republican George "Molly" Malone even defended hoarding as an "honest American trait" and charged that President Truman's criticism of wartime hoarders "echoes the thoughts of Communists who want to set up a welfare state." Ibid., Sept. 7, 1950, p. 2. "The moral climate of America seems to be getting worse and worse," lamented former New Dealer Harold L. Ickes. Ickes to Theodore F. Green, Sept. 2, 1950, box 1105, Green Papers.

devise or implement a political strategy to meet this challenge; and Congress took counsel in its fears. It was not the constitutional immunity of the Senate floor which protected Joe McCarthy, but the political immunity conferred upon him by the issues he had come to symbolize.

CONGRESS AND COMMUNISM: THE INTERNAL SECURITY ACT OF 1950

In September 1950 Congress passed the McCarran Internal Security Act, an omnibus "anti-subversive" bill with provisions for the registration of Communist-action and Communist-front groups, the emergency detention of persons believed likely to commit espionage and sabotage, and the tightening of laws against sedition and espionage. The bill was one with which Joe McCarthy was never closely identified, yet because it typified the collapse of congressional courage and good sense in the face of the Communist issue, it helps to explain a great deal about both McCarthy and "McCarthyism."

Throughout the late 1940s popular concern over domestic communism had been steadily increasing. Many constitutional lawyers argued that existing statutes were sufficient protection against potential espionage or subversion, but by 1950 it seemed obvious to even the most casual observers that some type of internal security legislation was in the works. In 1948 the House of Representatives passed a Communist registration bill sponsored by Congressmen Richard M. Nixon and Karl E. Mundt, and the following year the Senate Judiciary Committee gave detailed consideration to a similar measure co-sponsored by Republicans Karl Mundt and Homer Ferguson and Democrat Olin D. Johnston. In July 1950 the Republican Policy Committee placed a version of the Mundt-Nixon bill on its "must list," and the Democrats came under heavy pressure to support it lest they appear remiss in their patriotism.[2]

President Truman was adamant in his opposition to the Mundt-Nixon bill, which, he maintained, "adopted police-state tactics and

[2] Stephen J. Spingarn to Clark Clifford, May 2, 1949; Spingarn to Charles S. Murphy et al., July 20, 1950, National Defense—S2311; Spingarn to Murphy, Aug. 1, 1950, National Defense—Internal Security and Individual Rights, vol. 2, all in the Spingarn Papers.

unduly encroached on individual rights." The president believed that the situation in Congress was the worst it had been since the Alien and Sedition acts, with "a lot of people on the Hill . . . running with their tails between their legs." He promised to veto the bill "regardless of how politically unpopular it was—election year or no election year."[3] On August 8 he sent Congress a message on internal security and mounted a campaign for limited and moderate legislation. By then, however, it was too late. Congress was already stampeding toward the enactment of sweeping internal security measures, and the president was unable to establish any control over the flow of events.

In the Senate, the key figure was Pat McCarran, the silver-haired, seventy-four-year-old chairman of the Senate Judiciary Committee, and the leader of a coalition of conservative Republicans and Democrats demanding new and drastic legislation. McCarran was sometimes compared with McCarthy. Both were Irish Catholics and both played heavily upon the Communist issue. Though a Democrat, McCarran was usually aligned with the Republican right. But Joe McCarthy had no real sense of grand strategy. His genius was for turmoil and confusion, and for the excitement and notoriety they produced. What power he exercised was of an unconventional nature, derived from his symbolic role as exemplar of the anti-Communist persuasion and from his near monopoly of the mass media. McCarran, by contrast, had a swift and sure instinct for the traditional levers of congressional power. He exercised baronial authority over the Senate Judiciary Committee, and through his control of all judicial appointments he was able to exact tribute from the administration and his fellow senators alike. He could extort from Attorney General James P. McGranery, in return for the latter's confirmation, the promise that the Justice Department would press perjury charges against Owen Lattimore. And he could browbeat a deputy attorney general into promising that—"Cross my heart"—he would carry out a demand made by the chairman.[4]

[3] Stephen J. Spingarn, Memorandum for the Files, July 22, 1950, National Defense—Internal Security and Individual Rights, vol. 1, Spingarn Papers.

[4] Thurmond Arnold, *Fair Fights and Foul: A Dissenting Lawyer's Life* (New York, 1965), p. 217; Jack Anderson and Ronald May, *McCarthy: The Man, the Senator, the "Ism"* (Boston, 1952), p. 341. McCarran's power was increased by the institutional habits of the Senate. Most senators tend to

On August 17, just nine days after the president had warned
Congress that much of the legislation then pending before Congress
was "unnecessary, ineffective and dangerous," McCarran reported
from committee an omnibus internal security bill incorporating
not only the Mundt-Nixon bill but the provisions of four other
internal security measures as well. Opponents of the bill argued
that the registration provisions were cumbersome and ineffective,
and that they would, moreover, endanger traditional American
liberties guaranteed by the First and Fifth Amendments to the
Constitution. The editorial positions of liberal, moderate, and
even some conservative dailies were strongly against the measure.[5]
Yet in the Senate both the center and the left collapsed as the
"McCarran bill" carried by a vote of 70-7.[6]
On every side were reports of fear and gross hypocrisy. One
group of Democratic senators met and concluded that although
the bill was "a bad measure" which should not be supported under
ordinary circumstances, "those who faced the electorate THIS year
would be taking too great a risk if they voted right because of
the popular lack of understanding and hysteria over the issue."
One veteran newsman reported that he was "amazed in talking
privately to a number of conservative senators—both Republicans
and Democrats—that they voted with tongue in cheek for it and
with a lot of reluctance." The Democratic leadership, having done

specialize, concentrating their efforts in one legislative area and relying upon
the counsel of their friends and the party leadership in other matters. When
an especially powerful man such as McCarran dominates an area, there is
often no countervailing force to push and plead legislative alternatives.
"Senators, like myself, who are not members of the Judiciary Committee,
rely to a great extent, of course, upon the recommendations which it makes
after a thorough analysis of the particular matter under consideration," explained Texas Senator Tom Connally to an angry constituent. Tom T. Connally to Mrs. W. A. Nauwald, March 26, 1951, box 118, Tom T. Connally
Papers, Library of Congress.
    [5] *Washington Post*, Aug. 31, 1950; *New York Herald-Tribune*, Aug. 31,
1950; *New York Times*, Aug. 31, 1950; *Louisville Courier-Journal*, Sept. 1,
1950; *Philadelphia Inquirer*, Aug. 31, 1950; *Christian Science Monitor*, Sept.
15, 1950.
    [6] *Congressional Record*, 81st Cong., 2d sess., Sept. 12, 1950, p. 14628.
Voting against the bill were Democrats Graham, Green, Kefauver, Leahy,
Lehman, Murray, and Taylor. Republican William Langer would have voted
against the bill, but voted yea so that he might be able to move for reconsideration. Langer to Harry S. Truman, Sept. 18, 1950, PPF 5491, Truman
Papers.

little to keep the bill off the floor and even less to oppose it once it was reported out, now unanimously urged the president to sign it into law.[7]

The response of some Democratic liberals to the bill was more disconcerting to libertarians than the McCarran Act itself. Led by Paul H. Douglas of Illinois and Harley M. Kilgore of West Virginia, the Senate liberals proposed as a substitute for the McCarran bill an emergency detention plan for the internment of suspected subversives upon the declaration of an "internal security emergency" by the president.[8] This "concentration camp bill," as one White House aide labeled it, became the uneasy rallying point for those liberals who were trying to block the McCarran bill. It was a "very bad bill," confessed Julius C. C. Edelstein, the legislative assistant to New York Democrat Herbert H. Lehman. It had "profound" constitutional weaknesses in seeking to set aside the right of *habeas corpus*. Still, it would "certainly impress the public with the fact that you are determined to act against communists." The only real dangers which Edelstein foresaw were that the bill might actually be passed, and that Thomas E. Dewey might be able to dramatize it in order to show "that you are really more of a fascist that he is."[9]

On September 6, 1950, Douglas, Kilgore, Lehman, Hubert Humphrey, and several other liberal Democrats called on President Truman to explain their proposal. They told Truman that "they had to make a move of this sort as the only possible way of beating the McCarran bill." The president declined to commit himself, telling the senators to go ahead with their plans, but that he would

---

[7] John D. Erwin to Estes Kefauver, Sept. 24, 1950, in Legislative Files, 81st Congress, Estes Kefauver Papers, University of Tennessee. John Steele to Arthur Vandenberg, Sept. 27, 1950, Vandenberg Papers. Vice President Barkley, Scott Lucas, House Speaker Sam Rayburn, and House Majority Leader John W. McCormack had all urged Truman to sign the bill. Stephen J. Spingarn, Memorandum for the Files, Sept. 19, 1950, National Defense—Internal Security and Individual Rights, Spingarn Papers.

[8] S. 4130 was co-sponsored by Senators Douglas, Kilgore, Humphrey, Lehman, Graham, Kefauver, and Benton. Not all liberals, of course, were shocked by the Douglas-Kilgore proposal. Some, such as James Loeb, Jr., of Americans for Democratic Action, felt the bill was "justified both by realistic justice and by political expediency." James Loeb, Jr., to Miss Evelyn Dubrow, Nov. 1, 1950, Legislative File, box 34, ADA Papers.

[9] Memorandum, Julius C. C. Edelstein to Herbert H. Lehman, Sept. 4, 1950, Senate Files, Research—Drawer One, Herbert H. Lehman Papers, Columbia University.

reserve judgment until such time as the measure might reach his desk.[10]

In a series of complicated parliamentary maneuvers the concentration camp proviso was first rejected as a substitute for the McCarran bill, then later accepted as an addition to the measure. This last move followed a surprise motion by Majority Leader Scott Lucas which caught the liberals completely unprepared; as a result a number of them—Humphrey, Kilgore, Benton, Douglas, Clinton Anderson, Warren Magnuson, and Wayne Morse—voted for the McCarran bill on its final Senate passage.[11]

"As I look back on it I am very ashamed of my vote on the McCarran Act," confessed Connecticut Democrat William Benton. "I do have some excuses and alibis, though in retrospect they are not good ones." "I was very proud of you and your vote on the McCarran bill," wrote Hubert Humphrey to Tennessee's Estes Kefauver. "I wish I could say the same for myself."[12] A number of Senate liberals, including some who like Humphrey and Kilgore had voted for the bill, now urged Truman to veto it.[13]

The president needed no encouragement. He returned the bill to Congress with a strong veto message on September 22. In the House the veto was quickly overridden by a vote of 286 to 46. In the Senate, a vote was delayed by a last-minute attempt by William Langer and Hubert Humphrey to prolong debate in the hope of sustaining the president. Langer, who had earlier told the president that the bill was "one of the most vicious, most dangerous pieces of legislation against the people that has ever been passed by any Senate," spoke for nearly five hours before he collapsed near dawn. Humphrey took the floor for several more hours but fearing an "adverse reaction" finally allowed the measure to come before the Senate. The final vote was 57 to 10. Only a tiny band

[10] Stephen J. Spingarn, Memorandum for the Files, Sept. 6, 1950, National Defense—Internal Security and Individual Rights, vol. 3, Spingarn Papers.

[11] *Congressional Record*, 81st Cong., 2d sess., Sept. 12, 1950, p. 14628.

[12] William Benton to Ralph Flanders, Feb. 17, 1954, box 113, Ralph Flanders Papers, Syracuse University. Benton to Francis Biddle, Nov. 7, 1950, Legislative File, box 34, ADA Papers. Hubert H. Humphrey to Estes Kefauver, Sept. 19, 1950, Legislative Files, 81st Congress, Kefauver Papers.

[13] Harley Kilgore to Truman, Sept. 14, 1950; Senators Herbert Lehman, James Murray, and Estes Kefauver to Truman, Sept. 20, 1950, both letters in OF 2750-C, Truman Papers. Stephen J. Spingarn, Memorandum for the Files, Sept. 25, 1950, National Defense—Internal Security and Individual Rights, vol. 3, Spingarn Papers.

of liberals and one lone Republican, the irrepressible Langer, supported the president. The entire Democratic leadership of the Senate deserted the president, and of the eastern, "liberal" Republicans, not one was counted.[14] If the passage of the McCarran Act could be taken as an index to the strength of the Communist issue within the Senate and of the inability of either the administration or the Senate leadership to establish opposing centers of power, then it is clear why the Upper Chamber was vulnerable to McCarthy's brand of political adventure.

THE MYTH OF POLITICAL INVINCIBILITY

For those who remained to be convinced, there was the lesson of the ballot box. A senator's constituency may speak to him in many ways—through letters, newspapers, and personal contacts. In no instance does it speak with more finality than on election day. The Senate read the results of the 1950 elections and saw in them a reflection of its own worst fears. It seemed as though from one end of the country to the other, candidates for office were denouncing their opponents for being "soft on communism," for countenancing Reds in government, and indeed for being themselves dupes, fellow travelers, and "pinks." As a character from one of Herbert Block's cartoons plaintively asked, "Is Joe Stalin running in all these elections?"[15]

For McCarthy the campaign was strenuous and exciting. He was in demand as a speaker by Republican groups throughout the country, and in a few short months he delivered more than thirty major addresses in fifteen states.[16] In New York and in Illinois, in Connecticut and in Wisconsin, in Maryland and in Missouri, his message was the same. Drive from the Senate "those small-minded

---

[14] Voting nay were Senators Chavez, Graham, Douglas, Green, Humphrey, Kilgore, Leahy, Lehman, Murray, and Kefauver. Langer, who had been taken to the hospital, was announced as opposing the bill, and Glenn Taylor of Idaho was paired against it. *Congressional Record*, 81st Cong., 2d sess., Sept. 23, 1950, p. 15726.

[15] *New York Times*, June 18, 1950, sec. 4, p. 7. The campaign was following the "standard pattern," one Democratic congressman wryly noted. "I am the stooge of the CIO and of the Communists, the enemy of the middle class, and my patriotism is questionable. I have not checked *Mein Kampf*, but I think this is the recommended approach." Eugene J. McCarthy to James Loeb, Jr., Oct. 2, 1950, Political File, box 3, ADA Papers.

[16] *New York Times*, Aug. 19, 1950, p. 30; *Chicago Daily News*, Nov. 24, 1950.

men who have compromised country for party—who have covered up treachery and incompetence. . . . On their hands and on the hands of the men they have shielded is the blood of American youth." Drive from government the "Communists, dupes and fellow-travelers" who have "plotted the Communist victory in Asia." Drive from office the "Commiecrats," all who are "prisoners of a bureaucratic Communistic Frankenstein," and all the "parlor pinks and parlor punks" who still dance to the Moscow tune.[17]

Both Scott Lucas and Millard Tydings went down to defeat in the November elections. So did Majority Whip Francis J. Myers of Pennsylvania and Elbert D. Thomas of Utah. In many campaigns, including that of Richard M. Nixon of California, the Communist issue played a prominent role, and observers were quick to interpret the results as a vindication of McCarthy.[18]

The defeat of Tydings was particularly traumatic. What Roosevelt had failed to do in 1938, McCarthy had accomplished in 1950. And if Tydings could be defeated, then who was safe? Even the most conservative and entrenched Democrats began to fear for their seats, and in the months that followed, the legend of McCarthy's political power grew. By 1953 he was credited with nearly a dozen Republican Senate victories, and what one critic has called the "myth of political invincibility" was in full bloom.[19]

Communism and "McCarthyism" *were* factors in the 1950 elections. Indeed they reached their zenith as campaign issues in this election. The effect of both, however, has been overrated, and it is difficult to distinguish the influence of the Communist issue or McCarthy from the general disaffection for the entire Democratic administration.[20]

[17] *New York Times,* Aug. 13, 1950, p. 13; Sept. 16, 1950, p. 48; Oct. 17, 1950, p. 34; *Baltimore Sun,* Sept. 16, 1950; *Congressional Record,* 81st Cong., 2d sess., Sept. 23, 1950, pp. A6869–6901, A7246–49; radio address by Senator Joseph McCarthy, Nov. 6, 1950, press release in NCEC files.

[18] *Chicago Daily Tribune,* Nov. 8, 9, 10, 1950; *New York Times,* Nov. 9, 1950, pp. 28, 36; Nov. 10, 1950, p. 15.

[19] William S. White, *New York Times,* Jan. 18, 1953, sec. 4, p. 4; Cabell Phillips, March 8, 1953, sec. 4, p. 4; Maurice Rosenblatt to Arthur Schlesinger, Jr., April 24, 1953, in the NCEC files; *New York Post,* May 23, 1953.

[20] Louis Bean has shown that in selected counties in six states (Pennsylvania, Ohio, Indiana, Illinois, Wisconsin, and Maryland) Democratic candidates lost more heavily in counties with large concentrations of Catholic voters. His assumption is, of course, that the Communist issue and McCarthy's influence registered "most definitely" in areas of substantial Catholic concentration. Louis Bean, *Influences in the 1954 Mid-Term Elections* (Washington, D. C., 1954), pp. 25–32.

By 1950 the Truman administration was highly vulnerable. It bore the brunt of nearly twenty years of accumulated grievances against the New and Fair Deals. Its enemies were legion, and even its onetime friends were becoming restive. White southerners were in a predictable huff over the president's proposal for a permanent Fair Employment Practices Commission (FEPC); doctors and dentists were in arms over the prospect of national health insurance; and Farmer Jones was asking, "But what in the hell have you done for me lately?" Even the traditional Democratic strongholds in the great cities were showing signs of restlessness in the face of the continued prosperity of the late forties and early fifties. The scandals which touched the president's "Missouri gang" further contributed to Truman's declining popularity, until only 26 percent of the country approved the manner in which he ran the presidency. His "Give 'em hell, Harry" approach to politics, which had proved so effective in 1948, was wearing thin and now added to the growing disrespect for the office of the chief executive and for Truman himself. Finally, there was the fact of the Korean War. A series of brilliant victories during the early autumn had raised hopes for a swift end to the fighting, but during the first days of November the appearance of Chinese troops created doubt and uncertainty.

Not unexpectedly, the Democrats suffered heavy reverses in the election. Their losses were not as staggering as in the previous midterm election of 1946, however, and they still retained control of both houses of Congress.

If the impact of the Communist issue on the elections was difficult to determine, the influence of McCarthy himself was even more elusive. The senator spoke in at least fifteen states; in many of these, Republicans were indeed elected. But McCarthy could hardly claim these as personal achievements. Incumbents such as Robert A. Taft, Eugene Millikin, and Bourke B. Hickenlooper would have been elected no matter what the Wisconsin senator did. In Idaho McCarthy supporters Herman Welker and Henry Dworshak were almost assured election by a savage Democratic primary. In Pennsylvania, incumbent Democrat Francis J. Myers was defeated, but by a liberal Republican who had strongly criticized McCarthy. Even Richard M. Nixon, who had hammered away at the Communist issue, did not rise or fall on this alone, and his running mate, California's governor, Earl Warren, made no secret of his strong distaste for McCarthy. In one state in which McCarthy spoke the Republican incumbent was defeated by nearly 100,000 votes.[21]

McCarthy had singled out three Democratic incumbents for special attention—Brien McMahon of Connecticut, Millard Tydings of Maryland, and Scott Lucas of Illinois. They had been his chief antagonists during the Tydings Committee hearings, and he accused them of covering up for the State Department. "Lucas provided the whitewash when I charged there were Communists in high places," he declared. "McMahon brought the bucket; Tydings the brush."[22]

The Connecticut and Illinois contests presented many similarities. Each state had a strong two-party system—the Democrats relying on the big cities, the Republicans on the suburban and rural vote. In 1944 Roosevelt had carried both states, but in 1948 Dewey had won Connecticut and lost Illinois by less than a percentage point. In both states McCarthy made speeches denouncing the incumbent Democrats. In Illinois he spoke some half-dozen times in and around the Chicago area. In Connecticut he addressed Republican rallies in Bridgeport, New Haven, and Hartford. But here the comparison ends.

In Illinois the Republican nominee was Everett McKinley Dirksen, a veteran congressman and one of his party's very best orators and parliamentarians. His campaign was one of the most intensive in the state's history. He had begun in February 1949 and had continued almost without cessation, traveling some 250,000 miles and delivering nearly 1,500 major speeches. The Democrats realized their weakness early. Truman spoke on behalf of his majority leader in May 1950, and Vice President Barkley and other Democratic dignitaries joined the campaign during the closing weeks.[23]

Dirksen pounded away at the Communist issue ("A vote for

[21] For comments on McCarthy by James H. Duff of Pennsylvania and Earl Warren of California, see the *New York Times*, June 19, 1950, p. 1. Missouri Republican Forest C. Donnell was the only Republican incumbent defeated in the general election. Donald J. Kemper, *Decade of Fear: Senator Hennings and Civil Liberties* (Columbia, Mo., 1965), pp. 27–31.

[22] Speech to a Republican rally in Hyattsville, Md.; *Congressional Record*, 81st Cong., 2d sess., Sept. 23, 1950, p. A6901; *New York Times*, Sept. 24, 1950, p. 76.

[23] *Chicago Daily Tribune*, Nov. 2, 4, 6, 1950; Scott Lucas to Truman, May 25, 1950, PPF 1774, Truman Papers.

Dirksen is a vote against communism," declared one supporter.) and the "sellout of China to Stalin." His campaign was given an added boost by the military reversals in Korea.[24] The biggest issue in the campaign, however, was neither Korea nor communism, but "corruption." The Democrats had nominated for sheriff of Cook County (Chicago and environs) Daniel A. ("Tubbo") Gilbert, a Chicago police captain whom the *Tribune* called "The World's Richest Cop," and who had been a target for Senator Estes Kefauver's traveling investigation of crime and corruption. The Gilbert candidacy seriously damaged Lucas's chances in Chicago and was probably responsible for a record turnout in the surrounding suburbs. As a consequence the suburban vote canceled out the city vote and Dirksen coasted to an easy victory on a large downstate majority.[25]

In Connecticut the situation was quite different. Brien McMahon's Republican opponent was a relatively unknown former congressman. McMahon's religion and ancestry, moreover, may have served him well among the Irish who constituted the heart of the state's Democratic strength. Most importantly there was no taint of scandal as in Illinois. Despite Republican charges that he covered up for the State Department, McMahon won nearly 53 percent of the two-party vote and led the statewide Democratic ticket.[26]

It was not in Connecticut or Illinois that the legend of McCarthy's political invincibility originated, however, but in Maryland, where the Wisconsin senator's great antagonist, Senator Millard E. Tydings, was standing for his fifth consecutive term. Tydings had a record of impeccable conservatism, and in a state where the Democratic registration approached 70 percent he appeared unassailable. But the old issues and loyalties had paled beside the charges that Tydings had "whitewashed" the State Department and "covered up" for the administration. The accusa-

[24] *Chicago Daily Tribune*, Nov. 1, 4, 5, 8, 1950; earlier it had been believed that United Nations victories in Korea would hurt Dirksen's chances. *New York Times*, Oct. 28, 1950, p. 6.

[25] *New York Times*, Oct. 28, 1950, p. 6; Nov. 5, 1950, sec. 4, pp. 8–9; *Chicago Daily Tribune*, Nov. 1, 2, 8, 9; Lucas himself attributed his defeat to the Kefauver investigation of Gilbert. *New York Times*, March 11, 1951, sec. 4, p. 7.

[26] Brien McMahon and William Benton, who had also attacked McCarthy, ran one-two among the seven Democratic candidates for statewide offices. *New York Times*, Nov. 5, 1950, sec. 4, p. 8; John Howe to Kenneth Birkhead, July 15, 1953, box 4, Benton Papers.

tions first sounded by McCarthy echoed throughout the primary and general elections. One primary opponent accused Tydings of having "given the green light to Stalin's agents in this country to continue to gnaw at the foundations of our national security." Another accused him of "whitewashing" the entire affair.[27] And it was not just McCarthy's charges which dominated the election, but McCarthy himself, working behind the scenes in what a Senate subcommittee would later describe as "a despicable 'back street' type of campaign."

Tyding's opponent was John Marshall Butler, a Baltimore attorney who was making his first bid for public office. Although Butler had announced his candidacy in May, it was not until midsummer that his campaign really got underway. In July Butler met with McCarthy and his staff to plan campaign strategy. From this point Butler himself became a front for McCarthy and the "McCarthy lobby." He made speeches and posed for pictures, but effective control of the campaign passed into other hands.

From McCarthy's office the Maryland attorney was sent to Ruth McCormick ("Bazy") Miller, the niece of Colonel Robert R. McCormick and the editor of the McCormick-owned *Washington Times-Herald*. She enthusiastically agreed to help Butler; as a starter, she called in Jon M. Jonkel, a Chicago public relations man, to organize Butler's campaign. Although Jonkel did not technically become Butler's campaign manager (Maryland law specifically forbids this), he in fact ran the campaign in every way but in name.[28] Butler seldom appeared at campaign headquarters, and even large contributions would pass directly through Jonkel's office rather than through the campaign treasurer.[29] It was Jonkel who designed and implemented the strategy of "the big doubt." He exploited the general ignorance as to whether Tydings had in fact conducted an "impartial" investigation, and he attempted to discredit the senator's entire record in light of this uncertainty.[30]

The McCarthy-McCormick support was not limited to the pro-

[27] *Baltimore Sun*, Sept. 1, 17, 1950.

[28] U. S., Congress, Senate, 82d Cong., 1st sess., Committee on Rules and Administration, *Maryland Senatorial Election of 1950* (Washington, D. C., 1951), pp. 431–32, 436, 466 (hereafter cited as *Maryland Hearings*).

[29] U. S., Congress, Senate, 82d Cong., 1st sess., Committee on Rules and Administration, *Maryland Senatorial Election of 1950* (Washington, D. C., 1951), pp. 13, 15 (hereafter cited as *Maryland Report*).

[30] *Maryland Report*, p. 6. For a thoughtful analysis of Jonkel's role in the Maryland campaign see Stanley Kelley, Jr., *Professional Public Relations and Political Power* (Baltimore, Md., 1956), chapt. 4.

curement of Jonkel's professional services. From Chicago they imported an elderly Negro employee of the *Chicago Tribune* to work for Butler in Baltimore's black ghetto.[31] (Baltimore Negroes needed little convincing, since Tydings had opposed FEPC, anti-lynching, and practically every other measure designed to end racial injustice.) The Mutual news commentator Fulton Lewis, Jr., devoted a series of broadcasts to criticism of Tydings, chaired a meeting of Butler supporters, and helped with the layouts of Butler campaign advertisements. The *Times-Herald* provided Butler with cutrate editorial and printing services.[32] Even Colonel McCormick got into the campaign, charging that Tydings was "a supporter of the Iron Curtain and concentration camps for millions."[33]

Even more importantly, the McCarthy group tapped wealthy campaign contributors on Butler's behalf. A campaign against an incumbent senator, especially when there is no strong party or-ganization as was the case with the Republicans in Maryland, depends heavily upon the mass media and consequently requires a high level of expenditures. Butler spent nearly three times as much as Tydings, and a great deal of the money came from figures closely linked to McCarthy.[34]

McCarthy himself made three speeches in Maryland. In a typical performance before a Republican rally at Hyattsville, Maryland, he accused Tydings of "protecting Communists for political reasons," of whitewashing the State Department, and of shielding traitors "at a time when the survival of western non-atheistic civilization hangs in the balance."[35]

Behind this screen of platform oratory, McCarthy's staff worked hand in hand with Jonkel and the *Times-Herald* to provide help for the campaign. McCarthy's research assistant, Jean Kerr (later Mrs. McCarthy), was almost continuously in contact with the

[31] *Maryland Hearings,* pp. 439–49, 449–56; *Maryland Report,* pp. 36–37.

[32] *Maryland Hearings,* pp. 579–93; *Maryland Report,* pp. 21–26, 28, 30, 35–36.

[33] *Baltimore Sun,* Nov. 2, 1950.

[34] There was $10,000 from oilman Clint Murchison; $5,000 from Ruth McCormick Miller; $5,000 from Texas Republican H. J. Porter; $5,000 from Dan Gainey, a Minnesota supporter of Harold Stassen; $1,000 from Senator Owen Brewster; $1,000 from Alfred Kohlberg. *Maryland Report,* p. 16; Kelley, *Professional Public Relations and Political Power,* p. 132.

[35] *Congressional Record,* 81st Cong., 2d sess., Sept. 23, 1950, pp. A6899–6901; *New York Times,* Sept. 24, 1950, p. 76.

Butler headquarters. Don Surine, Ray Kiermas, and a handful of other McCarthy employees were also intermittently engaged in the undertaking. Toward the end of the campaign Mrs. Robert E. Lee, the wife of the Republican investigator and a close friend of Jean Kerr, supervised a mass mailing of Butler campaign literature. They used postcards, a McCarthy trademark, and the venture was underwritten by funds solicited by Miss Kerr on Butler's behalf.[36] Finally, McCarthy's office and the *Times-Herald* staff collaborated in the preparation of a campaign tabloid called "From the Record." The tabloid was a compilation of all the various charges and distortions previously made by McCarthy, and it contained the now famous "composite" photo of Tydings and Earl Browder, cropped and doctored so as to make it appear that the senator was in intimate conversation with the Communist leader.[37]

The results of the election shocked many. Tydings was defeated by more than 40,000 votes, and the shadow of Joe McCarthy loomed more ominously than ever across the nation's political horizons.

In retrospect it appears that Tydings was far more vulnerable than many had believed at the time. The sudden reversals in the Korean War, together with the general dissatisfaction with the Democratic administration, had taken a heavy toll. Maryland had tended to vote independently in national elections, moreover, despite its heavy Democratic registration. Dewey won the state's electoral vote in 1948, just as Eisenhower would in 1952 and 1956. The Democratic percentage of the two-party vote had been in a steady decline ever since 1938;[38] in 1946, the last senatorial election, Democrat Herbert R. O'Connor had come within a hairbreadth of defeat. In 1950 the state's Democratic organization was wracked by a fierce intraparty struggle. Democratic Governor W. Preston Lane had signed into law Maryland's first sales tax,

[36] *Maryland Report.* pp. 19–20.

[37] The tabloid was prepared by the *Times-Herald's* chief editorial writer, Frank Smith, who later became Butler's administrative assistant. The photograph was prepared by Garvin Tankersly, the assistant managing editor, later the husband of Ruth McCormick Miller. Butler's campaign treasurer, Cornelius P. Mundy, characterized the tabloid as "stupid, peurile, and in bad taste." Miss Kerr declared that it was "the type of literature that should go out in campaigns." *Maryland Report*, pp. 21–26.

[38] Bean, *Influences in the 1954 Mid-Term Elections*, p. 30.

and as a consequence had won renomination only after an extremely bitter primary contest. He was overwhelmingly defeated in the general election by the popular former mayor of Baltimore, Theodore McKeldin. Tydings led Lane in the general election, while Butler trailed far behind McKeldin.

Because of his extremely conservative record on economic and social legislation, Tydings had the support of neither labor nor the state's Negro population. The unions had supported one of Tyding's primary opponents, John A. Meyer, and they were at the very most lukewarm in the general election.[39] The Negro vote, despite a last-minute appeal by Democratic Congressman Adam Clayton Powell, went overwhelmingly for Butler.[40] Finally, Maryland's heavy Catholic population may have maximized McCarthy's impact. One of Tydings's primary opponents, Hugh J. Monaghan II, had been only a thinly veiled "Catholic" candidate, and his campaign had been pitched along lines similar to McCarthy's.[41] Jonkel had attempted further to exploit Catholic sentiments in a letter sent out over Butler's signature to the state's Roman Catholic clergy, promising to defend America against "atheistic Russia overseas" and from "Communists and their friends within our Government."[42] This strategy seems to have had some limited success. Tydings's margin in heavily Catholic and traditionally Democratic wards was sharply reduced from 1944,[43] although here again the sales tax and a variety of other issues may have also been involved.

Tydings himself believed that his defeat had been the result of a complex set of factors. He attached major importance to the demoralization of the Democratic organization and to the un-

---

[39] *Baltimore Sun*, Aug. 17, 1950. United Mine Workers President John L. Lewis, not untypically, endorsed Butler. Ibid., Nov. 9, 1950. There was some indecision among Tydings's supporters over whether to solicit labor support or use labor opposition as "a partial antidote for your anti-McCarthy record." James E. Ingram to Tydings, Aug. 22, 1950; Phillip W. Blake to Tydings, Oct. 26, 1950; Memorandum by "VK," Oct. 25, 1950, all in the Tydings Papers.

[40] By as much as 85 percent in the heavily Negro seventeenth ward where Tydings had won 51 percent of the vote in 1944. Kelley, *Professional Public Relations and Political Power*, pp. 140–41.

[41] *Baltimore Sun*, Sept. 1, 16, 17, 18, 1950.

[42] *Maryland Hearings*, exhibit 28, introduced at p. 149.

[43] Kelley, *Professional Public Relations and Political Power*, p. 140; Bean, *Influences in the 1954 Mid-Term Elections*, p. 28.

popularity of the sales tax, although he also admitted that the low ebb of the Korean War and the random charges of "whitewash" had their effect.[44]

But it was not the complexities of Maryland's Democratic factionalism, nor its patterns of voting behavior, which attracted nationwide attention following the election. It was McCarthy. Not John Marshall Butler, but McCarthy had defeated Tydings; or so the belief was. And this perception of reality was at the heart of McCarthy's increased strength within the Senate. There ran through the Democratic caucus, reported William S. White as the new Congress convened, "a general expression of fear that what had happened to Mr. Tydings, with all his standing in the Senate, could happen to any other man in the Senate." "For whom does the bell toll?" asked one senior Democrat. "It tolls for thee."[45]

SENATOR AT LARGE

McCarthy wasted little time in exploiting his new-found power and influence. As ranking Republican on the Senate Committee on Expenditures in the Executive Departments, he bumped Margaret Chase Smith from her position on the committee's investigating subcommittee and chose in her place freshman Republican Richard M. Nixon, a warm McCarthy supporter.[46]

McCarthy also badgered the Republican caucus to amend its rules in order to assure every freshman senator at least one major committee assignment, a move which would increase the influence of senators indebted to McCarthy for his support during the campaign. Although the proposal was rejected overwhelmingly,[47] McCarthy did secure for himself a position on the powerful Senate Appropriations Subcommittee, which had jurisdiction over the departments of State, Justice, and Commerce. Here, with Democrats

[44] Millard E. Tydings to William E. Boyle, Nov. 16, 1950, Tydings Papers; Tydings to Truman, March 27, 1952, PPF 445, Truman Papers; John Howe to Kenneth Birkhead, July 21, 1953, NCEC files; U.S. News & World Report 29 (Nov. 17, 1950): 33.

[45] New York Times, Jan. 7, 1951, sec. 4, p. 7.

[46] Ibid., Jan. 27, 1951, p. 9.

[47] Ibid., Jan. 4, 1951, p. 24; Jan. 8, 1951, p. 7; Jan. 12, 1951, p. 11. Ironically, Lyndon B. Johnson established a similar system in 1953 in order to give younger Democrats greater recognition in the Senate.

such as Pat McCarran and Kenneth McKellar and Republicans such as Styles Bridges and Kenneth Wherry, he was in a strategic position to launch new forays against the Executive Branch.[48] The Democrats quickly maneuvered to block McCarthy, however, and when the vacancy created by the death of Arthur Vandenberg was filled by a Democrat, they were able to bump McCarthy from the Appropriations Committee. After five years in the upper house, the junior senator from Wisconsin was once again without a single major committee assignment.[49]

But committee assignments in and of themselves were relatively unimportant to McCarthy at this point. One even suspects that the presence of such formidable inquisitors as McCarran and Bridges might have made the subcommittee uncomfortably crowded for him. In any case he had been on the outside far too long to worry over a committee seat. The power and influence which he enjoyed in the Senate was novel. It was not based upon an official position through which a senator such as McCarran, for example, might exercise life-and-death control over a piece of legislation. His influence derived instead almost entirely from his ability to dramatize and exploit the issues generated by Republican politics. Publicity and notoriety were both his means and his ends; he attracted notice by reducing everything, however unfairly, to the level of personal invective. He never for an instant denounced ideas, he denounced people! "It's a dirty, foul, unpleasant, smelly job," he would declare as he released the inner clutch on his inhibitions, "but it has to be done." It would be done, furthermore, "regardless of the high-pitched squealing of those left-wing bleeding hearts of the press and radio."[50]

Anyone in public office was fair game, and he denounced, debased, demeaned, and vilified without pause. He called the president a "son-of-a-bitch" and declared that the decision to dismiss MacArthur was "a Communist victory won with the aid of bourbon and benedictine." He called the secretary of state the "Red Dean of Fashion" and demanded, by turn, that Acheson

[48] Ibid., Jan. 31, 1951, p. 15.
[49] Ibid., May 22, 1951, p. 24. McCarthy regained his seat on the Appropriations Committee after the death of Kenneth Wherry. Ibid., Jan. 11, 1952, p. 22. Senator Hugh A. Butler to McCarthy, June 14, 20, 1951, both in box 120, Butler Papers.
[50] Quoted from a Lincoln Day speech, Feb. 1951, press release in the NCEC files.

resign, be fired, or be impeached. He even attacked British Prime Minister Clement Attlee, whom he accused of masterminding the dismissal of General MacArthur.[51]

For the most part, however, he only repeated and rehashed the old charges and accusations. He showed no great originality even in this. His speeches were loaded with almost every cliché and slogan developed by Republican orators since 1945. Time after time he denounced the "sellout of China," the "betrayal of Yalta," and the State Department's "crimson clique." Even his targets were the same, the State Department's Far Eastern Division and the Voice of America.

Only occasionally did he introduce a new angle to some warmed-over charge. Thus on August 9, 1951, he "named" twenty-six State Department officials whom he had accused of Communist leanings in his Senate speech of February 20, 1950. The address was carefully ballyhooed by a series of public letters to and from the Department of State, and by a press conference called to "announce" his speech in advance.[52] All those whom he named had been in State Department security channels well before the senator's speech at Wheeling; now, as the result of a presidential directive tightening security and loyalty criteria, each case was being restudied. Some of the suspects were no longer with the department, some had been cleared, and others were still under investigation.[53] Such distinctions meant little to the senator from Wisconsin. The twenty-six were targets of opportunity and fair game in his continuing hunt for headlines.

One of the most bizarre episodes in the campaign against the Truman administration was the attempt by McCarthy and his supporters to smear and discredit the United States Minister to Switzerland, John Carter Vincent. Like Owen Lattimore, Vincent had long been a target for Alfred Kohlberg and the "China lobby." He had played an important role in shaping American Far Eastern policy, first as counselor of the American Embassy in Chungking during the early 1940s, later as chief of the State Department's Division of Chinese Affairs, and then as director of Far Eastern

[51] *Time* 57 (April 23, 1951): 26; *New York Times,* March 15, 1951, p. 4; June 2, 1951, p. 9; June 17, 1951, p. 3; *Milwaukee Journal,* April 24, 1951.

[52] *New York Times,* July 26, 1951, p. 15; July 31, 1951, p. 1; Aug. 8, 1951, p. 8; Aug. 9, 1951, p. 16; Aug. 10, 1951, p. 7.

[53] See Memorandum for the President, n.d., in General Files, box 31, Alben W. Barkley Papers, University of Kentucky.

Affairs. In 1947 he was transferred from the Office of Far Eastern Affairs as a concession to Senator Styles Bridges and other Republican critics of the State Department.[54]

Vincent had been among the numbered cases lifted from the "Lee list" by McCarthy for his Senate speech on February 20, 1950, although the senator never returned to these first charges in his later attacks. Instead he accused Vincent of co-sponsoring the "Hiss-Acheson-Jessup-Lattimore-Vincent plan" to sell out Asia to the Communists. Vincent's objectives, declared McCarthy, were "identically the same as the publicly stated objectives of the Communist Party."[55]

While McCarthy attacked Vincent from the floor of the Senate, his supporters kept the beleaguered diplomat under almost continuous fire. As early as May 1950 Robert Morris, the minority counsel for the Tydings Committee, attempted to load Vincent's loyalty file by advising the Intelligence Office of the Third Naval District that he, Morris, had received information (he presented no source of evidence) that Vincent was a Communist. Subsequently, ex-Communist Louis Budenz testified before the McCarran Internal Security Subcommittee, whose counsel was Robert Morris, that in 1950 an unidentified naval intelligence officer had filed a report stating that Vincent was a Communist. When Senator McCarran wrote President Truman demanding that Vincent's file be turned over to the subcommittee, the White House caustically suggested that McCarran talk to his own subcommittee counsel.[56]

According to columnist Joseph Alsop, Morris was also involved

[54] Tang Tsou, *America's Failure in China* (Chicago, 1963), pp. 148–49, 221–22, 280–82. In this critical study of American policy in China, Professor Tsou concludes that Vincent was wrong in his analysis of Chinese affairs, but that his error resulted not from disloyalty but rather from the fact that his thinking embodied "the traditional policy of the United States." For Vincent's removal see H. Bradford Westerfield, *Foreign Policy and Party Politics: Pearl Harbor to Korea* (New Haven, Conn., 1955), pp. 259–60.

[55] No. 52 on the Lee list, No. 2 on McCarthy's list. The Lee investigators reported that a State Department security officer had been told by an unidentified informant that a special emissary for President Franklin D. Roosevelt had been told by an official of the OSS that No. 2 [Vincent] had been observed talking to a man who was later seen at the Soviet Embassy. This made the story, I believe, seventh-hand by the time it reached McCarthy. See *Tydings Committee Hearings*, pp. 178–79. Congressional Record, 81st Cong., 2d sess., Dec. 6, 1950, pp. 16177–78; 82d Cong., 1st sess., March 14, 1951, p. 2390.

[56] McCarran to Truman, Oct. 5, 1951; Matthew J. Connelly, Secretary to the President, to McCarran, Oct. 17, 1951, OF 1279, Truman Papers.

in a cloak-and-dagger plot to link Vincent to a well-known European Communist. The intrigue centered about Charles E. Davis,
an American traveling abroad. Davis had been active in Communist party affairs on the West Coast and was traveling in Europe
as the representative of *People's World,* a Communist paper published in California. He was also peddling information on his party
colleagues to anyone with the price. His buyers included American
intelligence agents in France, the United States consulate in
Switzerland, and Senator Joe McCarthy. Together with McCarthy's
European go-between, an attorney in Paris, Davis forged the name
of a Swiss Communist leader to a telegram addressed to John
Carter Vincent. The plot exploded, however, when Swiss authorities arrested Davis on charges of espionage. At his trial the Swiss
prosecution introduced a number of letters between McCarthy
and Davis and the records of several transatlantic telephone conversations. The Wisconsin senator simply wrote the case off as a
bad venture, and the State Department and American intelligence,
perhaps a little red-faced over their own support of an exposed
"papermill" informant, were only too happy to forget the incident.[57]

Although Vincent was repeatedly cleared by the State Department's Loyalty and Security Board, the attacks by McCarthy,
McCarran, and other right-wing politicians destroyed his career.
In 1951 Vincent was in line to become ambassador to Costa Rica,
but the administration, fearing a bitter Senate fight over confirmation, banished him instead to the American mission in Tangiers.
Following Louis Budenz's testimony that he knew from "official
reports" that Vincent was a Communist, the diplomat was examined
and once again "completely cleared." In December 1952 Vincent
was suspended upon the recommendation of the Loyalty Review
Board. Secretary of State John Foster Dulles subsequently cleared
Vincent of all loyalty and security charges, but demanded that
he resign "in the best interests of the U.S."[58]

McCarthy also made an abortive attempt to block the confirma-

[57] Carlisle H. Humelsine to William Benton, Oct. 16, 1951, box 4, Benton
Papers; Benton to Joseph Alsop, May 26, 1952, box 5, Benton Papers. "Report
of Preliminary Investigation of Senator William Benton's Charges against
Senator Joseph R. McCarthy Relating to Senate Resolution 187," Jan. 1952,
Case No. 10, Part 2, box 18, Hendrickson Papers.

[58] *New York Times,* Jan. 26, 1951, p. 4; March 4, 1951, p. 52; Feb. 20,
1952, p. 1; Jan. 4, 1953, p. 1; Feb. 1, 1953, p. 1; March 5, 1953, p. 1. John
Carter Vincent to William Benton, Feb. 25, 1954; Benton to John Howe,
March 9, 1954, both in box 5, Benton Papers.

tion of Anna M. Rosenberg as assistant secretary of defense. Mrs. Rosenberg was a well-known New York businesswoman with wide experience in the field of manpower utilization. She had been nominated by the president on the request of Secretary of Defense George C. Marshall for the express purpose of helping the Department of Defense meet the Korean emergency. Her background and credentials were impressive, and she had the strong support of a large number of influential business, political, and military leaders. On November 29, 1950, the Senate Armed Services Committee met briefly and recommended her confirmation unanimously.[59]

In the meantime, however, a vicious campaign against Mrs. Rosenberg's nomination had been launched by a group of professional anti-Semites. The leaders of the group were Benjamin H. Freedman, a retired New York businessman ("The Zionist pressure seems to kill off all my attempts to engage in business."), and Gerald L. K. Smith, the notorious leader of the "Christian Nationalist Crusade." These two men were in touch both with McCarthy's office and with J. B. Matthews and Fulton Lewis, Jr. The commentator had been charging Mrs. Rosenberg with Communist associations since early November.[60]

Freedman's "case" against Mrs. Rosenberg rested on a memorandum prepared for him by J. B. Matthews, and on the testimony of Ralph DeSola, a former Communist recently employed by Alfred Kohlberg as circulation manager of the *Freeman*.[61] It was arranged that DeSola would testify that he had seen Mrs. Rosenberg at a meeting of the John Reed club in the mid-1930s and that he had been told that she was a Communist.

[59] U. S., Congress, Senate, 81st Cong., 1st sess., Committee on Armed Services, *Nomination of Anna M. Rosenberg To Be Assistant Secretary of Defense* (Washington, D. C., 1951), pp. 1–23 (hereafter cited as *Rosenberg Hearings*). The most detailed account of the Rosenberg nomination appears in Arnold Forster and Benjamin R. Epstein, *The Troublemakers* (Garden City, N. Y., 1952), pp. 25–61.

[60] Forster and Epstein, *The Troublemakers*, p. 51; J. B. Matthews to C. Russell Turner, Nov. 27, 1950, photostat in NCEC files. The files of the House Committee on Un-American Activities indicated that an "Anna Rosenberg" had been a member of the John Reed club, as well as several other leftist groups. In 1950 the New York phone book listed forty-five "Anna Rosenbergs." *New York Times*, Dec. 20, 1950, p. 28.

[61] DeSola was a microfilm technician who had spent considerable time out of employment. Freedman apparently discussed the possibility of setting him up in business for himself. *Rosenberg Hearings*, p. 374.

Freedman arrived in Washington in early December and met over lunch with Gerald L. K. Smith and the "Reverend" Wesley Swift, another well-known anti-Semite. The group then set about buttonholing congressmen to support their campaign. The chronology of those first few days has been deliberately obscured by evasive testimony, but several facts stand out. Freedman told his story to Congressman Ed Gossett, a right-wing Texas Democrat who took him to see Senators Lyndon B. Johnson and Richard B. Russell, both on the Armed Services Committee. He also stopped by the office of Mississippi's John E. Rankin long enough to dictate a summary of what he had told Johnson and Russell. This "memorandum" was then taken by Swift to McCarthy's office and later to Colonel Mark H. Galusha, the staff director of the Senate Armed Services Committee. At the request of Smith, Freedman also stopped by Don Surine's office in the Senate Office Building, but not finding Surine there returned to New York that evening.[62]

McCarthy then moved into the picture himself, asking Republican floor leader Wherry to block a unanimous consent agreement which would have allowed the Rosenberg nomination to go through. That same afternoon, Senator Russell conferred with the ranking Democrats on the Armed Services Committee, and in hopes of heading off a McCarthy attack they hastily announced that the committee had determined to reconsider the nomination.[63]

That same evening McCarthy sent investigator Surine, along with reporter Edward K. Nellor from the office of Fulton Lewis, Jr., on a midnight visit to Freedman's home in New York. They carried with them a letter of introduction from Gerald L. K. Smith which began "Congratulations on the terrific job you are doing in helping to keep the Zionist Jew Anna M. Rosenberg from becoming the director of the Pentagon. This is to introduce two gentlemen who are helping in this fight."[64] Surine and Nellor conferred with Freedman, who then sent them to see DeSola. Arrangements were made for the ex-Communist to testify, and on December 8 Freedman was back again in Washington, this time with DeSola in tow. The two men checked in at McCarthy's office, left their luggage, and then headed for the hearing room.

[62] Ibid., pp. 145–201, 218–31, 372.
[63] Ibid., pp. 23–26; *New York Times*, Dec. 6, 1950, p. 28.
[64] *Rosenberg Hearings*, pp. 85, 179–85, 189, 307–23; Forster and Epstein, *The Troublemakers*, p. 56.

DeSola testified at length before the committee. The heart of his accusation was that he had met Anna Rosenberg at a meeting of the John Reed club in 1934. In a dramatic, face-to-face confrontation of the type so loved by committee investigators, he "identified" Mrs. Rosenberg as the woman he had seen at the meeting. That evening Fulton Lewis, Jr., was on the air declaring that it reminded him of another occasion "when Alger Hiss was confronted across the table with Whittaker Chambers."[65]

Unhappily for Lewis, McCarthy, and all concerned, the case began to collapse before it was even well established. The voluble DeSola supplied the committee with the names of several people whom he declared would verify his story. One by one they contradicted DeSola's testimony.[66] More importantly, the committee began to uncover all the various connections linking Freedman, Gerald L. K. Smith, Lewis, and McCarthy, and in almost no time at all everyone was ducking for cover. J. B. Matthews reluctantly appeared and denied statements attributed to him by Freedman. He did admit to preparing a memo on Anna Rosenberg, and he told the committee that former FBI man Theodore Kirkpatrick, the editor of *Counter-attack,* and William H. Harris, a researcher for the American Legion's Americanism division, would both corroborate his findings. But Kirkpatrick and Harris (whom Matthews had erroneously described as an "FBI agent") did just the opposite. They contradicted both Matthews and DeSola.[67]

The "case" had become a hot potato, and all concerned were trying frantically to cut their losses. Lewis went on the air to denounce Freedman as a "violent anti-semite." Edward Nellor expressed amazement and disgust over Freedman's fanaticism. Sources close to Matthews and Lewis, however, suggested that both men had been less than candid and were busily trying to cover their own tracks.[68]

[65] *Rosenberg Hearings,* pp. 37–93, 118–22; Anderson and May, *McCarthy,* p. 312.

[66] *Rosenberg Hearings,* pp. 93–113, 203–17, 271–84, 325–32; *New York Times,* Dec. 11, 1950, p. 18; Dec. 13, 1950, p. 25..

[67] *Rosenberg Hearings,* pp. 125–38, 286–90, 291–307.

[68] Ibid., pp. 314, 318, 376. "Report No. 27," Feb. 8, 1951, photostat in the NCEC files. The "report" is from one of Drew Pearson's informants within the Lewis-Matthews group, and included a photostat of a "hot" letter from Matthews to Russell Turner, another member of the Lewis staff. The

Mrs. Rosenberg was given the committee's unanimous endorsement and was promptly confirmed by the Senate. Among those expressing their unqualified support for her were General Dwight D. Eisenhower, former Secretary of State James F. Byrnes, former Secretary of War Robert P. Patterson, and Oveta Culp Hobby, later to become secretary of health, education, and welfare in the Eisenhower administration.[69]

The hearings themselves had been conducted with great skill by Senator Russell. The staff work by the Defense Department, by the committee, and by the individual senators was especially good. Democrat Estes Kefauver and Republicans Wayne Morse and Harry Cain were particularly effective in coaxing testimony from evasive and reluctant witnesses. Yet the very fact that the hearing was conducted, that fanatics like Freedman were accorded a hearing, was in itself symptomatic of the fear and confusion which permeated Washington during those first years of the mid-century.

And the senator from Wisconsin? Somehow this sort of thing never seemed to touch him, either personally or politically. He could easily shrug off the shabby intrigue involved in the Rosenberg case and hurry on to some new charge or accusation.

McCARTHY AND THE PRESS

Joe McCarthy nearly dominated the channels of mass communication during the early 1950s. Indeed, no senator in American history, even the most famous and powerful, has ever approached the sheer quantity of publicity and notice he was able to elicit. This notoriety was initially generated by his station ("Anything a senator says is news."), and by the continued excess and hyperbole of his charges. In time he became, with the aid of the right-wing reporters who surrounded his office, a master of senatorial press relations. He knew exactly when to time a release in order to catch the evening papers, how to "blanket" an unfavorable story,

anonymous informer declared that both the Matthews-Hearst group and Fulton Lewis, Jr., "covered up from the very start and engineered to have other people carry the ball and become the fall guys." Also see J. B. Matthews to C. Russell Turner, Nov. 27, 1950, photostat in the NCEC files. This letter is printed in *The Troublemakers*, pp. 52–53.

[69] *Rosenberg Hearings*, pp. 333–71.

and how to wring from each charge and accusation the maximum number of column inches.[70]

McCarthy was able to slip with casual ease from his guise of hail-fellow-well-met into his public role of crusader, and to "speak in headlines" for the benefit of the large band of reporters which inevitably pursued him through the Capitol's corridors. Yet even here there was a hollowness and ring of unreality, for his feelings and emotions never matched the rhetorical violence of the charges he hurled out, perhaps because there was no inner commitment to them. McCarthy never screamed, but the headlines did.

He turned to his own advantage the structure and functioning of the press itself. The "straight" news story, for example, played directly into his hands, for while it might not be a fact that Philip Jessup had "an unusual affinity for Communist causes," it *was* a fact that McCarthy had said so, and thus the story would be printed. Most reporters had neither the time nor the research facilities to evaluate properly the senator's many charges, and the wire service tradition of printing the most arresting facts at the head of a story distorted even the most intelligent presentations.

If the functioning of the press created publicity for McCarthy, so did the nature of his charges. Once leveled, an accusation did not wither and die, but tended to bounce back in the form of denials, qualifications, and countercharges, thus generating a chain reaction of publicity. This in turn would allow McCarthy opportunity for further comment, for a repetition of the charges, a well-chosen epithet, or some other new twist. If carefully managed, even the most unfounded charge could produce almost a week of notices. By 1951, moreover, the senator was becoming the beneficiary of "fallout" from the entire Communist issue. The charges he and others had made during the Tydings Hearings did not disappear when the committee brought in its report, but they continued to unfold through the capital's labyrinthine corridors of public and private power. Foreign service officers were returned from the field, or shifted to new positions; faceless panels of

[70] The most perceptive insights into McCarthy's use and abuse of the press have been offered by Douglass Cater, Elmer Davis, and Richard Rovere, but the subject needs detailed investigation. See Douglass Cater, "The Captive Press," *Reporter* 2 (June 6, 1950): 17–20; Cater, *The Fourth Branch of Government* (New York, 1965), pp. 68–74; Richard H. Rovere, *Senator Joe McCarthy* (New York, 1959), pp. 137–40, 162–67; Elmer Davis, *But We Were Born Free* (Indianapolis, Ind., 1952), pp. 147–77.

bureaucrats met to determine the loyalty of this or that employee; government officials were cleared, suspended, allowed to resign, and dismissed. John Stewart Service, for example, had been cleared several times by the State Department Loyalty Board and by the Tydings Committee. In 1951 he was recalled for yet another investigation by the Civil Service Commission's Loyalty Review Board. Service was also under attack by the McCarran Subcommittee investigating the Institute of Pacific Relations. In December 1951 the Loyalty Review Board recommended Service's dismissal. Service promptly appealed to the president to reverse the decision, but though some of the president's advisers described the board's action as a "miscarriage of justice," the administration was too timid to contest it.[71]

At each stage, McCarthy's role in the "case" was recapitulated. The senator was always available for a pungent comment, and even the most conscientious reader soon forgot that McCarthy was not the first (by far) to attack Service. At one point the senator even provided a running commentary on the case by reading to the Senate from the confidential minutes of the Civil Service Commission's Loyalty Review Board. When Service was finally cashiered it was a "triumph" and "vindication" of McCarthy.[72] This pattern was repeated time after time, only the names were different; and no matter what the final disposition of the case, the notoriety seemed only to increase McCarthy's stature and influence.

McCarthy discovered another, and equally rich, source of political notice in attacks upon the press itself. Many have argued that his aim was to intimidate the press, and perhaps this is true. More probably, these attacks were calculated—as were his attacks on high public officials—simply to drawn attention and publicity. At one time or another he accused of following the Communist party line all three major wire services, *Time, Life, Saturday Evening Post,* the *New York Times,* the, *New York Post,* the *Milwaukee Journal,* the *Washington Post,* the *St. Louis Post-Dispatch,* the *Denver Post,* the *Capital Times* (Madison), the *Sheboygan* (Wis.) *Press,* the *Syracuse Post-Standard,* and the

71 *New York Times,* May 2, 1951, p. 21; Dec. 14, 1951, p. 1; Dec. 23, 1951, sec. 4, p. 7; April 4, 1952, p. 10; Donald Hanson, Memorandum, Jan. 3, 1953, in Loyalty, Communism and Civil Rights, Spingarn Papers. In June 1957 Service was reinstated by order of the Supreme Court.
72 *New York Times,* Dec. 23, 1951, sec. 4, p. 7; Jan. 16, 1952, p. 19.

Christian Science Monitor. He made personal attacks on (among others) Drew Pearson, Elmer Davis, Marquis Childs, Edward R. Murrow, Herbert Block, Marvin Arrowsmith, Martin Agronsky, Richard Strout, and James A. Wechsler,[73]

If McCarthy's purpose was intimidation, then he fared badly, for the most prestigious sectors of the American press remained almost without exception strongly opposed to him. But if his object was publicity, then he enjoyed boundless success. By playing on the newsmen's traditional sensitivity to freedom of the press, he was able to provoke a storm of controversy.

Even McCarthy's strongest critics among the press may have given him unintended and unwilling aid. Some papers—the *New York Post,* the *Washington Post* and the *Capital Times* (Madison) come immediately to mind—expressed an almost obsessive hatred of McCarthy. They exposed his past and denounced his present, and above all gave him column after column of coverage. They suffered what one critic described as phobophilia: they were in love with their enemy.[74]

But the press did not create McCarthy or McCarthyism. It only reflected in exaggerated form the concerns and preoccupations of most Americans. If the battles and quasi-battles which the senator waged took place in the headlines, they usually originated on and eventually returned to the Senate floor. It was not in the editorial rooms of the great dailies, but in the Congress that McCarthy was vouchsafed his continued power and influence.

THE ILLUSION OF OMNIPOTENCE,
THE MYTH OF CONSPIRACY

At the heart of McCarthy's power was his mastery of the myths, stereotypes, and slogans created by the Republican attack on America's "failure" in China. United States policy in the Far

[73] "McCarthy: A Documented Record," *Progressive* 18 (April 1954): 59–62; Oliver Pilat and William V. Shannon, "How McCarthy Fights To Gag the Press," *New York Post,* Sept. 20, 1951; Anderson and May, *McCarthy,* pp. 271–86.

[74] Maurice Rosenblatt to Gifford Phillips, Aug. 31, 1953, NCEC files. By 1954 an edition of the *Washington Post* went to press with nearly ten stories and a half-dozen pictures and cartoons on the varied antics of the Wisconsin senator. *Washington Post,* March 13, 1954.

East has never been free from confusion and error, but the Republican critique began from fallacious assumptions and proceeded to erroneous conclusions. Refusing to recognize limits to American power abroad, Republican leaders concluded that American reversals in the Far East had been self-inflicted. From this conclusion it was but a short step to the charge of treason and betrayal within the government itself. The illusion of omnipotence fathered the myth of conspiracy.[75]

The China inquest continued throughout 1951, driven by the McCarran investigation of the Institute of Pacific Relations and by McCarthy's continuing philippics. Yet for all the controversy it stirred, the China debate was irrevocably tied to the past. What was needed was a new issue of dramatic and compelling urgency. The conduct of the Korean War was just such an issue, and when President Truman announced the dismissal of General Douglas A. MacArthur, the emotions and partisan drives which had fired the China debate flared hotly in support of the general. MacArthur offered the country a strategy for "victory" based upon the same illusion of omnipotence which had underlain the China debate. If betrayal and bungling had delivered China to the Communists, then the exercise of American power could easily reverse this course. In an age of simplification, MacArthur offered a seductively easy solution.

The China inquest and the MacArthur dismissal were the twin poles of the "great debate" over America's role in the Far East. They provided a political sanctuary for McCarthy's continuing assaults upon the administration, assaults which few senators on either side of the Chamber were willing to challange.

Perhaps the most celebrated of these broadsides was McCarthy's 60,000-word attack on General George Catlett Marshall. Marshall had been closely associated with American postwar policies in China, both as a special presidential envoy in 1946, and as secretary of state from 1947 to 1949. In the debate which followed MacArthur's dismissal, it was Marshall who argued most forcefully and persuasively for the concept of limited war. What Walter Lippman later described as the schism between "the generals of the Democratic Party and the generals of the Republican Party" existed long before the MacArthur hearings, however. As William

[75] See Norman A. Graebner, *The New Isolationism: A Study in American Foreign Policy since 1950* (New York, 1956), pp. 3–59.

S. White observed, McCarthy's attack on Marshall had long been foreshadowed.[76]

In September 1950 twenty Republican senators went on record against an amendment to the National Security Act which would enable Marshall, a career military officer, to become secretary of defense, and eleven voted against his confirmation. Missouri Congressman Dewey Short denounced Marshall as "a cat's paw and a pawn" for the Truman administration, while Republican floor leader Joseph Martin charged that Marshall was an "appeaser" who was responsible for the Communist victory in China. In the Senate, William E. Jenner called Marshall "a living lie" and a "front man for traitors." "Jenner made a complete ass of himself on the Marshall matter," wrote one newsman to Republican Senator Arthur Vandenberg. "Many Republicans were deeply disturbed and the Democrats played their righteous indignation up to the hilt. But on the more serious side the strong vote of Republican opposition to Marshall was not good."[77]

McCarthy himself had attacked Marshall on many occasions. As early as February 10, 1950, he had criticized Marshall for dismissing State Department security officer J. Anthony Panuch. In April 1950 he denounced him as "a pathetic thing . . . completely unfit" to hold high office, and in September he charged that Marshall was a man "whom Acheson could control" in his plans for a "sellout in Asia." In a speech on American foreign policy in December 1950, McCarthy urged that Marshall be retired to his farm in Leesburg, while MacArthur be given the discretionary authority for "speedy action of the roughest and toughest kind of which we are capable."[78] For McCarthy the crux of the "great debate" over military strategy in the Far East was "whether we approve the judgment of General MacArthur or whether we intend to follow the appeasement policies as enunciated . . . by General Marshall."[79]

McCarthy gave the Marshall speech a great deal of advertisement, promising reporters and fellow senators alike a documented

[76] *New York Times*, June 13, 1951, p. 12.

[77] Ibid., Sept. 16, 1950, p. 1; Sept. 21, 1950, p. 1; May 6, 1951, p. 1. John Steele to Arthur Vandenberg, Sept. 27, 1950, Vandenberg Papers.

[78] *Deseret News* (Salt Lake City), Feb. 11, 1950; *New York Times*, April 20, 1950, p. 3; *Baltimore Sun*, Sept. 16, 1950; *Congressional Record*, 81st Cong., 2d sess., Dec. 6, 1950, p. 16178.

[79] *Congressional Record*, 82d Cong., 1st sess., May 8, 1951, p. 5045.

picture of "a conspiracy so immense and an infamy so black as to dwarf any previous such venture in the history of man."[80] The galleries were filled as he began, but as he droned on in his flat, uninflected manner, the spectators gradually wilted and headed for the exits. He continued for nearly three hours, fumbling occasionally over an unfamiliar word or phrasing, and interrupting the speech at one point to snatch a glass of milk and a sandwich at his desk. Only a handful of senators were on the floor, and McCarthy, after wading through nearly a third of the promised 60,000 words, finally gave up and inserted the remainder of the speech into the *Congressional Record*.[81]

As Richard Rovere has noted, the Marshall speech was the product of the "Georgetown school" of revisionist historiography. Neither McCarthy nor his staff were capable of either the thought or the sustained research that went into the speech. It was written by men thoroughly conversant with the language and concepts of diplomatic and military strategy, and of scholarly disquisition. It is quite impossible, for example, to imagine McCarthy saying "I am reminded of a wise and axiomatic utterance in this connection by the great Swedish chancellor Oxenstiern, to his son departing on the tour of Europe. He said: 'Go forth my son and see with what folly the affairs of mankind are governed.' "[82]

Much of the speech was a reasoned, though meanly argued, critique of American military policy during World War II, relying heavily on Hanson Baldwin's *Great Mistakes of the War*.[83] Still other portions of the speech attacked United States Far Eastern policies (and Marshall's role in them) from Pearl Harbor to

[80] *Capital Times* (Madison), June 12, 1951; *New York Times,* June 13, 1951, p. 12.

[81] *Congressional Record,* 82d Cong., 1st sess., June 14, 1951, pp. 6556–6603; *Milwaukee Journal,* June 15, 1951; *Capital Times* (Madison), June 15, 1951; *New York Times,* June 15, 1951, p. 3.

[82] This example is cited both by Douglass Cater, "Is McCarthy Slipping," *Reporter* 5 (Sept. 18, 1951): 26, and by Rovere, *Senator Joe McCarthy,* p. 176.

[83] Baldwin, the distinguished military analyst for the *New York Times,* has strongly attacked the conspiratorial interpretations placed upon his works. This was not history, but politics, he declared, "a particularly reptilian form of politics which would have us believe that . . . our politicostrategic policies were part of a Great Conspiracy intended to hand the country over to Communism on a silver platter." "Churchill Was Right," *Atlantic* 194 (July 1954): 24.

Korea. At each point the author[s] would suggest, usually in the form of unanswered questions, that Marshall was driven by the foulest of motives.

". . . in whose interest did he exercise his genius?"

"Why . . . was Marshall so determined to follow Stalin and oppose Churchill?"

"Why did the War Department, meaning Marshall, leave us at the mercy of the Russians in Berlin?"

"Who constitutes the highest circles of this conspiracy?"

"What is the object of this conspiracy?"

There were some interpolations of pure McCarthy—attacks on "the left-wing bleeding-heart elements of the press" and their "high-pitched screaming and squealing," and on Marshall's "affinity for Chinese Reds." The speech concluded with the assurance that it had proved (as though saying so would make it so) the existence of "a conspiracy of infamy so black that, when it is finally exposed, its principals shall be forever deserving of the maledictions of all honest men."[84]

The real impact of the Marshall speech derived not from what was said, but rather from the fact that McCarthy had said it. It was never a widely read speech, and its extravagances were more widely broadcast by McCarthy's enemies (to prove his irresponsibility) than by his friends. Some Republicans were uneasy over the speech, and according to one reporter it played a role in blocking McCarthy's appointment to the Republican policy committee.[85]

For McCarthy it was just another sally against the administration, valuable for the sound and fury it occasioned, but no more. He had the speech published and distributed under the title of *America's Retreat from Victory*, but there is little else to suggest that he otherwise took it seriously. He was soon engaged in other battles, not the least of which was the fight to block the confirmation of Ambassador Philip C. Jessup as a delegate to the United Nations General Assembly.

The Jessup nomination had promised controversy from the very outset. Although the ambassador had been previously con-

[84] *Congressional Record*, 82d Cong., 1st sess., June 14, 1951, pp. 6556–6603.

[85] *New York Times*, July 1, 1951, sec. 4, p. 8; Cater, "Is McCarthy Slipping," p. 26.

firmed by the Senate on five occasions, three times as a delegate to the U.N. General Assembly, he had been since early 1950 under almost continuous attack by McCarthy and other right-wing Republicans. He had rather obvious political liabilities. He had edited the State Department's "White Paper" on United States relations with China, and he had testified as a character witness in the perjury trials of Alger Hiss. As Dean Acheson's chief diplomatic troubleshooter, he bore the brunt of much of the unreasoning and indiscriminate animus directed at the secretary of state. He had been a target of Republican attacks even before McCarthy's first charges. Styles Bridges had denounced him as an "appeaser," and Richard Nixon had called him "the architect of our Far-eastern policy."[86]

Jessup also had strong assets. He was a combat veteran of World War I and an honor graduate of Hamilton College and Yale Law School. He was a lecturer in international law at Columbia University, and he had wide diplomatic experience. During the 1920s he worked with such pillars of Republican respectability as former Secretary of State Elihu Root, Wisconsin Senator Irvine L. Lenroot, and Ambassador to Cuba Harry Guggenheim. He had been an isolationist and an America Firster during the late 1930s, but had later played an important role in the conferences which helped establish the United Nations. He was one of America's most effective spokesman in the United Nations and in 1948 had conducted the delicate negotiations for the lifting of the Berlin blockade. In 1949 he was appointed United States ambassador-at-large.[87]

Senator Tom Connally and a number of other senior Democrats had tried to dissuade Truman from nominating Jessup. "I do not care for Mr. Jessup," Connally bluntly informed one correspondent.[88] The president, however, was determined not to back away from the issue, and on September 3, 1951, he sent the Jessup nomination to the Senate, where it created the anticipated stir among Senate Republicans. McCarthy attacked the ambassador

---

[86] *Congressional Record*, 81st Cong., 2d sess., Jan. 24, 1950, p. 816; Jan. 26, 1950, p. 1003. Senator Mundt called Jessup Hiss's "friend and mental mentor." Ibid., Jan. 25, 1950, p. 909.

[87] *Tydings Committee Hearings*, pp. 227–29; *New York Times*, Oct. 14, 1951, sec. 4, p. 2; Bill Davidson, "The Surprising Mr. Jessup," *Colliers* 124 (July 30, 1949): 32, 67–70.

[88] Tom Connally to A. E. Amerman, Dec. 17, 1951, box 45, Connally Papers. *New York Times*, Sept. 18, 1951, p. 18; Oct. 18, 1951, p. 26.

in a radio address, and Senator Taft told reporters there had been "some discussion" of a Republican party position against confirmation. Pat McCarran added his opposition to Jessup, and Democratic leaders were soon conceding privately that they might not be able to secure the necessary majority for confirmation.[89]

The nomination was referred to a special five-man subcommittee of the Senate Foreign Relations Committee chaired by John J. Sparkman, a moderate Democrat from Alabama. McCarthy wasted no time in demanding to be heard. He arrived at the hearing room with a thick, red-bound file on Jessup and proceeded, in two days, to fill more than one hundred and fifty pages with testimony and exhibits. There was really nothing new in what he told the committee. The charges he made had been discussed, almost without exception, before the Tydings Committee in 1950. He claimed that Jessup had been associated with "six communist fronts" and that he had followed "the Communist line" in opposing aid to Great Britain during the Hitler-Stalin pact. In fact, only one of the organizations McCarthy named had been "cited" by the attorney general, and Jessup had not even belonged to that. As an isolationist, Jessup had indeed opposed aid to Britain, but he remained an isolationist, working with Republican Senators Hiram Johnson and Robert A. Taft, well after the German invasion of the Soviet Union. "You can put together a number of zeros and still not arrive at the figure one," declared Senator J. William Fulbright in evaluating McCarthy's testimony.[90] Had the subcommittee (or the Senate as a whole) been allowed to vote on McCarthy's charges alone, the ambassador would have been overwhelmingly confirmed.[91] But the Wisconsin senator's initial allegations were soon obscured by an acrimonious argument over Jessup's role in formulating American policy in China.

The new attack was launched by Harold E. Stassen, former governor of Minnesota and then president of the University of Pennsylvania, in testimony before the McCarran Subcommittee

[89] Ibid., Sept. 14, 1951, p. 4; Sept. 18, 1951, p. 18; Sept. 21, 1951, p. 1.

[90] U. S., Congress, Senate, 82d Cong., 1st sess., Committee on Foreign Relations, *Nomination of Philip Jessup To Be United States Representative to the Sixth General Assembly of the United Nations* (Washington, D. C., 1951), pp. 2–142 (hereafter cited as *Jessup Hearings*). *Tydings Committee Hearings*, pp. 226–27, 262–69; *New York Times*, Sept. 27, 1951, p. 11; Oct. 3, 1951, p. 1.

[91] *New York Times*, Oct. 18, 1951, p. 26.

investigating the Institute of Pacific Relations. Stassen made two major charges against Jessup: first, that Jessup had proposed ending all aid to Nationalist China in 1949, but had been blocked by congressional opposition; and second, that at a round-table discussion of Far Eastern experts in October 1949 Jessup had supported a group led by Owen Lattimore which favored recognition of Red China and a "soft" policy toward communism in Asia. A week later Stassen appeared before the Sparkman Subcommittee to "give the facts." His "facts," however, were rather meager. There had indeed been a proposal to stop aid to China in February 1949, but it had been made not by Jessup but by the senior American military adviser in China on the grounds that American supplies were likely to end up in Communist hands. The suggestion was rejected by congressional leaders at a White House conference at which Jessup was not even in attendance. As for the round-table conference on China, the 100,000-word transcript of the three days of meeting showed no statement by Jessup on the recognition question. The State Department position, as set forth by W. Walton Butterworth, was that the United States was asking all friendly nations to move slowly on the matter of recognition. About the only thing Stassen was left with was the vague and completely unsubstantiated charge that Jessup had been responsible for "a pattern of action" which undermined Chiang Kai-shek. As Chairman Sparkman bluntly suggested, Stassen had "put inference onto inference onto inference onto inference" and offered unproved assertions "to the fourth degree."[92]

---

[92] *Jessup Hearings*, pp. 685–872; *New York Times*, Oct. 2, 1951, p. 1; Oct. 4, 1951, p. 3; Oct. 9, 1951, p. 1; Oct. 12, 1951, p. 1; Oct. 18, 1951, p. 7. Stassen's motives were apparently political. He was a perennial presidential candidate whose very eagerness often proved his own undoing. His relationship with McCarthy remains mysterious. In 1948 McCarthy had worked hard to help Stassen win the Wisconsin Republican primary, and his first administrative assistant, a Republican professional named Victor Johnston, was originally a Stassen man. Dan Gainey, a Minnesota businessman who was Stassen's floor manager at the 1952 convention, was a heavy contributor to the Butler campaign in Maryland. Stassen was aligned with the conservative wing of the Republican party in Pennsylvania and had suffered setbacks at the hands of the liberal faction led by James H. Duff, a critic of McCarthy. The Communist issue was not new to Stassen (he had argued it at length in his contest with Dewey for the G.O.P. nomination in 1948), and in the wake of McCarthy's initial charges he had joined the growing Republican chorus, charging that the "blinded, blundering, bewildering" policies of the "spy-riddled" Truman administration were directly responsible for American casualties in Korea. He continued to support McCarthy until shortly after Robert

Yet such was the power of the China issue (and the Republican desire to pin upon the administration the charge that American losses in the Far East were brought about by a small group within the State Department) that this was enough. The subcommittee was soon embroiled in arguments over whether the United States had even considered recognizing Red China, whether the State Department had undermined Chiang Kai-shek, and whether Jessup was responsible, in Stassen's words, for a "pattern of action" which led to the fall of Nationalist China.

The subcommittee declined to approve the nomination by a vote of three to two. The reaction of the subcommittee was typical of the entire Senate. Sparkman and Fulbright voted for Jessup. From the outset there had been little doubt of their position, nor was anyone surprised when Owen Brewster, one of McCarthy's strongest supporters, voted against Jessup. The two men who held the balance of power on the committee were Guy Gillette, an Iowa Democrat, and H. Alexander Smith, a "liberal" Republican. Both affirmed their confidence in Jessup's loyalty, honor, and integrity. "He is one of the most honorable men I know," declared Smith, who was an old friend of the ambassador. But both voted against him. Gillette declared that Jessup had been the target of "unfair and unprincipled attacks," but because these attacks had destroyed public confidence in him, he should not be confirmed. Smith's statement was even more tortured, and it turned almost entirely on the China question. "He is a symbol of a group attitude toward Asia which seems to have proved completely unsound." He does not have "the confidence of our people." He is a "controversial figure" and his confirmation would "divide the country at a time when above all else we need unity."[93]

The Senate never voted on the Jessup nomination. The senators had little stomach for a vote which could be interpreted as supporting "McCarthyism" on the one hand, or as being "soft-on-communism" on the other. The nomination was held over until

---

A. Taft's victory in the Wisconsin presidential primary in 1952. He then "deplored" McCarthy's "wild-swinging recklessness." By 1953 Stassen was one of McCarthy's most prominent antagonists within the Eisenhower administration; and in 1956 he led an abortive movement to dump Richard Nixon from the Republican ticket on the grounds that the vice president was too closely identified with the Republican right.

[93] *New York Times*, Oct. 19, 1951, p. 1. H. Alexander Smith, COHC, pp. 189–92, 202, 256.

the Senate adjourned, allowing the president to give Jessup a recess appointment.[94] The result was a "triumph" for McCarthy. It was a victory won on the China issue, which the Republican party had adopted as its own; and it was a victory made possible only by the unwillingness of such moderates as Gillette and Smith to take a stand which might expose them to obloquy. Perhaps this was the real key to McCarthy's continued power—not the ranting of demagogues, but the fear and irresolution of honorable men.

[94] *New York Times,* Oct. 20, 1951, p. 1; Oct. 23, 1951, p. 1.

5

THE HISTORY OF AN INVESTIGATION

$\mathbb{D}$URING THE LATTER YEARS OF the Truman administration a few senators, never more than a handful, rose to challenge McCarthy. They tried to turn the slow, resistant wheels of political power, to trip the heavy balance which afforded McCarthy his privileged position, and even to drive him from the Senate. A few senators such as Herbert H. Lehman of New York and William Benton of Connecticut spoke out against McCarthy from the floor of the Senate itself.[1] Estes Kefauver of Tennessee sought to restrain McCarthy by tightening the rules governing senatorial conduct. Following McCarthy's August 9, 1951, speech "naming names" of those he charged were security risks, Kefauver introduced two resolutions—the first designed to protect the rights of citizens before congressional committees, the second to allow persons attacked on the floor of the Senate to file a reply for inclusion in the *Congressional Record*.[2] For the most part, however, McCarthy's opponents concentrated their efforts upon the Subcommittee on Privileges and Elections, an arm of the Senate Committee on Rules and Administration with jurisdiction over elections, credentials, and qualifications. In early 1951 this subcommittee was charged with the investigation of the Butler-Tydings election in Maryland. The subcommittee filed its report on the Maryland election on August 3, 1951. Less than a week afterwards, it received Senator William Benton's resolution calling for an investigation of McCarthy with a view toward his expulsion. The subcommittee struggled with the Benton Resolution throughout the remainder of the Eighty-second Congress, issuing its report on January 2, 1953, as that Congress expired.

Newsmen called it "the unhappy subcommittee," and indeed it was a pitifully weak weapon to wield against McCarthy. It was, however, all that was available, and for nearly two years it was the center of the only sustained attempt to challenge him.

PRELUDE: THE MARYLAND INVESTIGATION

In December 1950 Senator Millard E. Tydings filed oral and written complaints relating to the Maryland campaign with the Subcommittee on Privileges and Elections. Though he did not contest the election itself, he denounced the conduct of the campaign as "scandalous, scurrilous, libelous and unlawful," and urged the subcommittee to make a full investigation. Butler was allowed to take his seat "without prejudice" (thus reserving to the Senate as a whole the privilege of denying him his seat by a simple majority vote), and on February 3, 1951, the Subcommittee on Privileges and Elections voted unanimously to conduct public hearings on the election campaign.[3]

---

[1] *Congressional Record*, 82d Cong., 1st sess., Feb. 1, 1951, pp. 865–66; Feb. 12, 1951, pp. 1218–20. William Benton to Herbert H. Lehman, Feb. 17, 1951; McGeorge Bundy to Lehman, Sept. 24, 1951, both in Special File, Lehman Papers.

[2] *Congressional Record*, 82d Cong., 1st sess., Aug. 24, 1951, pp. 10602–10605. Kefauver to Herbert Monte Levy, April 14, 1951; Levy to Kefauver, April 30, June 12, 1951; Kefauver to Senators Blair Moody, Lester Hunt, Margaret Chase Smith, Robert Hendrickson *et al.*, Aug. 20, 1951; David S. Price to Kefauver, Aug. 29, 1951, all in Subject File, Congress 1, Kefauver Papers.

[3] *Maryland Report*, pp. 9–12; *New York Times*, Dec. 17, 1950, p. 48; Jan. 3, 1951, p. 1; Jan. 4, 1951, p. 24; *Congressional Record*, 82d Cong., 1st sess., *Daily Digest*, Feb. 5, 1951, p. D49.

The Democratic members of the subcommittee were Guy M. Gillette of Iowa, A. S. "Mike" Monroney of Oklahoma, and Thomas C. Hennings of Missouri. The Republicans were Margaret Chase Smith of Maine and Robert C. Hendrickson of New Jersey. Both Hennings and Monroney were newly elected, a fact which could not have escaped the shrewd chairman of the parent Rules Committee, Carl Hayden. Both had served in the House of Representatives, and both were skilled and effective senators in that quiet and undramatic manner so cherished by Senate traditionalists. Margaret Chase Smith was one of McCarthy's strongest critics within the Republican party. Her "Declaration of Conscience" of June 1, 1950, remained the strongest and most eloquent attack on the Wisconsin senator's tactics yet made from the Senate floor. Robert C. Hendrickson had also signed the "Declaration of Conscience," but he had blown hot and cold on McCarthy throughout the preceding Congress. He mirrored the ambivalence of most Republican "liberals" toward the Wisconsin senator. A good man of decent instincts, he never entirely mastered his fears.

The chairman of the subcommittee was Guy Gillette, a handsome, statuesque, and rather conservative midwestern Democrat. Gillette took no part in the investigation itself, but delegated it instead to a "hearings subcommittee" comprised of the other four members and chaired by Mike Monroney. While this may have been designed to provide the proper bipartisan balance to the investigation, it also allowed Gillette to remain at arm's length from the inevitable controversy.

The subcommittee began public hearings in February and continued throughout March and April, despite occasional criticism from McCarthy's supporters in the Senate.[4] The investigators concentrated on three major aspects of the campaign—its financing, its propaganda, and its "outside" help. The investigation revealed that Butler's campaign expenditures probably exceeded the limits set by the Federal Corrupt Practices Act. There were gross irregularities in the reporting of both contributions and expenditures. Some $27,000 was not even reported until after the hearings had begun.[5]

[4] New York Times, March 1, 1951, p. 14; March 7, 1951, p. 39.

[5] On June 4, 1951, Jon Jonkel pleaded guilty to violation of the Maryland election laws on six counts and was fined $5,000. Millard Tydings to Thomas Hennings, June 5, 1951, box 85, Thomas C. Hennings Papers, University of Missouri; New York Times, June 5, 1951, p. 24.

The subcommittee traced back to the offices of McCarthy and the *Washington Times-Herald* the campaign tabloid "From the Record." They exposed its manifest distortions and misrepresentations, including the famous "composite" picture which seemed to show Senator Tydings in intimate conversation with Communist party Chairman Earl Browder. The subcommittee explored in painstaking detail the influence of "outsiders" in the campaign. Most notable among these were Jon Jonkel, the Chicago public relations man hired to manage the campaign, Ruth McCormick Miller and the staff of the *Washington Times-Herald*, Fulton Lewis, Jr., and Joe McCarthy.

The subcommittee heard extensive testimony from almost everyone concerned—everyone, that is, but McCarthy himself. Monroney invited the Wisconsin senator to testify before the subcommittee, a right most senators would have demanded as a matter of personal privilege, but McCarthy artfully declined. The subcommittee, for reasons of its own, was reluctant to demand that he appear.[6]

The public hearings ended in April, but there was a long delay before the subcommittee finished its report. Neither Monroney nor Gillette showed great enthusiasm in pressing the investigation toward a conclusion, and in the meantime the Republican leadership placed McCarthy himself on the parent Rules Committee.[7] The significance of this maneuver was not lost on the more nervous members of the subcommittee. Gillette soon afterwards offered his resignation, complaining that the long delay in issuing a report "entailed a greater demand on my time than I felt justified in giving." Hendrickson threatened that he too would ask to be relieved of membership, or else he would write his own report. At an angry meeting of the full Rules Committee, Tom Hennings replied that the delay was because the subcommittee had been left without legal counsel. "I'm tired of fooling around with this committee without a counsel," he complained bitterly. "Senator Hendrickson and I are the only two lawyers on the committee, and we don't have time to go to the law libraries to do the research."[8]

[6] McCarthy to Mike Monroney, March 12, April 6, 1951, in *Maryland Report*, pp. 72–73; *New York Times*, March 13, 1951, p. 35.

[7] *New York Times*, June 23, 1951, p. 6. For criticism of Monroney's irresolution see Drew Pearson, *Washington Post*, July 15, 1951; Marquis Childs, *St. Louis Post-Dispatch*, July 19, 1951.

[8] Drew Pearson, *Washington Post*, July 5, 1951; *New York Times*, July 6, 1951; p. 8. For the role played by Hennings see Donald J. Kemper, *Decade*

The other members of the committee persuaded Gillette to withdraw his resignation, however, and the subcommittee began working in earnest on its report. Each of the four senators on the hearings subcommittee submitted an individual memorandum, and from these the final report was pieced together. There were many conferences and compromises, but the subcommittee finally agreed on a report sharply critical of McCarthy.[9]

There were in fact two campaigns in Maryland, they declared, a dignified "front street" campaign conducted by Butler, and a despicable "back street" campaign run by non-Maryland "outsiders." Foremost among these outsiders, the report made clear, were Senator McCarthy and his supporters. The subcommittee made no specific recommendations affecting either Butler or McCarthy. Instead, they urged the Rules Committee to formulate explicit standards for contesting the election of a senator (e.g., Butler) because of his campaign conduct, and for disciplining any senator (e.g., McCarthy) whose conduct and behavior rendered him unfit to hold the high office of United States senator.[10]

McCarthy's reaction to the report was predictable. He attacked Hendrickson and Smith, whom he charged had already gone on record "approving the Tydings whitewash" and denounced the members of the subcommittee as "puny politicians" who were willing to "ignore or whitewash Communist influences in our government." The report was accepted by the full committee on a 9-3 vote, with Smith and Hendrickson joining the Democrats against Wherry, Jenner, and McCarthy. Lodge, not untypically, was absent.[11]

The weakness of the Maryland report was its lack of specific recommendations. Its strength was its bipartisan unanimity. The

---

of Fear: Senator Hennings and Civil Liberties (Columbia, Mo., 1965), pp. 36–40.

[9] *Congressional Record*, 82d Cong., 1st sess., Aug. 20, 1951, pp. 10334, 10337; *New York Times*, Aug. 2, 1951, p. 24; Aug. 4, 1951, p. 1. "I just don't believe in that type of campaigning," declared Hendrickson to an irate McCarthy supporter. Robert Hendrickson to Mrs. Constantine Brown, Aug. 24, 1951, box 17, Hendrickson Papers.

[10] *Maryland Report*, pp. 6–9.

[11] Privately, Wherry told Senator Smith, "It was a whale of a report." *Congressional Record*, 82d Cong., 1st sess., Aug. 20, 1951, p. 10334; Marquis Childs, *Washington Post*, Aug. 22, 1951. McCarthy read his "Individual Views" into the *Record* on August 20. *Congressional Record*, 82d Cong., 1st sess., Aug. 20, 1951, pp. 10319–34; *Maryland Report*, pp. 41–74. Senator Jenner later circulated his own "views" in the form of a Senate document. *New York Times*, Nov. 1, 1951, p. 14.

two were not unrelated; given the political circumstances of the time, it was probably the strongest report which could have been achieved.

THE BENTON RESOLUTION

> *Somebody had to do this job.*
> *How were we to get it done?*
> Senator William Benton

On Friday, August 3, the Senate Rules Committee ordered the printing of the Maryland election report. That weekend Senator William Benton read the report and, fearing that it would be "filed and forgotten," decided on a dramatic follow-up. On Monday he returned to Washington and, after several brief conferences with Democratic Senator Lister Hill of Alabama and Secretary of the Senate Leslie Biffle, introduced into the Senate an unprecedented and unanticipated resolution calling upon the Rules Committee to conduct an investigation to determine "whether or not it should initiate action with a view toward the expulsion from the United States Senate of . . . Joseph R. McCarthy."[12]

Benton was a warm, ebullient, and sometimes impetuous man who had entered the Senate after a highly successful career in business and government. In 1929 he and Chester Bowles (later governor of Connecticut, ambassador to India, and under secretary of state) founded the New York advertising agency of Benton and Bowles. He served as vice president of the University of Chicago during the late 1930s and early 1940s, and in 1943 he became chairman of the board of *Encyclopaedia Britannica*. He served the Truman administration as assistant secretary of state from 1945 to 1947, and he was appointed to the Senate by Governor Chester Bowles in 1949 to fill the vacancy created by the resignation of Senator Raymond Baldwin of Connecticut. He was elected in 1950 to serve out the remaining two years of Baldwin's term.[13]

As a newcomer, Benton had little influence within the Senate itself. He was, in spite of his impressive credentials, an amateur in a body which respected professionalism and an "ad man" among

[12] *Congressional Record*, 82d Cong., 1st sess., Aug. 6, 1951, pp. 9498–9501. Bruce L. Felknor, assistant to William Benton, to author, July 10, 1967.
[13] *Biographical Directory of the American Congress, 1774–1961* (Washington, D. C., 1961), p. 546.

an assemblage of lawyers. He was a fervent defender of the State Department at a time it had few defenders on the Senate floor, and one suspects that not a few senators looked slightly askance at this former assistant secretary of state. He was a member of a small group of Senate liberals which strongly supported the Fair Deal and which chafed under the conservative leadership of the Senate "establishment." He supported New York Senator Herbert H. Lehman in his attempts to amend Senate Rule XXII to permit cloture, and he joined Senator Estes Kefauver of Tennessee in an attempt to establish firm rules for congressional investigations.[14] Both Lehman and Kefauver were "outsiders." They were men of exceptional ability, yet they were never accepted by the conservative inner leadership of the Senate. Neither was Benton, who was not intimidated by the traditions, precedents, or mystique which surrounded the Senate's operations. In early 1951, for example, he took the entire Republican Committee on Committees to task for appointing McCarthy to the Senate Appropriations Committee. This raised a storm of protest from the entire Republican leadership. The appointment had been made through the normal operation of seniority, they declared, and even Senator Edward J. Thye of Minnesota, a signer of the "Declaration of Conscience," defended the committee's action.[15]

Benton had long been one of McCarthy's sharpest critics. He had defended Ambassador Jessup, Anna M. Rosenberg, and Haldore Hanson from McCarthy's attacks, and he had denounced the senator himself as a "hit and run propagandist on the Kremlin model."[16]

By the criteria with which the Senate judged itself, the Benton resolution was probably impetuous and ill-conceived. "Most assuredly all the professional politicians opposed my attack on McCarthy," Benton soon afterwards declared. This itself was significant. The Senate preferred to pretend that McCarthy did

14 *Congressional Record,* 81st Cong., 2d sess., Aug. 24, 1950, p. 13264; 82d Cong., 1st sess., March 22, 1951, p. 2843; Aug. 24, 1951, pp. 10602–10605.

15 Ibid., 82d Cong., 1st sess., Feb. 1, 1951, pp. 865–68. During the colloquy Benton was called down twice for violating Senate rule XIX (which forbids the imputation of unworthy motives to a fellow senator), but was rescued in each instance by Majority Leader McFarland.

16 Ibid., 81st Cong., 2d sess., March 22, 1950, pp. 3763–69; March 27, 1950, pp. 4104, 4123–24; May 9, 1950, p. 6696; Aug. 14, 1950, pp. 12419–20. William Benton to John Howe, Feb. 21, 1955, box 4, Benton Papers.

not exist, and it took a nonconformist such as Benton to force the issue into the open. Politicians, like most other people, Benton later recalled, "too often underestimate the long-range values of boldness and stubbornness in defense of an ideal."[17]

Benton did not expect to win the necessary two-thirds majority needed for expulsion. He hoped instead to underscore the conclusions of the Maryland report, to focus attention directly on McCarthy himself, and "to encourage the voters of Wisconsin to expel him in 1952."[18]

The prospects for even preliminary action were not bright, however. To begin with, the resolution was as radical as it was unexpected. Since 1871 there had been but eight cases of expulsion or exclusion proceedings based on non-electoral conduct, and in no instance had the Senate actually expelled or excluded a member. Behind the Senate's traditional reluctance to discipline its members was the fear inspired by McCarthy himself. During the first week not one senator arose to support the Benton resolution, nor did any member defend the Connecticut senator against McCarthy's predictable countercharge that "Benton has established himself as a hero of every Communist and crook in and out of government."[19]

The resolution was referred to the Subcommittee on Privileges and Elections; Guy Gillette, who had been only too happy to unburden himself of the Maryland report, told reporters that he had no plans for hearings or any other action on the resolution. Several other members of the subcommittee expressed their private agreement.[20] The Democratic leadership, not forewarned of the resolution, had at least a dozen reasons for proceeding slowly. "These things require the most careful planning and strategy. An unsuccessful move can boomerang and help McCarthy; it is dynamite and might hurt many candidates."[21] Most observers agreed

[17] William Benton to John Howe, March 31, 1952, box 5, Benton Papers. Benton, "The Big Dilemma: Conscience or Votes," *New York Times Magazine,* April 26, 1959, p. 84.

[18] John Howe to William Benton, n.d. [c. March 21, 1952], box 4; Patrick S. Lucey to Benton, Aug. 7, 1951, box 1, both in Benton Papers; *New Republic* 125 (Sept. 17, 1951): 8.

[19] *Washington Post,* Aug. 7, 13, 1951.

[20] *New York Times,* Aug. 9, 1951, p. 16; *Washington Post,* Aug. 9, 1951.

[21] Quoted in John Howe to William Benton, n.d. [Aug. 1951], box 4, Benton Papers. Also see Douglass Cater, "Is McCarthy Slipping?" *Reporter* 5 (Sept. 18, 1951): 25; Kemper, *Decade of Fear,* pp. 41–42.

that the resolution would be shoved into a committee pigeonhole and forgotten.[22]

The Benton resolution was not buried, however, and a large part of the credit for this must be given to Joe McCarthy. It was one of his cardinal rules never to go onto the defensive, and his only answer to the Maryland report and Benton resolution was an indiscriminate series of counterattacks. On August 8, the same day the Rules Committee voted on the Maryland report, he called a press conference to announce that the following day he would "name names" on the Senate floor. An August 9 he read to the Senate the names of twenty-six past and present State Department officials whom he had previously accused of pro-Communist leanings.[23] When he had concluded, Senate Majority Leader Ernest W. McFarland of Arizona took the floor. The usually mild-mannered Democrat was flushed and angry. "It does not behoove the dignity of this Senate to smear any individual," he shouted. Such baseless and senseless attacks "tear at the very structure of government." In a very personal and immediate sense the majority leader had become converted to the anti-McCarthy cause.[24]

On August 14, five days later, President Truman made his strongest attack yet on McCarthyism, calling on the American people to rise up and put an end to character assassins and hate-mongers "who are trying to divide and confuse us and tear up the Bill of Rights." Although there is no evidence of cooperation between the White House and Benton's office, the administration's shift from Fabian to Napoleonic tactics undoubtedly strengthened the resolve of the Senate to tackle the McCarthy issue.[25]

On August 20, McCarthy made a long and largely irrelevant attack on the Maryland election report. He charged that both Senators Smith and Hendrickson were prejudiced, that they had already attacked "my exposure of Communists in the State Department," and that they should have disqualified themselves.

22 *New York Times,* Aug. 9, 1951, p. 16; Aug. 12, 1951, sec. 4, p. 2; *Washington Post,* Aug. 9, 1951; *Hartford Courant,* Aug. 8, 1951; *Newsweek* 38 (Aug. 20, 1951): 19.

23 See above, p. 133.

24 *New York Times,* Aug. 10, 1951, p. 7; *Washington Post,* Aug. 10, 1951; William White, *New York Times,* Sept. 9, 1951, sec. 4, p. 7.

25 *New York Times,* Aug. 15, 1951, p. 1; William S. White, ibid., Sept. 9, 1951, sec. 4, p. 7. Although not mentioned by name in the address, McCarthy demanded and received free broadcast time from the major networks in order to "reply" to Truman. Ibid., Aug. 23, 1951, p. 5.

Both Hendrickson and Smith were on their feet immediately. Hendrickson, as usual, was conciliatory, but Smith was angry and to the point. She reminded McCarthy that Minority Leader Kenneth Wherry had assigned her to the subcommittee and that he had praised the job she and Hendrickson had done. She would not be intimidated, she snapped, and defiantly placed the "Declaration of Conscience" once more into the *Congressional Record*.[26]

The reaction of McFarland, Smith, and Hendrickson to Mc-Carthy's attacks improved the outlook for the Benton resolution. Though McFarland was never one of the Senate's most powerful leaders, he was a respected member of the "inner club" and could exercise some influence. Smith and Hendrickson, the two minority members on the subcommittee to which the Benton resolution had been referred, were even more important. In such a delicate and controversial matter, their support was indispensable.

Benton's administrative assistant, John Howe, was soon conferring with McFarland's staff. The Democrats still seemed uncertain as to how to proceed. The general feeling was that the resolution for expulsion was too extreme. Some suggested that a resolution of censure would be preferable, and Benton quickly indicated his willingness to follow this course.[27]

By early September Benton had been tentatively promised a hearing before the subcommittee on his "bill of particulars" against McCarthy. If there remained any question, McCarthy quickly resolved it by his continued attacks on the subcommittee itself. On September 17 he released a letter to Chairman Gillette indicating that the subcommittee planned to hear Benton on Thursday, September 20, and demanding for himself the right of cross-examination. The subcommittee's staff denied that there was any certainty that Benton would be heard, and Gillette himself told reporters that the group planned to meet on Wednesday morning, September 19, "to decide when it wants to consider the Benton resolution, whether hearings will be held, and what procedure will be followed."[28]

[26] *Congressional Record*, 82d Cong., 1st sess., Aug. 20, 1951, pp. 10319–37.

[27] John Howe to William Benton, n.d. [Aug. 1951], box 4, Benton Papers; Thomas Hennings to Tom F. Baker, Aug. 31, 1951, box 73, Hennings Papers; *New Republic* 125 (Sept. 17, 1951): 8.

[28] McCarthy to Guy Gillette, Sept. 17, 1951, in U. S., Congress, Senate, 82d Cong., 2d sess., Committee on Rules and Administration, Subcommittee on Privileges and Elections, *Investigation of Senators Joseph R. McCarthy and*

Then on September 18 McCarthy released a letter to Senator Tom Hennings attacking and impugning his qualifications to sit on the Subcommittee on Privileges and Elections. It began like a personal note ("Dear Tom") though it had been given to the press hours before Hennings received it. McCarthy accused Hennings of bias on two accounts: first, because Hennings's law partner, John Raeburn Green, was now counsel for John Gates, the editor of the *Daily Worker,* in his appeal from a conviction under the Smith Act; and second, because Henning's law firm was counsel for the *St. Louis Post-Dispatch* which "has editorialized against my anti-Communist fight along the same lines followed by the *Daily Worker.*"[29]

Hennings replied to McCarthy's attack from the Senate floor on September 21, in a brief but eloquent address couched in the language and institutional values of the Senate. McCarthy's letter, he declared, was "an affront to the honor of the Senate and impugns the integrity of one of the Senate's committees." He spoke not as a citizen, he continued, but as "an elected representative of the people of Missouri" and he would be delinquent in his duty if he "ignored the ugly implications which so besmirch the reputation of this body." Green had undertaken the Gates appeal without fee, Hennings noted, because he believed that Communists could not be denied the basic rights guaranteed by the Constitution without endangering the rights of everyone. He pointed out that the *Journal* of the American Bar Association had hailed Green's action as "an example of advocacy at its purest and noblest." "These are the facts," Hennings concluded, "which confirm the integrity of the Senate Committee and the honor of the Senate."[30]

The attack on Hennings strengthened the determination of the subcommittee to grant Benton a hearing. There was no real hope of expulsion, but then this had never been the objective. The mere institution of such a proceeding was considered in itself a heavy blow to the accused member. It would give the Wisconsin

---

William Benton (Washington, D. C., 1952), p. 60 (hereafter cited as *Hennings Report*). *New York Times,* Sept. 18, 1951, p. 18; *Washington Post,* Sept. 18, 1951.

[29] *New York Times,* Sept. 19, 1951, p. 25; McCarthy to Thomas Hennings, Sept. 18, 1951, reprinted in *Congressional Record,* 82d Cong., 1st sess., Sept. 21, 1951, p. 11857; Kemper, *Decade of Fear,* pp. 43–46.

[30] *Congressional Record,* 82d Cong., 1st sess., Sept. 21, 1951, pp. 11855–57; *Washington Post,* Sept. 22, 1951.

senator's opponents a forum for attack and an opportunity to throw him onto the defensive.[31] The subcommittee voted unanimously to hear Benton and rejected McCarthy's demand to cross-examine. Simultaneously, Margaret Chase Smith addressed a letter to the chairman of the Rules Committee, Carl Hayden, asking for a vote of confidence from the full committee as to her qualifications to sit on the subcommittee. Like Hennings, she was placing McCarthy in a position of challenging the integrity of the Senate itself. The committee responded with a unanimous decision that Senator Smith was "well qualified."[32]

Benton testified before the subcommittee in open session on September 28, 1951. In some 25,000 words of prepared testimony he sought to establish that McCarthy's "pattern of conduct as a Senator" was unbecoming a member of the nation's highest legislative body. He presented ten specific "cases" to support his charge that the Wisconsin senator was guilty of corruption, dishonesty, and irresponsibility. He charged that McCarthy had perjured himself in telling the Tydings Committee he had used the number "57" rather than "205" in his speech at Wheeling, that he had misrepresented the source of the "81" cases he read to the Senate on February 20, 1950, that he had attempted to deceive the Senate as to who was responsible for public hearings before the Tydings Committee, that he had "deceitfully" claimed that he would repeat off the floor anything he said in the Senate, and that he had misled the Senate as to the nature of the phony "FBI Chart" which he had produced on the Senate floor in June 1950. Benton cited the tabloid "From the Record" and the McCarthy attack on George C. Marshall as examples of distortion and lies, and he singled out Don Surine's role in the Rosenberg hearings and Charles Davis's attempt to "frame" John Carter Vincent as incidents totally incompatible with the integrity of the United States Senate. He charged also that McCarthy had violated Senate

---

[31] William S. White, *New York Times*, Sept. 23, 1951, sec. 4, p. 9.

[32] Senator Smith to Carl Hayden, Sept. 24, 1951, copy in the NCEC files; John P. Moore and Israel Margolis, Memorandum [on the procedural background of the Benton resolution], Jan. 10, 1952, box 18, Hendrickson Papers; *New York Times*, Sept. 25, 1951, p. 1; Sept. 27, 1951, p. 28. McCarthy sent a proxy for Senator Smith while still demanding that she should withdraw, of her own volition. It was both a confession he was beaten and an attempt to obscure the issue. He sent another proxy favoring Hennings, a gratuitous action since the Missouri senator had not asked for a vote of confidence. *Washington Post*, Sept. 27, 1951.

ethics by accepting in payment for a pamphlet ten thousand dollars from the Lustron Corporation at a time the company was under intense congressional scrutiny.[33]

POLITICAL WARFARE

The release of the Maryland report and the introduction of the Benton resolution coincided with a momentary indecisiveness on the part of some Republican leaders over what to do about McCarthy. The G.O.P. Committee on Committees had still not found a place for McCarthy on any major Senate committee, and an attempt to put him on the Republican Policy Committee had been blocked by the powerful and conservative Eugene D. Millikin of Colorado. Even Minority Leader Kenneth S. Wherry, long a McCarthy ally, had praised Senators Smith and Hendrickson for doing "a whale of a job" on the Maryland election investigation.[34]

McCarthy harshly berated Wherry both publicly and privately. "While I realize that you were not attempting to criticize McCarthy in what you said this morning," he wrote the minority leader, "I could see it being repeated to the press by some of our left-wing friends and being reported that Wherry thought the McCarthy conduct was so bad that if the Senate made a sensible rule governing elections that was retroactive, there would be grounds for his dismissal." Nor did McCarthy appreciate Wherry's expression of gratitude to the subcommittee for its fine job. "I personally think they did the foulest conceivable political job," he declared. A week later, when Wherry tried to intervene on McCarthy's behalf during a meeting of the Rules Committee, the Wisconsin senator whirled on him angrily. "I don't need your protection and I don't want it. I can take care of myself."[35]

33 U. S., Congress, Senate, 82d Cong., 1st sess., Committee on Rules and Administration, Subcommittee on Privileges and Elections, *Investigation of Joseph R. McCarthy* (Washington, D. C., 1952), pp. 7–53 (hereafter cited as the *McCarthy Investigation*). *New York Times*, Sept. 29, 1951, p. 1. The impact of Benton's testimony was "blanketed" by McCarthy's sensational charges against Ambassador Jessup. McCarthy's two appearances before the Senate Foreign Relations Subcommittee on September 27 and October 2 (see above, p. 148) perfectly bracketed the September 28 Benton testimony.

34 Hugh A. Butler to McCarthy, June 14, 20, 1951, box 120, Butler Papers. Marquis Childs, *Washington Post*, Aug. 22, 1951.

35 Joe McCarthy to Wherry, Aug. 8, 1951, in the Wherry Papers. Robert S. Allen, *Capital Times* (Madison), Aug. 14, 1951.

In the end, party loyalty triumphed, and Wherry, following his temporary apostasy from the McCarthy cause, recovered in time to oppose the Maryland report in committee and on the floor. Following William Benton's appearance before the Subcommittee on Privileges and Elections, twenty-five Republican senators joined in a resolution condemning the use of "smear tactics" to silence political opposition. The resolution was ostensibly directed against the Truman administration, but because of the timing of its release it was also a convincing show of party support for Joe McCarthy.[36] With such support, McCarthy was able to battle the subcommittee to a standstill. McCarthy declined Chairman Gillette's repeated invitation to testify ("Frankly, Guy, I have not and do not intend to even read, much less answer, Benton's smear attack."). Although the subcommittee ordered its staff to conduct a preliminary investigation of each of Benton's charges, the resolution dropped from sight for nearly two months.[37] When it again became newsworthy, it was at McCarthy's instigation.

The Wisconsin senator was a consummate master of political guerrilla warfare. He had an unerring instinct for detecting the institutional weaknesses of Senate procedures—their slowness, their restraint, and their vulnerability to partisan exploitation. In late November he launched an attack designed to intimidate and discredit the Subcommittee on Privileges and Elections, even before it had begun its work.

He began with a series of public charges, accusing the subcommitttee of a "dishonest" attempt to prevent his reelection and warning them to remember what had happened to the Tydings Committee. On December 6 he released a letter to Gillette challenging the subcommittee's jurisdiction and accusing it of "stealing" from the taxpayers in order to "aid Benton in his smear attack upon McCarthy." He demanded to know the employment background and salaries of the subcommittee's staff and the "theory of law" under which the committee was proceeding. The members of the subcommittee, he charged in yet another letter, were "just as dishonest as though he or she picked the pockets of the taxpayers

36 *New York Times*, Aug. 9, 1951, p. 16; Oct. 1, 1951, p. 15. *Washington Post*, Aug. 22, 1951.

37 Guy Gillette to McCarthy, Sept. 25, Oct. 1, 1951; McCarthy to Gillette, Oct. 4, 1951, reprinted in *Hennings Report*, pp. 61–62; *New York Times*, Oct. 10, 1951, p. 6. In the meantime Benton asked that the inquiry be broadened to include McCarthy's presenatorial career. William Benton to Gillette, Oct. 5, 1951, in *Hennings Report*, p. 105.

and turned the loot over to the Democratic National Committee."[38]

Behind this barrage of charges McCarthy made a second move to subvert the investigation, this time through a former member of the committee's staff. On December 27 Daniel G. Buckley released a long statement to the press, charging that the investigation was all part of "an insidious campaign . . . to discredit and destroy any man who fights Communist subversion."[39] Buckley had served as assistant counsel to the subcommittee from October 15, 1951, until December 8, 1951, at which time his employment had been terminated as part of a normal reduction in staff following the conclusion of another investigation. He was not, as he later claimed, "summarily dismissed"; on the contrary, he remained on good terms with the committee staff. As late as December 22, 1951, he had lunched with the chief clerk and had talked with the chief counsel, who was trying to help him find another position. Telephone company records subsequently revealed that Buckley had been in close contact with McCarthy's assistant, Jean Kerr, and with radio commentator Fulton Lewis, Jr. The release was reportedly prepared in McCarthy's office, and its language and syntax contained more than a hint of the senator's touch. Buckley remained in contact with McCarthy's office for the next three weeks, and he was subsequently hired by the Republican National Committee.[40]

Despite McCarthy's attacks, the subcommittee continued to press its investigation. The entire membership of the subcommittee seemed to be taking an active role, and even Rules Committee Chairman Carl Hayden was reported to be "right on top" of the investigation.[41] The staff submitted a memorandum on the procedural background of the investigation on January 10, and on January 18 they brought in their long-delayed preliminary report. At the outset the investigators had eliminated those charges grow-

[38] McCarthy to Guy Gillette, Dec. 6, 7, 19, 1951, all reprinted in the *Hennings Report*, pp. 62–66; *New York Times*, Nov. 30, 1951, p. 14; Dec. 7, 1951, p. 17; Dec. 8, 1951, p. 2. William Benton to Thomas Hennings, Dec. 10, 1951, box 73, Hennings Papers.

[39] Press release, Dec. 27, 1951, reprinted in *Hennings Report*, p. 106; *New York Times*, Dec. 28, 1951, p. 8.

[40] *Hennings Report*, pp. 14, 108; John P. Moore, Confidential Memorandum to Senator Gillette, Jan. 11, 1952, photostats in box 18, Hendrickson Papers, and in NCEC files; Ralph Mann to William Benton, Jan. 3, 1952, box 4, Benton Papers.

[41] Ralph Mann to William Benton, Jan. 3, 1952, box 4, Benton Papers.

ing from McCarthy's attack upon General Marshall (case number three), both because it involved remarks made on the Senate floor and because they simply could not conclude a thorough investigation within the time limits set by the subcommittee. They confirmed Benton's charges in the two cases growing out of the Maryland investigation (case number five, case number ten-A), but they felt that additional hearings would serve no constructive purpose. They urged that hearings be held on five of Benton's "cases," although even here their conclusions were somewhat ambivalent. They conceded that what McCarthy actually said at Wheeling was "still shrouded in doubt" and that Benton had "overstated his case" in another instance. They came down most heavily on case number two, involving the Lustron Corporation. They pointed out that McCarthy had sold his overpriced brochure to a company almost exclusively financed by Reconstruction Finance Corporation (RFC) loans at a time when he was a member of two Senate committees charged with legislative oversight of RFC affairs.[42]

Before the subcommittee could act on its staff's recommendations, McCarthy launched the third phase of his attack. It began on January 10 as part of a general shift in Republican committee assignments following the death of Senator Wherry. McCarthy left the Rules Committee in order to return to the Appropriations Committee, on which he had briefly served during 1951. His place was taken by one of his most ardent supporters, Herman Welker. Everett M. Dirksen, another McCarthy ally, was also added to the committee. It was soon obvious what was afoot. With the support of Henry Cabot Lodge, the ranking minority member of the parent Rules Committee, the Republicans planned to replace Smith and Hendrickson, two anti-McCarthy Republicans on whom the investigation had depended heavily, with two strongly pro-McCarthy senators. Mrs. Smith announced that the change had been requested by Lodge, and that she would accede to the senior Republican's recommendation. Hendrickson balked, however, and decided to "stand pat."[43]

Benton and Gillette both protested the proposed shift. They

[42] "Report of Preliminary Investigation of Senator William Benton's Charges against Senator Joseph R. McCarthy Relating to Senate Resolution 187," Jan. 1952, in box 18, Hendrickson Papers.

[43] New York Times, Jan. 17, 1952, p. 17; Jan. 19, 1952, p. 6.

urged Smith and Hendrickson to remain on the subcommittee and
appealed to Hayden not to allow the Republicans to "change the
jury half way through the trial." At a meeting of the full Rules
Committee, Smith withdrew from the subcommittee and was
replaced by Welker. Hayden refused to interfere with what he
believed a Republican prerogative. "We deferred to the minority
and that's the way it is," declared the taciturn chairman. Hendrickson, under intense pressure from both sides, refused to be budged.
"I did not feel," he wrote his brother, "that I could run out in
the 'midst of a trial' so to speak, despite Joe McCarthy's wishes to
the contrary."[44]

The replacement of Smith with Welker was, in Mike Monroney's
words, "catastrophic." The prospects for a full investigation had
never been bright, and now they were even more uncertain. The
subcommittee met on January 28 to discuss the possibility and
scope of hearings, but the session was inconclusive and there were
strong indications that no action was likely to be forthcoming.
Welker extracted from Gillette the promise that nothing would be
done during February while the Idaho Republican was on an
extended speaking tour. Thus McCarthy and his allies appeared
to have succeeded in bringing the entire investigation to a halt.[45]

A VOTE OF CONFIDENCE

By late February 1952, the Benton resolution seemed hopelessly
stalled. "If there's one thing we've learned," complained Benton's
administrative assistant, "it's that there are a hundred ways of

[44] Ibid., Jan. 24, 1952, p. 13; Robert Hendrickson to Daniel J. P. Hendrickson, Jan. 25, 1952, box 21, Hendrickson Papers. Mrs. Smith claimed that she
wanted to take advantage of an opening on the Rules Subcommittee, another
arm of the Committee on Rules and Administration, which was nominally
charged with jurisdiction over Senate rules and procedures. It was what
Senator Hayden called a "pigeonhole committee." It had not met for more
than a year, and even when the controversial cloture resolution was referred
to the full committee, it was not sent to the Rules Subcommittee, but to a
"select" subcommittee appointed especially for that purpose. Margaret Chase
Smith to Carl Hayden, Jan. 22, 24, Feb. 19, 1952, all reprinted in *Congressional Record*, 82d Cong., 2d sess., March 18, 1952, pp. 2446–47; *New York
Times*, Jan. 24, 1952, p. 13; William Benton to John Howe, Jan. 6, 1955, box
4, Benton Papers.
[45] William S. White, *New York Times*, Jan. 27, 1952, sec. 4, p. 8; Jan. 29,
1952, p. 9; "Agenda for Meeting," Jan. 28, 1952, box 159, Hennings Papers;
McCarthy Investigation, p. 69; *Congressional Report* 1 (July 29, 1952);
William Benton to John Howe, July 22, 1953, box 4, Benton Papers.

delaying and sidetracking in the Senate for every way to push a cause." The subcommittee, he declared, was "leaderless, uncertain, and apparently regretful that the problem was dumped in its lap." Under Gillette's irresolute chairmanship, the prospect was for more delay and inaction.[46] At this point Senator Mike Monroney began a brilliant tactical maneuver designed to recover the initiative and to prod the subcommittee back to life. At a meeting in early March he proposed that the subcommittee go to the full Senate for a vote of confidence. Since McCarthy had repeatedly challenged both the jurisdiction and integrity of the subcommittee, Monroney suggested that McCarthy be asked to present to the Senate a motion that the Rules Committee be discharged from further consideration of the resolution. If he refused, as was expected, then the discharge motion would be presented by Chairman Hayden. In either case the Senate would be forced to choose between McCarthy and one of its own committees.

Monroney, like Hennings, had a fine appreciation of the traditions and mystique of the Senate, and he proposed to utilize these institutional loyalties against McCarthy. He believed that he could thus bring into the open against the Wisconsin senator the heretofore silent southerners and Senate conservatives, men who would never support a movement based on the merits of the Benton resolution or its political implications. The subcommittee approved the proposal, with only Welker dissenting, and passed it on to the full committee, which adopted it by an 8–3 vote.[47]

On March 21 McCarthy wrote Carl Hayden that although the subcommittee had spent "vast sums of money" in a "completely dishonest" investigation, it had nevertheless established a precedent and therefore should not be discharged from consideration of the motion. It was a remarkably nimble bit of maneuvering. McCarthy realized he was going to lose on the vote and was now trying to obscure the issue it involved.[48]

When it became obvious that McCarthy would not introduce the

[46] John Howe to William Benton, n.d. [c. March 21, 1952], box 4, Benton Papers.

[47] *New York Times*, March 6, 1952, p. 11; March 8, 1952, p. 1; Welker, Dirksen, and Jenner voted against the motion. Lodge was absent. William Benton to Mike Monroney, March 21, 1952; Benton to Thomas Hennings, March 21, 1952; John Howe to Benton, n.d. [c. March 21, 1952], all in box 4, Benton Papers.

[48] McCarthy to Carl Hayden, March 21, 1952, *Hennings Report*, pp. 67–68; *New York Times*, March 23, 1952, p. 32.

motion, Senator Hayden took the initiative himself and introduced Senate Resolution 300, the discharge motion.[49] The resolution was ordered to lie over, and debate opened on the motion on April 10. Once again McCarthy counterattacked. Before the debate began he introduced his own resolution, accusing Benton of harboring Communists while assistant secretary of state and calling for a sweeping investigation of the Connecticut senator's public and private affairs. The resolution was calculated to divert attention from the discharge debate and to throw Benton onto the defensive. It was perfectly timed to "blanket" coverage of the opening debate on the vote of confidence in the evening papers.[50]

Carl Hayden opened the discharge debate by calling up the resolution and urging the Senate to demonstrate its confidence in the jurisdiction and integrity of the Subcommittee on Privileges and Elections. He was followed by Gillette, mild and conciliatory as usual. Finally, Majority Leader McFarland made a strong and forthright statement. The issue was one between McCarthy and the subcommittee, he declared, and the Senate must choose.[51]

McCarthy countered that while he had "absolutely no con-fidence" in the subcommittee, he nevertheless intended to vote against discharging it from consideration of the resolution. He was supported by Styles Bridges, the newly elected minority leader, and by Everett M. Dirksen and Bourke B. Hickenlooper. The debate turned not on the vote, which was predetermined, but on the very meaning of the vote.[52]

The senior Democratic senators were followed by Monroney and Smith, who stated the subcommittee position in its strongest terms. The issue, declared Monroney, was whether the Senate had confidence in its subcommittee, or whether there was to be a con-tinuation of McCarthy's "performance." Senator Smith, still smart-ing from the rough handling she had received from the Republican leadership, made a blistering attack on McCarthy. "I say to the Members of the Senate that Senator McCarthy has made false accusations which he cannot and has not the courage to back up with proof." The issue, she repeated, was clear regardless of the

[49] *Congressional Record*, 82d Cong., 2d sess., April 8, 1952, pp. 3701–3708.

[50] Ibid., April 10, 1952, pp. 3833–3934; John Howe to William Benton, April 14, 1952, box 4, Benton Papers; *Milwaukee Journal*, April 10, 1952.

[51] *Congressional Record*, 82d Cong., 2d sess., April 10, 1952, pp. 3935–37.

[52] Ibid., pp. 3938–39, 3942–44, 3946–50.

"face-saving attempts" to confuse it. It was a vote on whether the Senate accepted or rejected McCarthy's charges.[53]

Nevertheless, McCarthy had succeeded in clouding the issue. The resolution was defeated, 0-60, thus upholding the subcommittee's position, but it was absolutely impossible to determine how many of the members were for, against, or neutral toward McCarthy's charges. And as the *New York Times* noted, "The feeling was that many Senators were just as well pleased that this vote was not a commitment one way or another."[54]

At the last moment of the debate, McCarthy made a gratuitous attack on Darrell St. Claire, the chief clerk of the full Rules Committee. He charged that St. Claire had helped to draft the Maryland report and the subcommittee's "preliminary report," that he had leaked the report to the "left-wing press," and that as a member of a State Department loyalty board he had "cast the deciding" vote in clearing one of McCarthy's accused "cases." Monroney hurried in from a corner of the Senate, red-faced and shouting, challenging McCarthy to prove his statement. Carl Hayden snapped that McCarthy's speech was "without any basis in fact whatsoever." But the grinning Wisconsin senator, having dragged yet another red herring through the debate, hurried off the Senate floor.[55]

If the discharge debate proved anything, it proved that McCarthy was an elusive and difficult target. It also showed that a majority of the Senate feared a direct confrontation with him, and it was on this fear that McCarthy's continued influence depended.

In spite of McCarthy's tactics, the "Monroney" resolution did strengthen the subcommittee's resolve. They voted to begin public hearings on Benton's charge that McCarthy had improperly accepted ten thousand dollars from the Lustron Corporation. Gillette told reporters that while there had been many delays, the subcommittee was now determined "to push the investigation through to a conclusion at the earliest possible time."[56]

In four days of detailed hearings, the subcommittee, led by Mike Monroney, confirmed the story of McCarthy's transactions

[53] Ibid., pp. 3938–39.
[54] Ibid., p. 3954; *New York Times*, April 11, 1952, p. 1; April 13, 1952, sec. 4, p. 2.
[55] *Congressional Record*, 82d Cong., 2d sess., April 10, 1952, pp. 3940–44.
[56] *New York Times*, May 8, 1952, p. 17.

with the Lustron Corporation. Lustron had been founded shortly after World War II to manufacture prefabricated homes and was almost totally subsidized by the Reconstruction Finance Corporation. Despite RFC loans totaling $37,500,000, the corporation went into bankruptcy in 1950. McCarthy had been a member of the Subcommittee on the Reconstruction Finance Corporation of the Senate Banking and Currency Committee, which was also constantly reviewing the controversial loan. In 1948 he proposed to the president of the corporation that the company publish a pamphlet on housing which had been prepared by the senator's staff. He asked ten thousand dollars for the brochure, and the company's president, Carl Strandlund, agreed.[57] Lustron then hired a professional writer who spent six weeks preparing the pamphlet for publication. Only a small number of copies were eventually distributed, however, and the remainder were sold for scrap paper when the firm went bankrupt.[58]

The conclusions seemed to be self-evident. Strandlund was playing for big money. The ten thousand for McCarthy doubtless seemed a pittance, especially if it would insure the good will of a strategically placed senator. For McCarthy it was an opportunity to capitalize, both politically and financially, on the work he had done on housing legislation during the Eightieth Congress. The conflict of interest involved was also obvious, but beyond this the investigation had revealed very little. The general outline of the Lustron "deal" had been public knowledge since J. William Fulbright's investigation of the Reconstruction Finance Corporation in 1950.[59] Limited by its own disinclination to face the "McCarthy issue" head on, all the subcommittee could do was to add detail to a somewhat threadbare story on the low state of congressional ethics. And there is little evidence to show that this seriously damaged Joe McCarthy.

McCarthy continued to refuse Gillette's repeated invitations to appear before the subcommittee. Instead, he accused both Benton and the members of the committee of using the hearings

[57] A well-known senator might have sold an article of a similar length to *Saturday Evening Post* for about one thousand dollars.

[58] *McCarthy Investigation*, pp. 108–20, 121–52.

[59] U. S., Congress, Senate, 81st Cong., 2d sess., Senate Committee on Banking and Currency, Subcommittee on the Reconstruction Finance Corporation, *Study of Reconstruction Finance Corporation, Lustron Corporation* (Washington, D. C., 1950), pp. 200–207.

as a sounding board for "smear attacks" and of carrying out the aims of the Communist party "insofar as McCarthy is concerned."[60] On May 8 he told reporters that he had offered to find the committee's "key witness" in the investigation, an offer he repeated in a letter to the subcommittee Democrats on May 11. The witness, he declared, was in an "institution for the criminally insane."[61] The individual in question was not at all a "key witness," nor for that matter was he in an "institution for the criminally insane." He had suffered a stroke the preceding year, however, and had been institutionalized. On May 7 the subcommittee counsel had asked investigator Jack Poorbaugh, who was assigned to the investigation of the 1950 Ohio senatorial election, to check on the witness's availability. Poorbaugh reported back that the witness had been institutionalized, and the subcommittee counsel decided, naturally enough, not to subpoena him. But Poorbaugh then apparently telephoned McCarthy, who in turn was able to make his spurious "offer" to the subcommittee.[62] Once again McCarthy had subverted the subcommittee through a member of its own staff.

A week later McCarthy made a second sally against the subcommittee, this time using a prospective witness as his catspaw. On May 15 Clark Wideman, a Columbus, Ohio, newspaperman, appeared in the Senate press gallery with a letter to Chairman Gillette accusing the subcommittee of bias and prejudice and declaring that he was "sickened and disillusioned" by the "innuendo and foul play" being used to discredit McCarthy. If Wideman ever had illusions, he must have lost them long before this. He had been in constant contact with McCarthy and his staff since arriving in Washington on May 11. The letter, which he distributed to the press, had been prepared in McCarthy's office, and Wideman backed all over himself later that day in repudiating it before an angry group of senators.[63]

The Lustron hearing exhausted the subcommittee's small supply of courage and energy, however; and as the uncomfortable Washington summer approached, the investigation languished once more. The next round would be McCarthy's.

[60] McCarthy to Guy Gillette, May 8, 1952; McCarthy to Gillette, Thomas Hennings, and Mike Monroney, May 11, 1952, *Hennings Report*, pp. 83–84.
[61] *New York Times*, May 9, 1952, p. 15; McCarthy to Guy Gillette, Thomas Hennings, and Mike Monroney, May 11, 1952, *Hennings Report*, pp. 83–84.
[62] *McCarthy Investigation*, pp. 72–73.
[63] Ibid., pp. 224–73; *New York Times*, May 16, 1952, p. 7.

THE PURSUERS AND THE PURSUED

Joe McCarthy believed almost obsessively that in politics the best defense is a good offense. He replied to charges only by countercharges, and Senator William Benton soon felt the full force of his attack. McCarthy's initial reaction to the Benton resolution was to call the Connecticut senator a "mental midget" who had made himself "the hero of every Communist and crook in and out of government."[64] In the early spring of 1952 he carried the attack further. Appearing on Edward R. Murrow's CBS television show, he accused Benton of hiding behind the shield of congressional immunity "to smear McCarthy." The taunt was probably calculated. In any case Benton quickly rose on the Senate floor to "waive any immunity which I may enjoy under the Constitution." After a brief exchange of letters confirming Benton's statement, McCarthy filed a two million dollar libel suit against him in Washington's federal court.[65]

McCarthy used the courts, like every other institution he touched, as an extension of the free-ranging political warfare he conducted in and about the Senate. At the time he filed the suit against Benton, he was already engaged as the plaintiff in a libel action against the *Syracuse Post-Standard* and as the defendant in a suit filed by Washington columnist Drew Pearson, no stranger to the courts himself. The intention of the suit was to place Benton on the defensive, and it succeeded splendidly. "McCarthy has very cleverly and skillfully tried to work this around so I am on trial with him as the prosecuting attorney," chafed Benton. The Connecticut senator was angered and frustrated by his inability to meet McCarthy's broad politico-legal challenge. "Who likes to be sued," he complained. "Who likes to be sued for $2,000,000?"[66]

[64] *New York Times*, Aug. 7, 1951, p. 6.

[65] *Congressional Record*, 82d Cong., 2d sess., March 18, 1952, pp. 2441–42; McCarthy to William Benton, March 18, 1952, box 5, Benton Papers; *New York Times*, March 19, 1953, p. 1; March 27, 1952, p. 1.

[66] William Benton to John Howe, April 2, 1952, box 4, Benton Papers. McCarthy had told reporters that he would be his own attorney. "I want to get people like Benton on the stand and make them either tell the truth or perjure themselves." *New York Times*, March 27, 1952, p. 1. McCarthy's case was handled by the celebrated Washington trial lawyer Edward Bennett Williams. Benton was represented by Theodore Kiendl, a well-known lawyer from the New York firm of John W. Davis, and by Gerhard P. Van Arkel, former general counsel for the National Labor Relations Board. Van Arkel worked chiefly on the political ramifications of the suit, while Kiendl handled the strictly legal aspects.

The litigation dragged on, with appropriate pyrotechnics on both sides, throughout the next two years. Finally, in March 1954, McCarthy suddenly dropped the suit before it came up on the federal district court's crowded docket.[67]

On April 10, 1952, McCarthy unleashed a second attack on Benton, this time by a resolution calling for a broad investigation of his service as assistant secretary of state and of his subsequent career as United States senator.[68] Like Benton's own resolution, the objective of the McCarthy resolution was political. What happened in Washington was seen by both sides as a problem pointing irresistibly and inevitably toward resolution in the general elections in Connecticut and Wisconsin. Once again Benton was forced to defend himself. To answer the charges in a face-to-face confrontation would be to give McCarthy the most dramatic setting possible. To leave them unanswered, however, would be an open invitation for the Connecticut G.O.P. to hammer at every one of the charges during the fall campaign, nor could the Rules Committee sidetrack the investigation without the inevitable screams of "whitewash."[69]

In July McCarthy appeared before the Subcommittee on Privileges and Elections to present his own "bill of particulars" on Benton. He wheeled into the hearings room a large cart stacked high with official-looking books and documents. He dramatically presented the subcommittee with "62 different exhibits" alleged to prove that Benton was a "clever propagandist" who for years had been "paralleling the Communist Party line down to the last period, the last comma." In reality, there were only twenty-four exhibits, hopefully numbered from one to sixty-one. Moreover, they didn't prove at all what McCarthy claimed. It was a typical McCarthy presentation of charges minus proof, a type of showmanship in which the Wisconsin senator excelled. He called Benton the "Chameleon from Connecticut" and accused him of packing the State Department with "a motley, Red-tinted crowd." "You have here today," declared Benton in a brief rebuttal, "an example of proof of my charge of perjury. You have had example after example of a pattern of fraud and deception. You have had the star witness."[70]

[67] New York Times, March 6, 1954, p. 1.
[68] Congressional Record, 82d Cong., 2d sess., April 10, 1952, pp. 3933–34.
[69] John Howe to William Benton, April 14, 21, 1952, box 4, Benton Papers.
[70] New York Times, July 4, 1952, p. 5; Newsweek 40 (July 14, 1952):

McCarthy followed his frontal assault on Benton with a back-room intrigue, once again involving a member of the subcommittee staff. During the summer of 1952 the subcommittee had hired, at the request of Senator Hendrickson, a Republican lawyer named Wellington H. Ware from Hendrickson's hometown of Woodbury, New Jersey. Ware had begun a study of Benton's tax records as a part of the preliminary investigation of McCarthy's charges. There was nothing unusual about this. What was unusual was that Ware was working hand in glove with McCarthy's chief investigator, Donald Surine, and had reportedly given Surine complete access to Benton's tax records. Benton was tipped off to the investigation by Luther H. Evans, the Librarian of Congress, and put his own counsel, Gerhard Van Arkel, to work exploring the situation. Van Arkel conferred with Monroney and with the subcommittee staff and reported back that "we must assume that McCarthy has access to your income tax records."[71]

Benton was furious. He protested to the subcommittee that, although he had nothing to conceal, he bitterly resented McCarthy's use of these records. The Wisconsin senator had shown such a talent for propaganda with no facts at all that there was no telling what mischief he might wreak with "facts" to give his charges an aura of authenticity. Only then was Ware reassigned to another investigation. Once again the McCarthy strategy had succeeded. "There couldn't be a better example anywhere to illustrate why experienced politcians don't get mixed up with fellows like McCarthy," concluded Benton ruefully. "Instead of pursuing McCarthy—I am the fellow who is being pursued."[72]

With Benton on the defensive, McCarthy made his final assault on the subcommittee, timed to coincide with his primary election contest in Wisconsin. On the evening before the primary, in-vestigator Jack Poorbaugh resigned from the subcommittee staff, charging that the subcommittee was conducting a biased investiga-

---

32. Benton's counsel, G. P. Van Arkel, made a point-by-point analysis of the McCarthy testimony. See draft of July 11, 1952, box 4, Benton Papers; also Van Arkel to William Benton, July 15, 1952, enclosed in Benton to Truman, July 18, 1952, OF 3371, Truman Papers.

71 Luther H. Evans to William Benton, Aug. 8, 1952; Gerhard Van Arkel to Benton, Aug. 11, 1952; John Howe to Benton, Aug. 12, 1952, all in box 4, Benton Papers.

72 William Benton to A. M. Gilbert, Aug. 14, 1952; John Howe to Benton, Aug. 22, 1952, box 4, Benton Papers; Paul J. Cotter to Thomas Hennings, Nov. 17, 1952, box 159, Hennings Papers.

tion and supplying information to newspapers for the "apparent political purpose of smearing Senator McCarthy." The timing of the resignation was hardly coincidental. Poorbaugh had helped McCarthy before, and on this occasion he had conferred with Fulton Lewis, Jr., and other McCarthy associates before the release of his resignation.[73] That same evening, McCarthy's staunch supporter, Herman Welker, also resigned from the subcommittee in a telegram given to the press in time to make the election morning editions in Wisconsin.[74] McCarthy, who scarcely needed this extra boost, was renominated by an overwhelming majority in the Wisconsin Republican primary.[75]

All this was too much for poor Guy Gillette. He had never wanted the McCarthy investigation from the beginning. He had tried to resign the previous spring, but had been prevailed upon to hang on. Then in early September he came under heavy pressure from Carl Hayden to stop pussyfooting and finish the investigation. McCarthy's renomination confirmed Gillette's worst fears, and the day after the primary he threw up his hands and resigned.[76]

With the abdication of Gillette, the last hopes for an investigation seemed to disappear. Chief counsel John P. Moore had already transferred from the subcommittee to the full Rules Committee. Hendrickson was in Europe on a congressional junket. Monroney was buried with work as chairman of the Speaker's Bureau of the Democratic National Committee, and Hennings was busy working on one of his own pet projects for a Missouri Valley Authority. Once again the journalistic insiders reported that the investigation was finished, and that the question would expire with the Eighty-second Congress on January 3, 1953.[77]

HALF A LOAF: THE HENNINGS REPORT

In spite of such predictions, the Gillette resignation did not signal the end of the inquiry. The subcommittee was reconstituted under

[73] Jack Poorbaugh to Guy Gillette, Sept. 8, 1952, *Hennings Report*, pp. 93, 14–15. In contrast to the tone of his resignation, note his request for a leave of absence on Sept. 6, 1952, ibid., p. 109.

[74] "Senator Raps Democratic Politics, Quits . . . Probe," page one headline in *Wisconsin State Journal* (Madison), Sept. 9, 1952; "Smear of McCarthy Boomerangs," page one headline in *Chicago Daily Tribune*, Sept. 9, 1952; Herman Welker to Carl Hayden, Sept. 9, 1952, *Hennings Report*, p. 94.

[75] *Wisconsin State Journal* (Madison), Sept. 10, 1952.

[76] Guy Gillette to Carl Hayden, Sept. 10, 1952, *Hennings Report*, p. 95.

[77] *New York Times*, Nov. 19, 1952, p. 22; Sept. 27, 1952, p. 23.

the chairmanship of Tom Hennings, and the investigation was placed in the hands of a new counsel, Paul J. Cotter, and a staff of experienced investigators.[78] Still there was no certainty as to how far or how fast the subcommittee intended to pursue the elusive Wisconsin senator. McCarthy was reelected to the Senate in November 1952, and many observers believed that this foreclosed any further action, at least as far as the Eighty-second Congress was concerned. Several of the subcommittee members apparently shared this view. Mike Monroney, who had been one of McCarthy's strongest adversaries on the committee, left for Europe following the election campaign, and he was loath to interrupt his vacation for anything as unpalatable as the on-again, off-again investigation of Joe McCarthy. "Tom was distressed that you've left the country, feeling that he needs you very badly on this major problem and assignment," wrote Benton reproachfully[79]

Hendrickson too remained a question mark. Benton urged him to press on with the inquiry, but the New Jersey senator's reply was not reassuring. "As you well know, there is little I can promise from our present committee because we are, in the fullest sense, a 'lame duck' corporation."[80] Even Hennings's position was unclear. "How aggressively he will proceed I don't know," confided Benton to Monroney. "I'm much concerned."[81]

In spite of the reluctance of individual senators, the subcommittee did proceed through the final stages of the investigation. On November 7, Senator Hennings instructed staff counsel Cotter to write both McCarthy and Benton, inviting them to appear before the subcommittee during the week beginning November 17. Benton accepted immediately, but Ray Kiermas, McCarthy's

78 *Hennings Report*, p. 11; Memorandum, Paul J. Cotter to Thomas Hennings, Nov. 17, 1952, box 159, Hennings Papers.

79 William Benton to Mike Monroney, Nov. 11, 1952, box 5, Benton Papers. Monroney himself was soon under attack from McCarthy, who had come into possession of a letter showing that the Oklahoma senator had received a $500 campaign contribution from Henry W. ("The Dutchman") Grunewald, then under indictment for contempt of Congress. McCarthy made the letter public in an attack on Monroney on January 7, 1953. *New York Times*, Jan. 7, 1953, p. 3; *Washington Post*, Jan. 7, 1953. McCarthy probably received the letter from Grunewald himself, who had close contacts with Senator Owen Brewster of Maine and Senator Styles Bridges of New Hampshire.

80 William Benton to Robert Hendrickson, Nov. 7, 1952; Hendrickson to Benton, Nov. 14, 1952, box 4, Benton Papers.

81 William Benton to Mike Monroney, Nov. 11, 1952, box 5, Benton Papers.

administrative assistant, replied after talking with McCarthy by telephone that it "appears that he will not be available during the time you mention."[82] Carl Hayden solved the problem of Monroney's absence by placing himself on the subcommittee. According to one member of the subcommittee's staff, the Arizonan became "the real force on the Committee."[83] Robert Hendrickson, despite intense pressure from Senator McCarthy and his supporters, remained on the subcommittee and thus insured its bipartisanship.

William Benton testified before a closed session of the subcommittee on November 24. ("Thank goodness Mr. Benton is now out of our hair for awhile," wrote a relieved Hendrickson.)[84] But McCarthy still refused to appear. Instead, he again accused the subcommittee of dishonest and improper proceedings. "I thought perhaps the election might have taught you that your boss and mine—the American people—do not approve of treason and incompetence and feel that it must be exposed."[85]

Hennings and Hayden briefly discussed the possibility of issuing a subpoena for McCarthy. There was no doubt that the subcommittee had the authority to issue such a subpoena, but there was a real fear that McCarthy would not respond to it and that the subcommittee would be powerless to enforce it. All three members of the subcommittee were, moreover, reluctant to issue a subpoena for a fellow senator, especially if that senator happened to be

[82] Paul J. Cotter to William Benton, Nov. 7, 1952; Cotter to McCarthy, Nov. 7, 1952; Ray Kiermas to Cotter, Nov. 10, 1952; all reprinted in *Hennings Report*, pp. 96–97.

[83] Paul J. Cotter to author, Dec. 20, 1967. Benton had urged that Hayden take Monroney's place on the subcommittee. Bruce L. Felknor to author, July 10, 1967. For the procedural problems raised by Monroney's absence see Memorandum, Grace E. Johnson to Hennings, box 159, Hennings Papers.

[84] Robert Hendrickson to Daniel J. R. Hendrickson, Dec. 3, 1952, box 21, Hendrickson Papers.

[85] McCarthy to Thomas Hennings, Dec. 1, 1952, *Hennings Report*, pp. 102–104. A long letter was delivered to McCarthy's office on Nov. 21, 1952, requesting his appearance before the subcommittee. A telegram of the same date was sent to Appleton, where the senator was vacationing. Hennings to McCarthy, Nov. 21, 1952, ibid., pp. 98–99. The correct text of the telegram from Hennings to McCarthy is reprinted in U. S., Congress, Senate, 83d Cong., 2d sess., *Report of the Select Committee To Study Censure Charges* (Washington, D. C., 1954), p. 15 (hereafter cited as *Watkins Report*). The more strongly worded telegram which appears in the appendix of the *Hennings Report* (p. 98) was never sent, and its inclusion in the record was possibly due to a clerical error.

Joe McCarthy. Instead, they turned to the preparation of the subcommittee's final report.[86]

The most important challenge facing the subcommittee was the absolute necessity of a bipartisan report. Both Hayden and Hennings were convinced that without Hendrickson's signature the report would be valueless, and Hendrickson himself was under great pressure from McCarthy. What influence Hendrickson exerted remains controversial. Benton believed that Hendrickson watered down the report and demanded that it include a section criticizing Benton as the price for his signature. Hendrickson denied this, declaring that he had not seen the report until it was in galley proofs and that he had made no alterations. He told Benton, somewhat ambiguously, "I only did for McCarthy what I would do for any other American citizen."[87]

Hennings and Hayden met with Hendrickson on December 22 and 23. Although one senator, probably Hendrickson, was reported to have been "very unhappy about some of the language" used in the report, the three reached virtual agreement on the terms of the final draft.[88] After an additional delay, the subcommittee issued its final report on the afternoon of January 2, 1953, the last day of the expiring Eighty-second Congress.[89]

In politics the imperatives of what should be are often compromised by the realities of what can be. No document better reflects this truism than the final report of the Subcommittee on Privileges and Elections. The political gales which had battered the subcommittee from its very beginning had not yet abated, and the political circumstances amid which the final report was

[86] James P. Radigan, Memorandum (on the authority of Senate committees to subpoena senators), Oct. 30, 1952, box 159, Hennings Papers; William Benton to Mike Monroney, Nov. 11, 1952, and Mary K. Garner (Benton's secretary) to Thomas Hennings, Sept. 13, 1954; Garner to Guy Gillette, Sept. 14, 1954; Garner to Monroney, Sept. 14, 1954; Benton to Robert Hendrickson, Sept. 15, 1954, all in box 5, Benton Papers.

[87] William Benton to Arthur Krock, Dec. 29, 1954, box 4; Benton to Mike Monroney, Nov. 11, 1952, box 5; Benton to Theodore Kiendl, Jan. 24, 1953, box 5; Hendrickson is quoted in Benton to John Howe, Sept. 17, 1954, box 5; all in the Benton Papers. For Hendrickson's disclaimers, see press release, Jan. 6, 1953, box 83, Hendrickson Papers.

[88] Press release, Jan. 6, 1953, box 83, Hendrickson Papers; New York Times, Dec. 25, 1952, p. 21.

[89] New York Times, Jan. 3, 1953, p. 5; Washington Post, Jan. 3, 1953; Willard Shelton, "The Shame of the Senate," Progressive 17 (Feb. 1953): 7–10; press release, Jan. 6, 1953, box 83, Hendrickson Papers.

drafted could hardly have been less favorable. McCarthy had been reelected, together with a Republican president and a Republican Congress, and on every side there were signs of his heightened prestige and power.[90] These circumstances created the natural limits beyond which the subcommittee would not proceed.

The subcommittee was especially reluctant to face the issues of "McCarthyism" or "communism in government" directly. In part this was because of an unwillingness to proceed against any senator on the basis of what he had said on the floor. More importantly, it was an admission that McCarthy had succeeded in entrenching himself behind a nearly impregnable political barricade. As the subcommittee itself admitted, some of the charges raised by Senator Benton "contained matters so controversial in nature that it would not be feasible for this subcommittee, or perhaps any other agency, regardless of its resources, to resolve."[91] Instead, the subcommittee preferred to continue along the oblique line laid out by Senator Monroney the previous spring. Monroney had argued that the only way to destroy McCarthy was through his spotty financial background. "Mike insisted," Benton later recalled, "that on every other count he was too clever, too smart, too dexterous—that he could evade us."[92]

The substantive part of the Hennings report dealt almost exclusively with McCarthy's finances. It posed once again the six questions Hennings had directed to McCarthy in his letter of November 21, 1952: Was it proper for McCarthy to receive ten thousand dollars from the Lustron Corporation? Were contributions sent to McCarthy for his "anti-Communist fight" diverted to other uses? (An examination of McCarthy's bank account had suggested that some such monies had been used to play the stock market, to buy flowers, to pay hotel bills, and for other miscellaneous expenses apparently unrelated to the task of "digging the Communists out of the federal government.") Did McCarthy use friends and relatives to conceal receipts, income, and stock speculation or other financial transactions? Did he use his influence on behalf of certain special interest groups? Did his financial tangles involve violation of federal and state tax and banking laws? Had he

90 *New York Times*, Nov. 21, 1952, p. 14; William S. White, ibid., Dec. 29, 1952, sec. 4, p. 5.
91 *Hennings Report*, p. 14.
92 William Benton to John Howe, Nov. 23, 1954, box 4, Benton Papers.

violated federal and state Corrupt Practice acts in his 1944 and 1946 senatorial campaigns?[93]

The report implied, without stating outright, that the answer to each of these questions was yes, and a long appendix of some 150-odd exhibits invited the reader to reach a similar conclusion.

The most damning part of the report was not the exposé of McCarthy's checkered finances, however, but the bare history of the investigation itself. The first fifteen pages of the report, nearly a third of the entire document, were devoted to a painstakingly detailed recital of the subcommittee's wavering attempts to conduct an investigation and of McCarthy's contemptuous response. This entire preamble was articulated in terms of the peculiar values and institutional loyalties of the Senate. The emphasis fell not upon McCarthy's real or alleged outrages against the American people, but those against the United States Senate. His behavior, the report declared, reflected "a disdain and contempt for the rules and wishes of the entire Senate body, as well as the membership of the Subcommittee on Privileges and Elections." The record of what had taken place, it continued, "leaves the inescapable conclusion that Senator McCarthy deliberately set out to thwart any investigation of him by obscuring the real issue and the responsibility of the Subcommittee by charges of lack of jurisdiction, smear, and communist-inspired persecution."[94]

The report concluded without recommendations. The subcommittee preferred to finesse the question and pass it on to the Senate itself. "The issue raised is one for the entire Senate," they declared. "[It] transcends partisan politics and goes to the very core of the Senate body's authority, integrity and the respect in which it is held by the people of this country."[95]

McCarthy replied that the report marked a "new low in dishonesty and smear." Hayden and Hennings were "left-wingers" and "lackeys" for the Truman administration; Hendrickson was "a living miracle in that he is without question the only man in the world who has lived so long with neither brains nor guts."[96] Liberals too were angry over the subcommittee's failure to make

[93] *Hennings Report,* pp. 15–45.
[94] Ibid., pp. 10–11.
[95] Ibid., p. 45.
[96] *New York Times,* Jan. 3, 1953, p. 5; *Watkins Report,* p. 17.

concrete recommendations. One critic called it "a pallid report which fizzled and sputtered like a wet firecracker."[97]

Behind the scenes in Washington, however, Senator Carl Hayden was attempting to organize a real challenge to the Wisconsin senator. Hayden planned to take the floor on the very first day of the new session to demand that McCarthy, when he presented himself to be sworn in, be asked to "stand aside" or else be administered the oath "without prejudice" to future Senate action.[98]

Hayden had worked on this procedure for several days, making long-distance calls to senators all across the country. The strategem might work, he had decided, even if it was brought to a vote. The Republicans held the Senate by only one precarious vote, and the presence of Wayne Morse, now an independent, nullified even this. Alben Barkley would remain in the chair, moreover, until January 20, when Richard Nixon was to be inaugurated as the new vice president.

Then on January 2 McCarthy (through Republican Majority Leader Taft according to one account) warned the Democratic Policy Committee that if they challenged him, the Republicans would ask that Dennis Chavez, a veteran Democrat from New Mexico who had narrowly defeated his Republican opponent amidst charges of fraud and irregularity, be asked to "stand aside" pending an investigation of the New Mexico election. The threat was enough to rattle the Democratic caucus. More importantly, a quick canvass of the Senate showed that only a few Republicans would cross over to support Hayden and that several Democrats would vote to sustain McCarthy. With this the entire attempt to challenge the Wisconsin senator collapsed, and once again McCarthy ducked behind the comfortable shield of party solidarity.[99] When his name was called, he walked in jauntily on the

---

[97] Shelton, "The Shame of the Senate," p. 7.

[98] When a senator "stands aside," he neither takes the oath of office nor assumes his seat. When he takes the oath "without prejudice," he is entitled to the privileges and prerogatives normally accorded a senator, but the right of the Senate to examine his *bona fides* is preserved. Some senators argue that a senator seated "without prejudice" may be removed from his seat by a simple majority rather than the two-thirds necessary for expulsion, but the issue is not entirely clear. See the colloquy between Vice President Alben Barkley and Senator Robert A. Taft in *Congressional Record*, 83d Cong., 1st sess., Jan. 3, 1953, p. 7.

[99] Part of this story appears in Marquis Childs, *Washington Post*, Jan. 6,

arm of Wisconsin's senior senator, Alexander Wiley. He clapped Hayden on the back and grinned down maliciously at the dour Arizonan, then strode on amid a patter of applause from the galleries overhead. He was, or at least so it appeared, more powerful than ever.[100]

The failure of the Senate to challenge McCarthy drew almost universal condemnation from the liberal press. A writer for the *Progressive* called it "the shame of the Senate"; the *Nation* described it as "a Senate sellout."[101] In fact, the subcommittee had simply come face to face with the unpleasant political realities underlying the McCarthy issue. As Senator Hennings patiently wrote one constituent: "The truth simply [was] that we did not have the votes to sustain such a move and any motion to that effect would have resulted in a vote of confidence in Senator McCarthy and a repudiation of the Subcommittee. In our opinion, such a result would have been bad for the country and for the Senate."[102]

AN EPILOGUE

The impact of the Hennings report was not entirely dissipated by the Senate's failure to challenge McCarthy. Hennings forwarded the report to the Justice Department, the Internal Revenue Service, and the Federal Deposit Insurance Corporation,[103] and Benton urged Truman to make a statement on the report in order "to leave it on the doorstep of Brownell, Humphrey, and the General." A few days later the president told a press conference

1953. The most complete account I have located is in John Howe to William Benton, Oct. 12, 1954, box 5, Benton Papers.

[100] *New York Times*, Jan. 3, 1953, p. 8; Jan. 4, 1953, p. 62. Chavez and Republican William Langer were both seated "without prejudice."

[101] Shelton, "The Shame of the Senate," pp. 7–10; H. H. Wilson, "The Senate Sellout," *Nation* 176 (Jan. 24, 1953): 64. Also see "Report on McCarthy," *Commonwealth* 57 (Jan. 23, 1953): 393; and *New Republic* 128 (Jan. 12, 1953): 3; all cited in Kemper, *Decade of Fear*, p. 60.

[102] Thomas Hennings to Ralph Torreyson, Feb. 2, 1953, box 85, Hennings Papers.

[103] Thomas Hennings to Attorney General James P. McGrannery, Jan. 6, 1953; Hennings to John S. Graham (IRS), Jan. 6, 1953; Hennings to Maple T. Harl (FDIC), Jan. 6, 1953; all in box 159, Hennings Papers. Hennings also forwarded to the Justice Department the subcommittee's voluminous but unpublished files on the McCarthy investigation.

that the Justice Department had ordered a full investigation of McCarthy based on the report, and here the issue rested as the Democratic administration left office. "I should say the matter is now squarely in the hands of the Republican Party," concluded Senator Hennings.[104] Following the inauguration, Benton and other Democrats began to prod and needle the new administration. Benton personally urged Eisenhower's new undersecretary of the treasury, Marion B. Folsom, to press the investigation, and Gerhard Van Arkel, his Washington counsel, worked hard to inspire external pressure on the administration.[105] Senator Carl Hayden tried to convince the new internal revenue commissioner, T. Coleman Andrews, to hire the subcommittee's former associate counsel to pursue the McCarthy investigation, but the Treasury Department wanted no part of antagonizing the Wisconsin senator. Former Attorney General Francis Biddle, chairman of Americans for Democratic Action, prodded the Justice Department in a letter citing a long list of possible violations of state and federal laws. Philip Horton of the *Reporter* magazine retained a Wall Street law firm to canvass the report.[106]

The result of all these labors was not impressive. The lawyers whom the *Reporter* engaged found that of all the possible state and federal statutes cited, only eight were applicable to a United States senator. In four of these instances the statute of limitations had already run out, and there was a possibility that it had also expired in two other cases. There was not much more hope for the remaining charges. The report did suggest that McCarthy's financial dealings may have resulted in tax evasion, but even here there was no conclusive proof.[107] Although the investigation had

---

[104] William Benton to Charles S. Murphy (counsel to the President), Jan. 10, 1953; Benton to Truman, Jan. 16, 1953; Truman to Benton, Jan. 19, 1953, all in box 5, Benton Papers; *New York Times*, Jan. 15, 1953, p. 12; Thomas Hennings to Ralph Torreyson, box 85, Hennings Papers.

[105] William Benton to Theodore Kiendl, Jan. 24, 1953, box 5, Benton Papers; Gerhard Van Arkel to Benton, Feb. 26, 1953; to Drew Pearson, Robert Baker, Frank Edwards, Lloyd Garrison, James H. Rowe, Philip Pearl, Jack O'Brien *et al.*, March 3-4, 1953, all in the NCEC files; Van Arkel, Memo (on McCarthy's finances and the Justice Department), n.d. [Feb.-March 1953], in NCEC files.

[106] *New York Times*, April 7, 1953, p. 13; Gerhard Van Arkel to Francis Biddle, April 9, 1953; John J. B. Shea to Philip Horton, June 8, 1953, both in NCEC files.

not been exhaustive and the firm had not had access to the subcommittee's files, the tentative conclusions were discouraging for those who hoped that the report might serve as the basis for legal action against McCarthy. The Justice Department confirmed this analysis in October 1953, clearing McCarthy and closing its investigation of the case.[108]

The Hennings report was somewhat more effective as a propaganda document; it added, if only by small measure, to the growing attack on McCarthy which would eventually shake the Senate and the Republican party to their foundations.

Much of the material collected by the subcommittee had already been leaked to columnist Drew Pearson and other Washington newsmen; Jack Anderson and Ronald May's muckraking biography, *McCarthy: The Man, the Senator, the "Ism,"* which appeared in the fall of 1952, had drawn heavily upon these documents.[109] The report itself became something of a bestseller by congressional standards. Some 2,500 volumes were originally printed. Hennings sent a copy to each member of the Senate and to the larger newspapers in Wisconsin. But he was deluged by additional requests from all over the country, and his own small supply was quickly exhausted.[110] It soon became impossible to obtain copies of the report, and there were ugly rumors that Senator William E. Jenner, the new chairman of the Senate Rules Committee, was deliberately suppressing the document.[111]

---

[107] "Memorandum of Law Regarding Report of the Subcommittee on Privileges and Elections to the Committee on Rules and Administration Pursuant to S. Res. 187," May 28, 1953, by the firm of Cleary, Gottlieb, Friendly and Hamilton; "Memorandum to the *Reporter* staff," Jan. 13, 1953 (a preliminary report); John J. B. Shea to Philip Horton, June 8, 1953; all in the NCEC files.

[108] Attorney General Herbert Brownell, Jr., to Senator William E. Jenner, Oct. 15, 1953, photostat in box 4, Benton Papers; *New York Times*, Oct. 17, 1953, p. 1; John Howe to William Benton, Oct. 23, 1953, box 5, Benton Papers.

[109] Jack Anderson was an associate of Drew Pearson. Ronald May was a reporter for the *Capital Times* (Madison).

[110] Thomas Hennings to George G. Connelly, Jan. 19, 1953, box 23; Hennings to Mrs. Clifford Ellsworth Conry, March 16, 1953, box 159, both in Hennings Papers. Box 82 of the Hennings collection contains many unfulfilled requests for copies of the report.

[111] Kenneth Birkhead (Democratic National Committee) to William Benton, n.d. [Jan.-Feb. 1953]; John Howe to Benton, March 30, 1953, both in box 4, Benton Papers. Also see Senator Wallace F. Bennett (R-Utah) to Robert G.

In late March the *New Republic* issued a condensation of the report, and by the following July reported total sales in excess of 150,000. Americans for Democratic Action reprinted the entire report and distributed nearly 7,000 copies within a few months.[112] The Hennings report became a staple for anti-McCarthy journalists, and as the "McCarthy issue" continued to rage, almost no month went by without some stern editorial demand that McCarthy answer the six questions posed by the subcommittee.[113]

The Hennings report, however, was not primarily intended as either a legal brief or a propaganda piece. Its audience was not a grand jury or even the general public. It was a document written by senators for their colleagues. Its harshest condemnation was reserved for McCarthy's willful and malicious obstruction of the internal processes of the Senate itself. Less than two years later, a Select Committee of United States Senators, speaking in much the same language as the Hennings report, would conclude that McCarthy's behavior had been contumacious and contemptuous in character and deserving of censure by the entire Senate body. In this legalistic sense, the Hennings report became the foundation for McCarthy's condemnation.

But censure itself would only come when the shifting balance of political power had turned, and when it was no longer possible to tolerate the disruptive presence of the junior senator from Wisconsin. Until then he would continue to trample the customs and traditions of the Senate, to abuse its authority, and to mock its high station.

Moore, Jan. 27, 1953, in Moore to Thomas Hennings, Feb. 2, 1953, box 30, Hennings Papers.

112 *New Republic* 128 (March 30, 1953); *New York Times,* July 16, 1953, p. 12; *Washington Post,* July 16, 1953; Memorandum, Edward D. Hollander to Robert R. Nathan, Oct. 5, 1953, NCEC files. There had been speculation that the *Progressive* might issue a condensation, but instead the magazine used the report in its full length "McCarthy issue" of April 1954. John Howe to William Benton, March 30, 1953, box 4, Benton Papers. "McCarthy: A Documented Record," *Progressive* 18 (April 1954).

113 See, for example, the *New York Times,* Jan. 10, 1953, p. 11; Feb. 1, 1953, sec. 4, p. 8; June 10, 1954, p. 30; *Christian Science Monitor,* June 17, 1954.

6

McCARTHY AND THE REPUBLICAN ASCENDANCY

T HE APPOINTMENTS OF THE Senate Chamber—the heavy wooden desks, the thickly carpeted floors, the admonitions against applause from the public galleries— all seem to suggest a dignified and aristocratic aloofness. But such an appearance is deceiving. The clash of party and faction is the inevitable backdrop to the drama of the floor, the sounds of the hustings are never distant, and the results of each election weigh heavily upon the members.

By 1952 Joe McCarthy had made his name synonymous with the issue of communism-in-government, an issue generated by more than a decade of Republican attacks on the administrations of Franklin Delano Roosevelt and Harry S. Truman. His extravagant charges had dramatized the issue as never before, but they had also stirred fierce opposition. The Republican party was faced with a difficult problem, and its response revealed the inner dynamics of the party issue with which McCarthy had become identified. Stated simply, the dilemma was this: to repudiate McCarthy entirely was to repudiate the G.O.P. contention that the Democrats had been "soft on communism"; to embrace him too eagerly was to invite a "boomerang" which might destroy McCarthy, the Communist issue, and all who stood too near. A few Republicans continued to criticize McCarthy, but as the 1952 elections drew near these faint protests disappeared. Prominent Republican leaders, including House Minority Leader Joseph Martin and National Committee Chairman Guy Gabrielson, joined in praising McCarthy for exposing "the tremendous infiltration of pinks and fellow-travelers into our government." In July 1952 McCarthy told a cheering Republican National Convention that he would never soften his fight against communism because "a rough fight is the only fight Communists understand." The Republican platform, shaped by McCarthy supporters, accused the Truman administration of "appeasement of communism at home and abroad."[1]

Both Robert Taft and Dwight Eisenhower had to contend with McCarthy in their quest for the presidency. Their reactions were an index to the power he had already achieved within the Republican party. Taft, the choice of most conservatives for the Republican nomination, was the first to meet the McCarthy issue. Although the Ohio senator's supporters included many enthusiastic McCarthyites, the relationship between the conservative and aristocratic Taft and the young and flamboyant McCarthy was always somewhat tenuous. During the autumn of 1951, Taft criticized McCarthy for overstating his case. In early 1952, however, he gave McCarthy a strong endorsement. Campaigning in the Wisconsin primary, Taft charged that the "pro-Communist" policies of the State Department "fully justified" McCarthy's demands for a thorough investigation.[2] Although McCarthy made no reciprocal

[1] McCarthy was criticized indirectly by Senator James H. Duff of Pennsylvania and by Governors Theodore R. McKeldin of Maryland and Earl Warren of California. See the *New York Times*, Oct. 19, 1951, p. 7; Oct. 24, 1951, p. 19; April 29, 1952, p. 24. Martin and Gabrielson are quoted in ibid., Nov. 11, 1951, p. 62, and Feb. 3, 1952, p. 45, respectively. The proceedings of the Republican National Convention are reported in ibid., July 10, 1952, p. 21; July 11, 1952, p. 1.

[2] *Milwaukee Journal*, Oct. 23, 1951; *New York Times*, Oct. 23, 1951, p. 14; Oct. 28, 1951, sec. 4, p. 10; Jan. 22, 1952, p. 15.

declarations of support for Taft, the Wisconsin G.O.P. organization remained solidly behind the Ohio senator. Tom Coleman, for years the most powerful figure in the state organization, was an early and ardent Taft supporter who subsequently became the senator's floor manager at the 1952 convention.

Eisenhower's confrontation with McCarthy did not come until the general's campaign train pulled into Wisconsin in the early fall of 1952. This meeting produced a microcosm of all those personal and political configurations which would swirl about the general during the next few years. Eisenhower himself was typically apolitical. He hated the details of party politics which would have intrigued a Lincoln or a Franklin Roosevelt, and he left these matters to his political retainers. McCarthy was energetic and pugnacious—fearing, yet at the same time daring, an attack from the general or anyone else. Between these two men were the professionals, the political managers to whom party harmony was the means to party victory. They blunted the sharp edges of conflict, muffled nascent controversy, and papered over real or apparent differences with homilies and truisms on party solidarity.

Eisenhower was sincerely opposed to McCarthy and all that he had come to symbolize. As president of Columbia University he had spoken out more than once against name-calling and hysteria. "Our problem is to defend freedom," he declared, ". . . in such fashion that we do not ourselves suffocate freedom in its own dwelling place."[3] As the candidate of his party's moderate wing, he numbered among his supporters many of McCarthy's strongest critics. Nor could he have forgotten or forgiven the Wisconsin senator's vicious attack upon his old friend and comrade-in-arms, General George C. Marshall. The McCarthy issue, however, raised difficult political problems. Eisenhower could ill afford, or so his advisers thought, to alienate the great mass of voters which McCarthy was believed to control. Even more importantly, the general faced the difficult task of soothing the feelings of the disgruntled party conservatives. Even though McCarthy was by no means popular with all conservatives, he had enough leverage within this faction to maintain his precarious but privileged position within the party at large. An attack by Eisenhower on McCarthy would only embitter the already strained relations between moderates and conservatives and introduce the

[3] *New York Times,* Oct. 20, 1950, p. 17.

specter of full-scale party warfare on the very eve of the election. At first Eisenhower simply attempted to ignore this dilemma. He told a press conference in Denver, Colorado, that he would never give a "blanket endorsement" to anyone (read McCarthy) whose views violated his own conceptions of what was "decent, right, just and fair." On the other hand, he promised he would "support" any properly nominated Republican candidate (again read McCarthy) "as a member of the Republican organization."[4] The general's position might have remained suspended in this semantic never-never land between "blanket endorsement" and "support" had the Republican National Committee followed his instructions and not scheduled a campaign trip into Wisconsin. The plans were laid, however, and the horns of the dilemma sharpened.

The conflict between the general and the senator crystalized about the figure of George C. Marshall. On this subject alone were reporters able to draw Eisenhower out from behind his platitudes about "un-American" methods and tactics. In Denver the general had hotly declared that he had "no patience with anyone who can find in his [Marshall's] record of service for this country anything to criticize." Then in late September, after he learned of the plans for the Wisconsin tour, he suggested to speechwriter Emmet John Hughes that they make this an occasion for a personal tribute to Marshall. The speech was to be one affirming Eisenhower's strong opposition to communism but balanced by warnings against "self-appointed censors" and "intellectual vigilantism." The draft continued:

The right to question a man's judgment carries with it no automatic right to question his honor.
Let me be quite specific. I know that charges of disloyalty have, in the past, been leveled against General George C. Marshall. I have been privileged for thirty-five years to know General Marshall personally. I know him, as a man and as a soldier, to be dedicated with singular selflessness and the profoundest patriotism to the service of America. And this episode is a sobering lesson in the way freedom must not defend itself.[5]

[4] Ibid., Aug. 23, 1952, p. 1.
[5] Ibid.; Emmet J. Hughes, *The Ordeal of Power: A Political Memoir of the Eisenhower Years* (New York, 1963), pp. 41–42; "Communism and Freedom," Sixth Draft, OF 101-GG, Eisenhower Papers, Eisenhower Library, Abilene, Kans.

The paragraph was a strong reaffirmation of Eisenhower's disagreement with McCarthy and—since it was to be delivered in Milwaukee—a direct challenge to the senator himself. But it was also a threat to the delicate balance of party unity both in Wisconsin and at large, and as the campaign train wound its way northward through Illinois, a heated debate broke out among the general's advisers. The political brokers argued that the passage was alien to the context of the speech, that it was an all-too-obvious affront to McCarthy, and that it might drag down to defeat Governor Walter J. Kohler and the entire Republican ticket in Wisconsin.[6]

On October 2, McCarthy, Kohler, and Wisconsin national committeeman Henry Ringling flew down from Madison to Peoria, Illinois, where the campaign train lay at a siding, ready to roll into Wisconsin. They were met at the Pere Marquette Hotel, where the general was resting, and taken up in a freight elevator to the room of Republican National Chairman Arthur E. Summerfield.[7] At 5:30 McCarthy was summoned to the general's suite, where he spent thirty minutes with the candidate. Afterwards, McCarthy told reporters that the question of the speech had not been raised.[8]

Early the following morning the train headed into Wisconsin, stopping briefly in Milwaukee to pick up party dignitaries and then speeding northward again toward Green Bay. Eisenhower met with McCarthy once again aboard the swaying train. It was by all accounts a strained interview. "I'm going to say that I disagree with you," Eisenhower told McCarthy. "If you say that, you'll be booed," replied McCarthy.[9]

[6] Robert Cutler, *No Time for Rest* (Boston, 1966), pp. 287–88. Robert Cutler to author, Oct. 13, 1966.

[7] Summerfield served in the last weeks of the campaign as the chief liaison between Eisenhower and the Republican National Headquarters. Only a few days before he had met with Tom Coleman of Wisconsin and praised McCarthy effusively before a luncheon meeting of the National Press Club. *Milkwaukee Journal*, Oct. 1, 1952.

[8] Walter J. Kohler, Memorandum to Sherman Adams, April 27, 1959, enclosed in Kohler to author, Oct. 3, 1966; *New York Times*, Oct. 3, 1952, p. 15; *Chicago Daily Tribune*, Oct. 3, 1952. "We had a very pleasant conversation," McCarthy told reporters. "If anything further is said, the General will say it." *Wisconsin State Journal* (Madison), Oct. 3, 1952.

[9] Sherman Adams, *Firsthand Report: The Story of the Eisenhower Administration* (New York, 1961), pp. 31–32; Dwight D. Eisenhower, *The White House Years: Mandate for Change, 1953–1956* (New York, 1965), p. 387.

In Green Bay Eisenhower called for the election of the entire Republican slate. McCarthy, shifting nervously from foot to foot just inside the rear compartment, broke into a broad grin. So did Governor Kohler. The general went on, however, to declare that while he agreed with McCarthy's aims, he could not agree with his methods. And although he would welcome congressional investigations, he declared that the primary responsibility for dealing with the question of loyalty and subversion rested with the Executive and not with Congress. McCarthy shook his head vigorously and frowned in disagreement and disapproval.[10]

When the train stopped at McCarthy's home town of Appleton, Wisconsin, a short while later, the senator bounced out, grinning broadly, to introduce Eisenhower. Eisenhower himself, though he made no further mention of McCarthy, once again called for the election of the entire Republican slate.[11]

Then, as the train turned south toward Milwaukee, Governor Kohler pressed Sherman Adams to remove the now controversial passage praising Marshall. He reminded Adams of the close ties between Wisconsin's Republicans and both Taft and McCarthy, and he argued that an attack on McCarthy would destroy the precarious solidarity of the party organization. He also pointed out that Wisconsin was politically unpredictable. The Republicans remained the majority party at the state level, but the Democrats had carried Wisconsin in four of the last five presidential elections. The alienation of ardent McCarthy backers might well lose the state and even the election. Adams and Kohler then called upon the general, who almost immediately agreed. "I handled that subject pretty thoroughly in Denver two weeks ago," he declared, "and there's no reason to repeat it tonight."[12]

The deletion of the Marshall paragraph was an open secret among the reporters on the Eisenhower train, and despite denials by Kohler, Coleman, and others, the news was soon embarrassingly

[10] Robert H. Fleming, *Milwaukee Journal*, Oct. 3, 1952; Walter J. Kohler, Memorandum to Sherman Adams, April 27, 1959, enclosed in Kohler to author, Oct. 3, 1966.

[11] *Milwaukee Journal*, Oct. 3, 1952.

[12] Walter J. Kohler, Memorandum to Sherman Adams, April 27, 1959; *Wisconsin State Journal* (Madison), Oct. 3, 1952, *St. Louis Post-Dispatch*, Oct. 4, 1952. McCarthy met with Eisenhower a third time that evening at the general's hotel. This last meeting was reported neither by the press nor by Eisenhower's biographers. See Cutler, *No Time for Rest*, pp. 287–88, and Cutler to author, Oct. 13, 1966.

flashed across the country. Without the balancing effect of the passage defending Marshall, the speech was duly interpreted as an endorsement of McCarthy and his "fight against communism." "Do I need tell you I am sick at heart?" wired Arthur Hays Sulzberger, the strongly pro-Eisenhower publisher of the *New York Times*. To be sure, Eisenhower had qualified his support, but the final comment on this came from a Wisconsin Republican leader: "I guess we can say he's for—but. And who's going to remember the but?"[13]

For the remainder of the campaign, Eisenhower's relation with McCarthy remained at this ambiguous point. In November McCarthy made an unsolicited television attack on Adlai E. Stevenson, whom he charged was the captive of "communist-line thinkers." When he had concluded, one of Eisenhower's friends wired, "Thank God it is over."[14] But for Eisenhower, unhappily, it was only the beginning.

The issue of McCarthy and McCarthyism also pressed upon Republican senatorial candidates. The Republican National Committee had decided quite early to use the Wisconsin senator for all he was worth, and by April 1952 McCarthy had made tentative commitments to speak in no less than sixteen states on behalf of Republican candidates.[15] Some Republicans, among them Barry Goldwater of Arizona and William A. Purtell of Connecticut, welcomed the Wisconsin senator enthusiastically. A few, such as Prescott Bush of Connecticut, went out of their way to disavow his methods. But for the most part, like Taft and Eisenhower, they granted Joe McCarthy the Republican party's *nihil obstat*.

The results of the election seemed to confirm McCarthy's power and influence. McCarthy himself was reelected by a wide margin,

13 Sulzberger's telegram to Sherman Adams is quoted in Adams, *Firsthand Report*, p. 31. The unidentified Republican leader is quoted in the *Milwaukee Journal*, Oct. 3, 1952. For typical press reaction to the speech see ibid., Oct. 4, 1952; *Wisconsin State Journal* (Madison), Oct. 4, 1952; *New York Times*, Oct. 4, 1952, p. 1; *Denver Post*, Oct. 4, 1952; *St. Louis Post-Dispatch*, Oct. 4, 1952. An exception to the general treatment of the address was the strongly pro-Eisenhower *Washington Post*, which stressed the general's "differences" with McCarthy and declared that he had "opened a wide gulf between himself and the notorious mud-slinger." *Washington Post*, Oct. 5, 1952.

14 *New York Times*, Oct. 28, 1952, pp. 1, 26; George A. Sloan to Eisenhower, Oct. 28, 1952, OF 99-R, Eisenhower Papers.

15 *Washington Post*, Sept. 16, 1951; *New York Times*, April 27, 1952, p. 10,

and four of the Democratic incumbents against whom he had campaigned went down to defeat, including William Benton, his strongest opponent in the Senate, and Ernest W. McFarland, the Democratic majority leader. The legend of his political power grew. Writing in the *New York Times*, William S. White declared that McCarthy had helped no less than eight senators to election, and other estimates ran even higher. This "simple fact," he declared, was not "overlooked in a political body."[16]

The "simple fact," however, was that McCarthy's political influence was vastly overrated. In a survey of the twelve non-southern states in which McCarthy campaigned, pollster Louis Bean discovered that *in every instance* the Democratic senatorial candidate ran well ahead of the national ticket. Three of McCarthy's strongest supporters were all ousted from the Senate despite his campaigning, and the senator himself ran considerably behind Eisenhower and the other Republicans on the Wisconsin ballot.[17]

It was not McCarthy who defeated Benton, McFarland, and the others, but Eisenhower. "I was absolutely confident that you would be reelected," wrote Herbert Lehman to the defeated majority leader. "Unfortunately, like so many others, you were caught in the irresistible tide which no one could stem." "The storm has struck," wrote Lehman's legislative aide to William Benton, "and the waves have receded, leaving us all pretty naked, indeed."[18] The "simple fact" of McCarthy's power was an illusion. In 1953, however, this was an illusion which many Americans accepted. What was important was not reality but how reality was perceived. In the newly elected Republican Congress McCarthy was believed to be more powerful than ever, and because of this "simple fact" he was.

[16] *New York Times*, Jan. 18, 1953, sec. 4, p. 4; also see Cabell Phillips, ibid., March 8, 1953, sec. 4, p. 10.

[17] Louis Bean, *Influence in the 1954 Mid-Term Elections* (Washington, D. C., 1954), pp. 1–2, 8–18. McCarthy ran 110,000 votes behind Eisenhower and 169,000 votes behind Republican Secretary of State Fred R. Zimmerman, who had played a prominent role in a statewide bipartisan movement to defeat McCarthy. Also see William Benton to Stanley Allen, Jan. 19, 1953, NCEC files.

[18] Herbert H. Lehman to Ernest W. McFarland, Nov. 11, 1952, Special File; Julius C. C. Edelstein to William Benton, Nov. 8, 1952, Senate Departmental File, Drawer 28, both in the Lehman Papers.

THE McCARTHY BALANCE

For nearly three years Joe McCarthy had ridden a political whirlwind created by the Republican struggle for power. Many Americans, including such perceptive and influential observers as Walter Lippman and Joseph Alsop, believed that the election of Dwight David Eisenhower would put an end to McCarthy and McCarthyism. The election, however, though altering certain elements in the political equation which had made McCarthy powerful, did not immediately change that equation itself. As before, McCarthy's immunity was underwritten by a complex balance of forces within the structure of national politics.

In the Senate, as in the country at large, the Republican party was divided into several fluid and ill-defined groups. McCarthy himself could count on the unflagging support of a handful of Republican bitter-enders. Some of these, such as Herman Welker and George "Molly" Malone, were notable primarily because of their vituperativeness in debate, but others held powerful positions within the Senate hierarchy. Styles Bridges was chairman of the Appropriations Committee and McCarthy's single most influential champion within the Republican leadership. William E. Jenner chaired both the Committee on Rules and Administration and the Internal Security Subcommittee. Everett Dirksen, who was already building a solid reputation among Senate conservatives, headed the Republican Senate Campaign Committee.[19] McCarthy's support among these and other right-wing Republicans was a powerful lever by which to multiply his influence both inside and outside the Senate.

Opposed to this nucleus of McCarthyites was a much less cohesive group of Republican "liberals." They had been early supporters of Eisenhower and were for the most part from the states along the eastern seaboard.[20] They shared with the con-

[19] McCarthy's strongest supporters usually included John W. Bricker of Ohio, H. Styles Bridges of New Hampshire, Homer E. Capehart and William E. Jenner of Indiana, Everett M. Dirksen of Illinois, Henry C. Dworshak and Herman Welker of Idaho, Barry Goldwater of Arizona, George W. Malone of Nevada, Karl E. Mundt of South Dakota, Bourke B. Hickenlooper of Iowa, and Andrew F. Schoeppel of Kansas.

[20] Usually included among the liberal Republicans were George D. Aiken and Ralph E. Flanders of Vermont, Charles W. Tobey of New Hampshire, Edward J. Thye of Minnesota, Robert C. Hendrickson and H. Alexander Smith of New Jersey, James H. Duff of Pennsylvania, Margaret Chase Smith

servatives the belief that most of the nation's problems were the result of Democratic appeasement and misgovernment. "McCarthy would never have had any influence had it not been for the fact that our late, departed saint, Franklin Delano Roosevelt, was soft as taffy on the subject of Communism and Uncle Joe," declared Ralph Flanders of Vermont. McCarthy was only trying to "clean out the State Department," recalled another G.O.P. moderate, "and we were all in favor of that, of course."[21] Although they were highly critical of McCarthy's rough-and-tumble tactics, few ventured to place their views in the public record. Occasionally someone such as the evangelical Charles Tobey would denounce McCarthy, but most of them were disinclined to do battle with him. "I shall have to leave to the Democrats the problem of making a case for the expulsion of a Republican Senator," wrote Ralph Flanders to a Vermont constituent in early 1953.[22]

The balance of power on the Republican side of the Senate was wielded by non-McCarthy conservatives, men such as Robert A. Taft of Ohio, Eugene D. Millikin of Colorado, and William F. Knowland of California, whose ranks had generally provided the party's Senate leadership. During the Eighty-second Congress they had used McCarthy and his followers to batter away at the Democrats. Now, willingly or not, they were unable to disengage themselves. The minimal responsibility of majority leadership— to maintain a majority—dictated that they conciliate McCarthy. They needed his support, moreover, in order to maintain a position of parity with the Executive, for Eisenhower was both the leader of an opposing faction within the party and the head of a competing

---

and Frederick G. Payne of Maine, Leverett Saltonstall of Massachusetts, John Sherman Cooper of Kentucky, Irving M. Ives of New York, and William Langer of North Dakota. Wayne Morse left the Republican party in 1952, becoming first an independent and then later a Democrat. Henry Cabot Lodge, one of the most prominent of the G.O.P. liberals, was defeated in the 1952 election. Robert Bendiner, " 'Liberalism' as G.O.P. Liberals Define It," *New York Times Magazine*, Sept. 23, 1951, p. 15. For a rudimentary roll call vote analysis see *Congressional Quarterly Almanac* (Washington, D. C., 1948), 4: 38–39; (1950), 6: 59; (1952), 8: 67.

[21] Ralph Flanders to Paul G. Hoffman, Oct. 15, 1951, box 105, Flanders Papers, Syracuse University. H. Alexander Smith, COHC, p. 189.

[22] Ralph Flanders to Freeman Keith, March 6, 1953, box 1, Flanders Papers, State Historical Society of Wisconsin. For Tobey's attack on McCarthy, see the *New York Times*, March 23, 1953, p. 12; William Benton to J. William Fulbright, March 28, 1953, box 4, Benton Papers.

branch of government. Though on occasion Taft acted as the president's spokesman in the Senate, he never forgot his competing obligations to the Upper Chamber.

It was not, however, a question of McCarthy's direct and effective influence over the internal processes of the Senate; this was never great. What was at issue was his role as a compelling personal symbol of Republican anticommunism. Senate Republicans could not divorce themselves from McCarthy without losing the burning appeal of the issues he personified, and this they were extremely reluctant to do. "McCarthyism is a kind of liquor for Taft," observed a friend of the Ohio senator. "He knows it's bad stuff, and he keeps taking the pledge, but every so often he falls off the wagon."[23]

The administration's response to McCarthy was conditioned by the same circumstances, framed in a somewhat different perspective. Victorious in an intense intraparty battle and the recipient of a large if vague popular mandate, the new president was faced with a Congress in which effective political power was exercised by those who had opposed his nomination. Indeed, it was to Robert Taft, the defeated leader of the Republican opposition and now majority leader of the Senate, that Eisenhower had no choice but to entrust his legislative programs. This peculiar relationship between the president and the majority leader insured McCarthy his privileged position. The administration could not attack him without endangering Republican control of the Senate and, beyond that, of opening up the possibility of large-scale factional warfare within the party.

Even before the election Taft had asked Eisenhower for assurances covering "the total expenditures of the budget after the first year, a reduction in taxes, a conservative foreign policy, a defense of the Taft-Hartley law and fair representation of Taft supporters in the cabinet." Eisenhower agreed to most of these points (the single exception was "a conservative foreign policy") at a highly publicized meeting with Taft on September 12, 1952, in which he promised his full cooperation with Congress.[24]

[23] Quoted by Richard H. Rovere, "What Course for the Powerful Mr. Taft," *New York Times Magazine*, March 22, 1953, pp. 9, 32–34. Also see William S. White, *The Taft Story* (New York, 1954), p. 239.

[24] Taft to Senator Hugh A. Butler, Aug. 13, 1952; Butler to Senator Frank Carlson, Aug. 23, 1952, both in box 363, Butler Papers. *New York Times*, Sept. 13, 1952, p. 1.

Cooperating with Congress, however, meant cooperating with McCarthy as well. It meant, for example, that the new president must appoint a number of conservative Republicans to positions within the administration, and this in turn opened the door to men who would make common cause with McCarthy. Appointments such as that of R. W. Scott McLeod, former administrative assistant to Styles Bridges and a close friend of McCarthy, as chief security officer for the State Department would prove particularly troublesome to the new administration. Working with Congress also involved working with its investigatory agencies and this too meant, and quite explicitly, cooperating with McCarthy.[25]

Beyond the question of "cooperating with Congress," the Eisenhower administration was committed, only a little less enthusiastically than Senate conservatives, to the use of the Communist issue against the Democrats. Richard Nixon, who early in the 1952 campaign had promised to make Communist subversion "the theme of every speech from now until the election," had charged that the Democrats were responsible for "the unimpeded growth of the Communist conspiracy within the U.S." Even Eisenhower, in his Milwaukee speech, had scored the Democratic party for tolerating treason and disloyalty.[26] Once in power, the Republicans in the White House were reluctant to give up this partisan issue, and their reluctance further contributed to McCarthy's continued influence.

The new president was a decent man, but he possessed neither the ability nor the inclination to deal with a political problem of this complexity. Urged by friends and advisers to speak out against McCarthy, he often replied: "I just will not—I refuse—to get into the gutter with that guy."[27] The real alternatives, of course,

[25] Robert J. Donovan, *Eisenhower: The Inside Story* (New York, 1956), pp. 83–86. John Robinson Beale, *John Foster Dulles: A Biography* (New York, 1957), p. 139. Alexander Wiley to R. W. Scott McLeod, March 10, 1953, Personal Correspondence, box f, Wiley Papers.

[26] *Evening Star* (Washington), Sept. 3, 1952; *New York Times*, July 12, 1952, p. 6; Oct. 4, 1952, pp. 1, 8; Oct. 19, 1952, p. 73.

[27] Quoted in Hughes, *The Ordeal of Power*, p. 92. "With respect to McCarthy, I continue to believe that the President of the United States cannot afford to name names in opposing procedures, practices and methods in our government," he wrote one friend. "This applies with special force when the individual concerned enjoys the immunity of a United States Senator. This particular individual wants, above all else, publicity. Nothing would probably please him more than to get the publicity that would be generated

were not limited to either standing aloof or gutter brawling. A more Machiavellian or manipulative president, a Franklin Roosevelt or a Lyndon Johnson, might have operated effectively against McCarthy while avoiding either extreme. But Eisenhower *was* president, and he was elected to office for reasons quite inseparable from his political naïveté.

Lacking strong leadership on the issue, the administration vacillated between opposition and appeasement of McCarthy. The White House staff itself was divided into warring factions. One group, led by special assistant to the president C. D. Jackson, argued that any compromise with McCarthy would only embolden him further, while costing the president support of the moderates and independents who had helped elect him. The other group was led by those involved in congressional liaison, especially Vice President Nixon and Major General Wilton B. Persons. They argued that an attack on McCarthy would only divide the party and publicize the senator even more. "The best way to reduce his influence to the proper proportion," declared one staff member in the vernacular of the Eisenhower years, "is to take him on as part of the team."[28]

Thus the multiple reflections of party factionalism, whether within the Congress, between Congress and the president, or within the Executive Office itself, produced on the part of the administration a pattern of ambivalence reminiscent of Eisenhower's 1952 encounter with McCarthy in Wisconsin. Nowhere was the operation of this "McCarthy balance" more clearly revealed than during the sharp debate which followed Eisenhower's nomination of Charles E. Bohlen as ambassador to the Soviet Union.

During the first weeks of the new administration, conservative disquietude over Eisenhower's future course in foreign affairs took the form of opposition to the president's appointments. Senate conservatives delayed confirmation of both General Walter Bedell Smith, whom Eisenhower had nominated as undersecretary of

---

by public repudiation by the President." Eisenhower to Harry A. Bullis, May 18, 1953, OF 99-R, Eisenhower Papers.

[28] John B. Oakes, "An Inquiry into McCarthy's Status," *New York Times Magazine*, April 12, 1953, pp. 9, 26–30; Adams, *Firsthand Report*, pp. 135–41; Robert J. Donovan, *Eisenhower*, pp. 247–48; Hughes, *Ordeal of Power*, pp. 66–67, 92–94.

state, and James B. Conant, whom he had named as United States high commissioner to Germany. General Smith, who had served as Eisenhower's chief of staff in World War II and later as ambassador to the Soviet Union and director of the CIA during the Truman administration, had defended diplomat John Paton Davies against the accusations of McCarthy and McCarran. He had also testified at a pretrial hearing in the Benton-McCarthy libel suit. Conant, then president of Harvard University, was attacked by McCarthy and his supporters for holding opinions contrary to "the prevailing philosophy of the American people" and for his criticism of Catholic parochial schools.[29] Both men were finally confirmed, but not before the conservatives had, by delay, made their point.

The Bohlen nomination promised to be far more explosive, for it involved not only the president's control over foreign policy but also that dearest of Republican themes, the "Yalta Betrayal." Bohlen was a career foreign service officer who had served as interpreter for Roosevelt at the wartime conference. Although he was considered to be the State Department's leading specialist in Soviet affairs, the very fact that he had been present at Yalta was enough to make him suspect in the eyes of many Republicans on the Hill. (The Republican platform had promised to "repudiate all commitments contained in secret understandings such as those of Yalta which aid Communist enslavements," and the White House and the Republican leadership in Congress were arguing, even then, over the precise wording of a resolution to implement this pledge.) In a day-long meeting of the Senate Foreign Relations Committee, Bohlen not only refused to endorse any blanket condemnation of the Yalta Conference, but defended it against Republican critics.[30]

Eisenhower, who had anticipated strong opposition to the Bohlen appointment, prevailed upon Senator Taft to set aside his

[29] Everett Dirkson to Alexander Wiley, Jan. 24, 1953, Personal Correspondence, box e, Wiley Papers. McCarthy to Eisenhower, Feb. 3, 1953; McCarthy to Sherman Adams, Feb. 4, 1953; Adams to McCarthy, Feb. 7, 1953, all in GF 9-D-1, Eisenhower Papers. William Benton to General W. B. Smith, Oct. 2, 1952, box 5, Benton Papers. New York Times, Jan. 22, 1953, p. 9; Jan. 30, 1953, p. 8; Feb. 4, 1953, pp. 1–14; Feb. 5, 1953, p. 1; Feb. 7, 1953, p. 1.
[30] New York Times, March 3, 1952, p. 1. Especially see Hughes, Ordeal of Power, pp. 76–77.

own feelings of opposition and support Bohlen's confirmation. With the majority leader's backing, the nomination was reported out of the Foreign Relations Committee by a vote of 15-0.[31]

The opposition to Bohlen was led by Styles Bridges and Pat McCarran. They not only denounced Bohlen's participation in the Yalta Conference, but McCarran went on to charge that Secretary of State John Foster Dulles had "summarily overridden" security chief Scott McLeod in granting Bohlen security clearance. McCarthy joined the battle relatively late, but quickly demonstrated his remarkable talent for capitalizing on the slogans and stereotypes of the Republican *risorgimento*. He accused Dulles of lying and demanded that the secretary appear before the Senate Foreign Relations Committee to testify under oath. He and Everett Dirksen tried to get Scott McLeod before the Permanent Investigations Subcommittee, presumably to testify against the nomination, only to be blocked by the White House, which placed the security officer under wraps.[32]

In a dramatic move to quell the uproar, Taft and Democrat John J. Sparkman of Alabama examined the FBI file on Bohlen and reported back to the Senate that there was nothing in the file to impeach his credentials. On the floor both Taft and Knowland angrily denounced McCarthy's tactics, while at a press conference Eisenhower praised Bohlen as the best qualified man for the difficult post. In the end Bridges and McCarthy were able to muster only thirteen votes against confirmation.[33]

Ostensibly, the Bohlen confirmation was a defeat for McCarthy

[31] Eisenhower, *Mandate for Change*, p. 267; Donovan, *Eisenhower*, p. 89.

[32] *New York Times*, March 14, 1953, p. 1; March 15, 1953, p. 23; March 16, 1953, p. 1; March 21, 1953, p. 1. McLeod, who was apparently working closely with Bridges, McCarran, and McCarthy (as well as the *Washington Times-Herald*), tried to resign during the midst of the controversy but was dissuaded by Special Assistant to the President Wilton B. Persons. Secretary of State Dulles, who was incensed at McLeod's meddling, wanted to fire the security officer, but was talked out of it by Undersecretary of State W. B. Smith. Donovan, *Eisenhower*, p. 88; Beale, *Dulles*, pp. 142–43. According to speechwriter Emmet John Hughes, the White House assigned a staff member to keep McLeod out of the reach of the McCarthy subcommittee. Hughes, *Ordeal of Power*, p. 75.

[33] *New York Times*, March 25, 1953, p. 1; March 26, 1953, p. 1; March 27, 1953, p. 1; March 28, 1953, p. 1. *Congressional Record*, 83d Cong., 1st sess., March 27, 1953, p. 2392. Voting against confirmation were Republicans Bricker, Bridges, Dirksen, Dworshak, Goldwater, Hickenlooper, Malone, McCarthy, Mundt, Schoeppel, and Welker, and Democrats McCarran and Edwin C. Johnson.

and a vindication of Eisenhower's leadership. In fact, the collateral cost of the fight had been high, and in the aftermath there was a coalescence of factions within the Republican party and with it a reassertion of the McCarthy balance. Taft, having discharged his responsibility to the president, now moved to reposition himself within the Senate. Publicly he assured the party faithful that there was no breach in Republican ranks. In private he bluntly warned the White House that there must be "no more Bohlens."[34] Other Republicans sought to minimize the significance of the division over confirmation. Ralph Flanders compared it to the "Shivaree"—the old rural custom of serenading a recently married couple by banging on pots and pans. It was not the end of the "honeymoon," he declared, but the beginning.[35]

The White House was also anxious to back away from its confrontation with McCarthy. Even during the height of the Bohlen controversy the administration had kept open its lines of communication with the Wisconsin senator. (McCarthy had gone to Vice President Nixon regarding which of two speeches opposing confirmation he should deliver, one that was rough or another that was "real dirty." Nixon prevailed upon him to use the former.[36]) Now the administration retreated by adopting a policy of extreme caution in its relations with Congress.[37]

The administration's retreat before McCarthy was nowhere more obvious than in its reaction to his announcement (only two days after the vote on Bohlen) that he had "negotiated" a secret pact

[34] White, *The Taft Story*, p. 239. Asked by reporters if the Bohlen fight signaled a break with McCarthy, Taft answered, "No, no, no, no." *New York Times*, March 28, 1953, p. 1.

[35] Radio broadcast, March 29, 1953, box 153, Flanders Papers, Syracuse University.

[36] Hughes, *Ordeal of Power*, p. 83.

[37] The State Department, for example, first named Mildred McAfee Horton, wartime head of the WAVES and former president of Wellesley College, to the United Nations Economic and Social Commission, but then allowed the appointment to die following right-wing attacks on Mrs. Horton. *New York Times*, May 20, 1953, pp. 1, 15; May 21, 1953, p. 20; May 29, 1953, p. 4. Senator Lehman to Donald B. Cloward, June 19, 1953, Senate Departmental File, drawer 30, Lehman Papers. Beale, *Dulles*, p. 143. On another occasion, after McCarthy had protested the appointment of career diplomat W. L. Beaulac as ambassador to Argentina, the White House promptly withdrew the nomination. Later, after the Senate had adjourned, Beaulac's name was resubmitted, this time as ambassador to Chile. McCarthy to Eisenhower, July 22, 1953; Memorandum, Dulles to the President, Sept. 3, 1953, both in OF 8-F, Eisenhower Papers. *New York Times*, July 31, 1953, p. 11; Aug. 4, 1953, p. 11; Aug. 23, 1953, p. 92; Jan. 20, 1954, p. 15.

with a number of Greek shipowners to halt all trade with Communist China and North Korea. The State Department quickly branded McCarthy's claims as "phony." Mutual Security Director Harold Stassen went even further, charging that McCarthy's heavy-handed tactics were "undermining" the administration's conduct of foreign affairs. Only two days later, however, Dulles and McCarthy met over lunch, and afterwards the secretary of state declared that while the execution of foreign affairs rested exclusively with the president, McCarthy's actions were "in the national interest." At a press conference the following day Eisenhower suggested that Stassen had in fact meant "infringed" rather than "undermined," and the dutiful Stassen agreed that he had not indeed meant what he had said and was now "happy" over the outcome.[38] As a result, senators on both sides of the aisle were unsure of the president's intentions and uncertain as to what course he might finally pursue; this uncertainty compounded in its turn the Senate's reluctance to deal with McCarthy.[39]

Senate Democrats, the third element in the McCarthy balance, were as acquiescent as the Republicans in the White House or on the other side of the aisle. Like the Republicans, they were divided between liberal and conservative wings, and again like the Republicans, they had moderately conservative leadership.[40] In the

[38] *New York Times,* April 2, 1953, p. 1; April 3, 1953, p. 1; April 4, 1953, p. 1; April 5, 1953, sec. 4, p. 2.

[39] William S. White, ibid., April 5, 1953, p. 9.

[40] Conservative Democrats, most of them Southerners, looked for leadership to men such as Walter F. George and Richard B. Russell, both of Georgia. The liberal bloc within the Senate included, at its very largest, the following: Warren G. Magnuson and Henry M. Jackson of Washington, John J. Sparkman and Lister Hill of Alabama, Estes Kefauver and Albert Gore of Tennessee, Clinton P. Anderson and Dennis Chavez of New Mexico, Matthew M. Neely and Harley M. Kilgore of West Virginia, Theodore F. Green and John O. Pastore of Rhode Island, Paul H. Douglas of Illinois, Hubert H. Humphrey of Minnesota, J. William Fulbright of Arkansas, Herbert H. Lehman of New York, Mike Mansfield of Montana, Guy M. Gillette of Iowa, Thomas C. Hennings, Jr., and Stuart Symington of Missouri, John F. Kennedy of Massachusetts, Wayne Morse (Ind.) of Oregon, A. S. (Mike) Monroney of Oklahoma, Lester C. Hunt of Wyoming, and Earle C. Clements of Kentucky. Blair Moody of Michigan, William Benton of Connecticut and Joseph C. O'Mahoney were all members of the liberal group before their defeat in 1952. See Memorandum, June 12, 1951, in box 4, Blair Moody Papers, Michigan Historical Collections, University of Michigan. Herbert Lehman to James E. Murray et al., Jan. 30, 1953, Senate Departmental File, drawer 33, Lehman Papers. Estes Kefauver to Edward R. Murrow, May 25, 1954, Subject File, Congressional 1, Kefauver Papers. Lister Hill to Theodore Francis Green, box 754, Green Papers.

Senate this leadership had been wielded during the 1940s and early 1950s by border state politicians, men whose first qualification was that they serve as honest brokers between the northern and southern wings. Alben Barkley, Scott Lucas, and Ernest McFarland, the Senate's successive majority leaders, had all typified this group. But the savage political warfare of the early 1950s had taken a heavy toll. Majority Leader Scott Lucas and Majority Whip Francis Myers were both defeated in 1950; Ernest McFarland was narrowly beaten in 1952. As a result the southern conservatives were more firmly in control than ever, and their designated leader—the youngest man ever to hold this post—was Lyndon Baines Johnson. "The South has the bit in its teeth," complained Adlai Stevenson, "and will bite the harder if it has anything to bite."[41]

During the Eighty-second Congress conservative Democrats, shut out from national power but unassailable within the Senate, had watched in silence as McCarthy and his cohorts lashed the Truman administration. In the Eighty-third Congress they remained just as quiet. Some of them undoubtedly shared McCarthy's aims and tolerated his methods, most certainly extreme right-wingers such as Pat McCarran and James O. Eastland. Some Senate traditionalists were perhaps reluctant to attack a fellow senator, although probably no member had brought more shame and obloquy upon the Senate and its customs than had McCarthy. Still others doubtlessly enjoyed seeing a Republican senator attacking a Republican president. In an unreported address to the Gridiron Club, Minority Leader Johnson ridiculed the administration for its inability to control McCarthy.

They have the Republican Party of President Eisenhower. They have the Republican Party of Senator Taft. They have the Republican Party of Senator Morse. And somewhere—way out behind the *Chicago Tribune* tower—is the Republican Party of Senator McCarthy with one foot heavy in Greece and the other foot in Secretary Dulles' security files.

It makes bipartisanship right difficult. We Democrats need to know which one of the Republican Parties to be bipartisan *with;* and which one of the Republican Parties to be bipartisan *against.*[42]

41 Adlai E. Stevenson to Frank Altshul, Dec. 29, 1952, Special File, Lehman Papers.
42 Reprint of an unpublished speech to the Gridiron Club, April 11, 1953, box 74, Hennings Papers.

The most important springs of Democratic behavior, however, were political. Individually the Democratic senators were badly shaken by the defeat of Millard Tydings and the others. The message seemed clear: "anti-McCarthyism" was a political dead end. "You may get a lot of moral support for fighting Joe," cautioned one senator, "but if you lose your seat in the Senate—as Millard Tydings or Bill Benton did—that's no good."[43] Collectively, the Democratic leadership was fearful of committing itself to a party-line battle against McCarthy and the Republicans. As a party they had been condemned as "commiecrats" and "the party of treason," and they feared that an attack on McCarthy would only strengthen these irrational accusations. A few Senate liberals such as Herbert H. Lehman wanted to launch an all-out attack on the issue of McCarthyism and civil liberties, but they found little support among their Democratic colleagues.[44] "Why don't we Democrats do anything about it," explained one southern leader. "Well, if the Democrats attacked him that would only help keep the Republicans lined up with him." "For a Democrat to take the lead at this juncture," declared J. William Fulbright, "would cause the Republicans to rally around McCarthy. . . . Unless some leading Republican is willing to take the curse of partisanship off the matter, I doubt that it is wise for a Democrat to make the move."[45] This was the real meaning of Lyndon Johnson's oft-quoted remark that McCarthy was a "Republican problem." "I will not commit my party," declared the minority leader, "to some high school debate on the subject, 'Resolved that Communism is good for the United States,' with my party taking affirmative."[46]

The issue thus returned full circle. Without substantial Republican leadership to remove "the curse of partisanship," the Democrats were unwilling to enlist in a campaign against the Wisconsin senator. On the Republican side there was even less enthusiasm for a political bloodletting. The administration's vacillating policies in this matter encouraged neither liberal Republican nor Democratic opposition to McCarthy. Today's

[43] Quoted in John B. Oakes, "An Inquiry into McCarthy's Status," pp. 26–30.

[44] New York Times, May 3, 1953, sec. 4, p. 3.

[45] The first senator is quoted in Oakes, "An Inquiry into McCarthy's Status," pp. 26–30; William Fulbright to William Benton, March 4, 1953, box 4, Benton Papers.

[46] Quoted in William S. White, The Professional: Lyndon B. Johnson (Boston, 1964), pp. 49–50.

ringing declaration might signal attack, but tomorrow's compromise would surely undermine any advanced position. Caution became contagious, and the politic actions of fearful men ensured McCarthy's continued power and influence.

THE SENATE COMMITTEE ON GOVERNMENT OPERATIONS

If the circumstances of McCarthy's continued rise to power were created by a delicate political balance, it remained for the senator himself to exploit these advantages through the institutional and technical levers of the Senate. As the newly elected Eighty-third Congress convened, there was a great deal of rather unseemly maneuvering among the victorious Republicans to determine just who would conduct the investigations which were to expose the sins and perfidy of "twenty years of treason." In the past, most investigations of communism had been conducted by the House Committee on Un-American Activities and the Internal Security Subcommittee of the Senate Judiciary Committee, the so-called McCarran Committee. The new chairman of HUAC was Harold R. Velde, an ex-FBI man from Illinois, who promised a busy schedule of inquiries. The future of the Internal Security Subcommittee was less clear. The new chairman of the Judiciary Committee was the unpredictable "Wild Bill" Langer, a maverick Republican who often voted with Democratic liberals on issues of civil liberties.[47] Now McCarthy too demanded a piece of the investigative pie.

McCarthy's public position was contradictory, perhaps deliberately so. A few nights after the election he assured Nixon and other Eisenhower aides that he would fully cooperate with the administration. He told reporters that he planned "an entirely different role for himself," investigating graft and corruption rather than subversion. Within a month, however, he was denying before a convocation of true believers that he might in any way soften "his fight" against communism. "That fight can't abate on my part or yours," he declared, "until we've won the war or our civilization has died."[48] In January, with his committee's appropriation up

47 New York Times, Jan. 4, 1953, sec. 4, p. 5. Herbert H. Lehman to Mrs. Agnes Meyer, July 12, 1954, Special File, Lehman Papers.

48 Earl Mazo, Richard Nixon: A Political and Personal Portrait, rev. ed. (New York, 1959), pp. 132–33; Richard H. Rovere, Senator Joe McCarthy (New York, 1959), p. 187; New York Times, Dec. 11, 1952, p. 27.

for Senate scrutiny, he was once again talking about graft and influence peddling, a carrot he would dangle every now and then before the hopeful eyes of the White House. But almost in the same breath he reaffirmed his determination to continue "his" battle. "No . . . No one can push me out of anything. . . . We have complete jurisdiction of the anti-Communist fight. . . . I'm not retiring from the field of exposing Communists."[49]

Behind the scenes McCarthy was waging an aggressive procedural fight for jurisdiction over the magnetic issue of communism-in-government. By seniority he could have become chairman of the powerful Senate Appropriations Subcommittee which passed on State Department funds. This would have given him an opportunity to make good on his now forgotten charge that there were "57" or "81" or "205" Communists in the State Department and to harass further that agency. Instead, he chose the chairmanship of the Committee on Government Operations.[50]

The Committee on Government Operations (formerly the Committee on Expenditures in the Executive Departments) was by definition a minor committee, but it had a Permanent Subcommittee on Investigations with wide discretionary authority to investigate "the operations of Government activities at all levels." Created by the Legislative Reorganization Act of 1946, the subcommittee was essentially a watchdog agency whose traditional function had been oversight of administrative procedures and organization. There were some precedents for inquiries such as McCarthy envisioned, however. In 1948 Homer Ferguson had chaired an investigation of "Export Policy and Loyalty" in which the star witness was Elizabeth Bentley, and in 1950 Democratic Senator Clyde R. Hoey had conducted a brief study on the employment of "homosexuals and other sex perverts" in government.[51]

McCarthy had far more ambitious plans, and in late 1952 he began throwing out feelers and claims to jurisdiction in all fields. He initially proposed dividing the committee into three separate subcommittees, each chaired by a veteran Republican investigator

[49] New York Times, Jan. 26, 1953, p. 8; Jan. 30, 1953, p. 7; Feb. 15, 1953, sec. 4, p. 2.
[50] Ibid., Nov. 21, 1952, p. 14.
[51] U. S., Congress, Senate, 80th Cong., 2d sess., Committee on Expenditures in the Executive Department, Export Policy and Loyalty (Washington, D. C., 1948); ibid., 81st Cong., 2d sess., Employment of Homosexuals and Other Sex Perverts in Government, Interim Report (Washington, D. C., 1950).

and among them possessing almost unlimited jurisdiction.[52] One of these subcommittees, he indicated, would direct its energies toward investigating "communism in government." He also tried to subvert the subcommittee's chief rival to jurisdiction over the Communist issue by hiring Robert Morris and the other staff members of the old McCarran Internal Security Subcommittee.[53] William Langer, now chairman of the parent Judiciary Committee, fought back against McCarthy's encroachments. He announced that the Internal Security Subcommittee would be reconstituted under Homer Ferguson, and he denied McCarthy's sweeping jurisdictional claims. The hapless Ferguson, who had also been offered a subcommittee chairmanship by McCarthy, was caught in a struggle between the two Republican chairmen, both of whom were using him as a pawn in a larger battle over committee jurisdiction.[54]

The Republican leadership supported Langer in rejecting McCarthy's claims, although they did assign the chairmanship of the Internal Security Subcommittee to William Jenner. Jenner was an ardent McCarthyite, but he was far more amenable to party discipline than was McCarthy. He could be trusted to pummel the Democrats without embarrassing the Republicans as well. As a result, the serious work of ferreting out the skeletons of the 1930s and 1940s was conducted by the "Jenner Committee," and the president, who in 1952 had felt only disgust and repulsion for Jenner, was now only too glad to cooperate.[55] The Republican leadership hoped that this decision would preclude McCarthy from the one issue with which he had been able to hit the headlines

[52] The proposed subcommittee chairmen were to be Karl Mundt, a veteran of HUAC, John J. Williams, a conservative Delaware Republican who had already shown a talent for tracking down Democratic scandals, and McCarthy himself. *New York Times*, Nov. 21, 1952, p. 14. Williams demurred. "He doesn't dislike Joe, (he) just doesn't want to get too close," declared newsman Clark R. Mollenhoff. Mollenhoff to James S. Pope, Dec. 4, 1952, box 1, Clark R. Mollenhoff Papers, Manuscripts Division, State Historical Society of Wisconsin. Williams later told William Benton of McCarthy, "I despise him." Benton to John Howe, April 27, 1955, box 4, Benton Papers.

[53] *New York Times*, Nov. 21, 1952, p. 14; Dec. 11, 1952, p. 27; Jan. 4, 1953, sec. 4, p. 5; Jan. 6, 1953, p. 3.

[54] Ibid., Jan. 6, 1953, p. 3.

[55] On July 30, 1953, the Jenner subcommittee issued its report on "Interlocking Subversion in Government Departments." The report was widely circulated by the Republican National Committee and by Texas oilman H. L. Hunt. *Congress and the Nation*, (Washington, D.C., 1965), p. 1715.

day after day. "We've got McCarthy where he can't do any harm," boasted Majority Leader Taft.[56] Such self-congratulation was, to say the least, premature. McCarthy had failed of his declared goal of winning "exclusive jurisdiction" over the Communist issue and had even entered into an agreement with Jenner acknowledging the Internal Security Subcommittee's primary authority in this field, but he had won for his own committee a tentative role investigating "Communists" and had covered his retreat so well that few observers even noticed it.[57]

Having wrung from the Senate a grudging part in the "investigation" of communism, the senator quickly pressed a wide variety of demands on the incoming Republican administration. He requested, and was speedily granted, access to all "Federal income tax returns and other related documents" in the files of the Bureau of Internal Revenue.[58] The authorization was normal enough; such power had been granted to several congressional committees during the previous Congress, including the Committee on Expenditures in the Executive Departments and the Subcommittee on Privileges and Elections which was investigating McCarthy.[59] In McCarthy's hands, however, even the routine became explosive. By 1954 it was widely charged (without denial) that McCarthy had made photostats of the tax returns of all important government officials.[60] He also demanded access to the classified files of the Federal Communications Commission, and if this indicates a general pattern, then it is probable that the senator was casting his investigative nets exceedingly wide.[61]

The Committee on Government Operations and its "investigations subcommittee" gave McCarthy a nearly impregnable political

[56] Quoted in Rovere, *Senator Joe McCarthy,* p. 188.

[57] The *New York Times,* for example, ran a story almost certainly based on a McCarthy handout, entitled "McCarthy To Share Red Investigation." *New York Times,* Jan. 8, 1953, p. 16.

[58] McCarthy to Eisenhower, Jan. 21, 1953; Secretary of Treasury George M. Humphrey to Eisenhower, Feb. 3, 1953, in OF 148-B, Eisenhower Papers. Executive Order 10435 authorizing access to the files was issued on Feb. 7, 1953. *Code of Federal Regulations, Title 3, The President, 1949–1953* (Washington, D. C., 1958), p. 929.

[59] *Code of Federal Regulations,* pp. 832–33, 848–49, 851; Memorandum, Charles S. Murphy to Thomas Lynch [c. early 1952], OF 252-U, Truman Papers.

[60] *New York Times,* July 16, 1954, p. 6; William Benton to John Howe, July 28, 1954, box 4, Benton Papers.

[61] Memorandum, Charles Willis to Bernard M. Shanley, April 22, 1953, OF 103-P, Eisenhower Papers.

base from which to operate. Within the Senate the balkanization of power makes almost every committee chairman a law unto himself. Majority Leader Taft tried to insist that all investigations be cleared through the party leadership, but he was almost powerless to enforce this demand in McCarthy's case. The Wisconsin senator was simply not amenable to the informal restraints upon which party leadership depends; the only formal control (which Taft was certainly not disposed to use) was committee appropriations, which in turn meant going through the Senate Rules Committee, now chaired by William Jenner.[62]

Minority Leader Johnson, in his own cautious way, tried to counterbalance McCarthy's power by adding to his committee three newly elected Democrats, W. Stuart Symington of Missouri, Henry M. Jackson of Washington, and John F. Kennedy of Massachusetts. Each of these young, aggressive senators had ousted a Republican incumbent in the 1952 election, and none would face the voters again until 1958. Each had impressive credentials. Symington had served as secretary of the air force under the Truman administration. Jackson was a veteran of the House of Representatives who had defeated McCarthy supporter Harry P. Cain by over 134,000 votes. Kennedy had ousted Eisenhower's campaign manager, Henry Cabot Lodge.[63] Still, they were poorly equipped to deal with the strong-minded McCarthy, who for the first six months of the new Congress very much ran his own show.

[62] *New York Times*, Jan. 1, 1953, p. 40; Jan. 4, 1953, sec. 4, p. 5; Jan. 18, 1953, sec. 4, p. 4.

[63] The relationship between McCarthy and the late president remains shrouded in legend. In 1950 Kennedy reportedly told a group of Harvard students that he "knew Joe pretty well, and he may have something." Ambassador Joseph P. Kennedy was a warm devotee of McCarthy, and the senator visited the family at Hyannis Port. The persistent story that McCarthy received $50,000 from the ambassador to stay out of Massachusetts in 1952 is not impossible, but rests only on the testimony of Westbrook Pegler. The editor of the nominally Democratic but strongly pro-McCarthy *Boston Post* endorsed Kennedy in the election, and in early 1953 the senator's younger brother, Robert, became assistant counsel to the Permanent Investigations Subcommittee. Senator Kennedy never spoke out against McCarthy, though he voted rather consistently against him in the Senate. According to Theodore Sorenson, Kennedy prepared a speech favoring censure for delivery on July 31, 1954, but did not deliver it because the issue was turned over to the Watkins Committee. When the censure vote did come, Kennedy was hospitalized. John P. Mallan, "Massachusetts: Liberal and Corrupt," *New Republic* 127 (Oct. 13, 1952): 10–12; Westbrook Pegler, *New York Journal-American*, Dec. 9, 1960; Theodore C. Sorenson, *Kennedy* (New York, 1965), pp. 34–35, 45–49; Arthur M. Schlesinger, Jr., *A Thousand Days: John F. Kennedy in the White House* (Boston, 1965), pp. 12–13, 693.

The powers of committee chairmen are formidable, and Mc-Carthy exercised these powers to their limit. He assumed the chairmanship of the Permanent Investigations Subcommittee and filled it with close supporters—Everett M. Dirksen of Illinois, Karl E. Mundt of South Dakota, and Charles E. Potter of Michigan. The Democrats included John L. McClellan, a powerful Arkansas conservative, Henry Jackson, and Stuart Symington. But neither Republicans nor Democrats were able to restrain their impetuous chairman.

The "McCarthy subcommittee" met at its chairman's call. Both Democrats and Republicans often learned of a new investigation less than twenty-four hours before the hearings began. On some occasions they did not find out at all; the chairman controlled the subcommittee's investigative agenda, and senators and witnesses alike were often summoned to the committee's hearing room with only the barest knowledge of why they were there.[64] The chairman controlled the subcommittee's staff; he hired as chief counsel Roy M. Cohn, a bright and abrasive young graduate of Columbia Law School who had already won a wide reputation for work on various internal security cases. Thus in addition to the informal man-hours contributed by *Chicago Tribune* reporters, Hearst sleuths, and other members of the "McCarthy lobby," and the compliant help of Executive Department officers at all levels, McCarthy now had the technical assistance of a large and industrious committee staff. As a result the senator had at his command a type of expertise in the "Communist issue" which made him all the more formidable; and he wasted little time in exploiting these newly won advantages.

THE INVESTIGATOR

Joe McCarthy's reputation as a grand inquisitor rests almost entirely on the tumultuous events of 1953. Both before and following that memorable year the senator was more often than not the object of investigation. In early 1953, however, Republican inquisitors all across Capitol Hill were preparing their exposés, and McCarthy's subcommittee quickly captured the nation's attention by hurrying from one "startling revelation" to another. By its own count, the

[64] On this point see John Howe to William Benton, Feb. 2, 1954, box 4, Benton Papers.

subcommittee initiated 445 "preliminary inquiries" and 157 "investigations." Seventeen of these investigations reached the stage of public hearings, most of them conducted by McCarthy himself. Congressional security "investigations" are, of course, fundamentally different from the operations of security services; this was especially true of the McCarthy subcommittee. Cohn, McCarthy, and company conducted their inquests into subjects long explored by the FBI and other security agencies and often well known to key congressional personnel. The senator's declared purpose was to "expose Communists." His unstated objective was to garner publicity and to reaffirm the myth of "Joe McCarthy's fight against communism."

His first target, now rapidly becoming his favorite, was the State Department. The new secretary of state, John Foster Dulles, had hardly settled in when McCarthy embarked on a whirlwind investigation of the department's loyalty and security files. He called before his committee a number of disgruntled file clerks who agreed that the files were in a "deplorable" mess and who hinted that a dark conspiracy lay at the bottom of it all.[65] In mid-February he turned upon the department's information program—first the Voice of America and then the overseas information program.

The Voice of America had been under close congressional scrutiny since the late 1940s. Jurisdiction over the Voice usually fell to a subcommittee of the Senate Foreign Relations Committee.[66] Still, it was a vulnerable target. Powerful Republican leaders were convinced it was filled with "Communists, left-wingers, New Dealers, radicals and pinkos," and McCarthy simply could not let it pass by unexploited.[67] For a month and a half he conducted a caricature of an investigation, weaving from the petty gossiping

[65] U. S. Congress, Senate, 83d Cong., 1st sess., Committee on Government Operations, Permanent Subcommittee on Investigations, State Department—Files Survey (Washington, D. C., 1953); New York Times, Feb. 5, 1953, p. 6; Feb. 7, 1953, p. 6; Feb. 15, 1953, p. 26; Feb. 17, 1953, p. 18.

[66] In fact, Senator Bourke B. Hickenlooper directed a balanced survey of the entire information program during this very period. His report was generally favorable to the program. Washington Post, Feb. 4, 1954.

[67] Martin Merson, The Private Diary of a Public Servant (New York, 1955), p. 38; New York Times, March 16, 1953, p. 1; John Taber to Eisenhower, May 13, 1953, OF 8-D, Eisenhower Papers. There was some discussion within the administration as to liquidating the Voice altogether. See C. D. Jackson to John Foster Dulles, Feb. 19, 1953, OF 8-D-2, Eisenhower Papers.

of department bureaucrats a fanciful tale of conspiracy and intrigue designed to titillate the press and capture still more publicity. In two reports filed in early 1954 (when the question of funds for the committee was again before the Senate) the subcommittee accused the Voice of waste and mismanagement in its engineering projects and of harboring employees who were not "dedicated to the American way of life."[68]

The senator and his aides then turned upon the State Department's overseas information libraries. At point was another pseudo-issue of McCarthy's creation, the presence of books by "Communists, fellow-traverels, et cetera" in American libraries abroad.[69] In April Roy Cohn and his young friend, G. David Schine, the subcommittee's unpaid "chief consulant," took off on a whirlwind tour of American information centers—forty hours in Paris, sixteen in Bonn, twenty-three in Belgrade, six in London. The two brash young men left Americans abroad alternately laughing and grinding their teeth. "My recent trip through Europe was extremely interesting," wrote Schine solemnly to presidential assistant Charles F. Willis, "and much of what was uncovered will be brought out in hearings during the next several weeks."[70] This new investigation allowed McCarthy even greater latitude than before, and he called before the subcommittee a long list of writers whose books and articles supposedly were found in the overseas libraries. Some were or had been Communists; others patently were not. But their appearance before the subcommittee created the anticipated tumult and shouting.[71]

In at least one instance the hearings were used to settle an old score by McCarthy and some of his entourage from the Hearst Corporation. They called before the subcommittee James A. Wechsler, the editor of the liberal New York Post, and one of

[68] Congress and the Nation, p. 171.

[69] The language is that of State Department Information Guide 272, drafted under pressure from McCarthy and sent to the field on Feb. 19, 1953. Merson, Private Diary, p. 14.

[70] G. David Schine to Charles F. Willis, Jr., May 15, 1953, OF 99-P, Eisenhower Papers; Ray M. Hudson, Paris, to Senator Ralph Flanders, April 23, 1953, box 1, Flanders Papers, State Historical Society of Wisconsin.

[71] U. S., Congress, Senate, 81st Cong., 1st sess., Committee on Government Operations, Permanent Subcommittee on Investigations, State Department Information Centers (Washington, D. C., 1953); New York Times, March 25, 1952, p. 1; March 26, 1953, p. 9; March 27, 1952, p. 9; March 28, 1953, p. 1; April 2, 1953, p. 16; April 3, 1953, p. 10.

McCarthy's most frequent critics. Wechsler had joined the Young Communist League in the mid-1930s, while a student at Columbia University. He had left the party in 1937, age twenty-two, following the Moscow trials, and later became a distinguished and influential journalist. Ostensibly he was hailed before the subcommittee to be questioned about a book he had written which was found in an overseas library. But in two days of hearings the subcommittee never indicated which of Wechsler's four books was in question, a point of some importance, since two had been written while he was a Communist and two sometime later. McCarthy later told reporters that the book was *Labor Baron*, a critical biography of John L. Lewis which Wechsler had written well after he had left the party, but Roy Cohn denied even this.[72]

As always there was no rancor, no anger, not even personal animus in McCarthy's cross-examination. It was a performance played to a giant and invisible audience waiting somewhere at the end of the wire services. McCarthy himself seemed to sense subconsciously the hollowness of his charges, for there was an ambivalence in his language which was remarkable even by congressional standards. "You see your books, *some of them*, were paid for by taxpayer's money. They are being used, *allegedly*, to fight communism. Your record, *as far as I can see it*, has not been to fight communism. You have fought every man who has ever tried to fight communism, *as far as I know*. Your paper, *in my opinion, is next to and almost paralleling the Daily Worker*."[73] And yet he drove ahead, circling the editor in a "ring of fantasy," suggesting his break with the party was "phony" and that Communist criticism of the editor was inspired perchance by Wechsler himself.[74]

The State Department, like some wounded prehistoric animal, aroused itself first in puzzlement and then in panic. Between

[72] James A. Wechsler, *The Age of Suspicion* (New York, 1953), pp. 3–10, 309.

[73] Quoted in ibid., p. 277. Emphasis added.

[74] The chairman of the American Society of Newspaper Editors (ASNE) appointed a special committee to study the Wechsler hearings, but the group was unable to reach a unanimous conclusion as to whether the hearings had constituted a "clear and present danger to freedom of the press." When four members of the committee released a report condemning McCarthy's actions, the senator counterattacked by demanding that the ASNE investigate the group's chairman, J. R. Wiggins of the *Washington Post*. *New York Times*, Aug. 13, 1953, p. 23; Aug. 16, 1953, p. 51.

February and June there was a steady stream of directives and counterdirectives on book policy in library centers across the world. Books were removed, replaced, and even in some instances burned. Among the volumes whisked from library shelves were books by Joseph E. Davies, former ambassador to the Soviet Union; by Bert Andrews, head of the Washington Bureau of the Republican *New York Herald-Tribune;* and by Foster Rhea Dulles, cousin of the secretary of state.[75] At last even Eisenhower was compelled to acknowledge the mess which McCarthy had precipitated, and in an impromptu statement made during a commencement address at Dartmouth College the president warned Americans not to "join the book burners," but to explore every thought on its own merits.[76]

During the summer of 1953 McCarthy thrashed about for new targets. He held a one-day hearing on a bogus "plot" to assassinate him. He told reporters that he intended to subpoena former President Truman to testify about a supersecret list of spy suspects which he charged the Democrats had suppressed. In mid-July, after he was thrown onto the defensive in a rough procedural battle over control of the subcommittee staff, he countered with a series of sensational proposals to investigate the Atomic Energy Commission, the Central Intelligence Agency, and the military establishment.[77]

In August, after the Congress had recessed and while most of the members were resting and mending political fences, McCarthy plunged ahead into yet another investigation. This time his target was a suspiciously pink bookbinder in the Government Printing Office.[78] The GPO, of course, was not an executive agency but a subsidiary of Congress itself. Jurisdiction over it belonged to the Joint Committee on Printing, headed by McCarthy's fellow in-

[75] Merson, *Private Diary,* pp. 14–15; *New York Times,* June 22, 1953, pp. 1, 8; Joseph Alsop, *Washington Post,* June 14, 1953.

[76] *New York Times,* June 15, 1953, p. 1. The problem was discussed at length at cabinet meetings on June 26 and July 10; Donovan, *Eisenhower,* pp. 92–93; John Foster Dulles, Memorandum for the President, June 27, 1953; Eisenhower to Senator William Benton, July 13, 1953, both in OF 8-D, Eisenhower Papers.

[77] *New York Times,* July 10, 1953, p. 1; Aug. 11, 1953, p. 12.

[78] U. S., Congress, Senate, 83d Cong., 1st sess., Committee on Government Operations, Permanent Subcommittee on Investigations, *Security–Government Printing Office* (Washington, D. C., 1953). The chief witness was a veteran of an HUAC investigation in 1951.

vestigator, William E. Jenner. The inquiry produced no hard facts not already known to the FBI and other security agencies, but this hardly mattered. The objective was publicity, and this the investigation achieved.

By the autumn of 1953, however, McCarthy's showmanship was wearing thin. The frenetic and desperate quality of his activities was becoming more apparent. The Democrats had walked off his subcommittee in late July, and even his closest supporters on the Republican side were increasingly anxious to disassociate themselves from his investigations. Still he pressed on ("He always raises on the poor hands . . ."), driven by some distorted picture of himself and unable to release the whirling merry-go-round of politics and publicity.

In September he began a broad and unrelated series of "one man" investigations into the army and the Defense Department. First it was civilian personnel—a clerk in the purchasing department, a man working for the quartermaster corps, a security guard. McCarthy would quiz them in private, then hurry outside to give the waiting newsmen a breathless version of what had taken place in the hearing room. Then the senator followed his "leads" up the bureaucratic ladder—first demanding the personnel files of those whom he had questioned, then demanding the names of those who were responsible for giving them clearance.[79]

On September 9, the senator quickly changed his tack, releasing photographic copies of a restricted army intelligence document entitled *Psychological and Cultural Traits of Soviet Siberia,* which he charged contained pro-Communist propaganda. He brought Louis Budenz before the subcommittee to testify that the publication was indeed slanted, and that, most damning of all, it contained in its bibliography several volumes by writers Budenz "knew" to be Communists. McCarthy then berated the army's chief intelligence officer (G-2), Major General Richard C. Partridge, as "completely incompetent" for his job.[80]

[79] Part of these hearings are reprinted in U. S., Congress, Senate, 83d Cong., 1st sess., Committee on Government Operations, Permanent Subcommittee on Investigations, *Communist Infiltration among Army Civilian Workers* (Washington, D. C., 1953). *New York Times,* Sept. 1, 1953, p. 9; Sept. 2, 1953, p. 4; Sept. 3, 1953, p. 13; Sept. 4, 1953, p. 8; Sept. 5, 1953, p. 7; Sept. 8, 1953, p. 5; Sept. 9, 1953, p. 1.

[80] U. S., Congress, Senate, 83d Cong., 1st sess., Committee on Government Operations, Subcommittee on Permanent Investigations, *Communist In-*

On September 29 McCarthy married his onetime research assistant and longtime girl friend, Jean Kerr. It was a gala affair, even by Washington standards, and afterwards the couple hurried off to a vacation retreat. But the magnetic lure of the hearing room drew him back, and he cut short his honeymoon for yet another investigation, this time of civilian scientists employed by the Army Signal Corps Engineering Laboratories at Fort Monmouth, New Jersey.

Like almost all of McCarthy's "investigations," the facts behind the Monmouth case were old and dusty, arising from charges and accusations dating back to 1946 and all well known to military intelligence and the FBI. The House Committee on Un-American Activities had sniffed about the Monmouth premises in 1952, and finding nothing spectacular had let the matter drop.[81] Joe McCarthy, however, had a talent with unpromising materials and he quickly turned the Monmouth investigation into a showy and farcical spectacular. The hearings were held in executive session, and as before, the senator would hurry outside after each session to give the press his version of what had happened. Though the hearings themselves produced little, the senator's impromptu briefings continued to feed the press. There was an "extremely dangerous espionage" situation which might envelop the entire Signal Corps, he told reporters. A wartime spy ring set up by Julius Rosenberg was still in operation. There was perhaps a link to Alger Hiss. Or, an important witness "broke down and agreed to tell all he knew about spy rings."[82]

---

filtration in the Army (Washington, D. C., 1953), p. 105; *New York Times,* Sept. 10, 1953, p. 9; Sept. 12, 1953, p. 1; Sept. 22, 1953, p. 29; Sept. 24, 1953, p. 1; Sept. 29, 1953, p. 20.

Roy Cohn, who tried half-heartedly to sidetrack the general's appearance, warned Secretary of the Army Robert T. Stevens that once the hearings began, it would be difficult to keep them from turning into a spectacle. "You might want a nice gentle fight, but once you get in the ring and start taking a couple of pokes, it gets under your skin." Transcript of telephone conversation, Sept. 23, 1954, in U. S., Congress, Senate, 83d Cong., 2d sess., Committee on Government Operations, Permanent Subcommittee on Investigations, *Special Senate Investigation on Charges and Countercharges Involving: Secretary of the Army Robert T. Stevens, John G. Adams, H. Struve Hensel and Senator Joe McCarthy, Roy M. Cohn, and Francis P. Carr* (Washington, D. C., 1954). Hereafter cited as *Army-McCarthy Hearings.*

[81] *Washington Post,* Jan. 2, 1953; *New York Times,* Jan. 22, 1952, p. 9; Jan. 30, 1953, p. 7.

[82] *New York Times,* Oct. 13, 1953, p. 10; Oct. 16, 1953, p. 1; Oct. 17, 1953, p. 1; Oct. 27, 1953, p. 18. The testimony taken by McCarthy in

In November McCarthy veered briefly into an investigation of "subversion and espionage" in defense plants, calling before his subcommittee members of the United Electrical, Radio and Machine Workers Union, a Communist-led union which had long been a target of congressional investigators and had been expelled from the CIO in 1949.[83] In December he again returned to the Monmouth investigation for two more weeks of testimony and headlines. But as both the Monmouth and the Defense probes spilled over into 1954, the long-delayed confrontation between McCarthy and the administration rapidly approached. The way in which it came about, however, could hardly have been anticipated.

Throughout 1953 it was becoming increasingly obvious that a collision between the Wisconsin senator and the administration was inevitable. The skirmishes over the Bohlen nomination and the Greek ships gave way during the summer of 1953 to more ominous bumpings. An open break came perilously close in November 1953, after Attorney General Herbert Brownell charged that former President Truman had nominated Harry Dexter White as executive director of the International Monetary Fund at a time when the White House had in its possession detailed FBI reports alleging that White had been engaged in Soviet espionage activities.[84] Truman lashed back at the administration for embracing "McCarthyism," and McCarthy, picking up his cue, demanded that he be allowed free television time to reply. As before,

---

executive session does *not* appear in U. S., Congress, Senate, 83d Cong., 1st and 2d sess., Committee on Government Operations, Permanent Subcommittee on Investigations, *Army Signal Corps—Subversion and Espionage* (Washington, D. C., 1954). For an evaluation of the facts behind the Fort Monmouth investigation, see Scientists Committee on Loyalty and Security, Federation of American Scientists, "Fort Monmouth: The Scientists Examine the Investigation" (mimeographed report released in New Haven, Conn., 1954); and "Fort Monmouth One Year Later," *Bulletin of the Atomic Scientists* 11 (April 1955): 148.

[83] U. S., Congress, 83d Cong., 1st and 2d sess., Committee on Government Operations, Permanent Subcommittee on Investigations, *Subversion and Espionage in Defense Establishments and Industry* (Washington, D. C., 1954); *New York Times*, Nov. 13, 1953, p. 10; Nov. 14, 1953, p. 8; Nov. 18, 1953, p. 18; Nov. 20, 1953, p. 1; Nov. 25, 1953, p. 4.

[84] From the timing, immediately after Republican defeats in New Jersey and immediately before an off-year election in California, it would appear that the speech represented an attempt by the administration to regain the initiative on the Communist issue. Brownell had told the president that his attack "would take away some of the glamour from the McCarthy stage play." Adams, *Firsthand Report*, p. 137. Also see the remarks of Republican National Chairman Leonard W. Hall in the *New York Times*, Nov. 16, 1953, p. 1.

the networks gave in without protest. McCarthy's "reply," however, turned out to be not so much an attack on Truman as on
Eisenhower. He criticized the administration for allowing the
continuation of a "blood trade" between American allies and Red
China, and for its failure to dismiss John Paton Davies, a foreign
service officer who had long been under attack by McCarthy. To
Eisenhower's recently expressed hope that the Communist issue
would play no role in the 1954 election McCarthy replied, "The
raw, harsh, unpleasant fact is that communism is an issue and will
be an issue in 1954." An Eisenhower aide described the speech
as "a declaration of war against the President."[85]

Eisenhower still refused to accept McCarthy's challenge, however,[86] and the Republican pacificators in both the White House
and the Senate continued their ministry between president and
senator. In late 1953 McCarthy met with Vice President Nixon
and Deputy Attorney General William P. Rogers in Miami, where
Nixon was vacationing. The meeting was cordial. McCarthy, before leaving Miami, told a news conference that he planned to
broaden his investigations to include tax cases which had been
compromised "at ridiculously low figures." Back in Washington,
Nixon told reporters off-the-record that McCarthy planned a new
role for his subcommittee. McCarthy rejected the report as false,
but with his committee's appropriation once again before the
Senate, he continued to foster the illusion that he might lay off
both the administration and the Communist issue.[87] But the
euphoria of early 1954 was short-lived, and by the middle of
February the administration and the Senate were facing a major
crisis.

[85] *New York Times*, Nov. 25, 1953, pp. 1, 5; Nov. 26, 1953, p. 1.
[86] Eisenhower angrily refused to blast back at McCarthy. "I will not get in
the gutter with that guy," he told C. D. Jackson when the latter proposed a
strong attack on the senator. Donovan, *Eisenhower*, p. 249. For Jackson's
proposed attack, see the draft of a statement notated "C. D. Jackson, 12-2-53,"
in OF 3-A, Eisenhower Papers. Also see Stanley M. Rumbough, Jr., and
Charles Masterson, Memorandum to Murray Snyder, Dec. 1, 1953, OF 99-R,
Eisenhower Papers.
[87] *New York Times*, Dec. 31, 1953, p. 4; Jan. 6, 1954, p. 1; Jan. 7, 1954,
p. 10; Jan. 9, 1954, p. 6; Mazo, *Richard Nixon*, pp. 147–48.

7

THE
OPPOSITION

THE WINTER OF 1952-1953 WAS a time of ripe despair for most American liberals. McCarthy's victory in Wisconsin shattered the last hopes that the voters of that state might repudiate their junior senator, and the collapse of the Senate drive to seat him "without prejudice" confirmed his continued power in the Upper Chamber. A few of the new president's more moderate supporters still hoped that the election of a Republican chief executive would somehow exorcise "McCarthyism," but the White House itself was diligently working to get the Wisconsin senator onto the Eisenhower "team."

In the Senate itself there was little sign of opposition. "They realize what kind of a person he is, but they don't believe much can be done about him," declared one Democratic staff member. "You hear practically no discussions of him in the bull sessions around the Hill. They are watching his current investigations, I am sure, but he has to go much further than he is currently going before they will do much to oppose him."[1] Only a handful of senators challenged McCarthy's growing power within the Senate, and in the absence of substantial support from their colleagues, their challenge was largely ineffectual.

The most outspoken of McCarthy's Senate antagonists was New York's Herbert H. Lehman. During the last years of the Truman administration Lehman had been, together with William Benton, McCarthy's most frequent critic. In the Republican Eighty-third Congress he stood almost alone among those whose opposition to McCarthy was both persistent and public. "I cannot condone or ignore the disregard for the standards of public office; the privileged, irresponsible tirades against many patriotic and devoted public servants; the distraction of the executive, the Congress and much of the country from its proper business," he wrote in a long and angry letter to Judge Albert Cohn, father of Roy Cohn, McCarthy's chief staff assistant. Time and again Lehman spoke out against what he called "Creeping McCarthyism" and the "Strait Jacket of Fear" which threatened to destroy traditional rights and liberties.[2]

Most senators preferred to be more circumspect in their opposition. Some, like Mike Monroney and Guy Gillette, sought to restrain McCarthy through the administrative machinery of the Senate. Gillette introduced a resolution (Senate Resolution 65) tightening the Senate's control over appropriations for congressional investigations. The resolution was aimed directly at the McCarthy subcommittee, whose budget had been doubled by a $189,000 appropriation from the contingent fund of the Senate Monroney introduced a resolution (Senate Resolution 146) to empower the presiding officer of the Senate to dismiss an investigating committee from any investigation which he ruled, subject to appeal, was beyond its jurisdiction. By increasing the authority of the Senate body over its committees, the resolution would provide a means of restraining McCarthy's freewheeling investigatory

[1] Kenneth Birkhead to William Benton, [c. Feb. 1953], box 4, Benton Papers.
[2] Herbert Lehman to Albert Cohn, Aug. 1, 1953, Special File, Lehman Papers; Allan Nevins, *Herbert H. Lehman and His Era* (New York, 1963), pp. 332–51. Also see Morris H. Rubin to Lehman, July 23, 1953; Herman Edelsberg to Lehman, July 30, 1953, Washington Miscellaneous File, McCarthy and McCarthyism, drawer two, Lehman Papers. "Here in Wisconsin we are glad to know that there is at least one United States Senator who had the courage to stand up against the ugly evil of McCarthyism," wrote the *Capital-Times* (Madison) editor. "Frankly, those of us who have been making the fight here in Wisconsin have been disappointed in the liberal members of the United States Senate who should have spoken out long ago against this threat to the American way." William T. Evjue to Lehman, June 23, 1953, ibid.

forays.[3] Both the Gillette and Monroney resolutions were referred to William Jenner's Committee on Rules and Administration.

Other senators, led by Estes Kefauver, tried to check McCarthy by codifying the rules for congressional investigations. Kefauver reintroduced two resolutions which he had sponsored during the previous Congress. The first (Senate Resolution 10) provided for a uniform code for the conduct of congressional investigations; the second (Senate Resolution 11) sought to protect the rights of individuals before congressional committees. Wayne Morse and Herbert Lehman sponsored a similar resolution (Senate Resolution 83) establishing uniform rules to insure orderly and fair procedures by Senate committees, and Morse and eight other senators joined Kefauver as co-sponsors of Senate Resolution 10. All three resolutions were referred to the Rules Committee, which under Jenner's direction declined to consider them.[4]

Criticism of McCarthy from the Republican side of the Senate was even less frequent and usually more indirect. Charles Tobey sharply rebuked McCarthy in a television appearance during the Bohlen controversy. Ralph Flanders, Alexander Wiley, and John Sherman Cooper were all critical of the attacks made by McCarthy and others on British Labour party leader Clement Attlee. But for the most part Republicans, liberal and conservative alike, were in no mood to chastise their party's most controversial member. "I am not going to be forced into a position publicly critical of

[3] *Congresional Record,* 83d Cong., 1st sess., Feb. 6, 1953, p. 891; July 20, 1953, p. 9185; Guy Gillette to Theodore F. Green, Feb. 12, 1953, box 751, Green Papers; Memorandum, Tom Wheeler to William Benton and John Howe, July 31, 1953, box 4, Benton Papers.

[4] *Congressional Record,* 83d Cong., 1st sess., Feb. 10, 1953, p. 982; Feb. 20, 1953, p. 1327; April 1, 1953, p. 2605. Kefauver to William E. Jenner, June 16, 1953; Jenner to Kefauver, June 23, 1953; both in Subject File, Congressional 1, Kefauver Papers. Brooklyn Congressman Emanuel Celler proposed the establishment of a Joint Committee on Subversive Activities which would have preempted both McCarthy's Permanent Investigations Subcommittee and the House Committee on Un-American Activities from investigations of "subversion." Many liberals, however, were wary of creating any new investigating committee. *Congressional Record,* 83d Cong., 1st sess., May 15, 1953, p. 4954. Emanuel Celler to Theodore F. Green, May 25, 1953; Green to Celler, May 29, 1953, both in box 718, Green Papers. Celler to Thomas C. Hennings, May 25, 1953, box 30, Hennings Papers. Celler to Herbert H. Lehman, May 25, 1953; Lehman to Celler, June 10, 1953, both in Senate Legislative File, drawer 27, Lehman Papers. "Frankly, however, I'm not sure that the creation of a Joint Committee is the best answer to the problem." Lehman to Walton Butterfield, July 7, 1954, ibid., drawer 27.

McCarthy," declared one powerful Senate leader, banging his fist on the desk for emphasis.[5]

Thus the question remained: Who will bell the cat? Not the Democrats until the Republicans made their move. Not the Republicans while there was still party profit. And if not the Democrats and not the Republicans, then who? Perhaps there was no alternative but that reached by former President Truman, who concluded that the only way to beat McCarthy was to let him "run his course because he will destroy himself."[6]

AN ANTI-McCARTHY LOBBY

Against this discouraging background, a small group of political activists in and about Washington began in early 1953 a series of discussions aimed at rethinking the entire "McCarthy problem." From these meetings emerged a fresh analysis of "McCarthyism" and a new strategy for combating it.

Most of these meetings were initiated by an energetic Washington lobbyist named Maurice Rosenblatt and a small organization he had helped to found, the National Committee for an Effective Congress (NCEC). This group had been organized in 1948 to raise and distribute campaign funds to "men of caliber whose general outlook is liberal."[7] Though nonpartisan, its support of

[5] New York Times, March 23, 1953, p. 12; May 14, 1953, p. 8; May 15, 1953, p. 1; May 17, 1953, sec. 4, p. 1. William Benton to J. William Fulbright, March 28, 1953; Benton to Stuart Symington, March 28, 1953, both in box 4, Benton Papers. Ralph Flanders to Robert Sharp, May 18, 1953, box 1, Flanders Papers, State Historical Society of Wisconsin. E. W. Richardson to Alexander Wiley, May 25, 1953, Personal Correspondence, box g, Wiley Papers. Wiley was under intense attack from the isolationist and McCarthy-oriented leadership of the Wisconsin Republican party. See Wiley to Harold R. Wilde, April 23, 1953, Personal Correspondence, box f, and Wiley to Henry E. Ringling, July 6, 1953, Personal Correspondence, box g, both in the Wiley Papers. The powerful Republican Senate leader quoted by John B. Oakes was probably Robert Taft. "An Inquiry into McCarthy's Status," New York Times Magazine, April 12, 1953, p. 28.

[6] President Truman's remarks are reported in William Benton to John Howe, Nov. 3, 1953, box 4, Benton Papers.

[7] Congressional Quarterly Weekly Report 11 (March 6, 1953): 308–309. Recipients of the committee's support or endorsement included Democrats Paul H. Douglas, Hubert H. Humphrey, Estes Kefauver, Guy M. Gillette, James E. Murray, Matthew M. Neely, William Benton, Blair Moody, and Joseph C. O'Mahoney; and Republicans Charles W. Tobey, Ralph E. Flanders, John Sherman Cooper, and Frederick G. Payne. For a comprehensive dis-

liberal and internationalist candidates soon involved the NCEC in the savage political warfare of the early 1950s. In 1952 it helped organize the Harvard Civil Liberties Appeal, a fund-raising drive on behalf of Judge Thomas R. Fairchild, who was McCarthy's opponent in Wisconsin, Governor Henry F. Schricker, who was challenging Jenner in Indiana, and William Benton, who was running for reelection.[8]

Although the NCEC boasted the usual letterhead of prominent liberal personalities, it was essentially a staff organization, directed by Rosenblatt in Washington and George E. Agree in New York. Rosenblatt himself was a veteran political activist who had been involved in the McCarthy controversy from its beginning. In 1950 he had helped prepare Senator Dennis Chavez's widely publicized speech criticizing former Communist Louis Budenz. The following year he had provided research support for Senators Wayne Morse and Brien McMahon in their attacks on the "China lobby."[9] It was his enthusiasm and commitment which carried the NCEC into the fight against McCarthy in early 1953.

For Rosenblatt and his associates, the shadow of the Third Reich loomed ominously across America during these years. They saw in "McCarthyism" not simply anticommunism, but a "radical movement aimed at destroying the foundations, liberal and conservative, of our democratic society." "In our view," declared Gerhard Van Arkel, a prominent Washington lawyer and a member of the NCEC, "the parallel is close between present developments and those in Germany in the late 20's and early 30's. The German conservatives were, by and large, contemptuous of Hitler; yet . . . they tolerated, and to a degree cultivated him." Rosenblatt later recalled: "My own personal experience, and that of several of my associates, was in the pre-war fight combating the Coughlinite, pro-Franco, anti-Semitic, anti-intellectual, para-military forces that joined under the big tent of the America First Committee. Many elements that were so vociferous in that period appeared incarnate

---

cussion of the origins and activities of the NCEC, see Harry M. Scoble, *Ideology and Electoral Action: A Comparative Case Study of the National Committee for an Effective Congress* (San Francisco, 1967).

[8] George E. Agree, "Memorandum #1," [c. Sept. 1954], NCEC files. Scoble, *Ideology and Electoral Action*, pp. 103–104.

[9] Author's interview with Maurice Rosenblatt, June 13, 1966. Scoble, *Ideology and Electoral Action*, p. 32.

in Joe McCarthy."[10] Rosenblatt saw in William Bolithos's essay on Cataline a model for Joe McCarthy, and in Hannah Arendt's essay on Stalinism in *The Origins of Totalitarianism* an analysis of McCarthyism. The real tactical problem, he declared, was to juxtapose McCarthyism against "the majority elements of society which are its real targets, not the shadow targets it sets up" and to "make known to the conservative elements the real nature of the McCarthy attack."[11]

But if their analysis of McCarthyism was based on a worried reading of European history, their tactics and strategy were largely drawn from their day-to-day experience as political technicians in and around the nation's capital. They saw that much of McCarthy's power came not from active support, but from the lack of active and informed opposition within the Congress itself. The political balance which checkmated the Senate, the novelty of the issues of communism and loyalty in America's interest-group-oriented politics, the slow-moving internal procedures of the Senate itself, all created opportunities for McCarthy and his supporters. A case in point was internal security legislation. "To date all the liberals have done for the loyalty program is fight it and grumble," complained Rosenblatt. They should accept the fact that there was going to be legislation of some kind and draft a "good bill" of their own, rather than leave the field open to "totalitarians" like

[10] Maurice Rosenblatt, "The Clearing House," [c. Nov. 1953]; Gerhard Van Arkel to William Benton, Feb. 26, 1953; Rosenblatt to Harry M. Scoble, n.d. [1966], all in the NCEC files. Many liberals readily compared McCarthy with Hitler. "As I see it, all the ingredients which were present in Germany when Hitler began his rise to power are present in the United States. It CAN happen here." William T. Evjue to Herbert Lehman, June 23, 1953, Washington Miscellaneous File, McCarthy and McCarthyism, drawer two, Lehman Papers. "The time to have stopped Hitler was when he went into the Rhineland. There is a time to stop McCarthy." G. Bromley Oxnam to William Benton, March 11, 1954, box 5, Benton Papers.

[11] By McCarthy's "real targets," Rosenblatt meant "the Protestant Church, the Eastern universities, the Wall Street financial community, the CIA, the West Point professional soldiers." Maurice Rosenblatt, "The Clearing House," [c. Nov. 1953]; Rosenblatt to Gifford Phillips, Aug. 31, 1953, both in the NCEC files; interview with Rosenblatt, June 13, 1966. Memorandum, Rosenblatt to author, April 16, 1968. As Harry M. Scoble has pointed out in *Ideology and Electoral Action,* the NCEC's analysis of McCarthyism was identical with that popularized by Daniel Bell, David Riesman, and the other contributors to *The New American Right.* For a brilliant and provocative critique of this analysis see Michael Paul Rogin, *The Intellectuals and McCarthy: The Radical Specter* (Cambridge, Mass., 1967).

McCarran and McCarthy. Nor could McCarthy be fought at the invective level. The exposés and denunciations, the gossip about Joe's low morals, served in many instances only to inflate him further, to help him become identified as "the figure around whom you rally if you don't like communists, or selling atomic secrets, or perverts in Government, or even Stevenson and the Democrats." What was necessary was a tough, sustained, and yet unemotional fight within the Senate itself.[12]

At first Rosenblatt proposed a broad and ambitious program to preempt McCarthy's entire drive for power and publicity in the Senate—in essence an "anti-McCarthy lobby." Such a plan called for skilled "operators" and "technicians" ("You can't use hacks or fanatics to work the Hill."), men with entree to key senators and committee executives, researchers, press relations men, and all the other appurtenances of a large, modern lobby. Working through the Senate itself, they could help create positive centers of power and thus preclude McCarthy and his followers from such key areas as internal security, broadcasting, and education. Rosenblatt especially emphasized the necessity of providing senators, newsmen, and other Hill workers with the type of technical assistance which McCarthy received in abundance from the McCormick and Hearst organizations. Precisely because the Communist issue was unique in American politics, none of the traditional interests or ethnic groups were deeply involved in "operations" affecting it. This was a vacuum which Rosenblatt proposed to fill. "Can't liberals use the simple techniques of a god damned power company?" he demanded.[13]

In fact, nothing approaching this original program ever materialized. There was no money to finance it. Rosenblatt estimated that such an operation would cost $125,000. Liberal "money people" remained cautious and skeptical, however, and the very nature of the plan prevented a publicized fund drive.[14] But the discussions

[12] Maurice Rosenblatt, Memorandum to Robert R. Nathan, March 4, 1953; Rosenblatt to Gifford Phillips, Aug. 31, 1953, both in the NCEC files.

[13] Rosenblatt's plan is developed most fully in a detailed memorandum to Robert R. Nathan, then chairman of the executive committee of Americans for Democratic Action and a member of the National Committee for an Effective Congress. Rosenblatt to Nathan, March 4, 1953, NCEC files.

[14] Interview with Maurice Rosenblatt, June 13, 1966; Rosenblatt to Robert R. Nathan, March 4, 1953; George E. Agree, "Memorandum #1," [c. Sept. 1954], both in the NCEC files.

did generate the formation of a small group of Hill technicians, knowledgeable in the processes of Congress and determined at a minimum to collect and make available political intelligence on the McCarthy issue. With this technical function in mind, they called themselves the "Clearing House."

The membership of the Clearing House was fluid and constantly changing, but it centered about Rosenblatt and several other members of the NCEC; Kenneth Birkhead, the staff director of the Senate Democratic Campaign Committee; John Howe, a political aide to former Senator William Benton; and Gerhard Van Arkel, a member of the NCEC who had also served as Benton's attorney. Benton played an active though indirect role in the Clearing House through his political aides and through his many contacts with well-to-do sympathizers such as Marshall Field and Paul G. Hoffman who were willing to help finance Clearing House operations. Former Senator Millard Tydings also met with the group on occasion to plan and execute strategy.[15]

The Clearing House employed a full-time researcher, Lucille Lang, in June 1953 and set about consolidating an inclusive file on McCarthy and McCarthyism.[16] Jack Anderson and Ronald May contributed the voluminous notes and clippings they had collected while preparing their biography of McCarthy. Van Arkel turned over the material he had accumulated while working for Benton. Warren Woods, an attorney for Drew Pearson and on occasion a participant in the Clearing House, added the files he had gathered for the Pearson-McCarthy suit. The research center was first set up in downtown Washington, then later moved to the Hill, where Senator Earle C. Clements nervously agreed to provide room in the offices of the Democratic Senate Campaign Committee. From here Miss Lang was able to provide instantaneous research support to any senator or aide who requested it.[17] Beyond this the

[15] Maurice Rosenblatt, "The Clearing House," [c. Nov. 1953]; George E. Agree, "Memorandum #1," [c. Sept. 1954]; William Benton to Rosenblatt, March 9, 1953; Rosenblatt to Kenneth Birkhead, March 16, 1953, all in the NCEC files. Benton to John Howe, April 8, 1953, box 4; Agree to Benton, June 23, 1953, box 5, both in the Benton Papers.

[16] [Mrs.] Lucille Lang [Olshine] was a former assistant to Senator Blair Moody of Michigan. Marshall Field contributed $1,500 for the original undertaking, and the NCEC promised to pay Miss Lang's salary. See George Agree to William Benton, July 23, 1953, box 5, Benton Papers.

[17] George E. Agree, "Memorandum #1," [c. Sept. 1954]; "The Clearing House History," Memorandum, n.d., both in the NCEC files.

Clearing House could operate only sporadically whenever Mc-
Carthy overreached himself and offered a clear "target of opportunity." The Wisconsin senator presented such a target on
June 18, 1953, when he announced the appointment of a new
subcommittee staff director, Joseph Brown Matthews.

A TOUGH, KNOWING FIGHT

The Legislative Reorganization Act of 1946 provided that staff
members of congressional committees be appointed by a *majority
of the committee.* In fact, this power was usually exercised by
the committee chairman, sometimes by formal agreement, often
by tacit understanding. The chairman might, if he desired, confer
with the ranking member of the minority on questions of committee personnel; he might also earmark specific positions to be
filled by staff members responsible to the interests of the minority.
But these last provisions depended on the chairman's own tempera-
ment and desires and upon his responsiveness to Senate folkways.[18]
McCarthy had hired and fired with a free hand throughout early
1953, and the Democrats had acquiesced in his decisions.

McCarthy's choice of Matthews to head the committee staff,
however, was another matter. Matthews was another of those
disillusioned radicals who had abandoned the absolutes of the
far left only to embrace those of the far right. During the thirties
he had been active in dozens of Communist-front organizations
and was chairman of the American League against War and
Fascism. By 1938 he had renounced his old ties and become a star
witness before the Dies Committee. He served as the committee's
research director from 1938 to 1945, when he left the committee
to become a consultant for the Hearst Corporation. It was in this
capacity that he had first rushed to McCarthy's aid in March 1950,
when the senator was faced with the herculean job of finding some
sort of substantiation for his wild charges against the State Department.[19] Though Matthews himself had once been a Methodist
minister, he was one of the Protestant clergy's harshest critics.

[18] Donald Matthews, *U. S. Senators and Their World* (Chapel Hill, N. C.,
1960), p. 160; Kenneth Korfmehl, *Professional Staffs of Congress* (West
Lafayette, Ind., 1962), pp. 70–71.
[19] Murray Kempton, *Part of Our Time: Some Ruins and Monuments of the
Thirties* (New York, 1955), chapt. 5; Ralph Lord Roy, *Communism and the
Churches* (New York, 1960), pp. 249–51.

In 1935 he denounced them as "Partners in Plunder" with American business capitalism; after 1938 he attacked them for conspiring with the Kremlin. By coincidence he had only recently completed an article for the July 1953 issue of the *American Mercury* entitled "Reds and Our Churches." The first and operative sentence of the article declared, "The largest single group supporting the Communist apparatus in the United States today is composed of Protestant Clergymen."[20]

The appointment of Matthews to the McCarthy subcommittee was potentially explosive. Protestant clerics across the nation were resentful of the attacks made by Matthews and others, and the leaders of most of the major denominations were especially suspicious of McCarthy. Yet the Matthews appointment remained only a *potential* issue. Political disputes of this kind do not just happen; they are consciously shaped. The catalyst in this instance was the Clearing House.

Shortly after McCarthy announced the appointment, Lucille Lang prepared an extensive dossier on Matthews. The dossier was given to Senator Mike Monroney, a veteran opponent of McCarthy who had already expressed an interest in the Clearing House. Initially, Monroney planned to deliver a Senate speech on the appointment, but after the appearance of the article in the *American Mercury* the matter was taken directly to Senator John McClellan and the other Democratic members of the Permanent Subcommittee on Investigations. McClellan was so enraged by the article that he promptly assumed leadership of the group and insisted on an immediate showdown with McCarthy. On July 2, after an early-morning planning session, McClellan, Stuart Symington, and Henry Jackson marched into McCarthy's office and demanded that Matthews be fired. The chairman hedged, tried to put them off, and then finally refused. Both sides quickly issued press releases. The Democrats denounced the article as "a shocking and unwarranted attack against the American clergy" and demanded that the subcommittee meet at once "to consider appropriate action." McCarthy defended Matthews and declared that he had no intention of firing him.[21]

[20] J. B. Matthews, "Reds and Our Churches," *American Mercury* 453 (July 1953): 3–13; *New York Times*, July 3, 1953, p. 1.

[21] Press release (McClellan, Symington, and Jackson), July 2, 1953; press release (McCarthy), July 2, 1953, both in the NCEC files. John Howe to William Benton, July 10, 1953, box 4; George E. Agree to Benton, July 23,

Meanwhile, the members of the Clearing House alerted the press and a number of influential Protestant clergymen. By evening the story had broken on page one, and by the next day senators were already receiving calls and telegrams from concerned ministers across the nation. Through the Episcopal Bishop of Detroit, the Clearing House put pressure on Senator Charles E. Potter, a Republican member of the subcommittee, and the following day Potter announced that it was his "present" opinion that Matthews should not be retained.[22] Over the weekend, reaction to the appointment continued to mount. Officials of the National Council of Churches, the United Lutheran Church, the Southern Baptist Convention, and other prominent religious leaders denounced the new appointment, and on Sunday morning a number of ministers spoke directly to the issue from their pulpits.[23]

On Tuesday, July 7, the subcommittee met for an hour and a half of bitter debate. The Democrats, now joined by Potter, demanded that Matthews resign. Dirksen was absent and Mundt disappeared shortly after the meeting began, leaving McCarthy alone to defend his controversial appointment. The chairman refused to allow the issue to come to a vote by declaring that Matthews was a "non-professional" staff member and thus could be hired or fired at his discretion. The meeting finally broke off with both sides vowing to continue the fight.[24]

On July 8 McClellan, who had consulted with leading southern Democrats, again challenged McCarthy's interpretation of the Legislative Reorganization Act and declared that if necessary he would take the issue to the full Committee on Government Operations, or as a last expedient, to the Senate itself.[25] The following

1953, box 5, both in the Benton Papers; *Congressional Report,* 2 (July 22, 1953).

[22] *New York Times,* July 4, 1953, p. 1. John Howe to William Benton, July 10, 1953, box 4; George E. Agree to Benton, July 23, 1953, box 5; both in the Benton Papers.

[23] *New York Times,* July 5, 1953, p. 18; July 6, 1953, p. 1; Rt. Rev. William Horstick to Alexander Wiley, n.d., box 54, Wiley Papers.

[24] McCarthy's argument was spurious on two grounds. First of all Matthews, who would head the committee's staff at a salary of $11,600 per year, was manifestly a "professional" staff member. But the distinction was meaningless anyway because even clerical staff were subject to approval by the majority under the terms of the Legislative Reorganization Act of 1946.

[25] *New York Times,* July 9, 1953, p. 9. The Clearing House had worked out alternative strategies for a fight in the full committee or on the floor. John Howe to William Benton, July 10, 1953, box 4, Benton Papers.

morning McCarthy told the Senate that he would abide by the subcommittee's decision as to whether he had the power to hire and fire staff personnel. There were rumors that the Republicans had compromised their differences and that Potter had agreed to support a motion delegating McCarthy full powers to hire and fire in return for the removal of Matthews.[26]

Meanwhile, even the White House had stirred itself into action. On July 8 a handful of White House advisers, including speechwriter Emmet John Hughes, Vice President Nixon, and Deputy Attorney General William P. Rogers, arranged for a telegram protesting Matthews's attack on the clergy to be sent the president by three prominent leaders of the National Conference of Christians and Jews. On July 9 the telegram arrived at the White House, where a draft reply was already awaiting the president's signature. It denounced as "unjustifiable and deplorable" recent attacks on the American ministry. There then followed a frantic race between McCarthy, who had already decided to let Matthews go, and the White House, which wanted the credit, to see whose release would reach reporters first. The White House won. The president's letter was given to the press less than an hour before McCarthy reached reporters with his own handout.[27]

McCarthy's instinctive response to these combined attacks was diversion. On July 4, shortly after his first confrontation with the angry Democrats, he released a committee report on the long-finished investigation of the State Department filing system. On July 9, the same day he accepted Matthews's resignation and was denounced indirectly by the White House, he attacked Allen Dulles and called for a full-scale investigation of the CIA.[28]

The administration could have joined the issue at this point. It probably could have marshaled overwhelming Senate support against an investigation of the CIA. As it was, gentler counsels prevailed, and Nixon and the other conciliators went to work. On July 10 McCarthy and Dulles met in the senator's office, and afterwards they announced that the investigation would be "temporarily" postponed. On July 13 Mike Monroney made a blistering speech, challenging the Senate to take responsibility for

[26] *New York Times,* July 10, 1953, p. 1.

[27] Ibid., Eisenhower to Msgr. John A. O'Brien, Rabbi Maurice H. Eisendrath, and Rev. Dr. John Sutherland Bonnell, July 9, 1953, OF 133-E-1-A, Eisenhower Papers; Emmet John Hughes, *The Ordeal of Power: A Political Memoir of the Eisenhower Years* (New York, 1963), pp. 95–96.

[28] *New York Times,* July 5, 1953, p. 18; July 10, 1953, p. 1.

its investigating committees and denouncing the proposed CIA inquiry as a dangerous fraud. Although Monroney won the public praise of Republican John Sherman Cooper of Kentucky and the private support of Alexander Wiley of Wisconsin, the administration still preferred the soft line. Dulles and McCarthy met once more and this time announced that they planned to work out a formula whereby the Senate inquisitors could question CIA personnel.[29]

In the Senate events took a different turn. On July 10, the day following Matthews's resignation, the subcommittee met, and, as predicted, the Republicans passed a face-saving motion giving the chairman exclusive power to hire and fire staff personnel. Mc-Clellan listened quietly as the motion was made, then suggested that it lie over until the following week. McCarthy demanded an immediate vote, and after the motion carried on a straight party vote the angry Arkansas conservative led the Democrats out of the committee room in an unprecedented minority boycott.[30]

By the time the press began its postmortems of the incident, it was obvious that McCarthy had suffered a setback. He had been indirectly rebuked by the president and challenged by a majority of his own subcommittee. It was, as Murray Marder of the *Washington Post* declared, "the first major blow to McCarthy in his role as chairman of the Government Operations Committee and its Permanent Investigations Subcommittee."[31]

The real questions, however, involved the underlying meaning of the encounter. What did it reveal about McCarthy and the complex balance of political forces which supported him? What lessons and illustrations could be drawn from it? For the Clearing House it proved that McCarthy could be beaten, that the "myth of invincibility" was just that. It confirmed their belief in the importance of technical assistance in defining issues, and it showed that McCarthy could and indeed had to be fought within the Senate itself. "Not once was there an alarmed speech about a 'reign of terror,' nor the use of an elaborate apparatus to 'educate

[29] Ibid., July 11, 1953, p. 7; July 14, 1953, p. 1; July 15, 1953, p. 16; Earl Mazo, *Richard Nixon: A Political and Personal Portrait*, rev. ed. (New York, 1959), p. 146; *Congressional Report*, 2 (July 22, 1953).

[30] *New York Times*, July 11, 1953, p. 1; Doris Fleeson, *Evening Star* (Washington), July 15, 1953.

[31] Murray Marder, *Washington Post*, July 10, 1953; William S. White, *New York Times*, July 12, 1953, sec. 4, p. 3; Thomas L. Stokes, *Evening Star* (Washington), July 17, 1953.

the public.' It was a tough, knowing internal procedural battle over the firing of an employee of a subcommittee of a minor Senate committee."[32] The incident also produced a prophetic alignment of forces against McCarthy. The Democrats, led by conservative southerners, were solid in their opposition; the moderate Republicans, who were the third force both in the subcommittee and in the Senate as a whole, joined the issue; and the president openly arrayed himself against a powerful senator from his own party.

The encounter also demonstrated, however, that the time had not yet arrived for the Wisconsin senator's final defeat. Though the Democrats were now off the subcommittee and publicly committed against McCarthy, there remained many reservations. Some Democrats still worried that party fortunes might suffer from the appearance of a purely partisan attack and that a Democratic alignment against McCarthy would only strengthen him. "If he suddenly becomes a partisan issue," fretted ex-Senator Benton, "the Republicans may hesitate much longer before they attack him. Even the best of Republicans may stand by him for party reasons. This is the danger."[33] Senator Potter, after his brief show of independence, quickly scurried back under the McCarthy banner, and the last signs of moderate Republican opposition also disappeared. The White House too suffered a case of nerves. The conciliators held the upper hand, and the administration still preferred conferences and compromises to open warfare.

As for the junior senator from Wisconsin, he recovered quickly if not quite gracefully. After his threatened investigation of the CIA was "postponed," he plunged back into an on-again-off-again attack on the United States Information Agency and its retiring director, Robert L. Johnson. He accused an unnamed State Department official of conducting a $150,000 shakedown of a friendly Latin American government. He announced that he would *not* subpoena former President Truman, whom he had earlier accused of suppressing information on Soviet espionage, and he released two long overdue subcommittee reports. He had, as one reporter observed, adopted as his own the motto of the French revolutionary, Danton: "Audacity, more audacity, always audacity."[34] Or; in words with

---

[32] *Congressional Report*, 2 (July 22, 1953).

[33] William Benton to John Howe, July 20, 1953, box 4, Benton Papers. Also see William S. White, *New York Times*, July 12, 1953, sec. 4, p. 3.

[34] *New York Times*, July 5, 1953, p. 18; July 10, 1953, pp. 1, 6; July 11, 1953, p. 7; July 14, 1953, p. 11; July 15, 1953, p. 16; July 16, 1953, p. 12; July 19, 1953, p. 1; July 19, 1953, sec. 4, p. 2.

which the senator himself would have been more familiar: "He raises on the poor hands and always comes out the winner."

SKIRMISHES

Buoyed by the tentative success of the Matthews fight, the members of the Clearing House continued their scattered operations into the fall of 1953. They initiated a study by pollster Louis Bean of the political campaigns in which McCarthy had intervened, a study designed to explode the legend of McCarthy's political invincibility. They set about documenting McCarthy's abuse and manipulation of subcommittee records and transcripts in order to lay the groundwork for an attempt to block the committee's appropriation in 1954. They also encouraged the administrative assistants of four Democratic senators to undertake an extensive review of antisubversion legislation in hope of introducing a "liberal" internal security bill.[35]

On October 6, 1953, the Clearing House discovered another "target of opportunity" when the White House announced the interim appointment of Robert E. Lee to the Federal Communications Commission. Lee was a former FBI man who had worked since 1946 for the House Appropriations Committee. He had compiled the famous "list" from which McCarthy had drawn so freely in his first major speech on the Communist issue on February 20, 1950. Both Lee and his wife were close personal friends of the Wisconsin senator. His wife had played an active role in the Maryland senatorial campaign against Millard Tydings. Lee's only experience with communications came from three broadcasts he had moderated for *Facts Forum*, the ultra-right-wing program sponsored by Texas oilman H. L. Hunt.[36]

The Clearing House interpreted the appointment as a bid by McCarthy for influence over the broadcasting industry and decided to make it an operational issue in hopes of handing the Wisconsin senator another defeat.[37] They worked once again through Mike Monroney, a member of the Senate Committee on Interstate and

[35] Maurice Rosenblatt to Gifford Phillips, Aug. 31, 1953, NCEC files.

[36] *Washington Post*, July 7, 1953; "Preliminary Report on Robert E. Lee," Dec. 17, 1953, NCEC files. Lee was hailed by *Aware, Inc.*, an ultraright organization headed by Godfrey P. Schmidt, as "an anti-Communist for the FCC." Press release enclosed in Paul M. Milton to Herbert H. Lehman, Jan. 18, 1954, Senate Department Files, drawer 31, Lehman Papers.

[37] Maurice Rosenblatt to William Benton, Oct. 9, 1953, NCEC files.

Foreign Commerce, whom they provided with a detailed resumé of Lee's background and activities. They called particular attention to a recent FCC decision involving the Hearst Corporation, whose newspapers were among McCarthy's strongest supporters. Since 1948 the Hearst interests had been engaged in a fight with the Milwaukee Board of Vocational Education over the allotment of Channel 10 in that city. McCarthy had interested himself in this issue earlier by calling FCC chairman Paul A. Walker before his committee in a supersecret executive session. Less than a week after Lee's appointment, the Hearst group stopped bidding for Channel 10 and filed a new application for Channel 6, to be located in a Milwaukee suburb. Though there had been no previous plans for another commercial channel in the Milwaukee area, the request was speedily granted.[38]

Monroney agreed that an issue should be raised on the appointment, and he publicly demanded that Lee's role in the Maryland election campaign be reinvestigated.[39] The Clearing House tried to stir up opposition to the appointment within the radio and television industry, but without notable success. The prospects of a losing fight and a vengeful FCC commissioner were more than most industry executives cared to contemplate.[40]

Ironically, the Lee nomination was not a "McCarthy appointment" at all, not at least in a literal sense. Lee was a close personal friend of McCarthy, to be sure. "I like him. I think he's a great guy," Lee told senators. But he had far more powerful patrons than the junior senator from Wisconsin. His candidacy was being pushed strongly by Senator Styles Bridges and by Congressman John Taber, the respective chairmen of the Senate and House appropriations committees.[41] The Lee appointment was a tithe

---

[38] Maurice Rosenblatt to William Benton, Oct. 9, 1953; Lucille Lang to Senator Mike Monroney, Oct. 16, 1953; "Preliminary Report on Robert E. Lee," Dec. 17, 1953, all in the NCEC files. *Washington Post*, Oct. 7, 19, 1953; *Milwaukee Journal*, Oct. 8, 1953. Also see Paul A. Walker [chairman, FCC] to Alexander Wiley, March 4, 1953, in reply to a letter of Feb. 9, 1953, from "you and Senator McCarthy," and Wiley to Rep. Charles Kersten, April 3, 1953, both in box 72, Wiley Papers.

[39] *Washington Post*, Oct. 19, 1953; John Howe to William Benton, Nov. 27, 1953, box 5, Benton Papers. Monroney had chaired the "hearings subcommittee" which investigated the Maryland campaign.

[40] George E. Agree to Maurice Rosenblatt, Nov. 16, 1953; Agree to Lucille Lang, Nov. 25, 1953, both in the NCEC files. John Howe to William Benton, Nov. 13, 1953, box 4, Benton Papers.

[41] Memorandum, Charles F. Willis, Jr., to Sherman Adams, July 11, 1953,

levied upon the new administration by these powerful congressional barons and demonstrated once again the identification between "McCarthyism" and conservative Republicanism.

Monroney fought the appointment almost singlehandedly in the Commerce Committee, but it was a near hopeless struggle. The administration was still basking in the false euphoria which followed McCarthy's New Year's conference with Vice President Nixon. Few liberal Republicans were inclined to oppose their party leadership, and Minority Leader Lyndon Johnson had returned from the holiday recess preaching patience and pacifism to all the Democrats. On the final roll call only twenty-five senators voted against confirmation. Though this was the strongest show of opposition yet made to an Eisenhower nominee, the appointment carried by a better than two-to-one margin.[42] For the Clearing House the lesson remained clear, even in defeat. "It demonstrated also the lack of political know-how among responsible influences in Washington, which, with a few exceptions, are completely unable to unite on matters not relating to their specific fields of interest."[43]

While the Lee nomination slipped through the Senate, yet another battle on the "McCarthy" front was taking shape, an effort to reestablish control over the Investigations Subcommittee by denying its annual appropriation. As early as August 2, Senator John McClellan had intimated that he might lead a move to block the committee's funds, and during the autumn of 1953 rumors of an impending battle over appropriations multiplied. Once again the Clearing House was operating in the background, gathering evidence of McCarthy's abuse of Senate procedure and passing it on to Allen J. Ellender, the economy-minded Louisiana Democrat who was determined to slash McCarthy's appropriations.[44]

By the end of 1953, moreover, a number of powerful senior

OF 99; Leonard Hall [?], Memorandum, n.d., OF 16, both in the Eisenhower Papers; Sinclair Weeks to Ralph E. Flanders, Jan. 10, 1953, box 112, Flanders Papers, Syracuse University.

[42] *New York Times,* Jan. 19, 1954, p. 12; Jan. 20, 1953, p. 15; Jan. 26, 1953, p. 13; *Congressional Record,* 83d Cong., 2d sess., Jan. 25, 1954, pp. 693–98.

[43] *Congressional Report,* 3 (Feb. 17, 1954).

[44] Maurice Rosenblatt to William Benton, Oct. 9, 1953; Rosenblatt, "The Clearing House," [c. Nov. 1953]; George E. Agree, "Memorandum #1," [c. Sept. 1954], all in the NCEC files; *New York Times,* Nov. 8, 1953, p. 76. Ellender had earlier opposed the unusually large appropriation which was given McCarthy's subcommittee in 1953. *New York Times,* Jan. 30, 1953, p. 7.

Democrats were moving toward a partywide confrontation with McCarthy. The opposition to the Wisconsin senator broke out along a broad front involving internal Senate procedures. Several Democrats attacked McCarthy's repeated invasions of committee jurisdiction. From such an improbable source as Pat McCarran came the charge that McCarthy's subcommittee had "stepped over into a field where it was not intended to function at all." Guy Gillette announced he would seek to strip the Government Operations Committee of jurisdiction over American United Nations employees, one of the many areas in which McCarthy had preempted operations of the Senate Foreign Relations Committee. There were even more complaints over McCarthy's investigation of the military and his wholesale invasion of an area normally under the jurisdiction of the Armed Services Committee. Unless McCarthy was curbed, declared Senator Ellender, he would eventually violate the prerogatives of every committee on the Hill. Other senators attacked McCarthy's highhanded "one-man rule" of the Investigations Subcommittee and the waste and duplication which his flashy and fast-moving inquiries had produced.[45]

The debate produced a variety of solutions for the "McCarthy problem." Some senators suggested that the Senate deny further authorization to the Permanent Subcommittee on Investigations after its authority expired on January 31, 1954, unless the chairman agreed to take back the dissenting Democrats on their own terms. McClellan, with the support of Richard Russell and several other powerful senior Democrats, proposed the establishment of a "Joint Committee on Subversive and Un-American Activities," designed to unify the various investigations of communism and to exclude McCarthy altogether. Ellender, Carl Hayden, and several others proposed to restrain the subcommittee by blocking its appropriations.[46]

Intensive political maneuvering continued for nearly three weeks. The administration, still hoping that McCarthy might join the Eisenhower "team," was quiescent and gave no encouragement to liberal or moderate Republicans. Majority Leader William F. Knowland declared that the leadership would "discuss" the

---

[45] *New York Times,* Dec. 31, 1953, p. 1; Jan. 2, 1954, p. 24; Jan. 3, 1954, p. 41; Jan. 5, 1954, p. 1; Jan. 10, 1954, sec. 4, p. 2.
[46] Ibid., Dec. 31, 1953, p. 1; Jan. 5, 1954, p. 1; Jan. 7, 1954, p. 1.

unification of the investigations of communism, but the G.O.P. hierarchy continued to defer to McCarthy by strategically placing him on the Senate Rules Committee, the group charged with initial jurisdiction over funds for Senate investigations. Minority Leader Johnson continued to preach caution and restraint to his colleagues. Pressed by newsmen, he declared: "I have nothing to say except that he is a Republican problem."[47]

McCarthy bobbed and weaved as usual. He released two long-delayed reports on his stewardship as chairman of the Permanent Subcommittee on Investigations, and he denounced his opponents, in one of his stock phrases, as "men of little minds and less morals."[48] But in the end he capitulated. At a subcommittee meeting on January 25 he joined the Republican majority in repealing the rule delegating him exclusive authority to hire and fire the subcommittee's staff. He agreed to Democratic demands for staff counsel and clerical help for the minority, and he accepted a rule whereby the Democrats on the subcommittee could block any public hearing unless overruled by the full committee.[49]

With the Democrats back on the subcommittee, Ellender's fight to cut the group's appropriation quickly ran out of steam. On the final roll call only one senator, J. William Fulbright of Arkansas, voted against the appropriation.[50] Like the Matthews incident, the battle over appropriations showed that McCarthy was not invincible and that he could be defeated. It also revealed again, however, the enervating political deadlock which continued to protect him from more direct attack.

THE MYTH OF INVINCIBILITY

One of the greatest deterrents to Senate action against McCarthy was the legend that he had defeated Millard Tydings and William Benton and had "decorated his pike" with the scalps of half a dozen other Senate colleagues. The fear of reprisal and loss of

---

[47] Ibid., Jan. 1, 1954, p. 34; Jan. 3, 1954, sec. 4, p. 5; Jan. 7, 1954, p. 10; Jan. 10, 1954, sec. 4, p. 4; Jan. 11, 1954, p. 9; Jan. 13, 1954, p. 6.

[48] Ibid., Jan. 6, 1954, p. 1; Jan. 18, 1954, p. 1; Jan. 25, 1954, p. 11.

[49] Ibid., Jan. 26, 1954, p. 1; Washington Post, Jan. 26, 1954; John Howe to William Benton, Feb. 2, 1954, box 4, Benton Papers.

[50] New York Times, Jan. 28, 1954, p. 15; Feb. 3, 1954, p. 1. Also see Senator Thomas C. Hennings, Jr., to William H. Biggs, Jan. 18, 1954, box 30, Hennings Papers; John Howe to William Benton, Feb. 2, 1954, box 4, Benton Papers.

office weighed heavily upon every member and lay like a dead hand across any action the Senate might take.[51]

The Clearing House worked hard with reporters and columnists —the men who interpret the news and in consequence do much to shape it—in an effort to overcome the fear inspired by this widely held belief. McCarthy could not be credited with the defeat of seven senators, or even of Benton and Tydings, wrote Rosenblatt to Arthur Schlesinger, Jr., who was then writing a column for the *New York Post*. Instead, he survived through perpetuation of "the myth of his political invincibility."[52]

For William Benton the question of McCarthy's "political invincibility" was immediate and personal. Defeated in the Eisenhower landslide of 1952, he had been forced to listen time after time to those who attributed this defeat to his campaign against McCarthy and to the latter's intervention in Connecticut.[53] As early as January 1953 Benton was urging that "some organization" take up the question of McCarthy's political power. What was needed, he declared, was a quick memorandum showing that neither he nor Tydings was defeated by McCarthy and that the Wisconsin senator by himself was powerless to defeat incumbent senators. "This little memo," he concluded, "would be enormously helpful in generating more courage in some circles where courage greatly needs to be generated."[54]

[51] William S. White, *New York Times*, Jan. 18, 1953, sec. 4, p. 4; Cabell Phillips, ibid., March 8, 1953, sec. 4, p. 10; John B. Oakes, "An Inquiry into McCarthy's Status," pp. 9, 26–30.

[52] Maurice Rosenblatt to Arthur Schlesinger, Jr., April 24, 1953, NCEC files; *New York Post*, May 23, 1953. Also see John Howe to the editor, *Leader and Press* (Springfield, Mo.), July 28, 1953; Howe to William Evjue, Jan. 19, 1954; Howe to George Bye,.March 12, 1954; William Benton to Howe, Dec. 23, 1953, all in box 4, Benton Papers.

[53] Nineteen fifty-two was an overwhelmingly Republican year in Connecticut. Benton was defeated, as was Connecticut's other Democratic senatorial nominee, the popular Abraham Ribicoff. But Benton also ran ahead of Stevenson and the national ticket. Though he undoubtedly was hurt among the state's traditionally Democratic Irish Catholics, he received a "backlash vote" from the normally Republican towns and villages in the western part of the state. William Benton to Stanley Allen, Jan. 19, 1953; NCEC files; Benton to John Howe, April 19, 1954, Oct. 19, 1954, both in box 4, Benton Papers; Louis Bean, *Influences in the 1954 Mid-Term Elections* (Washington, D. C., 1954), pp. 23–24.

[54] William Benton to Stanley Allen, Jan. 19, 1953, NCEC files; Benton to John Howe, April 21, 1953, box 4, Benton Papers. By May the ex-Senator was complaining: "The myth that Joe McCarthy defeated Tydings and me is gaining ground steadily. It is adding enormously to McCarthy's power." Benton to Howe, May 16, 1953, box 4, Benton Papers.

Both Benton and the Clearing House went to work collecting material on the senatorial campaigns in which McCarthy had intervened. They solicited statements from Tydings and from John M. Bailey, the state Democratic chairman from Connecticut, dismissing McCarthy's influence in the elections, and they arranged for influential liberal Republicans to pass their information along to the White House.[55]

In July 1953 the Clearing House enlisted the services of Louis Bean, an expert electoral statistician, who was to prepare a persuasive document which would smash the myth of McCarthy's invincibility.[56] After several long delays, Bean's analysis was finally published in the late spring of 1954, at the height of the army-McCarthy controversy, under the disarming title of *Influences in the 1954 Mid-Term Elections*. The study emphasized that *in every one* of the twelve non-southern states in which McCarthy had campaigned in 1952, the Democratic candidate had run well ahead of the national ticket, while in the states in which McCarthy did not campaign the vote for the local and national ticket was roughly equal. It also pointed out that McCarthy himself had run far behind Eisenhower and the remainder of the state ticket in Wisconsin, and it argued that neither Benton nor Tydings was necessarily the victim of McCarthy's *blitzkrieg*.[57]

The Clearing House gave the study wide distribution. They sent copies to senators, to key political reporters, and through former presidential aide C. D. Jackson to Sherman Adams and the White House staff. The pro-Eisenhower Cowles publications ran a summary of the report in *Look* magazine, and there was a brief flurry of stories inspired by the study in other newspapers and periodicals. "If you will read my column in the *Monitor* for tomorrow, June 23," wrote Joseph C. Harsch of the *Christian Science Monitor*, "you will find that your missionary work has not been wasted."[58]

[55] John Howe to Kenneth Birkhead, July 15, 1953, box 4; Howe to William Benton, July 21, 1953, box 4; George E. Agree to Benton, July 23, 1953, box 5, all in the Benton Papers.

[56] John Howe to William Benton, July 16, 1953, box 4, Benton Papers. Howe to Lucille Lang, Sept. 18, 1953, NCEC files. Robert R. Nathan, then chairman of the executive committee of Americans for Democratic Action and a member of the NCEC, persuaded Bean to undertake the assignment.

[57] Bean, *Influences in the 1954 Mid-Term Elections*, pp. 1–18.

[58] Louis Bean, "The Myth of McCarthy's Strength," *Look* 18 (June 1, 1954): 108; Joseph C. Harsch to John Howe, June 22, 1954, box 4, Benton Papers; Ernest K. Lindley, "McCarthy and the Campaign," *Newsweek* 43

The impact of the Bean study was quickly swallowed up in the turmoil surrounding the end of the army-McCarthy hearings. Yet because it coincided with letters and statements from worried Republican leaders across the nation, it did suggest that the dynamic which McCarthy had mastered for more than four years was at last falling apart. The *New York Times* announced, with abundant documentation, that the Wisconsin senator henceforth would be more shunned than sought after by Republican organizations locked in hot partisan campaigns, and Democratic Senator Monroney predicted that McCarthy's support in the 1954 election would mean "the kiss of death" for the Republican candidates.[59]

Beyond this, the efforts of the Clearing House remained sporadic throughout 1953 and early 1954. In November 1953, after Herbert Brownell's sensational charges against the Truman administration, they ran a survey of congressional mail which showed little public concern over the issue. Their hopeful conclusion was that the issue of "communism-in-government" was at last beginning to fade from the public mind.[60] General Telford Taylor, the American prosecutor at the Nuremberg trials and a member of the National Committee for an Effective Congress, was working independently on a detailed analysis of the havoc wreaked by McCarthy's "investigation" at Fort Monmouth.[61] But the Clearing House was clearly limited by its own meager resources and by McCarthy's considerable strength. "I don't believe that anything our committee can do, or you can do, will be decisive at this moment," wrote John Howe to ex-Senator Benton in late 1953. "The big tide has not yet begun to turn against McCarthy. We have a moral obligation to continue to work at this, and we may be able to hasten the turn and speed the flow when the turn comes. But please don't look for any major victories."[62]

Even as Howe was writing, the junior senator from Wisconsin was turning down the long road to his final confrontation with the army, the administration, and the United States Senate.

(June 7, 1954): 33. Also see John Howe to Drew Pearson, July 7, 1954; Howe to Lester Markel, Aug. 2, 1954; Howe to James Reston, Sept. 27, 1954, all in box 4, Benton Papers.

[59] *New York Times,* June 14, 1954, p. 11; Cabell Phillips, ibid., June 20, 1954, sec. 4, p. 7.

[60] Press release, Nov. 26, 1953, NCEC files.

[61] John Howe to Gerhard P. Van Arkel, Dec. 29, 1953, box 5; Howe to William Benton, Feb. 8, 1954, box 4, both in the Benton Papers.

[62] John Howe to William Benton, Oct. 23, 1953, box 5, Benton Papers.

8

THE ARMY-McCARTHY HEARINGS

THE ARMY-MC CARTHY HEAR-
ings were unique in the annals of Congress and the nation. Never
before had the polite facade of parliamentary decorum been lifted
to expose such a bewildering tangle of personal, political, and
constitutional issues. Never before had an audience of eighty
million been made privy to the inner secrets of government. The
hearings resembled drama of a sort and the principals actors. Yet
the origin and evolution of the proceedings lacked the precise,
clear movement of the stage. Individual lines of cause and effect
were inextricably wrapped one about another until the total effect
was diffuse and elliptic. There was all the thunder of conflict,
but only occasional glimmers of meaning.

PRIVATE SCHINE, MAJOR PERESS, AND
OTHER AFFAIRS OF STATE

Throughout the autumn of 1953, McCarthy had pressed hard upon the Defense Department for access to the army's confidential files on loyalty and security. His demands raised a basic constitutional conflict between the right of the president to withhold information and the right of Congress to know, a conflict which had wound its way through almost every investigation of "communism-in-government" since 1948.[1] Neither the claims of Congress nor the Executive were absolute, but rather depended on cooperation, trust, and moderation by members of both branches of government. But Joe McCarthy had never been noted for restraint or moderation, and the "cooperation" which he demanded was strictly a one-way affair. Throughout the first few months of his "investigation" of the army he pushed and bullied the secretary of the army, Robert T. Stevens. The harried secretary gave in to or evaded most of the senator's demands until January 1954, when McCarthy threatened to subpoena the entire Loyalty and Security Appeals Board which had passed on the cases of the Fort Monmouth scientists. The challenge to the prerogatives of the president was inescapable, and there was a flurry of scattered conferences between army counsel John G. Adams and various Republican leaders. Adams met with Sherman Adams,

---

[1] The presidential position had been articulated as early as 1792, when George Washington declared that "the Executive ought to communicate such papers as the public good would permit, and ought to refuse those the disclosure of which would endanger the public." See a Justice Department brief prepared in 1948 entitled "Is a congressional committee entitled to demand and receive information and papers from the President and the heads of departments which they deem confidential, in the public interest?" and "Demands of congressional committee for executive papers: A study of the 'Incidents,' debates in the Congress, court decisions, and the statutes during the years 1948–1953," both with Deputy Attorney General William P. Rogers to Eisenhower, March 2, 1954, in the Files of Special Counsel to the President David W. Kendall, box 2, Eisenhower Papers. The second study was completed during the autumn of 1953 by Assistant Attorney Generals J. Lee Rankin and Warren E. Burger and first sent to the White House with Brownell to Eisenhower, Oct. 19, 1953, ibid. Congress, of course, has never accepted this principle of Executive privilege. As Senator Mundt noted during a pause in the army-McCarthy hearings, "If I were President Eisenhower or Brownell, I'd do everything I could to stop it [information leaks]. I'm down here [in Congress] and I do all I can to get it. That's the way you play the game." *Congress and the Nation* (Washington, D.C., 1965), p. 1725.

Herbert Brownell, and Henry Cabot Lodge from the White House, and with the majority members of the Permanent Subcommittee on Investigations. The Republicans finally prevailed upon McCarthy to draw back, and on January 22 the chairman announced that he was deferring the calling of the loyalty board members.[2]

At this same series of meetings, army counsel John Adams revealed yet another dimension to the long-simmering dispute between McCarthy and the army. Even while the senator and his young aides had been busily investigating the army, they had been almost equally diligent in trying to secure special treatment for the subcommittee's sometime "chief consultant," G. David Schine. When Schine had first been called by his draft board on July 1953, both Cohn and McCarthy had tried unsuccessfully to arrange a commission for the young college dropout.[3] After the army, the navy, and air force had all turned him down, Roy Cohn had proposed to General Walter B. Smith that Schine be tapped for the Central Intelligence Agency, which McCarthy was at that very time proposing to investigate. Schine himself suggested that he be made special assistant to the secretary of the army, and Cohn urged that he be assigned to check the textbooks used in the United States Military Academy.[4]

Schine's career as an army recruit was no less unusual. He was given sixteen passes during a period in which most enlisted men received three. He was excused from drill to place or accept 250 long-distance phone calls. On occasion, Roy Cohn would call up the commander of Fort Dix, or the general counsel of the army, or even the secretary of the army himself and upbraid them for their treatment of young Schine. On one occasion Private Schine patronizingly threw his arm around the shoulder of his commanding officer and told him that it was his purpose "to remake the American military establishment along modern lines."[5]

In mid-December 1953 Drew Pearson broke portions of the

---

[2] *Army-McCarthy Hearings*, pp. 1177–79, 1186–89, 1194–95; Sherman Adams, *Firsthand Report: The Story of the Eisenhower Administration* (New York, 1961), pp. 143–45; *New York Times*, Jan. 23, 1954, p. 1.

[3] See, for example, Major General W. B. Persons to McCarthy, Aug. 15, 1953, OF 11-H-5, Eisenhower Papers.

[4] *Army-McCarthy Hearings*, pp. 82–85, 89–97; Michael Straight, *Trial by Television* (Boston, 1954), pp. 30–31.

[5] *Army-McCarthy Hearings*, p. 1482; Adams, *Firsthand Report*, p. 144; *New York Times*, March 12, 1954, pp. 1, 9A.

"Schine story" in his syndicated column. A week later the *Baltimore Sun* ran a long article on the same subject, and in late January 1954, the *New York Post* ran its own exposé. The army, at the suggestion of Sherman Adams, prepared a detailed "chronology" of Cohn and McCarthy's attempts to gain preferential treatment for their young friend.[6] By early February high-ranking Democrats were demanding a report from the army on the entire affair.[7] Their inquiries went unanswered. It was neither McCarthy's challenges to Executive privilege nor Roy Cohn's string-pulling on behalf of Private Schine which shoved the reluctant Republican administration into a final confrontation with McCarthy. Rather, it was an event of almost monumental significance.

In October 1952 the army had commissioned Irving Peress, a New York dentist and a member of the left-wing American Labor party. In November 1953 Peress was promoted to the rank of major through the automatic provisions of the Doctor Draft Law. By the following month, however, the armed forces bureaucracy had discovered that the dentist had declined to answer questions regarding his political beliefs, and the adjutant general ordered the First Army to discharge him within ninety days. At this point Senator McCarthy landed on the "case" feet first. He summoned Peress before his subcommittee for questioning, and when the major claimed immunity by the Fifth Amendment in answer to questions about his politics, McCarthy wrote the secretary of the army demanding that he be court-martialed. On February 2, the day after McCarthy's letter was written, Peress requested that his discharge become effective immediately, and the Department of Defense followed the path of least resistance in easing the dentist from the service.[8]

On February 18 McCarthy called Brigadier General Ralph W. Zwicker before the subcommittee and demanded from him the

<hr>

[6] Adams, *Firsthand Report,* pp. 144–45.

[7] *Army-McCarthy Hearings,* p. 1142. The Democrats included Senator McClellan of the Government Operations Committee and Senator Richard B. Russell of the Senate Armed Services Committee. *New York Times,* March 5, 1954, p. 1.

[8] Robert Stevens to Joseph McCarthy, Nov. 3, 1954, with enclosed memorandum prepared by the army on the Peress case, Subject File, McCarthy Censure, Wiley Papers. *New York Times,* Jan. 31, 1954, p. 57; Feb. 3, 1954, pp. 1, 9; Adams, *Firsthand Report,* p. 145; Straight, *Trial by Television,* pp. 57–58.

names of all the officers who had been involved in Peress's discharge. When Zwicker refused on advice of army counsel John Adams, McCarthy berated the officer as "not fit to wear that uniform" and charged that he did not have "the brains of a five-year-old."[9] Secretary Robert Stevens, who by now was under intense pressure from General Matthew J. Ridgeway and other army leaders, denounced McCarthy's behavior as unwarranted and ordered Zwicker not to reappear before the subcommittee as the senator had ordered. "Just go ahead and try it, Robert," threatened McCarthy over the phone. "I am going to kick the brains out of anyone who protects Communists! . . . You just go ahead. I will guarantee you that you will live to regret it."[10]

Behind the scenes the Republican managers were still laboring mightily to head off a final collision between McCarthy and the White House. Vice President Nixon and "Jerry" Persons urged the Republicans on the subcommittee—Everett Dirksen, Karl Mundt, and Charles Potter—to make a last attempt to heal the breach between McCarthy and the army. As a result, Stevens and the Republican senators met on February 24 over fried chicken in the offices of the Senate Republican Campaign Committee. Secretary Stevens was, in one reporter's wry phrase, like a goldfish in a tankful of barracuda, and when the dinner was over Senator Mundt read to waiting newsmen a "memorandum of understanding" in which the secretary gave in to practically all of McCarthy's demands. As for McCarthy, he later told a reporter that Stevens could not have surrendered "more abjectly if he had got down on his knees."[11]

The reaction to Stevens's "chicken dinner" was sharp, both publicly and privately. "From here it looks as though Stevens' complete cave-in has splattered more mud on the U. S. Army uniform than have all our enemies in all our wars," wired the

[9] U. S., Congress, Senate, 83d Cong., 1st sess., Committee on Government Operations, Subcommittee on Permanent Investigations, *Communist Infiltration in the Army* (Washington, D. C., 1953), pp. 146–53; *New York Times*, Feb. 19, 1954, p. 1; Feb. 20, 1954, p. 1; Feb. 21, 1954, p. 1.

[10] *New York Times*, Feb. 21, 1954, p. 1; transcript of phone conversation between Secretary Stevens and Senator McCarthy, Feb. 20, 1954, in *Army-McCarthy Hearings*, p. 2155.

[11] *New York Times*, Feb. 25, 1954, pp. 1, 10; Feb. 26, 1954, p. 1. McCarthy later denied the quote attributed to him.

strongly pro-Eisenhower publisher of the *Denver Post.* "The Secretary didn't mean to surrender to the Senators," quipped one Washington wit, "he merely thought they wanted to look at his sword."[12] The next day the agitated Stevens tried to salvage his position. After Dirksen and others had failed to work out a compromise satisfactory to both the army and McCarthy, the secretary read to the press a statement approved by the president, reaffirming his determination not to allow army personnel to be "browbeaten or humiliated."[13]

There arrives a point in the political process when no leader or group of leaders can any longer determine the course of events. When the presidential leadership is weak or the majority party divided, this point is reached more quickly. This was the case in the army-McCarthy controversy. Neither the president nor the party leadership welcomed this divisive display of party disunity, yet neither was able to prevent it. The controversy unfolded by a dynamic all its own.

During the next two weeks the clash ran its final course amid a scene of turmoil and confusion. On every side there were conferences and huddles among Republican leaders. On March 2 Republican National Chairman Leonard W. Hall, who had only a few weeks before praised McCarthy as a "great asset" to the party, emerged from a conference with the president and criticized McCarthy's fight with Stevens.[14] The following day, in remarks prepared for his press conference, the president himself insisted that fair treatment be accorded all witnesses.[15] The party pacificators, however, were still hard at work. The president's statement was generally moderate in tone. He had rejected a more strongly worded attack on McCarthy which declared that "only under tyranny is error equated to treason" and that "people who import such methods into our free country are helping Communism not hurting it." Vice President Nixon and House Leader Charles A. Halleck met with nervous Republican legislators to explain the

[12] Palmer Hoyt to Sherman Adams, Feb. 24, 1954, GF 171, McCarthy (1954), Eisenhower Papers; *New York Times,* Feb. 26, 1954, p. 1; Feb. 28, 1954, sec. 4, p. 1. Also see press statement written but not released by Estes Kefauver's office, Feb. 25, 1954, General Correspondence, Kefauver Papers.
[13] *New York Times,* Feb. 26, 1954, p. 1.
[14] Ibid., Feb. 8, 1954, p. 8; March 3, 1954, p. 1.
[15] Ibid., March 4, 1954, p. 1.

background of the controversy and "why the President did not break with McCarthy regardless of pressure from certain groups that this be done."[16]

McCarthy, however, left little room for compromise. Replying sharply to the president's statement, he charged that Peress was the "sacred cow of certain Army brass" and that any "stupid, arrogant or witless man" appearing before the subcommittee would receive his just deserts. He had established "beyond any possibility of a doubt," he declared, that "certain individuals in the Army have been promoting, covering up, and honorably discharging known Communists," a charge Secretary of Defense Charles E. Wilson promptly labeled as "just damn tommyrot."[17]

There were more conferences, more charges and countercharges, and then finally, on March 11, the army released its celebrated "chronology," accusing McCarthy and Cohn of seeking preferential treatment for G. David Schine.[18] The following day McCarthy countercharged that the army had tried to "blackmail" him into halting his exposure of Communists by holding Schine as a "hostage."[19] Thus the power and prerogatives of two coordinate branches of government, the prestige of the world's most powerful military establishment, the cry of "communism-in-government," and the tangled affairs of one young army recruit had all met upon one stage, all inextricably bound to that strange and unparalleled drama soon to begin, the army-McCarthy hearings.

GROUND RULES

Because the procedures under which Congress investigates are broad and ill-defined, nearly every hearing has its own style, organization, and procedural ground rules. These rules and the men selected to carry them out are crucially important, for they

[16] Draft of Press Statement, n.d.; Memorandum, Earle D. Chesney to Sherman Adams, March 4, 1954, both in OF 99-P, Eisenhower Papers.

[17] *New York Times*, March 5, 1954, p. 1.

[18] Ibid., March 12, 1954, pp. 1, 9A. To ensure that the Republicans on the subcommittee received the report first, Secretary of Defense Wilson phoned Senator Potter and arranged for the senator to "request" the information from the army. The report was in Potter's office in less than thirty minutes. *Army-McCarthy Hearings*, pp. 394–96. Charles E. Potter, *Days of Shame* (New York, 1965), pp. 31–32.

[19] *New York Times*, March 13, 1954, p. 1.

pattern and determine the way a particular set of hearings will develop. Consequently, they are often arrived at only after a prolonged internal struggle within the committee. In the case of the army-McCarthy investigation this procedural fight, the battle before the battle, did much to shape the outcome of the hearings themselves.

The permanent Subcommittee on Investigations was faced at the outset with the question of whether there would be an investigation at all and, if so, who would conduct it. Although the pressure for some type of hearing was strong, the Republicans on the subcommittee were extremely hesitant to take up the issue. The day after the army "chronology" was released, Senator Everett Dirksen attempted to set up a private meeting at which the subcommittee itself would interrogate Cohn. After this fell through, the Illinois Republican suggested in executive session that it might not be wise to "ventilate" the matter any further, but instead to let "the grass grow over it."[20]

Karl Mundt, easily the most unhappy man on the subcommittee, simply did not want to conduct the investigation himself and suggested that another committee—any committee—should investigate the charges and countercharges. There was a small possibility that the investigation might be conducted by the Senate Armed Services Committee. Republican Ralph Flanders and Democrat Estes Kefauver had both been pressing Chairman Leverett Saltonstall to reassert his committee's jurisdiction over matters relating to the armed forces. This proposal, however, was resisted by Democrats and Republicans on the McCarthy Subcommittee and on the Armed Services Committee as well.[21]

The Democrats on the subcommittee argued that the inquiry should be conducted by the full Senate Committee on Government Operations, where the presence of Margaret Chase Smith would

[20] *Army-McCarthy Hearings,* pp. 5, 10.
[21] Ibid., pp. 12–13; *New York Times,* March 10, 1954, p. 1; March 13, 1954, p. 1; March 14, 1954, p. 1; March 15, 1954, p. 16; March 18, 1954, p. 15. Saltonstall faced reelection in 1954. The 1952 defeat of Henry Cabot Lodge, which many observers had credited to McCarthy, made the Massachusetts senator extremely wary of taking a prominent role in the McCarthy controversy. See draft of Senate resolution, n.d., in Legislative File, Armed Services Committee, 4, Kefauver Papers. Alfred A. Knopf to Herbert H. Lehman, April 29, 1954; Lehman to Knopf, May 6, 1954, both in Washington Files, McCarthy and McCarthyism, drawer one, Lehman Papers.

ensure an anti-McCarthy majority. The Republicans successfully defeated this maneuver, however, and in the end the subcommittee itself voted to investigate the charges raised against and by its chairman and chief counsel.[22]

There remained other important questions of procedural detail. As soon as the controversy began to break, McCarthy had quite typically set out to stir up diversions. He called for new investigations of corruption in Alaska and income tax settlements in Washington, of Communists in defense plants, and of cheese prices in Wisconsin. But the Democrats on the subcommittee refused to budge, and for the first time the subcommittee operated effectively to check its chairman. On March 16, McClellan successfully demanded that the army-McCarthy investigation "proceed to the exclusion of all other hearings." When McCarthy tried to slip this limitation a week later, all six of his subcommittee colleagues protested. The army-McCarthy charges and the army-McCarthy charges alone were to be the focus of the investigation.[23]

The Democrats also insisted on public hearings, despite Dirksen's arguments that "ventilating" the case would serve no good purpose. The subcommittee also rejected Mundt's suggestion that the committee follow the procedure of the MacArthur hearings.[24] The Democratic members, prompted by Lyndon B. Johnson, forced the hearings before the television cameras.

Still another key question involved the subcommittee's staff. Roy Cohn quite obviously could not conduct an investigation of Roy Cohn, and so the subcommittee resolved to find a new "unbiased" counsel to direct its inquiry. Few reputable lawyers were eager for an assignment which offered low pay and high risks. Still, the committee thought it had discovered a satisfactory can-

---

22 *Army-McCarthy Hearings,* p. 24; *New York Times,* March 17, 1954, p. 1.

23 *Army-McCarthy Hearings,* p. 25; *New York Times,* March 17, 1954 p. 1; March 24, 1954, p. 1. The administration too showed occasional starts of political sense. When Adlai E. Stevenson denounced the administration for endorsing McCarthyism, the senator, as usual, demanded network time to reply. This time, however, the administration stirred itself more quickly. Vice President Nixon was assigned the task of answering Stevenson, and McCarthy was effectively shut out. Ibid., March 7, 1954, p. 1; March 8, 1954, p. 1; March 9, 1954, p. 1; March 10, 1954, p. 14. Earl Mazo, *Richard Nixon: A Political and Personal Portrait* rev. ed. (New York, 1959), p. 149.

24 The MacArthur hearings were conducted in the absence of press or public, but a censored transcript of the proceedings was made available to newsmen almost immediately. *Army-McCarthy Hearings,* pp. 3, 24.

didate in Samuel P. Sears, a Boston Republican who was unanimously approved by the subcommittee on April 1.[25]

The Sears appointment had all the markings of a put-up job by McCarthy and company. Sears had been an unsuccessful candidate for the Republican gubernatorial nomination in 1952, and he was a strong supporter of McCarthy. Although he assured Senator McClellan and other members of the subcommittee that he had never expressed himself on the McCarthy issue, he had in fact made many laudatory statements on the Wisconsin senator's "great job" of driving "the pinks and Commies out of the Government." He had actively solicited the appointment through Senators Leverett Saltonstall and John F. Kennedy of Massachusetts and Mike Monroney of Oklahoma. Kennedy had attested to his "good reputation in Massachusetts."[26]

On the same day the subcommittee announced Sears's appointment, the newspapers broke the story of his strong pro-McCarthy background. The Democrats were incensed over the manner in which he had misrepresented his views to the subcommittee, and after a second hearing the group agreed unanimously to receive his resignation.[27] Finally, Everett Dirksen came up with an acceptable counsel, Ray H. Jenkins, a Tennessee trial lawyer and Taft Republican whose chief qualification appears to have been that "I have no record, publicly or otherwise, with regard to Senator McCarthy or what has come to be called McCarthyism."[28]

Perhaps the most important problem facing the subcommittee was the role of McCarthy himself. At the very beginning the senator demanded the right to cross-examine all witnesses. Congressional hearings are technically nonadversary. The committees are ostensibly engaged in collecting information, not conducting trials. Yet many congressional "investigations" have

[25] *New York Times,* April 2, 1954, p. 1.

[26] Ibid., April 2, 1954, pp. 1, 10; April 4, 1954, p. 84; April 4, 1954, sec. 4, pp. 2, 7; April 7, 1954, p. 1; April 11, 1954, p. 37.

[27] Ibid., April 7, 1954, p. 1. Estes Kefauver to Sharon Mauhs, April 8, 1954, 1954 Miscellaneous Correspondence, Kefauver Papers.

[28] *New York Times,* April 8, 1954, p. 1. Jenkins was somewhat less guarded after the hearings had ended, declaring that he would welcome McCarthy's help in his planned campaign for the Senate seat then held by Democrat Estes Kefauver. Ibid., June 21, 1954, p. 1. Kefauver to Sharon Mauhs, April 8, 1954; Kefauver to Worth M. McCown, April 8, 1954; Kefauver to Edward D. Smith, April 21, 1954, all in 1954 Miscellaneous Correspondence, Kefauver Papers.

come to assume a quasi-judicial nature, and there have consequently been demands that the rights of witnesses be protected
by the privilege of cross-examination.[29]   McCarthy himself had
regularly denied the right of cross-examination to witnesses appearing before his subcommittee, and now McClellan and others urged
that McCarthy be heard as a witness and nothing else.[30]   Nevertheless, McCarthy won the privilege of cross-examination, and a
similar right was extended to the army. The decision was crucial,
for it assured McCarthy easy entree to the drama of the hearings.
Conflict is the spring which drives the play, and conflict, thanks
to McCarthy's insistence on the right of cross-examination, was
built into the very structure of the hearings.

McCarthy also put up a hard fight to stay on the subcommittee
itself. Although he had relinquished the chairmanship to the
reluctant Mundt almost immediately, he insisted that he would
play an active role in the investigation.[31]   Stuart Symington replied
for the Democrats with a strong statement challenging McCarthy's
proclaimed intention of sitting as witness, prosecutor, and judge,
all in one. He was soon supported by Senators Knowland and
Ferguson, who spoke for the Republican leadership in urging
McCarthy to step down from the subcommittee. Even President
Eisenhower, who intervened only rarely in congressional affairs,
told a press conference that in America a man who was a party to
a dispute should not sit in judgment on his own case.[32]

McCarthy gave in to this demand, but not until he had turned
it to his own advantage. He "stepped down" from the subcommittee and appointed in his place a strong supporter, Senator
Henry C. Dworshak of Idaho. Once the hearings began, however,
he quickly rendered this concession meaningless, for by his repeated "points of order" he was able to interrupt the proceedings
at will. Although he was no longer technically on the subcommittee, he remained very much at the center of its investigation.

[29] Most proposals for the reform of congressional investigations during the
1950s included provisions for at least limited cross-examination. See the
proposals of Senator Estes Kefauver in *Congressional Record*, 82d Cong.,
1st sess., Aug. 24, 1951, p. 10602, and those of Senator Prescott Bush in
ibid., 83d Cong., 2d sess., July 31, 1954, p. 12897.

[30] *New York Times*, March 23, 1954, p. 1.

[31] Ibid., March 15, 1954, p. 16; March 16, 1954, p. 1; March 17, 1954, p. 1.

[32] Ibid., March 21, 1954, p. 32; March 22, 1954, p. 19; March 25, 1954,
p. 1.

THE HEARINGS

The army-McCarthy hearings sprawled out through nearly two months of confusion and turmoil. In a special sense they were a dramatization of all which had come to be associated with Joseph R. McCarthy. And yet their meaning remained cryptic and elusive. The issues, both real and contrived, were more often than not obscured and muddied by the torrent of words poured forth during the hearings themselves.

Did Roy Cohn exert improper pressure in seeking preferential treatment for his friend and traveling companion, G. David Schine? The answer was yes. Cohn had been by turn arrogant, insulting, and abusive in his demands that Schine be given special favors, though Senator McCarthy's role in all of this was as much one of acquiescence as of actual connivance. Had the army sought to end McCarthy's investigations? The answer here too was yes, although not at all in the way McCarthy alleged. The idea that the United States Army was actively "coddling Communists" was absurd. If anything, the army had plunged overboard in the opposite direction. The secretary of the army was, in McCarthy's words, "a fine, naive, not-too-brilliant" Republican businessman who had tried to appease the senator and to deflect his energies elsewhere. Six months later these very acts of appeasement were exhibited by McCarthy as proof that the army was surely trying to hide something. No one questioned the primary assumption that McCarthy's "investigation" had been a valid attempt to guard the national security, and as a consequence the entire debate was delivered over into the realm of fantasy.

From the very beginning McCarthy dominated the hearings. He was a participant because of the charges made by and against him, a cross-examiner by virtue of the privileges won during the battle over procedures, and the center of continuing controversy by the sheer exercise of will with which he overpowered Chairman Mundt and the other members of the subcommittee. McCarthy had always lacked a sense of inner restraint, and in the lax and permissive atmosphere of the Senate caucus room he roamed almost at will.

The hearings proceeded awkwardly. Subcommittee counsel Ray Jenkins would first interrogate a witness on direct examination, then cross-examine him. The large-boned Tennessean was, despite a handsome criminal practice in his home state, ill equipped for the demands of his position. A more acute mind might have challenged the presuppositions of both McCarthy and the army. Jenkins was content to share in the collective unreality of the hearings and to lead the subcommittee into countless time-consuming digressions and superfluities.

When Jenkins had finished, the senators would direct their own questions to the witness. Each man was a study in the politics of the situation. Mundt, who had always supported McCarthy in the past and who was now up for reelection, was plainly unhappy with his duty. He had wanted neither the investigation nor the chairmanship which had been thrust upon him, and in the face of conflict he usually retreated into a cloud of midwestern geniality. Dirksen was at his oratorical best, supporting McCarthy and yet trying to minimize and muffle the conflicts between the senator and the Republican administration. Dworshak usually favored McCarthy also, although on occasion even he was harried by the senator's repeated "points of order." Potter was the only Republican truly ambivalent toward McCarthy. Like Hendrickson and other Republican moderates, he was a decent enough man, but he was torn between competing factional loyalties. As a freshman member of HUAC during the Eighty-third Congress he had won a reputation as "something of a junior McCarthy." In 1952 he had received aid from McCarthy in his narrowly successful campaign against Democratic incumbent Blair Moody. But he was also responsive to the demands of the administration, and at the end of the hearings this ambivalence proved an important factor in helping to check McCarthy.[33]

The Democrats were cautious and circumspect. Each went to extreme lengths to establish his own *bona fides* as an anti-Communist, and not one of them directly challenged the assumption that McCarthy was a great Communist hunter. Still, they furnished the brunt of the opposition to McCarthy. Together with special army counsel Joseph L. Welch, they acted as the "prosecution," a role which inevitably led them into conflict with McCarthy.

John L. McClellan led the minority, and both Democrats and

[33] Kenneth Birkhead to William Benton, n.d. [Jan. 1953], box 4, Benton Papers. For Potter's none-too-candid recollections of the hearings see Potter, *Days of Shame*. But also see Richard H. Rovere, "The Untold Story of McCarthy's Fall," *New York Review of Books* 5 (Oct. 28, 1965): 3–5; and Robert W. Griffith, "Senators Potter, Hennings, and McCarthy: A Review Article," *Wisconsin Magazine of History* 49 (Summer 1966): 334–37.

Republicans alike deferred to this wiry and unsmiling senior senator. He was restrained, judicious, even unimaginative, yet when he spoke it was with force and authority. Jackson was moderate and direct, a good lawyer and an intelligent parliamentarian. But McCarthy's most intransigent foe on the subcommittee was Stuart Symington of Missouri. Symington remained doggedly in opposition throughout the hearings, and the clashes between the two men became increasingly bitter and violent.[34] On June 4 the transcripts of the early March conversations between Symington and Stevens were introduced into the record. "If you are going to play with McCarthy, you have to forget about any of those Marquis of Queensberry rules," Symington had advised the secretary of the army; now McCarthy demanded that the Missouri senator be disqualified from the investigation. The following evening, in Ripon, Wisconsin, he accused Symington of instigating the entire controversy in order to destroy Eisenhower and the Republican party.[35]

The hearings themselves developed through a series of incidents, rather than by any logical exploration of the issues involved. There were typical McCarthy gambits—a cropped photograph of Schine and the secretary of the army, a phony letter from J. Edgar Hoover to Army Intelligence (G-2) "condensed" from a 15-page memorandum stolen from the files of the FBI or military intelligence. And there were violent personal attacks, for as McCarthy explained to one of the participants, he always followed a maxim taught him by "Indian Charlie," which was "that if one was ever approached by another person in a not completely friendly fashion, one should start kicking at the other person as fast as possible below the belt until the other person was rendered helpless."[36]

Some of McCarthy's attacks were aimed at people in no way involved in the hearings. On the very first day, for example, he demanded of General Miles Reber if he was aware that his

[34] Willard Edwards, a friend of McCarthy, recalls that one evening during the hearings he dropped in at McCarthy's home and was surprised to find Symington there having a drink with the Wisconsin senator. Author's interview with Willard Edwards, May 26, 1966.

[35] *Army-McCarthy Hearings*, pp. 2123, 2127; *New York Times*, June 6, 1954, p. 1.

[36] *New York Times*, June 21, 1954, p. 1. One suspects that McCarthy rendered the story in more graphic and colorful language.

brother, the former deputy high commissioner of Germany, "was allowed to resign when charges that he was a bad security risk were made against him as a result of the investigations of this committee?" The charge was outrageously false, but it served McCarthy's purpose, temporarily diverting the hearings and casting a shadow on General Reber's testimony.[37]

More often than not, however, McCarthy's attacks were directed at the other participants in the hearings. His office had prepared dossiers on each person, and in the fire of battle the senator would use these charges, whatever their nature, to bludgeon his opponents and throw them onto the defensive. He gathered some unspecified charges against Senator McClellan from enemies of the senator in Arkansas,[38] but even McCarthy never quite dared to attack a senator so powerful and conservative. Nor did McCarthy himself attack Senator Jackson. After one especially acrimonious hearing, however, Roy Cohn marched over to minority counsel Robert F. Kennedy, and brandishing aloft a large folder marked "Jackson's record" he loudly threatened to "get Jackson."[39]

McCarthy's strongest blasts were directed against Stuart Symington. One of the charges in the Symington dossier stemmed from a teenage joyride Symington and two other boys had taken in a neighbor's car. The charge had been used against Symington during the 1952 campaign, and now McCarthy threatened to bring it up again. He would stride into the hearing room, throw his arm casually around Symington, and maliciously ask, "Stole any cars lately, Stu?"[40] On June 9, before the cameras, McCarthy charged that the former secretary of the air force had "associated" with a Communist in a "study group" and that this was what lay behind his "smears" against the subcommittee and his attempts

[37] *Army-McCarthy Hearings*, pp. 62, 72; *New York Times*, April 23, 1954, pp. 1, 8, 9.
[38] For enigmatic references to these charges, see Bradley Taylor to McCarthy, June 3, 19, 1954, both in box 5, Taylor Papers. "Every man in public life lives in a glass house," declared a Democratic senator in 1953. "There are few if any people who haven't done something in the past that could be used against them in a political fight by an opponent willing to bar no holds." Quoted by John B. Oakes, "An Inquiry into McCarthy's Status," *New York Times Magazine*, April 12, 1953, pp. 9, 26–30.
[39] *New York Times*, June 12, 1954, p. 1; Straight, *Trial by Television*, p. 192.
[40] Drew Pearson, *Capital Times* (Madison), Oct. 1, 1952; Pearson, *Washington Newsletter*, June 12, 1954; author's interview with Walter Trohan, May 26, 1966.

"to force an end to our investigation." This was also an accusation which McCarthy had first hurled at Symington in 1952 when he campaigned in Missouri on behalf of James P. Kem. The so-called study club referred to a series of meetings sponsored by Episcopalian Bishop Will Scarlett of Missouri. The Communist mentioned was William Sentner, the head of the United Electrical Workers of Missouri and the union representative with whom Symington had to deal as an executive for the Emerson Electric Manufacturing Company of St. Louis.[41]

Then on one of the last days of the hearings McCarthy rose to another "point of order" and again accused Symington of trying to "smear" the subcommittee's staff and their work on the committee's files. The other senators were already gathering their papers and preparing to answer a roll call when Symington stood up, faced McCarthy, and angrily replied that "the files of what you call my staff, my director, my chief of staff, have been the sloppiest and most dangerously handled files that I have ever heard of since I have been in the Government."[42] The caucus room burst into applause—not so much because of what Symington said but because of the sheer emotion with which he said it. The senators threaded their way through the crowd while McCarthy sputtered through his now familiar superlatives. "He runs away . . . the most dishonest . . . and most unfounded . . . upon some of the most outstanding young men . . . (whereupon, at 4:40 P.M. the hearing was recessed, to reconvene at 10 A.M. the following day, Tuesday, June 15, 1954)."[43]

McCarthy's most celebrated attack was made on Frederick G. Fisher, a young member of army counsel Welch's law firm of Hale and Dorr in Boston. On the thirtieth day of the hearings, after a heated exchange between Welch and Roy Cohn, McCarthy interrupted with a "point of order" to charge that Fisher "has been for a number of years a member of an organization which was named, oh, years and years ago, as the legal bulwark of the Communist Party."[44] When he finished, he was grinning at Welch across the table. Fisher had been originally chosen by Welch's

41 *Army-McCarthy Hearings*, pp. 2354–61; *New York Times*, June 10, 1954, pp. 1, 14–16.

42 *Army-McCarthy Hearings*, p. 2707.

43 Ibid.; *New York Times*, June 15, 1954, p. 1.

44 *Army-McCarthy Hearings*, p. 2427.

assistant, James D. St. Clair, to help with the army defense and had accompanied Welch and St. Clair to Washington in early April. He had belonged, while a student at Harvard Law School, to the National Lawyer's Guild, an organization now charged with Communist leanings. Although Fisher was an entirely respectable and very Republican member of Hale and Dorr, Welch had decided to send him back to Boston lest there be any unpleasantness. The decision was hardly secret. McCarthy had even alluded to the incident in the formal countercharges he filed with the subcommittee on April 20. His lawyer, Edward Bennett Williams, and Roy Cohn had both prevailed upon him not to drag Fisher into the hearings, and the senator had promised them that he would not bring the matter up.[45]

Once before the cameras, however, the senator seemed to slip all restraints. While Cohn pleadingly shook his head, McCarthy plunged into his attack on the young lawyer. Welch's reply was charged with emotion. "Until this moment I think I never really gauged your cruelty or your recklessness," he told McCarthy. He explained Fisher's background, his position in Hale and Dorr, and his brief membership in the Guild. Then he turned to McCarthy again: "Little did I dream you could be so reckless and so cruel as to do an injury to that lad. . . . If it were in my power to forgive you for your reckless cruelty, I [would] do so. I like to think I am a gentleman, but your forgiveness will have to come from some one other than me." McCarthy persisted, but Welch again cut him short. "Have you no sense of decency, sir, at long last? Have you left no sense of decency?" He arose and walked from the room, while the spectators broke into loud applause. As the subcommittee briefly recessed, McCarthy turned questioningly to those around him, turning his palms upward to ask "what did I do?"[46]

[45] *New York Times*, April 3, 1954, p. 1; April 16, 1954, p. 1; April 21, 1954, p. 1; Edward Bennett Williams, *One Man's Freedom* (New York, 1962), p. 61.

[46] *Army-McCarthy Hearings*, pp. 2428–30; Straight, *Trial by Television*, p. 253; *New York Times*, June 10, 1954, p. 1. Roy Cohn, in his recent memoir, argues that he had made a "deal" with Welch not to bring up Fred Fisher in return for Welch's promise not to explore Cohn's military record. Roy Cohn, "Believe Me, This Is the Truth about the Army-McCarthy Hearings. Honest," *Esquire* 69 (Feb. 1968): 128–29.

Some cynics suggested that Welch had anticipated the exchange and carefully prepared his response in advance. William Benton to John Howe, June

Throughout the course of the hearings President Eisenhower remained determined not to be drawn into the controversy. When he had to deal with McCarthy at all, he did so obliquely and through subordinates. Yet despite the president's determination, despite the best efforts of members of the Senate and the White House staff, Eisenhower was slowly but inevitably pulled into the conflict.

On May 14 army counsel John Adams refused to testify on the details of the January 21 meeting at which Sherman Adams had first directed him to prepare the army "chronology." Three days later, on May 17, Eisenhower told Republican congressional leaders that he would permit no testimony on private discussions within the Executive Department, and in a strong public letter to Secretary of Defense Wilson he directed that no such confidences be revealed, in order to preserve the integrity of the presidency, to maintain the proper separation of powers between the Executive and Congress, and to "preclude the exercise of arbitrary power by any branch of the Government."[47]

McCarthy denounced the presidential order as an "iron curtain," and even the Democrats were reluctant to accede to this broad statement of executive privilege. McCarthy could not rest here, however, and on May 27 he declared that all federal employees should know that "it is their duty to give us any information which they have about graft, corruption, communism, treason, and that there is no loyalty to a superior officer which can tower above and beyond their loyalty to their country."[48] His call was a plea for insubordination, a threat to the processes of orderly government, and a challenge to presidential prerogative which the administration could not ignore. The following day, in a statement approved by the president, Attorney General Brownell declared that the execution of laws was the sole and fundamental duty of the executive and "that responsibility can't be usurped by an

---

11, 1954, box 5, Benton Papers. The cynics were right. A lawyer who accompanied Welch out of the committee room recently recalled: "We walked out of the hearing together, down the hall, around the corner, around another corner, through the corridors of the Senate office building until finally reporters had quit trailing us and the flash bulbs had quit exploding. Then Welch looked at me and without changing his expression, the tears still streaming down his face, asked: 'Well, how did it go?'" Confidential source.

[47] *Army-McCarthy Hearings*, p. 1249; *New York Times*, May 18, 1954, p. 1; Adams, *Firsthand Report*, pp. 149–50.

[48] *Army-McCarthy Hearings*, p. 1575.

individual who may seek to set himself above the laws of our land."[49] For one brief instant the long-awaited confrontation between McCarthy and Eisenhower appeared to be at hand. The administration, however, crept back into its shell of protective silence, and the center stage was returned to the principals.

By May the Republicans were already working hard to bring the hearings to a close. On May 3 Senator Dirksen proposed that testimony be limited to McCarthy and Stevens, but immediately met strong opposition from the Democrats, who were determined to see the hearings continue until the administration faced up to McCarthy. The president, however, still had no intention of getting "into the gutter" with the senator. "I agree completely with your hope that the McCarthy-Army hearings be brought speedily and effectively to an end," he wrote a friend and supporter. "The Senate has sought means to bring this about; so far, unhappily, they have been unsuccessful."[50]

On May 8 Dirksen again offered a plan for limiting the hearings, this time suggesting that the public phase of the investigation be closed after the Stevens and McCarthy testimony was taken and that any subsequent hearings proceed behind closed doors. McClellan and the Democrats resisted this maneuver, and after some initial wavering the army joined them in oppositon to the motion. The proposal was defeated 4-3, with Chairman Mundt casting the tie-breaking vote.[51]

On May 17, after John Adams had read President Eisenhower's letter to Secretary Wilson, Dirksen was ready with still another motion. This time he called for a one-week recess, ostensibly to study the procedural problems raised by Adams's refusal to testify about the January 21 conference with White House leaders. The motion read "recess," but the Republicans obviously hoped to use it to cool down the controversy, to take it behind closed doors, or perhaps to end it altogether. It passed on a straight party vote after Symington had denounced it as a "transparent device" to take McCarthy and Cohn off the hook.[52]

[49] New York Times, May 29, 1954, p. 1.
[50] Ibid., May 4, 1954, p. 1; May 5, 1954, p. 1; Eisenhower to Harry A. Bullis, May 6, 1954, OF 99-R-1, Eisenhower Papers.
[51] According to news reports, the motion had been prepared in consultation with Styles Bridges and other Senate Republicans. It drew guarded statements of support from Nixon and other White House advisers. New York Times, May 9, 1954, p. 1; May 10, 1954, p. 1; May 11, 1954, p. 1.
[52] Army-McCarthy Hearings, p. 1280; New York Times, May 18, 1954, p. 1.

The reaction to the maneuver was strong. McClellan reaffirmed the determination of the minority not to be diverted by side issues, and President Eisenhower now reversed himself in a news conference on May 19 and urged that the hearings be continued. Chairman Mundt scoffed at the idea that the recess was designed to end the hearings, and the following week the subcommittee resumed its work.[53]

Senator Henry C. Dworshak presented yet another Republican motion on May 26, following a private conference by the majority members of the subcommittee. The Idaho Republican proposed that the charges against Assistant Secretary of Defense H. Struve Hensel and subcommittee staff director Francis Carr be dropped and that neither man be called to testify. The motion was important, not simply because it eliminated the two men as principals to the controversy, but because it also removed them as witnesses. Although Hensel's only part in the army-McCarthy controversy had been to sign a letter of transmittal forwarding the army "chronology" to Senator Potter, McCarthy had made him a main target for the formal countercharges he filed with the subcommittee on April 20. At an executive session on May 17, McCarthy admitted he had no evidence to show that Hensel had been involved in the controversy, but he refused to withdraw the charges because, as he told Hensel, he would look like "a damn fool."[54]

The case of Frank Carr was quite different, for although the army testimony showed that he had been a rather passive accomplice to Cohn's improprieties, he remained one of the most important witnesses to the various activities of McCarthy, Cohn, and others. Welch pleaded with Dworshak to split his motion in two, and he begged the majority not to pass it, but to no avail. The motion carried on a straight party vote.[55]

[53] *New York Times*, May 19, 1954, p. 1; May 20, 1954, pp. 1, 18; May 21, 1954, p. 1. Millard Tydings and Maurice Rosenblatt conferred with McClellan and Earle C. Clements to warn against the possibility of the hearings being called off by a diversionary move involving the committee's right to know what transpired at the January conference. Other "Clearing House" members contacted other senators. See "Chronology" included in Maurice Rosenblatt to Dean Clara Mayer, June 22, 1954, NCEC files.

[54] Potter, *Days of Shame*, pp. 223–25; Straight, *Trial by Television*, pp. 150–66. Hensel subsequently submitted an affidavit which was released to the press on June 20. *New York Times*, June 21, 1954, pp. 1, 17.

[55] *Army-McCarthy Hearings*, pp. 1531–32, 1546–50; *New York Times*, May 27, 1954, p. 1. According to one source very close to the army-McCarthy hearings, Welch's protests were purely forensic. He and the army had

By June 8 both the army and McCarthy had given up any hope of a clear-cut decision and were moving toward an agreement with the subcommittee majority on ending the hearings. Once again Dirksen took the initiative, proposing that the hearings be ended in one week. Private Schine, the amazing young man who had done so much to precipitate the hearings, was not to be called at all. The Democrats were just as determined to keep the investigation open. "I am not going to be a party to eliminating the subject of the controversy," declared Senator Jackson. Once again, however, the motion carried on a party vote, and the hearings at long last wound toward an end.[56]

EPILOGUE

The meaning of the army-McCarthy hearings is difficult to assess because the events of 1954 crowded close upon one another. It seems clear that Senator McCarthy lost little of his hard-core support, either in the Senate or the nation as a whole. There was heavy attrition, however, among moderates who had long tolerated McCarthy, despite of or in ignorance of his methods.[57] The coun-

---

already agreed to the elimination of Hensel and Carr. McCarthy later permitted Carr to testify toward the end of the hearings. His testimony generally supported that of Cohn and McCarthy, although under cross-examination he was incredibly vague about matters in which he was an intimate participant. *Army-McCarthy Hearings,* pp. 2626–2802.

[56] *Army-McCarthy Hearings,* pp. 2538, 2544; *New York Times,* June 11, 1954, p. 14.

[57] In 1954, the Gallup Poll reported the following summary of public response to McCarthy:

Date	% Favorable	% Unfavorable	% No Opinion
June 1953	35	30	35
August 1953	34	42	24
January 1954	50	29	21
March 1954	46	36	18
April 1954	38	46	16
May 1954	35	49	16
June 1954	34	45	21
August 1954	36	51	13

Washington Post, Nov. 12, 1954. The release of the army "chronology" and the events of March 1954 seem to have deflated the temporarily high rating McCarthy received in January 1954. By May his support had returned to 35 percent and remained more or less constant thereafter. The opposition to McCarthy steadily increased as the number of those having "no opinion" declined. Also see John Fenton, *In Your Opinion* (Boston, 1960), pp. 135–37. For a somewhat different view, see G. D. Wiebe, "The Army-McCarthy Hearings and the Public Conscience," *Public Opinion Quarterly* 44 (Winter 1958–1959): 490–502.

try's newspapers, most of which had long been hostile to McCarthy, now assailed him in ever-increasing numbers. And in his home state a recall movement led by a small town newspaper editor threatened the senator in his own backyard.[58]

The political stress created by the hearings was felt most acutely by the moderate Republicans who had long tried to avoid or ignore the McCarthy problem altogether. From across the entire country, storm warnings from Republican leaders poured into the White House. "There is a growing impatience with the Republican Party," declared Congressman George H. Bender, the Republican candidate for the Senate in Ohio. "McCarthyism has become a synonym for witch-hunting, star-chamber methods and the denial of those civil liberties which have distinguished our country in its historic growth." If we don't do something about McCarthy, warned a New Hampshire national committeeman, "we are going to lose a lot of votes." In Nebraska a Republican leader reported that everyone on the State Central Committee had agreed "that our candidates are being harmed by this public spectacle." "If we are to win the November election, we shall need the support of the Independents, many Democrats and the 'liberal' Republicans," complained an Iowa Republican leader to Sherman Adams. "It is now time for the Republican Party to repudiate Joe McCarthy before he drags them all to defeat," declared Palmer Hoyt of the *Denver Post*. From California to New York, from Tennessee to Vermont, Republican leaders expressed worry, anger, and frustration over the disruption McCarthy had caused. "If the facts could be proven," grumbled one Texas banker, "I am sure he is in the employ of the New Dealers."[59]

In the Senate, Republicans felt the same pressures. "I cannot

---

[58] For an excellent study of the recall movement, see David P. and Esther S. Thelen, "Joe Must Go: The Movement To Recall Senator Joseph R. McCarthy," *Wisconsin Magazine of History* 49 (Spring 1966): 185–209. Working from March 18 until June 5, the recall workers gathered an estimated 400,000 signatures on petitions urging McCarthy's recall. Significantly, McCarthy returned to campaign in Wisconsin almost every weekend during the army-McCarthy hearings.

[59] Rep. George H. Bender to Eisenhower, May 7, 1954, OF 138-Ohio; Frank J. Sulloway to Sherman Adams, May 17, 1954; Adams to Sulloway, May 21, 1954, GF 171; Jim Schramm to Adams, Feb. 22, 1954, GF 171; Palmer Hoyt to Paul G. Hoffman, May 17, 1954, in Hoyt to Eisenhower, May 24, 1954, OF 99-R; Frank Wood to Eisenhower, May 16, 1954; Eisenhower to Wood, May 19, 1954, OF 99-U, all in the Eisenhower Papers. J. C. Tye to Hugh A. Butler, box 287, Butler Papers.

begin to tell you how many people I have heard around these parts expressing their intention to vote for a Democratic senator as a means of supplying the necessary votes to eliminate the Junior Senator from Wisconsin," wrote a New Jersey Republican to Senator Robert C. Hendrickson. "If my mail reflects any degree of accuracy, we are in for trouble as a result of the hearings," agreed Hendrickson. "I wonder if you gentlemen there in Washington fully realize what this is doing to the Republican party," complained a Nebraska Republican to Senator Hugh Butler. "I will guess with you that hereabouts it is making more Democratic votes than helping the Republican party," added a local banker. "My own personal views coincide with the general run of Republicans who are engaged in fund raising," wrote the chairman of the Republican National Finance Committee to Karl Mundt. "The opinion of a large majority . . . is that the McCarthy-Stevens hearings are a disgraceful affair and the sooner they finish the better for the party."[60]

But all this did not change the underlying balance of power. McCarthy still had the unyielding support of eight to ten Senate bitter-enders and through them considerable leverage over the Republican leadership in Congress and the White House. McCarthy had remained in power through the acquiescence of the Senate body, not its active support. The army-McCarthy hearings had increased the instability of the "McCarthy balance," but they had not destroyed it altogether. McCarthy had recovered on countless other occasions and even now, as the hearings closed, he was already talking of new and expanded investigations of the army, the CIA, and the defense industry.[61]

But none of the senator's proposed investigations ever materialized. Before the army-McCarthy hearings ended, Senator Ralph Flanders arose in the Senate to initiate a resolution which would ultimately lead to McCarthy's condemnation. The Flanders resolution was a dramatic and probably decisive attempt to end the

[60] Herbert J. Hannoch to Robert C. Hendrickson, June 14, July 6, 1954; Hendrickson to Hannoch, June 21, July 9, 1954; Hendrickson to David Baird, Jr., June 23, 1954, boxes 17, 83, in the Hendrickson Papers. John L. Mattox to Hugh A. Butler, April 30, 1954; J. Y. Castle to Butler, April 30, 1954, both in box 287, Butler Papers. F. Peavey Heffelfinger, chairman, Republican National Finance Committee, to Karl E. Mundt, May 5, 1954 (copy), GF 171, Eisenhower Papers.

[61] Army-McCarthy Hearings, pp. 2973–77; New York Times, June 17, 1954, p. 1; June 19, 1954, p. 1.

McCarthy interregnum and to reclaim the honor and dignity of the Senate. It was not, however, the only struggle. There was another front to the battle—less dramatic, less decisive, certainly less publicized—but which was nevertheless a piece with the broad movement to check McCarthy's power. Involved were the internal affairs of McCarthy's own committee.

Since the Democratic walkout of 1953, there had been steadily increasing pressure on the members of the Investigations Subcommittee to restrain their chairman. The rule changes adopted in January 1954 had been a partial response to this demand, but it still remained for the members to operate effectively on a day-to-day basis to oppose the chairman. While the focus of publicity shifted to the Senate floor and the Flanders resolution, the subcommittee faced two major problems left over from the hearings: what to do with Roy Cohn and the subcommittee staff, and what kind of a report to prepare on the hearings themselves.

By June the Democratic members of the subcommittee were lined up in a firm phalanx under the cautious leadership of John McClellan. Without Republican support, however, they could only operate with limited effectiveness. Then on the very last day of the hearings, freshman Republican Charles Potter issued a hard-hitting statement calling for an overhaul of the subcommittee staff and suggesting that the attorney general explore the possibility of perjury.[62]

The following day the Democrats joined the issue with a joint statement demanding a staff shake-up and urging the Justice Department to press perjury prosecutions. They also revealed that two members of the subcommittee staff (subsequently identified as Donald A. Surine and Thomas La Venia) had never received security clearance from the Department of Defense.[63] Thus, as the hearings ended, Chairman McCarthy was faced with a revolt within his own subcommittee.

McCarthy chaired his first meeting of the rebellious subcom-

[62] *New York Times*, June 18, 1954, p. 1; Potter, *Days of Shame*, pp. 263–64. The origin of Potter's statement has itself become a matter of controversy. According to Richard Rovere, the statement was drafted by Potter's administrative assistant, Tom McIntyre, a fiery Irishman who had set for himself the task of toppling Joe McCarthy. Fearing that Potter might back down at the last moment, McIntyre distributed the release to the press without the senator's knowledge, thus locking him into an anti-McCarthy position. Richard H. Rovere, "The Untold Story of McCarthy's Fall," pp. 3–5.

[63] *New York Times*, June 18, 1954, p. 11; June 19, 1954, p. 1.

mittee on July 15. Potter, Jackson, and Symington all demanded that the subcommittee take action on its staff, but the chairman successfully defeated the move by simply refusing to accept McClellan's proxy. He then rode roughshod over the other senators by ordering an unexpected hearing on "Communist activities" in defense plants near Boston. Outside in the corridor he loudly taunted his opponents: "If you want to keep me from exposing Communists, go ahead."[64]

The senator's triumph was short-lived. From Arkansas came McClellan's angry mutterings that the chairman's decision was arbitrary and that he would insist on firings among the staff. Republican Majority Leader Knowland phoned McCarthy to demand that he call off the Boston hearing. Since the Senate would be in session, the hearing would require unanimous consent. "I will say the Majority Leader himself would object to any committees meeting outside Washington," declared Knowland.[65]

On July 19 Roy Cohn, who was under intense pressure from Republicans to spare the subcommittee the embarrassment of having to ask him to leave, announced his resignation. Shortly before a subcommittee meeting the following day, McCarthy "reluctantly" accepted the resignation, denouncing those who had sought it and declaring that it was "a great victory" for communism. He also transferred Don Surine back to his own staff after one of the Democrats raised questions about the ex-FBI man's personal fitness. Reporters noted this as one of the few reversals ever suffered by McCarthy within the subcommittee.[66]

A few days later another McCarthy aide was in trouble. Thomas La Venia, it now appeared, had once belonged to the American Law Student's Association, an organization which had been "identified" by HUAC as a Communist front and which McCarthy had publicized in his attack on Ambassador Philip C. Jessup in 1950. Under pressure from several members of the subcommittee, La Venia was reassigned to a "non-sensitive" position on the subcommittee staff.[67]

Yet another battle erupted a week later, this time in the full Committee on Government Operations, after McCarthy announced

---

[64] Ibid., July 16, 1954, p. 6. McClellan was in Arkansas in the middle of a primary campaign.

[65] Ibid., July 16, 1954, p. 6; July 17, 1954, p. 1.

[66] Ibid., July 20, 1954, pp. 1, 6; July 21, 1954, p. 1.

[67] Ibid., July 22, 1954, p. 1; July 24, 1954, p. 1.

the appointment of ex-Senator Owen Brewster as chief counsel. Brewster was a right-wing Republican and a strong McCarthy supporter who had been defeated in the 1952 primary by Maine's popular and moderate governor, Frederick G. Payne. Still, as a former member of the Senate he commanded a certain amount of support in the Upper Chamber. The minority members of the committee at first delayed approval of the appointment, and then on August 10 McClellan announced the unanimous opposition of the five Democrats to the appointment. Several Republicans joined the Democratic-led opposition, and the appointment was finally withdrawn.[68] Once again Chairman McCarthy was set on his heels by a group which heretofore had been responsive to his slightest commands.

Meanwhile, the so-called Mundt subcommittee worked hard to finish its final report on the army-McCarthy hearings. The Democrats were determined to file a report sharply critical of McCarthy. The senator's Republican supporters on the subcommittee were equally intent upon absolving him. Jackson and Dirksen met briefly in an attempt to draft a bipartisan report, but they quickly split over irreconcilable differences.[69] The only real question was the course of Senator Potter, who managed, typically, to be on both sides of the issue. His June 17 statement criticizing both sides was almost identical with the Democratic position, and there were rumors that he might join the minority in its report. He was also under pressure from Dirksen, however, to compromise for the sake of party unity.[70] In the end Potter uncomfortably straddled the entire question. He signed a moderately worded majority report, but then filed his own "supplementary views" reaffirming his June 17 charge that "the principal accusation of each side . . . was borne out."[71]

The struggles within the Permanent Subcommittee on Investigations were eclipsed by the drama of the Flanders resolution. They

[68] Ibid., July 30, 1954, p. 18; Aug. 4, 1954, p. 8; Aug. 11, 1954, p. 101. Theodore C. Sorenson assigns a major role in this battle to John F. Kennedy, whom he declares "was responsible for delaying and defeating the appointment." Sorenson, *Kennedy* (New York, 1965), p. 46. While this is certainly possible, it is rather difficult to imagine John McClellan taking his cues from a freshman senator.

[69] *New York Times*, Aug. 15, 1954, p. 34; Aug. 20, 1954, p. 1.

[70] Ibid., Aug. 21, 1954, p. 7; Aug. 22, 1954, p. 1.

[71] Ibid., Aug. 24, 1954, p. 1; Sept. 1, 1954, p. 1; *Congress and the Nation*, (Washington, D.C., 1965), p. 1725.

were nonetheless an important part of the growing movement to end McCarthy's long-suffered abuse of senatorial power. He would still chair a few meetings of the Investigations Subcommittee, but for all intents and purposes the grand inquisitor had been hamstrung within his own committee. The men who had fought him were neither idealistic nor especially courageous. They made no impassioned pleas against "McCarthyism" or in defense of civil liberties. They did not even attack McCarthy himself, but rather his lieutenants. Nevertheless, they fought a politically wise inner battle over procedures and appointments which had the net effect of blocking the Wisconsin senator at almost every point. While the sustained pressure behind the Flanders resolution mounted, the steady and continued rebellion within the subcommittee threatened to devour McCarthy's most important political base within the Senate. "He can't sit still any longer," declared one compassionate senior senator. "They are hitting him everywhere and from every angle. He feels caged. He has it coming to him in my book. But believe me, I don't take pleasure in this sight."[72]

[72] Quoted by William S. White in the *New York Times,* Aug. 15, 1954, sec. 4, p. 3.

CENSURE

> *Resolved, That the conduct of the Senator from Wisconsin, Mr. McCarthy, is unbecoming a Member of the United States Senate, is contrary to senatorial traditions, and tends to bring the Senate into disrepute, and such conduct is hereby condemned.*
>
> SENATE RESOLUTION 301.

WHILE THE ARMY-MC CARTHY hearings were dramatic and spectacular, they were not conclusive. They threatened the now delicate balance which had for so long assured the Wisconsin senator's continued power and influence, but they did not destroy it. This was why the resolution Senator Ralph E. Flanders introduced on June 11 was so important. The "McCarthy balance" was created by acquiescence, not by support, and its prolongation depended upon the Senate's continued evasion of a direct confrontation with McCarthy. The Flanders resolution, quite simply, threatened to make further evasion impossible.

SENATOR FROM VERMONT

On June 11, 1954, Ralph Flanders entered the crowded Senate caucus room and slowly threaded his way through the spectators and cameramen until he arrived at the long table where Joe McCarthy was seated. The elderly Vermont Republican showed no sign of his customary humor as he handed the Wisconsin senator an invitation to be present that afternoon when Flanders addressed the Senate. McCarthy read the invitation aloud and dismissed it. "I think they should get a net and take him to a good quiet place," he told reporters. But he couldn't dismiss the resolution Flanders introduced that afternoon. The Vermont senator called upon the Senate to remove McCarthy from his chairmanships unless he "purged" himself of his contempt of the Senate by answering the questions raised eighteen months earlier by the Hennings report.[1]

What sort of a man would challenge McCarthy? The question was posed rhetorically by Paul G. Hoffman at a dinner meeting of prominent businessmen, educators, and literary figures in the autumn of 1954.

"For a long time," declared Hoffman, "I knew there would come forth an individual to do battle with this evil man. And I thought that this individual would have to be the complete opposite to McCarthy. He would have to be literate, a humanist, a man of deep values rather than pragmatic politics . . . and I did not know who this could be. But when I saw him hand McCarthy the invitation to be present on the floor, I realized that my *old* friend Ralph Flanders met these specifications."[2]

The senator from Vermont was an engineer and an inventor who had worked his way from apprentice to board chairman along the lines of the classic success story. He even married the boss's daughter. He combined with the flinty conservatism of his native state a broader concern for social values and an intelligent interest in foreign affairs. He served in a wide variety of public and quasi-public organizations during the 1930s and 1940s, and in 1942 he joined Paul Hoffman, William Benton, and a number of other internationally minded business leaders in founding the Committee for Economic Development. He was elected to the Senate in 1946 and overwhelmingly reelected in 1952. He would be seventy-eight years old when this second term expired, and he had already decided not to seek reelection.[3]

[1] *Congressional Record,* 83d Cong., 2d sess., June 11, 1954, pp. 8032–33; *New York Times,* June 12, 1954, p. 1.

[2] Author's interview with Maurice Rosenblatt, June 13, 1966.

[3] Ralph E. Flanders, *Senator from Vermont* (Boston, 1960); *New York Times,* July 31, 1954, p. 4; Flanders to W. L. Beale, Jr., Dec. 28, 1954, box

Flanders was probably a true conservative, though his conservatism was often masked by the peculiarities of American political usage. He usually described himself as a Republican "liberal," but this liberalism was more intuitive than intellectual. "I have found great difficulty in defining to myself just what a liberal is," he confessed to Norman Cousins, the editor of *Saturday Review*, a few months after the censure debate.[4] He strongly supported Dwight Eisenhower for the Republican nomination in 1952, and he worked hard for the general's election. He enjoyed speaking to college students, young Republicans, and Democrats on behalf of Eisenhower, but not to "dyed-in-the-wool" Republicans. "I am no good at talking with life long Republicans," he told Sherman Adams. "We don't see eye to eye and I stir no enthusiasm."[5]

Like most "liberal" Republicans, Flanders had for a long time been critical of McCarthy in private but had said very little in public. In the autumn of 1951 he had gone so far as to draft a resolution aimed at McCarthy and McCarthyism, but he continued to hope that the nomination and election of Eisenhower would somehow eliminate the Wisconsin senator from the political scene. "I believe McCarthy can be washed out as thoroughly as a Kansas flood washes out the stockyards," he wrote Paul Hoffman, who was soon to organize "Citizens for Eisenhower." As for the resolution against McCarthy, he declared, "I am keeping the gun loaded but not taking it out just yet."[6]

In early 1953 he wrote one Vermont constituent, "I shall have to leave to the Democrats the problem of making a case for the

---

101, Flanders Papers, Syracuse University. Many of McCarthy's strongest critics were members of the Committee for Economic Development, an organization that is the very embodiment of what is sometimes called that "American establishment." In addition to Benton, Hoffman, and Flanders, its board of trustees included cotton merchant W. L. Clayton, newspaper publisher Gardner Cowles, Harry A. Bullis, chairman of the board of General Mills, Harry Scherman, president of the Book-of-the-Month Club, Fred Lazarus, Jr., president of Federated Department Stores, Inc., and J. D. Zellerbach, president of Crown Zellerbach. These and other leaders of the CED became increasingly opposed to McCarthy as the senator turned his fire upon Eisenhower.

[4] Ralph Flanders to Norman Cousins, March 15, 1955, box 103, Flanders Papers, Syracuse University.

[5] Ralph Flanders to Sherman Adams, July 30, 1952, box 115, Flanders Papers, Syracuse University.

[6] Ralph Flanders to Paul G. Hoffman, Oct. 15, 1951, Oct. 21, 1951, both in box 105, Flanders Papers, Syracuse University.

expulsion of a Republican Senator. I hope you will not think that I am cynical on this matter because I am disturbed by the situation," he continued. "But I have to decide what is the wisest use of my time."[7] Two months later he indirectly rebuked McCarthy for his intemperate attack on British Labour party leader Clement Attlee, but he declined to go further. "Senator McCarthy is within the law and within his rights," he wrote, "though he toes to the extreme limit in both respects."[8]

He became more deeply concerned in late 1953, when he went abroad to visit his daughter and her husband and found everywhere the persistent question: "What about McCarthy?"[9] Flanders made his first attack on McCarthy on March 9, 1954, just two days before the army released its famous "chronology." He accused him of deserting the Republican party and ridiculed his celebrated hunt for Communists in government. "He dons his warpaint. He goes into his war dance. He emits his warwhoops. He goes forth to battle and proudly returns with the scalp of a pink Army dentist. We may assume that this represents the depth and seriousness of the Communist penetration in this country at this time."[10] When he had finished speaking, John Sherman Cooper of Kentucky rose to praise him and that evening the president himself sent his congratulations. "I was very much interested in reading the comments you made in the Senate today," declared Eisenhower. "I think America needs to hear from more Republican voices like yours."[11]

Two weeks later Flanders appeared to weaken. He praised McCarthy's Lincoln Day "indictment" of the Democratic party

[7] Ralph Flanders to Freeman Keith, March 6, 1953, box 1, Flanders Papers, State Historical Society of Wisconsin.

[8] Ralph Flanders to Robert Sharp, May 21, 1953, box 1, Flanders Papers, State Historical Society of Wisconsin.

[9] Ralph Flanders to author, June 27, 1967; Flanders, *Senator from Vermont,* p. 254. Ralph Flanders to William Knowland, Aug. 4, 1954, box 25, Arthur V. Watkins Papers, Brigham Young University.

[10] *Congressional Record,* 83d Cong., 2d sess., March 9, 1954, pp. 2886–87; *New York Times,* March 10, 1954, p. 1.

[11] Eisenhower to Ralph Flanders, March 9, 1954, OF 99-R, Eisenhower Papers. In reply to one correspondent who implied that his remarks had been inspired by left-wingers, Flanders wryly answered that he had discussed the matter only with his wife and son. "Being an inventor and a machine designer, I have had ideas of my own in the past and they still come to me." Flanders to J. W. Brandt, March 31, 1954, box 1, Flanders Papers, State Historical Society of Wisconsin.

as a good "Republican speech." But he continued to insist that America faced no real threat of internal Communist subversion, and he redoubled his criticism of McCarthy's abuse of office.[12] Then on June 1, in the midst of the army-McCarthy hearings, Flanders attacked the Wisconsin senator once again. This time his remarks were harsh and unsparing. He compared McCarthy to Hitler and denounced him for spreading division and confusion throughout the land. "Were the Junior Senator from Wisconsin in the pay of the Communists he could not have done a better job for them," he charged. Behind Flanders sat Majority Leader William F. Knowland, red-faced and angry yet powerless to stop Flanders's arraignment. The leadership bitterly resented Flander's speech, for in attacking McCarthy, he threatened to drive into the open the division in Republican ranks which they had been trying so desparately to avoid. When their argument failed to sway the Vermonter, they ostracized him. On the floor, in the cloakroom, in the Senate dining room, Flanders was treated to that deliberate and studied silence reserved for those troublesome senators who breach the Senate's mutually protective folkways. As the senator himself later recalled, "Mrs. Flanders and I were left in Coventry."[13]

But stop him they could not. A week later he returned to the floor once again, this time to introduce Senate Resolution 261, calling upon the Senate to remove McCarthy from the chairmanship of both the Committee on Government Operations and its Permanent Subcommittee on Investigations.

FLANDERS AND THE CLEARING HOUSE

According to a popular Capitol Hill truism, seven-eighths of the "iceberg" of congressional politics exists below the surface in a demi-world peopled by lobbyists, administrative assistants, speechwriters, and pressmen. And it was because of this reality that the unlikely alliance between the impeccably Republican Senator from

[12] *New York Times,* March 21, 1954, p. 44. Radio broadcast, week of March 28, 1954, box 154; Flanders, "Personalities and Policies," draft of undelivered remarks on Senator McCarthy, prepared for April 7, 1954, box 144; both in the Flanders Papers, Syracuse University.

[13] *Congressional Record,* 83d Cong., 2d sess., June 1, 1954, p. 7389; *New York Times,* June 2, 1954, p. 1; radio broadcast, week of June 6, 1954, box 154, Flanders Papers, Syracuse University; Ralph Flanders to author, June 27, 1967. Flanders, COHC, p. 10.

Vermont and the liberal enthusiasts of the Clearing House was fashioned. Flanders had taken the initiative in challenging McCarthy. "He is completely motivated by principle," declared one observer.[14] Nevertheless, he scarcely had the staff support to force an issue of this magnitude upon the Senate. His office was organized on a modest basis, as befitted the representative of a small, largely one-party state. It was certainly not a citadel from which to do battle with the Senate's most controversial member.

The NCEC Clearing House, on the other hand, had developed a political strategy which emphasized the role of technical support in battling McCarthy inside the Senate—the application to the McCarthy issue of techniques "which have hitherto been generally confined to winning a pork barrel or a gas franchise."[15] Soon after Flanders introduced his original resolution he turned to the Clearing House for support, and that group, having assured themselves of the Vermonter's determination to see the issue through, readily agreed to furnish the necessary "technical" assistance.

Throughout 1954 the activities of the Clearing House had remained piecemeal and peripheral. Lucille Lang had continued to supply Democratic senators with research material from Earle Clement's office, but there were no major "operations" such as the group had long envisioned. The Clearing House and its parent organization, the National Committee for an Effective Congress, did work closely with William Benton in the organization of "I Believe," a propaganda campaign begun after McCarthy dropped his $2,000,000 libel suit against Benton with the declaration that he could find no one who believed Benton's charges.[16] The "I Believe" committee placed full-page advertisements in the *New York Times* and the *New York Herald-Tribune* soliciting both contributions and "witnesses" who believed Benton's charges. The highly successful response to this appeal was used in turn to finance more advertisements in major dailies across the country.[17]

On occasion the Clearing House had intervened more directly in the McCarthy controversy. Shortly after the Republican major-

---

[14] Maurice Rosenblatt to Dean Clara Mayer, June 22, 1954, NCEC files.

[15] Maurice Rosenblatt to Paul G. Hoffman, Jan. 20, 1955, NCEC files.

[16] *New York Times*, March 6, 1954, p. 1. William Benton to John Howe, March 8, 12, 16, 1954; Orton H. Hicks to Walter H. Wheeler, Jr., March 10, 1954; Benton to Edward R. Murrow, March 18, 1954, all in box 5, Benton Papers.

[17] John Howe to Morris Rubin, June 16, 1954; Howe to George E. Agree, July 9, 1954; press release, July 1954, all in box 5, Benton Papers.

ity voted its "temporary" recess in the army-McCarthy hearings, for example, Millard Tydings, Maurice Rosenblatt, Dean Francis P. Sayre of Washington Cathedral, and several others met for a worried consultation. Tydings was distressed over the possibility that the Democrats on the subcommittee were falling into a trap designed to end the hearings altogether. Afterwards, Tydings and Rosenblatt met with John McClellan, who immediately issued a strong statement declaring that the subcommittee would not be diverted. Dean Sayre met with Stuart Symington, who also made a categorical declaration that the hearings would continue.[18] This pressure from the Democrats, together with a strong declaration from the White House, foreclosed the possibility that the hearings might be ended or diverted at that point.

By early June Rosenblatt and others were busy at work with William Macomber, administrative assistant to John Sherman Cooper, on a resolution to strip McCarthy of his chairmanships for his *prima facie* violations of law and Senate procedure. The Kentucky Republican had steadfastly refused to make speeches, but he declared that the time had at last come for action. Before Cooper could act, however, Ralph Flanders had already introduced Senate Resolution 261.[19]

Before June 1954, the Clearing House had had only minimal contact with Flanders. In 1952 the National Committee for an Effective Congress had endorsed him and sent him a small contribution. Flanders had returned their check, however, since he was almost assured of election and was not even actively campaigning. In March Rosenblatt had written him on behalf of the NCEC, congratulating him on his remarks on McCarthy, but only after Flanders had introduced his original resolution did he turn to the Clearing House for help.[20]

On June 14, three days after the Flanders resolution was introduced, the Clearing House group met with some twenty-five lawyers, legislative directors, and Hill functionaries in the Washington home of Gerhard P. Van Arkel. Dean Sayre opened the meeting by declaring that an issue between McCarthyism and

[18] "Chronology," in Maurice Rosenblatt to Dean Clara Mayer, June 22, 1954, NCEC files.
[19] Ibid., interview with Maurice Rosenblatt, June 13, 1966. Cooper immediately issued a press release supporting the Flanders resolution.
[20] Maurice Rosenblatt to Ralph Flanders, March 12, 1954; George E. Agree, "Memorandum #1," [c. Sept. 1954], both in the NCEC files.

democracy had to be drawn. Rosenblatt explained the nature and operation of the Clearing House and declared that the Flanders resolution was the best opportunity yet offered for a showdown with McCarthy. The group reached a general agreement that the Flanders resolution should be supported, and they promised to contribute time, money, and energy to force the issue.[21]

THE FLANDERS RESOLUTION AND THE SENATE

Action on the Hill is never easy, and when the issues involved are highly controversial the obstacles are legion. While the Clearing House was preparing to muster technical support for the Flanders resolution, the resolution itself was meeting stiff opposition from both sides of the Chamber. Majority Leader Knowland denounced the resolution at a hastily called press conference on June 12. Flanders had not consulted him about the resolution, and the Republican leader was not at all happy about it. "I don't believe the motion entered was justified," he declared. "I think it is contrary to established procedure in the Senate." "I agree that this is embarrassing to the Republican leadership," retorted Flanders, "but it's past time for them to be talking about that now."[22]

The Democratic leadership did not want a division on the McCarthy issue either, although Democrat Herbert H. Lehman had followed Flanders's lead by entering his own resolution calling upon the Senate to remove McCarthy from his chairmanships. The Democrats still fretted over the possibility of a party-line confrontation, and some even urged a complete abdication of responsibility. McCarthy was part of the "Republican mess" in Washington, and it was up to Eisenhower and the G.O.P. to get rid of him. Many southern Democrats were particularly opposed to the form of the resolution. They feared that it might establish a precedent which would threaten not only party control of the Senate but the seniority system as well. "If we get back in power," declared one senior Democrat, "we don't want a simple motion like Senator Flanders' to throw us out of joint."[23]

---

[21] "Chronology," in Maurice Rosenblatt to Dean Clara Mayer, June 22, 1954, NCEC files.

[22] *New York Times*, June 13, 1954, p. 1.

[23] Ibid., June 16, 1954, p. 1; "Memorandum regarding the Flanders Resolution," June 23, 1954, NCEC files.

For members of both parties, however, the root problem was political and not procedural. The Senate would not act to remove McCarthy from his chairmanships unless the Republicans requested it, declared Guy Gillette, and this was highly improbable. "They certainly would oppose any action initiated from the Democratic side."[24] McCarthy, moreover, had polarized opinion throughout the country. For many he remained a symbol of fearless opposition to communism; for others he stood for illiberalism incarnate. No matter how a senator voted, he stood to antagonize a large part of his constituency. "It is, I think, a rule followed by most politicians that you never antagonize any group, no matter how small, if you can avoid it," declared *New York Times* columnist James Reston a few months later. "If you have to choose between two groups, you always choose to antagonize the one that is less vindictive and organized than the others. And in this case that is certainly not the pro-McCarthy crowd."[25]

On June 15 Flanders met with Republican leaders and then acquiesced as Knowland referred the resolution to the Senate Rules Committee. This meant that Flanders himself could no longer call the resolution to a vote at will and that the parliamentary obstacles to a division were greater than ever. The Vermont Republican could certainly expect little assistance from Rules Committee Chairman William E. Jenner. Nevertheless, this procedure answered the technical objections raised by some Republicans that Flanders had given McCarthy no forum before which he might "purge" himself, and it prevented McCarthy and his supporters from calling up the resolution themselves in an effort to catch Flanders unprepared. The press, sensing the strong opposition to the resolution, quickly concluded that there would be no showdown.[26]

Behind the scenes, however, the half-dozen activists who comprised the Clearing House had already set about creating support and viability for the resolution. Turning from their regular jobs, they plunged into a broad operation designed to turn the wheels of power and force a division.

[24] Guy Gillette to Robert Edberg, July 9, 1954, Legislative File, box 39, ADA Papers. Also see John W. Bricker to Wilbur D. Peterson, June 22, 1954, Bricker Papers, Ohio Historical Society.

[25] James Reston to John Howe, Sept. 29, 1954, box 4, Benton Papers.

[26] *New York Times*, June 15, 1954, p. 24; June 16, 1954, p. 1; Arthur Krock, ibid., June 27, 1954, sec. 4, p. 3. John W. Vandercook, radio broadcast of June 15, 1954, transcript in NCEC files.

The most immediate problem was that of finances. Flanders had asked for a key Hill "operator," a man whose services would generally run from $20,000 to $30,000 a year. In addition the campaign required a public relations man, a leg-man to maintain liaison with senators and committee executives, and a modest clerical staff. These were things that money could buy. "History must not record that a battle as serious as this was lost in its critical moment because nobody organized the latent sentiment of the country and struck at the right time at the right place," declared Rosenblatt.[27]

The Clearing House secured $12,000 to cover operations between mid-June and the end of July. Most of this money was raised by Paul G. Hoffman, a liberal Republican businessman and an ardent Eisenhower suporter. During the Truman administration Hoffman had served as administrator of the Economic Cooperation Agency (Marshall Plan). Afterwards, he had directed the Ford Foundation and still later the Studebaker Corporation. In 1952 he organized "Citizens for Eisenhower" and played a key role in the battle for the Republican nomination. Although he was shunted aside by the professionals who surrounded Eisenhower after the convention, he remained one of Senator McCarthy's most persistent critics within the Republican party. On June 2, after Flanders's sharp attack on the Wisconsin senator, he wired Flanders three short words: "You are wonderful." Now, with the future of McCarthy and possibly the Republican party hanging in the balance, he eagerly joined the battle for the Flanders resolution. The money he raised was not a great sum, but it was enough to enable the Clearing House to scrape together its campaign against McCarthy.[28]

The Clearing House began its operation like any modern lobby. Well, almost like any lobby. Most powerful pressure groups are well-financed and maintain large permanent staffs. This by contrast was an ad hoc operation, and its participants were enlisted only for the duration. They started by hiring Laurence Henderson, a veteran congressional technician and former administrative assistant to both Senators Flanders and Benton, to head the cam-

[27] Maurice Rosenblatt to Seniel Ostrow, June 23, 1954, NCEC files.
[28] George E. Agree, "Memorandum #1," [c. Sept. 1954]; Paul G. Hoffman to Maurice Rosenblatt, July 9, 1954; Rosenblatt to Hoffman, July 8, 12, 1954; Joseph D. Shane to Rosenblatt, July 8, 1954, all in the NCEC files. Hoffman to Ralph Flanders, June 2, 1954, box 105, Flanders Papers, Syracuse University.

paign. A few weeks later they added several more Hill workers and set up a suite of offices in the Carroll Arms Hotel.

The entire operation was conducted simultaneously on several fronts. At one level they sought to stimulate and mobilize public opinion. Working through the press and through the leadership of a wide variety of civic, religious, and labor groups, they attempted to organize maximum pressure behind the resolution. "The most vital thing is to get as many of your individual members [as possible] to write their senators calling for a showdown in this session," wrote Rosenblatt to the legislative director of a key CIO union. To the editor of an influential Democratic newspaper he appealed: "Anything which you can do to build a bonfire under the Democrats will be most helpful." The Clearing House worked especially hard to keep the press well informed of the day-to-day progress of the resolution. Whenever Flanders had an important statement they arranged for a press conference (on occasion a luncheon), and they carefully briefed the reporters on the political and parliamentary background of the struggle. They also distributed copies of speeches by Flanders and reprints of favorable editorials in an effort to overcome the initial skepticism which had greeted the resolution.[29]

But mass pressure is only one way, and not always the most effective, to influence the legislative process. Most of the mail which arrives in a senator's office never goes past the desk of his administrative assistant. But a personal communication—a phone call, wire, or visit—from an influential constituent cannot be ignored. The Clearing House tried to bring this type of pressure to bear on the Senate.

A good example was the case of John McClellan. As a southerner, a conservative, and the ranking minority member of McCarthy's committee, McClellan held the key to much of the uncommitted Democratic vote. Not only southerners but midwesterners such as Thomas A. Burke of Ohio and easterners such as John F. Kennedy of Massachusetts tied their votes to McClellan's lead. Senator Fulbright knew of several Arkansas businessmen who were "definitely key people in determining McClellan's course," and Rosenblatt urged Paul Hoffman to exert his own in-

---

[29] Maurice Rosenblatt to John J. Flynn, June 26, 1954; Rosenblatt to Mark Ethridge, July 14, 1954; Rosenblatt to Frank Edwards, July 6, 7, 1954; Rosenblatt to Evans Clark, June 25, 1954; Rosenblatt to James A. Wechsler, July 15, 1954, all in the NCEC files.

fluence on them. The Clearing House also urged the powerful Philadelphia businessman C. Jared Ingersoll to ask his friends in Arkansas to help win McClellan's support. "I am endeavoring to pass the word on to our people in Arkansas, who may be helpful," replied Ingersoll.[30] The Clearing House inspired a strong letter to Democratic Senator Earle Clements from the president of the Kentucky Chamber of Commerce, and they once again alerted leading Michigan clergymen who put pressure on Republicans Charles Potter and Homer Ferguson.[31]

Paul Hoffman worked especially hard to line up Republican support for the resolution. He came to Washington in mid-July for lunch with the president, and he spent much of the remainder of the day conferring with key Republican liberals. Two weeks later, as debate on the resolution neared, he urgently appealed to the White House to use its influence on several wavering Republicans.[32] Together with the Clearing House, Hoffman and C. D. Jackson, a former Eisenhower aide, drafted an open telegram to every senator from twenty-three "prominent citizens" urging support for the resolution. The signers, many of whom had been strong supporters of Eisenhower in 1952, urged the Senate to end at long last McCarthy's "flagrant abuse of power."[33]

The National Committee for an Effective Congress itself released a letter to Minority Leader Lyndon Johnson demanding that the Democrats support the resolution. The mercurial Texas Democrat was angered, and there was a good deal of criticism from Hubert Humphrey and several others who thought that the maneuver was heavyhanded and illadvised. The Clearing House had acted deliberately, however, on the assumption that the only way to influence the minority leader was to put him on the spot.[34]

[30] Maurice Rosenblatt to Paul Hoffman, July 8, 1954; Donald Jenks to C. Jared Ingersoll, July 22, 1954; Ingersoll to George E. Agree, July 23, 1954, all in the NCEC files.

[31] Joseph A. Getzow to Senator Earle C. Clements, July 21, 1954; Getzow to George E. Agree, July 21, 1954; Maurice Rosenblatt to Agree, July 20, 1954; Agree to Rosenblatt, July 23, 1954, all in the NCEC files.

[32] Schedule for Mr. Hoffman, July 14, 1954, in the NCEC files; Memorandum, Charles F. Willis, Jr., to Sherman Adams, July 27, 1954, OF 99-R, Eisenhower Papers; Newsweek 44 (July 26, 1954): 15.

[33] Press release, July 22, 1954; Maurice Rosenblatt to Marshall Field, July 22, 1954; Donald Jenks to C. Jared Ingersoll, July 22, 1954, all in the NCEC files; New York Times, July 23, 1954, p. 5; Baltimore Sun, July 23, 1954.

[34] Maurice Rosenblatt to Lyndon B. Johnson, July 27, 1954; press release in NCEC files; John Howe to William Benton, Aug. 5, 1954, box 5, Benton Papers.

The mobilization of public opinion was only a part of the McCarthy operation. Even more time and energy had to be devoted to planning and executing strategy on the Hill itself. For the campaign the Clearing House established a loose and informal organization through the operational leaders of what has been called the "Lib-Lab lobby," a coalition of liberal and labor groups hung together by common interests and ideology. Thus the battle for the Flanders resolution eventually involved not just the original members of the Clearing House and the staff hired on for the "operation," but also the administrative assistants of a half-dozen Democratic and Republican senators, the legislative directors of several large labor unions, and the Washington representatives of a wide variety of liberal pressure groups.[35] This large and informal alliance provided the Clearing House with continuous liaison, political intelligence, and support throughout the operation. As the showdown on the resolution approached, many of them moved onto the Hill itself to help line up votes.

The Clearing House also had to help organize leadership within the Senate proper. The Republican hierarchy was vehemently opposed to the resolution, and the Democrats were unenthusiastic. Consequently, support for the resolution had to be marshaled on bipartisan grounds *outside* the normal channels of Senate leadership. William Fulbright took the initiative on the Democratic side of the Chamber, with help from Tom Hennings, John Sparkman, Mike Monroney, Herbert Lehman, and a few others. Flanders and John Sherman Cooper led the Republicans, with occasional help from James H. Duff and a few other G.O.P. liberals.[36]

[35] The administrative assistants included Langdon West (Hennings), William Macomber (Cooper), Jack Yingling (Fulbright), Julius Edelstein (Lehman), Stuart McClure (Gillette), and several others. The labor representatives included Donald Montgomery (UAW-CIO) and John W. Edelman (United Textile Workers-CIO) who were among the most active. Others included George Nelson (United Machine Workers); John Flynn (IUE-CIO), William Hanscom (Oil Workers), David Brody (Steelworkers). Several unions also made small contributions to the Clearing House. The liberal organizations included Americans for Democratic Action, the Anti-Defamation League, the Friends Service Committee, the National Farmers Union, the Public Affairs Institute, the American Veterans Committee, and others. In most instances it was not the organizations themselves but their legislative directors who aided the Clearing House. Nor were their contributions as great as one might have expected in such a crucial battle.

[36] "Memorandum regarding the Flanders Resolution," June 23, 1954; Maurice Rosenblatt to Seniel Ostrow, June 23, 1954; Rosenblatt to Joseph D. Shane, June 30, 1954, NCEC files.

The initial task facing the Clearing House was to overcome the widespread belief among "knowledgeable" congressional observers that the resolution had no chance. Although Flanders had given reporters repeated assurances that he intended to force the issue, the belief persisted, especially after the resolution was referred to the Rules Committee, that there would be no showdown. Even Herbert Lehman, whose own resolution, like that of Flanders, had been sent to committee, confessed that "it is very unlikely that the full Senate will now have an opportunity to consider either of these measures."[37]

The Clearing House arranged a press conference for June 21 at which Flanders emphatically reiterated his determination to force a division, either by calling for the Rules Committee to discharge the measure or else by introducing a substitute resolution. "I will not let this session of Congress end without providing the Senate with an opportunity to go clearly on the record on this issue," he declared.[38]

During the following week the resolution began to pick up momentum. The *New York Times* demanded that the McCarthy issue be brought to a vote in some form, no matter what Knowland and Johnson thought was "smart politics," and other editorial writers and columnists began to take the resolution more seriously.[39] An initial canvass of the Senate showed about twelve Republicans and twenty-five Democrats for the resolution and about nineteen Republicans and one Democrat, McCarran, against it. The rest of the senators were not *for* McCarthy, but they would not vote unless compelled to.[40]

Most Republicans were anxious to avoid a confrontation with

[37] Lehman to Catherine McPartland, July 12, 1954, Washington Miscellaneous File, McCarthy and McCarthyism, drawer one; Lehman to Francis B. Sayre, June 25, 1954, Special File, both in Lehman Papers. *New York Times,* June 13, 1954, p. 1; June 14, 1954, p. 1; June 16, 1954, p. 1.

[38] Press release, June 21, 1954, box 144; broadcast for week of June 20, 1954, box 154; both in the Flanders Papers, Syracuse University; "Chronology," in Maurice Rosenblatt to Dean Clara Mayer, June 22, 1954, NCEC files; *New York Times,* June 22, 1954, p. 9; *Congressional Report* 3 (July 2, 1954).

[39] *New York Times,* June 25, 1954, p. 20; Thomas Stokes, *Evening Star* (Washington), June 28, 1954; Roger Stuart, *New York World-Telegram,* July 8, 1954.

[40] "Confidential Memorandum on Possibility of Senate Floor Action on McCarthy during Remaining Weeks of 83d Congress," June 21, 1954; Maurice Rosenblatt to Dean Clara Mayer, June 22, 1954, both in NCEC files.

McCarthy. The White House, for example, showed at best a passive interest in the resolution, even though Attorney General Brownell told Flanders that "your matter is the most important thing before the Congress today." Republican senatorial candidate Clifford P. Case was an exception to this general trend. The former New Jersey congressman and head of the Fund for the Republic declared that if elected he would vote against continuing McCarthy as chairman of the Government Operations Committee or any other committee with similar functions. "I'm sure I can't tell you what the political effect will be," he wrote William Benton, "but it was something I had to get off my chest in any event."[41]

The real battle lay within the Senate itself, however, and it was here that the Clearing House began to rally its shaky forces. "Until now, the fight against McCarthy was hopeless because there was nobody who was willing to stand firm and force the issue," declared Rosenblatt. "Now Flanders is compelling both the administration and the timorous Democrats to recognize that they will have to stand up and be counted."[42] On July 7 the Clearing House held a luncheon at the Willard Hotel with some twenty members of the "Lib-Lab lobby." The meeting was chaired by Robert R. Nathan, executive committee chairman of Americans for Democratic Action and a member of the National Committee for an Effective Congress. Larry Henderson explained Flanders's position, and Rosenblatt stressed the need for public support and for direct work on the Hill. Afterwards the group spread out across the Capitol, visiting various senators and urging support of the resolution.[43]

By mid-July the resolution had picked up enough strength to force the Republican leadership into action. On July 13 Flanders met with the Senate Republican Policy Committee, and Knowland assured him that he would not attempt to block the resolution by procedural or parliamentary diversions. Capitalizing on Democratic hesitations, however, the Policy Committee went on to record its *unanimous* opposition to the resolution. Knowland announced that he would personally make the motion to table.[44]

[41] *New York Times,* July 8, 1954, p. 10; Clifford P. Case to William Benton, Aug. 2, 1954, box 4, Benton Papers.
[42] Maurice Rosenblatt to Frank Edwards, July 6, 1954, NCEC files.
[43] Memorandum on Luncheon of July 7, 1954; Maurice Rosenblatt to Frank Edwards, July 7, 1954, both in the NCEC files.
[44] *New York Times,* July 14, 1954, p. 1; July 15, 1954, p. 1.

Flanders quickly countered the Republican move. At a press luncheon called by the Clearing House on July 16, he announced that he was changing the resolution from one stripping McCarthy of his chairmanships to one of censure. Rather than risk any possible confusion, he declared, he would introduce a new resolution "that will permit a clear-cut vote on McCarthyism." The following day he appeared on network television and predicted that the new resolution would win strong bipartisan support.[45] On July 18 Flanders released in advance the text of the new resolution and accompanying remarks which he had prepared for delivery in the Senate on July 20. The resolution was privileged, he explained, and thus was subject neither to reference to a committee nor to the stipulation that it lie over for one legislative day. It was clear that the Vermont senator was determined to force a vote and was now trying to focus maximum pressure on the Senate. A vote to amend or table would be as important as a vote on the resolution itself, he stressed. "Even absence has significance." That same day William Fulbright appeared on "Meet the Press" to announce his own support for the resolution.[46]

The Democratic leadership remained cautious, but a number of southerners loyal to the rule of seniority were favorably impressed by the new resolution. "This is something I can go along with," declared Senator Walter F. George, the dean of the southern Democrats.[47] Nevertheless, the issue was far from decided. Only three times in 165 years had the Senate invoked censure on one of its members, and not one of these cases established a clear precedent for the Flanders resolution. Advocates and opponents alike were venturing out onto an unchartered sea. The political force of the "McCarthy balance," moreover, still weighed heavily upon the Senate. By the evening of July 18 the Clearing House counted twenty-four "sure" and eighteen "very probable" votes for censure, a total of forty-two. Twenty senators remained committed against the resolution, with the rest somewhere in between.

[45] Press release, July 16, 1954, NCEC files; transcript, "Youth Wants to Know," NBC, July 17, 1954, in box 144, Flanders Papers, Syracuse University; New York Times, July 17, 1954, p. 1; July 18, 1954, p. 31.
[46] Press release, "The Problem of the Junior Senator from Wisconsin," for release July 19, 1954, NCEC files; New York Times, July 19, 1954, pp. 1, 7, 18. The New York Times reprinted the entire text of Flanders's remarks.
[47] Maurice Rosenblatt to Marshall Field, July 22, 1954, NCEC files; New York Times, July 18, 1954, sec. 4, p. 2.

Most of them would vote for censure if a vote could be compelled, but they would support any motion, even one to table, in order to avoid a direct vote.[48]

At this point Fulbright arranged a personal meeting between Flanders and John McClellan, the Arkansas Democrat who held the key to much of the uncommitted Democratic vote. McClellan told Flanders that he was vitally interested in the censure resolution, but that his primary campaign would keep him away from the Senate until after July 27. Although he made no definite commitments to Flanders and Fulbright, he asked that the final showdown be postponed until after his return to Washington. After conferring with Rosenblatt, Fulbright, and Stuart Symington, Flanders agreed to the delay. McClellan's support might very well mean the difference between victory and defeat, so on the morning of July 19 Flanders announced that he would not force a vote until July 30.[49]

During the final week before debate began the Clearing House and the "Lib-Lab" technicians set about the difficult task of committing votes to the resolution. By late July they had some thirty-one senators definitely committed to the resolution and some fifteen others in the "very probable" category. McCarthy still retained about twenty votes. Between these two groups remained a large, uncommitted center of about forty-five senators. Many of them were moderate Republicans whose support was absolutely necessary in order to ensure the bipartisanship of the movement. Homer Ferguson was "wobbly." Charles Potter was "believed favorable" but needed to be encouraged by Michigan labor and church leaders. H. Alexander Smith was worried and undecided but could be "persuaded by conscience." Irving Ives was "hairsplitting" but probably favorable "if tactfully persuaded by all represented groups." Prescott Bush was favorable but needed encouragement. Leverett Saltonstall was "very much on the fence." Facing re-election in Massachusetts, he made his own position contingent

[48] Maurice Rosenblatt to Marshall Field, July 22, 1954; Donald Jenks to C. Jared Ingersoll, July 22, 1954, both in the NCEC files; *New York Times,* July 18, 1954, sec. 4, pp. 2, 3; July 19, 1954, p. 1.

[49] John J. Gunther to James E. Doyle, July 20, 1954, Legislative File, box 21, ADA Papers. Maurice Rosenblatt to Marshall Field, July 22, 1954; Donald Jenks to C. Jared. Ingersoll, July 22, 1954; William Frye, Memorandum [for the press], July 23, 1954; press release, July 19, 1954, all in the NCEC files; *New York Times,* July 20, 1954, p. 6.

on how John F. Kennedy voted. He declared that he would vote for the resolution as a matter of conscience if he had to, but that he would do everything in his power to keep it from coming to a vote.[50]

On the Democratic side the situation was even more complicated. Henry M. Jackson was "wearing the judicial mantle" and arguing that he could not take a stand on censure until the Mundt Subcommittee reported on the army-McCarthy hearings. Stuart Symington, although he had promised to "fight this thing through in the interests of American decency and integrity," was now reportedly "all over the lot" and beginning to weaken because of Jackson's legalisms. Earle Clements was trying to "straddle" the issue. Both Thomas Burke of Ohio and John Kennedy of Massachusetts looked to the Democratic leadership. Kennedy, Theodore Green, and John Pastore, all Democrats with large Irish Catholic constituencies, were particularly fearful of being identified with the McCarthy opposition. Kennedy declared that he would support the motion if Lyndon Johnson or McClellan did, but that otherwise he would be absent. Johnson was the "root of all difficulties on the Democratic side," according to a Clearing House memorandum. The resolution was gaining strength, but "when Knowland starts attacking and Johnson aids him, this structure of reluctant senators could very easily fall apart." The Democratic Policy Committee met with five of McCarthy's strongest critics on July 29, but decided against a party position for fear of alienating Republican support for the resolution.[51] By the end of July, moreover, groups

[50] There are several breakdowns of the prospective Senate vote in the NCEC files. The most comprehensive is Donald Montgomery (UAW-CIO) to John W. Edelman (United Textile Workers-CIO), July 26, 1954. Also see John Howe to William Benton, Aug. 5, 1954, in box 5, Benton Papers. Potter and Ferguson were both extremely cautious. See Ferguson to Josephine Gomon, July 7, 1954; and Potter to Mollie Tendler, July 14, 1954, both in Legislative File, box 39, ADA Papers. Both Ives and Bush tried to avoid a direct confrontation over McCarthy by calling, somewhat belatedly, for reform of committee procedures. Ives to Mrs. Bernard Chertow, July 13, 1954, in ibid.; *Congressional Record*, 83d Cong., 2d sess., July 31, 1954, p. 12897. On Saltonstall, see the Montgomery memorandum cited above and John J. Gunther to Mrs. Barbara Cikins, July 19, 1954, Legislative File, box 39, ADA Papers.

[51] Memorandum, Donald Montgomery to John W. Edelman, July 26, 1954, NCEC files. John F. Kennedy to Evelyn Stiles, July 16, 1954; Stuart Symington to Fred A. Schoen, July 20, 1954, both in Legislative File, box 39, ADA Papers. On Kennedy see John J. Gunther to Mrs. Barbara Cikins, July 19,

within the White House were pressing Flanders to relent. Secretary of the Treasury George M. Humphrey, a powerful spokesman for the Eisenhower administration, told Flanders that he should lay off McCarthy for the sake of party harmony.[52] The impact of such pressures could not but have an enervating effect on the delicate coalition committed in support of the resolution.

Debate began on Friday evening, July 30. On the steps of the Capitol the army band played its regularly scheduled concert. But inside, the Senate wing was crowded and tense. Flanders opened the debate by introducing his resolution of censure, Senate Resolution 301, and briefly imploring the Senate to act. Then the initiative passed to the opposition. Guy Cordon of Oregon and Everett Dirksen of Illinois each delivered a major address against the resolution. The two speeches reveal in part how the Senate fulfills its multiple functions. The first speech, by Cordon, was a restrained and scholarly appeal for due process and orderly procedure. The second, by Dirksen, was a harsh attack on Flanders himself. Cordon addressed himself to the Senate and its traditions. He argued that a censure resolution should be supported by a bill of particulars and that the entire issue should be referred to a committee in order to give McCarthy "his day in court." The Senate should act like "a judicial body and not like a mob," he declared. Dirksen, by contrast, spoke not so much to the Senate as to the public at large, denouncing the censure movement as a contrivance of Communists and left-wingers. Flanders, like Brutus, was "an honorable man," declared Dirksen, behind whom the Communist party, Americans for Democratic Action, the CIO and the National Committee for an Effective Congress had joined hands in an unfair attempt to besmirch the senator from Wisconsin. Flanders rose indignantly to answer Dirksen's charges, but Majority Leader Knowland cut him off by asking for a recess. McCarthy sprang to his feet and pumped Dirksen's hand.[53]

1954, box 39, and Gunther to James E. Doyle, July 20, 1954, box 21; on Johnson see Gunther to George Lambert, July 1, 1954, box 39, all in Legislative File, ADA Papers. Called in by the Democratic Policy Committee were Symington and Jackson, McCarthy's sharpest critics within the Committee on Government Operations, and Fulbright, Monroney, and Lehman, the Democratic leaders of the censure movement. *Washington Post*, July 30, 1954.

[52] Flanders, *Senator from Vermont*, p. 262. Author's interview with Maurice Rosenblatt, June 13, 1966.

[53] *Congressional Record*, 83d Cong., 2d sess., July 30, 1954, pp. 12729–42; *New York Times*, July 31, 1954, pp. 1, 4.

It was not Dirksen's oratory which set the terms of the debate, however, but Cordon's powerful arguments for orderly procedure. The Oregon senator raised a broad political and legal question. Could the Senate properly condemn McCarthy for his abuse of due process and orderly procedure if in so doing the Senate itself violated those concepts? Many senators believed it could not. Even Wayne Morse strongly endorsed Cordon's plea for "basic procedural safeguards." Morse asked both for a bill of particulars and for committee referral.[54]

Flanders and Fulbright both resisted attempts to amend the resolution by adding particulars. "You can't be specific about an ism," Fulbright told Symington in private. What was involved was not any one specific act but a whole pattern of action. The Scripps-Howard newspapers had only recently taken more than 8,000 words to draw their own indictment of McCarthy. Such an attempt to spell out "McCarthyism" in the resolution would simply kill it. A bill of particulars, moreover, would make committee referral unavoidable, and this Flanders and Fulbright believed would only lead to an evasion and postponement of the Senate's duty. McCarthy had practically wrecked five previous committees, observed Mike Monroney a little later in the debate. The prospects were not good for a sixth.[55]

Nevertheless, the speeches by Cordon and Morse made a deep impression, and on the second day of debate Fulbright himself introduced six specific charges in the form of amendments to the resolution. Later Wayne Morse added his own bill of seven particulars. Flanders, once it was clear that debate on specifics was inescapable, added thirty-three more.[56]

[54] *Congressional Record*, 83d Cong., 2d sess., July 30, 1954, pp. 12735–36. Symington, Ellender, and Kennedy were also known to favor a bill of particulars. Maurice Rosenblatt to Ralph Flanders [c. July 28, 1954], NCEC files. According to biographer Theodore C. Sorenson, Kennedy prepared, but did not deliver, a speech supporting censure but emphasizing the need to specify concrete censurable actions. Sorenson, *Kennedy* (New York, 1965), pp. 47–48.

[55] *Congressional Record*, 83d Cong., 2d sess., July 30, 1954; pp. 12729–31; July 31, 1954, pp. 12903–19; Aug. 2, 1954, p. 12844; Maurice Rosenblatt, Memorandum on the Censure Movement, July 22, 1954; William Frye, Memorandum [for the press], July 23, 1954; Rosenblatt to Ralph Flanders [c. July 28, 1954], all in the NCEC files.

[56] *Congressional Record*, 83d Cong., 2d sess., July 31, 1954, pp. 12903–19; *New York Times*, Aug. 1, 1954, pp. 1, 47, 48. Rosenblatt put together the thirty-three additional charges in a hurried, last-minute effort to ensure that the committee would have wide jurisdiction. The response to them was not

For two days confusion and uncertainty prevailed. The pro-censure senators had demonstrated enough strength to force the McCarthy issue before the Senate, but it was impossible to deter-mine whether they had the votes to carry the resolution. Then on August 2, the third day of debate, William Knowland introduced a motion to refer the Flanders resolution to a select committee composed of three Republicans and three Democrats. The majority leader had earlier brushed aside a similar proposal by H. Alexander Smith, but now he seized upon it as the only possible alternative to an almost certain show of party disunity on the very eve of the 1954 elections. And as Knowland began his move, the long inert Democratic leadership also sprang to life. There were rumors that Johnson and Knowland had reached an accord. The minority leader denied this, but he did admit conferring with New York Republican Irving Ives. Ives played a crucial role by insisting, with strong Democratic support, that the select committee report back *before* the Eighty-third Congress adjourned. This amend-ment, agreed to reluctantly by Knowland, meant that the Senate could not long delay its final reckoning with McCarthy. Flanders and Fulbright fought a rearguard action against the motion, but the Senate eagerly adopted it by a vote of 75-12.[57]

The battle for the Flanders resolution had forced the Senate to act, though not quite along the lines that Flanders and the Clearing House had wanted.[58] The powerful arguments for orderly

---

uniformly favorable. "I wouldn't vote to put down a dog on such an array of charges," declared one Democrat. Author's interview with Maurice Rosen-blatt, June 13, 1966. Arthur Krock, *New York Times*, Aug. 8, 1954, sec. 4, p. 3.

[57] *Congressional Record*, 83d Cong., 2d sess., Aug. 2, 1954, p. 12989. Those opposed included Republicans Flanders, Duff, and Cooper, and Democrats Chavez, Douglas, Fulbright, Hennings, Hill, Humphrey, Lehman, Magnusen, and Monroney. On the Smith proposal see H. Alexander Smith to Herbert H. Lehman, July 29, 1954, Washington Miscellaneous File, McCarthy and McCarthyism, drawer 1, Lehman Papers; and Smith to Alexander Wiley, July 29, 1954, Personal Correspondence, box 1, Wiley Papers. The Smith resolution differed from that finally adopted in three important particulars: 1) The Smith resolution called for a seven-man committee (three Republicans and three Democrats) chaired by Vice President Nixon. The resolution adopted established a six-man committee without the vice president. 2) The Smith resolution called for a report "not later than February 1, 1955." The final resolution, as amended by Ives, called for the committee to report *to the current session.* 3). The mandate given by the Smith resolution was vague—to investigate "disunity in the Senate . . . over the alleged good or evil of so-called McCarthyism." The final resolution specifically charged the committee with consideration of S. Res. 301, the Flanders resolution.

procedure and the fervent desire of a majority of the Senate to evade or postpone a showdown on the McCarthy issue led to the establishment of a select committee of United States senators, headed by Utah Republican Arthur V. Watkins. Some of the procensure senators were disappointed. "Unfortunately, we who fought for the Flanders resolution have been temporarily defeated," declared Herbert Lehman. "I am not very optimistic regarding the outlook." Flanders, Fulbright, Hennings, and Monroney all expressed some degree of pessimism over the future of the select committee. But if the result was less than they had hoped, it was still more than many observers had believed possible a few months earlier. There was still the fear that the resolution might get sidetracked, reported one newspaperman. "But generally the anti-McCarthy forces regarded the outcome as a substantial victory."[59]

CONGRESS AND COMMUNISM (II): THE COMMUNIST CONTROL ACT OF 1954

Because the Senate had at last begun, however reluctantly and distastefully, to move toward a confrontation with Joe McCarthy did not at all mean that it was also prepared to face up to the Communist issue, or what was frequently although mistakenly called "McCarthyism." In fact, it seemed almost as though the opposite were true. Even while the Senate was debating what to do about Joe McCarthy, it was rushing through, virtually unopposed, a wide variety of so-called anti-subversive bills which, in the opinion of one liberal senator, were "broad enough to

---

[58] It is difficult to say what the outcome would have been had the Flanders resolution been forced to a direct vote. Rosenblatt and the Clearing House group believed that if there had been enough strength to compel a vote, then such strength would have carried the resolution itself. Other observers believed that a tabling motion, which would have taken precedence, would have been defeated, but that the censure resolution would have failed as well. Still others believed that any action at that point would have resulted in a vote of confidence for McCarthy. Maurice Rosenblatt to Marshall Field, July 22, 1954, NCEC files; Rosenblatt to author, April 28, 1967; John Howe to William Benton, Aug. 5, 1954, box 5, Benton Papers; William S. White, *New York Times*, Aug. 6, 1954, p. 6.

[59] Herbert H. Lehman to Harry Stanfield, Aug. 3, 1954, Washington Miscellaneous File, McCarthy and McCarthyism, drawer 1, Lehman Papers. *New York Times*, Aug. 3, 1954, p. 1. Also see John Howe to William Benton, Aug. 5, 1954; Benton to Howe, Aug. 20, 1954, both in box 5, Benton Papers.

endanger the civil liberties of all Americans."[60] Prodded by the Eisenhower administration, both Senate and House quickly approved legislation to strip citizenship from persons convicted of conspiracy to advocate the violent overthrow of government, to make peacetime espionage a capital offense, to require Communist organizations to register all printing equipment, to grant immunity to witnesses before courts, grand juries, and congressional committees in order to compel testimony, to increase the penalties for harboring fugitives and jumping bail, and to broaden and redefine espionage and sabotage laws.[61]

The most controversial of these new measures was the Communist Control Act of 1954. Originally introduced by Maryland Republican John Marshall Butler, the bill was designed to amend the McCarran Internal Security Act of 1950. The McCarran Act had required that organizations designated as "Communist-action" and "Communist-front" by the Subversive Activities Control Board register with the attorney general. Butler proposed to add a third category of groups that must register—those which the SACB decided were "Communist-infiltrated."[62]

When the Butler bill reached the floor, a small group of liberals led by Hubert Humphrey introduced a substitute in the form of an amendment which declared that the Communist party was an "agency of a hostile foreign power" and therefore was not entitled to the rights, privileges, and immunities attendant upon legal bodies. "I do not intend to be a half patriot," declared Humphrey. "I will not be lukewarm. . . . Either Senators are for recognizing the Communist Party for what it is, or they will continue to trip over the niceties of legal technicalities and details."[63]

Like the "concentration camp" amendment to the McCarran Internal Security Act, the Humphrey amendment illustrated the tendency of cold war liberals to adopt as their own the policies and programs of the right. Implicit in the Humphrey amendment were

[60] Herbert H. Lehman to Lloyd R. Shaw, May 6, 1955; Lehman to R. M. Stein, Sept. 3, 1954, both in Senate Legislative File, drawer 21, Lehman Papers.

[61] *Congress and the Nation* (Washington, D.C., 1965), pp. 1656–58.

[62] *Congressional Record*, 83d Cong., 2d sess., July 6, 1954, p. 9708.

[63] The Humphrey amendment was attached to the Butler bill on August 12 and then to the House version of the measure when it came before the Senate on August 17. *Congressional Record*, 83d Cong., 2d sess., Aug. 12, 1954, p. 14234, and Aug. 17, 1954, p. 14727. Humphrey is quoted in Frank J. Kendrick, "McCarthy and the Senate" (Ph.D. diss., University of Chicago, 1962), p. 114.

two of the cardinal assumptions of the McCarthy era—that the Communist party constituted a real and immediate threat to the nation's security and that the way to meet this threat was through repression. "Liberalism, in its noble and historic sense, did not have one spokesman in the Senate last week," declared the *Chicago Daily News*. "The self-styled Democratic liberals could think of no answer to their detractors except to out do them in the sponsorship of repression."[64]

Civil libertarians protested that the Humphrey amendment constituted a denial of the right to vote, an abridgment of free speech and association, and a denial of due process. They charged that it was both a bill of attainder and an *ex post facto* law. Humphrey was not impressed. "I anticipated some of the rather emotional reaction from the liberal community because I was hitting somewhat of a sacred cow," he later confided. With the strong support of Lyndon Johnson, he rammed the amendment through the Senate by a narrow 41-39 vote. On the final roll call only one senator, Estes Kefauver, voted against the amended bill.[65]

The language of the bill was weakened and made more imprecise in conference. "It is not as strong a blow as Hubert Humphrey would like to have struck," declared the Minnesotan.

[64] *Chicago Daily News*, Aug. 16, 1954.
[65] *Congressional Record*, 83d Cong., 2d sess., Aug. 17, 1954, p. 14727. The vote on the Humphrey amendment would have been tied (and consequently defeated by the chair) had not Kefauver and Alton Lennon (D.-N.C.) withdrawn their votes against the amendment and allowed themselves to be paired with absent Democrats. Thus Kefauver, who received a great deal of praise for opposing the amended bill, was also responsible for the form of its final passage. *Washington Post and Times-Herald*, Aug. 21, 1954. Immediately following the roll call, Lyndon Johnson moved to forestall opposition by calling for reconsideration. His motion was then quickly tabled by a vote of 43-49.

Humphrey's statement on liberal reaction is taken from Hubert Humphrey to Marvin Rosenberg, Aug. 27, 1954, in Legislative File, box 16, ADA Papers. In this long and highly revealing document Humphrey declared that it was time American liberals quit relying on the thinking of John Stuart Mill and do some "20th century thinking in order to face 20th century problems." He dismissed the argument that the amendment might become a precedent for the repression of other political parties, declaring that the amendment would stand on its own merits and that "it is not necessary for me to defend any possible abuse of that amendment at a later date." Although Humphrey denied any political motivation in offering the amendment—"the people of Minnesota can never be fooled into thinking Hubert Humphrey is a Communist"—he did boast in later years that the vote of one liberal Democrat on the bill saved that senator's political life. See Winthrop Griffith, *Humphrey: A Candid Biography* (New York, 1965), p. 223.

Still it remained, again in Humphrey's words, "a great blow" for freedom and against the "evil conspiracy" which was menacing American institutions. The conference report was agreed to by a vote of 79-0. Even Estes Kefauver, who earlier had been the Senate's only dissenter, now "supported and voted for it whole-heartedly."[66]

Thus the Senate continued its bipartisan obeisance to the accumulated slogans, stereotypes, and mythologies of the anti-Communist persuasion. Wayne Morse, a co-sponsor of the Humphrey amendment, declared, "In the Senate there is no division of opinion among liberals, conservatives and those in between when it comes to our utter detestation of the Communist conspiracy and our united insistence that as a Senate we will fight the growth of the Communist conspiracy."[67] Because the Senate remained transfixed by this anti-Communist consensus, the problem of dealing with Joe McCarthy became an exercise in circumvention—to strike at McCarthy while leaving intact the issues and assumptions upon which he had built his political career.

THE WATKINS COMMITTEE

The fate of Joe McCarthy now rested in the hands of a select committee of his fellow senators. But how well would that committee execute its mandate? Would it at long last resolve the question of Joe McCarthy? Or would the dictates of partisan politics force yet another evasion? "I certainly don't want the Republican Party to compound its own difficulties by creating new ones," declared Alexander Wiley. "We have got enough of a job combating the Democrats in November, without getting into a hassle among our own members if we can possibly avoid it."[68] As in most such proceedings, the lines of debate were laid out well in advance by the tough, internal politicking which preceded the hearings themselves. The crucial questions of personnel and procedure inevitably determined the substantive debate. "If the

---

[66] *Congressional Record,* 83d Cong., 2d sess., Aug. 19, 1954, pp. 15101–21. Arthur Schlesinger, Jr., *New York Post,* Aug. 29, 1954. Estes Kefauver to William R. Ross, Oct. 22, 1954, Subject File, National Security 1, Kefauver Papers.

[67] *Congressional Record,* 83d Cong., 2d sess., Aug. 16, 1954, p. 14565.

[68] Alexander Wiley to Philip G. Kuehn, n.d., Legislative File, 1953-1954, box 147, Wiley Papers.

committee is tough (No Mundts, I hope!), limits its sphere at the start, controls McCarthy, and drives hard, it might have something in a few weeks," declared one observer.[69]

The most immediate problem facing the Democratic and Republican leadership was the selection of the committee itself. No senator volunteered for this odious duty. Although the members were to be appointed by the vice president, they were selected by Knowland and Johnson respectively. Each leader deferred to the other, moreover, so that all six men were approved by both. The men whom they selected were without exception members of the moderately conservative group which held the balance of power within both parties. All of them were from the South and West, where McCarthyism was considered a less inflammable issue, and none had taken a strong stand with either the bitter-enders or the liberals. They were, moreover, what William S. White has called Senate "types," men deeply respected within the inner councils of the Senate itself.[70]

The ranking Democratic member of the committee was Edwin C. Johnson of Colorado, a veteran of seventeen years in the Senate and a close friend and adviser of Minority Leader Lyndon Johnson. The other two Democrats were John C. Stennis, a highly regarded conservative from Mississippi, and Sam J. Ervin, Jr., a sprightly North Carolinian who had only recently begun his Senate career. The Republicans were led by Arthur Vivian Watkins, a thin and ascetic Mormon from Utah with an unbending devotion to order and propriety. As chairman of the committee, Watkins would set the tone of the entire proceeding. The other members of the committee were Frank Carlson of Kansas, a moderate Republican who had been one of Eisenhower's earliest supporters, and Francis H. Case of South Dakota, a cautious and dimly inconspicuous conservative.[71]

McCarthy launched his fight for control over procedures before the committee was even named. On August 2 he demanded that those senators filing charges against him (Flanders, Fulbright, and Morse) be called to testify, and he insisted that he be allowed the

[69] John Howe to William Benton, Aug. 5, 1954, box 5, Benton Papers.

[70] William S. White, New York Times, Aug. 6, 1954, p. 6; William S. White, Citadel: The Story of the U. S. Senate (New York, 1956), pp. 128–31.

[71] New York Times, Aug. 6, 1954, p. 6. "I am well satisfied with the committee which has been appointed," declared Flanders. Radio broadcast, week of Aug. 15, 1954, box 154, Flanders Papers, Syracuse University.

right of cross-examination. His antagonists, he declared, would "either indict themselves for perjury, or . . . prove what consummate liars they are." Three days later, when Johnson and Knowland announced the membership of the select committee, McCarthy repeated his demands and raised the clear threat of a diversionary action by declaring that he intended to call before his subcommittee a long list of high-ranking army officers. "I would not want to have the [select] committee meet on a day I had an executive session scheduled with a large number of witnesses called," he brashly announced. Instead, he suggested that he meet with the committee that very afternoon to iron out conflicts and decide "the method of proof, the nature of proof, and what they want." Flanders, on the other hand, urged that the committee's procedure become one of "stark simplicity."[72]

The select committee, which had wide discretion in the formulation of its internal procedures, refused to be intimidated by McCarthy. "We are not unmindful of *his* genius for disruption," Watkins assured Flanders.[73] The committee stonily ignored McCarthy's demands, and in the weeks that followed they hammered out a set of rules designed to check him at every turn. On August 9 they announced that McCarthy "or his lawyer" could exercise the right of cross-examination, but they stipulated that only *one of them* could examine a given witness. Even this carefully hedged concession became meaningless in the context of other rulings. The committee decided, for example, to function somewhat like an "appellate court," passing more on questions of procedure than on questions of fact. Only "firsthand" testimony would be taken, they declared, thus eliminating Flanders, Fulbright, and Morse as prospective witnesses. The proceedings were "judicial" and McCarthy was "sort of a defendant because charges have been leveled against him," said Watkins; Flanders, Fulbright, and Morse, however, were not in the position of "complaining witnesses or even plaintiffs." McCarthy would therefore have no one to attack. There would be no "Flanders-McCarthy" hearings as there had been "Benton-McCarthy" and "army-McCarthy" hear-

[72] *New York Times,* Aug. 3, 1954, p. 11; Aug. 6, 1954, p. 1. Ralph Flanders to William Knowland, Aug. 4, 1954, box 25, Arthur V. Watkins Papers.

[73] William Knowland to Arthur Watkins, Aug. 10, 1954, box 25, Watkins Papers. Watkins is quoted in Maurice Rosenblatt to Paul G. Hoffman, Aug. 26, 1954, NCEC files.

ings. The senator might cross-examine, but much of what was to be introduced was technical and legal. McCarthy was not a good lawyer, either by training or inclination, and if he chose to conduct the cross-examination himself he would be putting himself against some of the best lawyers in the Senate. If he allowed his attorney to cross-examine, however, he gave up his own right to occupy stage center. Finally, the committee insisted that the rules of the Senate itself be applied in the committee room. The hearings would be open, but no television would be allowed.[74]

In short, the committee denied McCarthy all the familiar props for his earlier performances. There was no audience to play to and no antagonist to harass and intimidate. There was no drama, no hovering specter of a foreign conspiracy. There were only six stern men and Joe.

The committee also began the difficult task of narrowing the charges against McCarthy and establishing explicit and concrete foundations for censure. At the very outset they indicated that the number of counts would be drastically reduced, but they also made it clear that they would "reserve the right to go into other charges if new evidence develops." Privately, some committee members placed McCarthy on notice that should the hearings stray beyond the bounds they were establishing, the committee would then exercise its right to explore other accusations.[75]

The most immediate problem facing the select committee was the difficulty of documenting McCarthy's entire pattern of actions with concrete censurable acts. "It was not his breaches of etiquette, or of rules or sometimes even of laws which is so disturbing," wrote Flanders to Watkins. "It was his breach of society, his threat to the very traditions and foundations of our orderly democratic procedures, which makes the conduct of Mr. McCarthy so all-embracing in its gravity. No one of the single actions with which the Senator is charged is as dangerous by itself as it is arrayed alongside the total sequence of his behavior."[76]

The Senate was an assemblage of lawyers, however, and most

[74] *New York Times,* Aug. 7, 1954, p. 1; Aug. 8, 1954, p. 1; Aug. 11, 1954, p. 1; Aug. 16, 1954, p. 1. John Howe to William Benton, Sept. 1, 1954, box 5, Benton Papers.

[75] *New York Times,* Aug. 3, 1954, p. 8; Aug. 7, 1954, p. 1; Aug. 23, 1954, p. 1.

[76] Ralph Flanders to Arthur V. Watkins, Sept. 11, 1954, NCEC files. Also see William Benton to John Howe, Aug. 31, 1954, box 5, Benton Papers.

of its members demanded a bill of particulars. The specific charges hurriedly entered by Fulbright, Flanders, and Morse were an attempt to meet this demand. The Watkins Committee approached these charges cautiously. Some of the particulars were vague and insubstantial. Others, even if true, were probably not cause for censure. Even liberals such as Wayne Morse and ex-Senator Benton were indisposed to condemn McCarthy for remarks made on the floor.[77] McCarthy had so wrapped about him the powers and prerogatives of his office that it was difficult to disavow the senator without also disavowing the privileges which he had so badly abused. The necessity of filing a report before the Senate adjourned placed upon the committee the added burden of proceeding as expeditiously as possible, and tactical considerations dictated that the committee narrow the charges in order to prevent McCarthy's all-too-familiar diversions. At the heart of the committee's circumspection, however, was the necessity imposed by the anti-Communist consensus of striking at McCarthy but not "McCarthyism." The Watkins Committee would not, and given the circumstances probably could not, address itself to the nervous assumptions of the postwar decade.

On August 24 Watkins announced that the committee would reduce its scope to thirteen charges divided into five general categories: incidents in contempt of the Senate; encouragement of federal employees to violate the law; receipt of classified information; abuse of Senate colleagues; and abuse of General Ralph W. Zwicker.[78]

The hearings opened on August 31. Chairman Watkins began with a long statement on the rules and procedures which the committee had adopted. "We realize that the United States Senate, in a sense, is on trial," he declared, and he promised to maintain the "high traditions and dignity" of that body. When the chairman had finished, he allowed McCarthy to read a statement also, but not until he had dryly observed that "most of it is not material and relevant to the issues in this hearing as we understand them."[79]

---

[77] *New York Times*, Sept. 23, 1954, p. 1; William Benton to John Howe, Aug. 31, 1954, box 5, Benton Papers.

[78] *New York Times*, Aug. 25, 1954, p. 1.

[79] U. S., Congress, Senate, 83d Cong., 2d sess., Select Committee to Study Censure Charges, *Hearings on S. Res. 301* (Washington, D. C., 1954), pp. 11–14 (hereafter cited as *Watkins Committee Hearings*). *New York Times*, Sept. 1, 1954, p. 1.

Immediately after McCarthy's statement, committee counsel E. Wallace Chadwick, a thin, elderly trial lawyer from Pennsylvania, began to drone testimony and exhibits into the record. It was about as exciting, declared one observer, as reading from a telephone directory.[80] The only flash of drama came toward the end of the two-hour session. McCarthy's lawyer, Edward Bennett Williams, attempted to question Senator Edwin Johnson's impartiality but was ruled out of order by Watkins. McCarthy, who had nervously fidgeted throughout the session, could contain himself no longer. He snatched the microphone from William's grasp and cried, "Just a minute, Mr. Chairman, just 1 minute." Watkins brought his gavel down once, then a second, and yet a third time. "The Senator is out of order. . . . We are not going to be interrupted by those diversions and sidelines. We are going straight down the line." And the committee adjourned to reconvene the following day. McCarthy rushed outside into the crowded corridor where the banned television crews had set up their lights and cameras. He grabbed a microphone and sputtered into it: "I think it's the most unheard of thing I ever heard of."[81]

According to Edward Bennett Williams, Senator McCarthy promised his lawyer that he would behave well during the hearings and, Williams continues, McCarthy "meticulously" kept this promise. But it was not the assurances given to Williams which silenced Joe McCarthy. Oral agreements meant very little to him under such circumstances. It was not Edward Bennett Williams who restrained McCarthy, but the strong-willed Mormon senator who conducted the hearings. Watkins's stern ruling, declared one reporter, was "the gavel crack heard round the world."[82]

Outside the hearing room, McCarthy pursued his customary tactics. He began by attacking Senator Edwin Johnson's right to sit on the committee. He brought into the committee room a clipping from the *Denver Post* of March 12, 1954, which quoted the Colorado senator as saying, "In my opinion, there is not a

[80] James Reston, *New York Times*, Sept. 1, 1954, p. 15.
[81] *Watkins Committee Hearings*, pp. 37–38; *New York Times*, Sept. 1, 1954, pp. 1, 15.
[82] Edward Bennett Williams, *One Man's Freedom* (New York, 1962), pp. 60–63. Apparently Watkins was the one senator whom McCarthy never forgave for his part in the censure proceedings. Flanders, *Senator from Vermont*, p. 268.

man among the Democratic leaders who does not loathe Joe McCarthy." Both McCarthy and Williams avoided a direct challenge, however, and they explicitly refused to enter a motion seeking Johnson's disqualification. (Such a motion would have been roundly defeated.) Their purpose was simply to impeach the credibility of the Select Committee. Watkins and the other members of the committee rejected McCarthy's protests out of hand. "We are human beings," the chairman declared, "and . . . we haven't been living in a vacuum. But we are like jurors, and can set aside any impressions and consider the matter fairly and equitably." McCarthy described the chairman's defense of the committee as "the most fantastic" statement he had ever heard.[83]

A few days later another Democrat on the committee, Sam Ervin, was also attacked, although not by McCarthy directly. The attack came from the Hearst broadcaster and gossip columnist Walter Winchell, a close friend of McCarthy's, who read from the *Winston-Salem Journal and Sentinal* of August 1, 1954, quoting Ervin as saying that he had "formed an unfavorable opinion of the Junior Senator from Wisconsin since going to Washington."[84] McCarthy also attacked committee counsel Chadwick. He charged that Chadwick had taken an adversary position during the hearings and should therefore be disqualified from drafting the committee's report. "I don't think the district attorney should try to write an opinion when trying to prosecute the case," he declared,[85] but this the Watkins Committee ignored.

The hearings unfolded with a conspicuous absence of drama. The difference between the army-McCarthy hearings and the Watkins Committee hearings, declared one reporter, was like that between a Hollywood premiere and a coroner's inquest. Watkins himself declared: "Let us get off the front pages and back among the obituaries."[86] The first days were largely devoted to reading documentation into the record. Then the committee allowed McCarthy and his counsel to present their case. Even here, however, Chairman Watkins pressed hard upon McCarthy. Time after

[83] *New York Times,* Aug. 31, 1954, p. 1; Sept. 1, 1954, p. 1; Sept. 2, 1954, p. 1; Sept. 3, 1954, p. 1; Sept. 4, 1954, p. 5.

[84] Ibid., Sept. 8, 1954, p. 17.

[85] Ibid., Sept. 14, 1954, p. 1; Sept. 15, 1954, p. 1.

[86] Anthony Leviero, ibid., Sept. 12, 1954, sec. 4, p. 9; *Congress and the Nation,* p. 1727.

time McCarthy and his attorney were brought up short by rulings of irrelevancy and immateriality, or by admonitions that they were stating conclusions, being argumentative or unresponsive. At one point Watkins even ordered McCarthy's remarks stricken from the record.[87] And when these brief public hearings were over, the committee retired to its chambers to draft its final report on Joseph R. McCarthy.

The work of Flanders, Fulbright, and the Clearing House during this second phase of the censure movement was largely peripheral. The National Committee for an Effective Congress was especially handicapped by the publicity it had received during the last days of debate over the Flanders resolution. They learned in late July that Fulton Lewis, Jr., planned a series of attacks on the group, and tried to defuse them by planting discreet news items in several large dailies.[88] Lewis began his broadcasts on July 25, and Everett Dirksen tore into the group during the Senate debate. In the House, Republican Kit Clardy of Michigan introduced a resolution calling for a full investigation. Hubert Humphrey and a number of other senators were irritated because the NCEC had not remained in the background.[89]

The Clearing House continued to provide Flanders and other friendly senators with limited technical assistance. On August 24 Watkins had asked Flanders, Fulbright, and Morse to provide documentation in support of their bills of particulars. With the help of Marshall MacDuffie, a well-known constitutional lawyer and a member of the National Committee for an Effective Congress, Flanders's office produced a steady stream of "briefs" on

[87] *Watkins Committee Hearings*, pp. 299–433; *New York Times*, Sept. 12, 1954, sec. 4, pp. 1, 9.

[88] See, for example, the *New York Times*, July 20, 1954, p. 6.

[89] *Congressional Record*, 83d Cong., 2d sess., July 30, 1954, pp. 12736–42; Aug. 16, 1954, p. 14661; John Howe to William Benton, Aug. 5, 1954, box 5, Benton Papers; Maurice Rosenblatt to Ralph Flanders, Aug. 4, 1954, NCEC files. Both Hennings and Cooper were hesitant to appear working in concert for the resolution. "I merely wish to point out . . . that my own activities with respect to the Flanders motion," declared Hennings, ". . . were without reference to the plans and actions of other Senators." Hennings to the editor, *New York Times*, Aug. 9, 1954, in box 23, Hennings Papers. Cooper declared on the floor: "I have consulted with no groups, either for or against the resolution." *Congressional Record*, 83d Cong., 2d sess., July 31, 1954, p. 12922. In fact, the administrative assistants of both men were active on an almost day-to-day basis during the censure movement.

the various charges against McCarthy.[90] The Select Committee did not enter the Flanders briefs into the record. They were "acknowledged" but not formally accepted as evidence. They formed, rather, what was in effect a political reserve which the committee might use if it had to. After the last brief had been filed, Fulbright congratulated Flanders: "You have done a fine job and we all owe you a debt of gratitude."[91]

Former Senator Benton also worked to strengthen potential points of weakness. As the Watkins Committee steadily narrowed the scope of its case against McCarthy, it became clear that the most important charge was that McCarthy had been in contempt of the Senate when he refused to appear before the Gillette-Hennings Subcommittee in 1952. On September 9, however, McCarthy testified that he had told Guy Gillette that he would not appear unless subpoenaed. Benton immediately wired Gillette, Hennings, Hayden, Hendrickson, and Monroney, all of whom confirmed his own recollection that McCarthy had made no such statement. He then quickly brought this to the attention of the Watkins Committee and several influential newspaper columnists.[92] In the end, the Watkins Committee ruled that it was McCarthy's "duty" as a senator to have appeared and that the question of a subpoena was irrelevant. Nevertheless, like Flanders's "briefs," Benton's quick action provided the Select Committee with a strong second line of defense. "In view of that and all else," concluded Flanders, "it is hard to see how a clean bill of health can be given our mutual friend from Wisconsin."[93]

[90] Arthur V. Watkins to Ralph Flanders, Aug. 24, 1954; Memorandum, Joan Eldredge to Flanders, Sept. 13, 1954; both in the NCEC files. John Howe to William Benton, Sept. 7, 1954, box 5, Benton Papers. Copies of the various briefs may be found in the NCEC files.

[91] William Fulbright to Ralph Flanders, Sept. 20, 1954, copy of hand-written note in NCEC files; Flanders to William Benton, Sept. 22, 1954, box 5, Benton Papers. *New York Times,* Sept. 19, 1954, p. 36.

[92] William Benton to John Howe, Sept. 13, 16, 22, 1954. Mary K. Garner (Benton's secretary) to Thomas C. Hennings, Sept. 13, 1954; to Carl Hayden, Sept. 13, 1954; to Guy Gillette, Sept. 14, 1954; to Mike Monroney, Sept. 14, 1954. William Benton to Gillette, Sept. 15, 1954; to Arthur V. Watkins, Sept. 15, 21, 1954; to Robert Hendrickson, Sept. 15, 1954. Gillette to Garner, Sept. 15, 1954; Gillette to Benton, Sept. 20, 1954. Howe to Marquis Childs, Sept. 17, 1954; Howe to Stanley Allen, Sept. 21, 1954. All the above letters and telegrams are in box 5, Benton Papers. Other fragments of this voluminous correspondence may be found in the Robert C. Hendrickson Papers, the Thomas C. Hennings Papers, and the NCEC files.

[93] Ralph Flanders to William Benton, Sept. 21, 1954, box 5, Benton Papers.

The Clearing House continued to aid the small group of liberals who had forced the McCarthy issue on the Senate. They prepared a detailed analysis of the legal foundations for censure and they continued their consultations with friendly senators. They even prepared a study of "Ten Million Americans Mobilizing for Justice," a short-lived anticensure organization which William S. White described as the largest reemergence of the far right since the late 1930s.[94] Beyond this, however, their activities were minimal. The political center of gravity had shifted, and the issue had been joined by more conservative forces.

The unanimous report of the Select Committee was released to the press on September 27. The committee recommended that McCarthy be censured on two counts—for contempt of the Senate because of his refusal to appear before the Subcommittee on Privileges and Elections in 1952, and for his abuse of General Ralph W. Zwicker before his own subcommittee in early 1953. On the three remaining counts the committee denounced McCarthy but declined to recommend censure.

Two of the five categories involved the long and troublesome issue of Congress's right to information originating in the Executive Department—McCarthy's appeal to two million federal employees to deliver information to him "even though some little bureaucrat has stamped it 'secret' to protect himself," and his receipt, during the army-McCarthy hearings, of classified government information. Faced with the dilemma of disavowing McCarthy and his abuse of senatorial power without disclaiming the power and prerogatives of the Senate itself, the committee chose to condemn McCarthy in the strongest possible language, but to stop short of recommending censure. His actions, they declared, were "disruptive of orderly governmental processes, violative of accepted comity between the two great branches of our Government . . . and incompatible with the basic tenets of effective democracy." They tended "to create a disruption of the orderly and constitutional functioning of the executive and legislative branches of government, which tends to

[94] "Analysis of Watkins Committee Discussion of Alleged Incidents of Contempt of the Senate or a Senatorial Committee," copy of legal brief in NCEC files; Maurice Rosenblatt to Ralph Flanders, Oct. 7, 1954; Rosenblatt to Marshall Field, Oct. 21, Nov. 19, 1954, all in the NCEC files. John Howe to William Benton, Oct. 12, 1954, box 5, Benton Papers. "Ten Million Americans . . .," press release, Nov. 23, 1954, in NCEC files. William S. White, *New York Times*, Nov. 21, 1954, sec. 4, p. 3.

bring both into disrepute." Nevertheless, they gave McCarthy the benefit of all reasonable doubt and "mitigating circumstances" and declined to recommend censure.[95]

With an eye to a long and colorful legacy of congressional name-calling, the committee also refused to censure McCarthy specifically for the abuse of his colleagues. But the senators found his treatment of General Zwicker "reprehensible" and concluded that he should be condemned for this disgraceful episode.[96]

The heart of the report, however, was the committee's recommendation that McCarthy be censured for his refusal to appear before the Subcommittee on Privileges and Elections in 1952 and for his repeated abuse of the members of that body. "It was the duty of Senator McCarthy to accept the repeated invitation by the subcommittee and his failure to appear was obstructive of the processes of the Senate," the report declared, "for no formal order or subpoena should be necessary to bring Senators before Senate committees when their own honor and the honor of the Senate are at issue." The key words were "honor" and "duty." Like the Hennings Committee before it, the Watkins Committee spoke in the institutional idiom of the Senate itself. "When persons in high places fail to set and meet high standards, the people lose faith," the report continued. "If our people lose faith, our form of Government cannot long endure." The Select Committee found McCarthy's actions "contemptuous, contumacious, and denunciatory" and obstructive to the legislative process. And for this reason they recommended that he be condemned.[97]

Once the Select Committee released its report, censure in some form and to some degree became almost inevitable. It was no longer a question of voting confidence or no in Joe McCarthy, but of voting confidence or no in the Senate itself.

Flanders, Fulbright, and the tiny band of liberals who spearheaded the censure movement hoped that the Senate would be called back into session in late September to consider the Select Committee's report. They feared that any delay would afford

<hr />

[95] U. S., Congress, Senate, 83d Cong., 2d sess., *Report of the Select Committee to Study Censure Charges* (Washington, D. C., 1954), pp. 39, 44–45 (hereafter cited as *Watkins Report*).

[96] *Watkins Report*, pp. 46, 60–61. McCarthy's attacks on Robert Hendrickson and the other members of the Gillette-Hennings Subcommittee were incorporated into another category and did become grounds for censure.

[97] Ibid., pp. 27–31.

McCarthy and his partisans an opportunity for diversion. There had been a certain "earnestness and solemnity" about the committee proceedings, and they had produced a momentum which a long delay might interrupt.[98]

Neither Republicans nor Democrats were especially eager to meet the issue before the November elections, however. Senators such as Ives, Staltonstall, Ferguson, Douglas, and Gillette were all engaged in tough campaigns in which a stand one way or the other on the censure might mean defeat. "October will not provide a wholesome atmosphere for discussion of such a question," declared Senator Edwin C. Johnson, the ranking Democrat on the Watkins Committee, and a number of Republicans were only too happy to concur. "I have been afraid of this all along, since I know the Democratic leader in the Senate as well as the Republican leader wish to defer the matter," concluded Fulbright.[99]

The final decision to delay reconvening the Senate was left to Majority Leader Knowland and the Republicans. Lyndon Johnson shrewdly declared, "We are ready to meet now—as soon as the report is presented." But Styles Bridges and other McCarthy supporters issued strong statements against recalling the Senate, and Everett Dirksen hurried out to California to confer with Knowland. While the issue was still unresolved, McCarthy entered the Naval Medical Center for treatment of a "sinus condition," in what was perhaps a final move in the campaign for delay. Knowland bowed, not unreluctantly, to the pressure from McCarthy and the others to postpone recalling the Senate until after the election so that the "ulimate action of the Senate would take place in an atmosphere free from pre-election tensions."[100]

The elections themselves seemed to reinforce the belief that McCarthy's star had at last fallen. In 1950 and 1952 he had been the most sought-after campaigner on the Republican side of the Senate. By 1954 he was an embarrassment to the entire party. He gamely told reporters that he was receiving "hundreds of invitations" but was turning them down in order to devote his full

---

[98] Maurice Rosenblatt to Ralph Flanders, Sept. 20, 1954; William Benton to Rosenblatt, Sept. 27, 1954, both in the NCEC files.

[99] William Fulbright to William Benton, Sept. 18, 1954, box 5, Benton Papers; Maurice Rosenblatt to Ralph Flanders, Sept. 20, 1954, NCEC files. Irving Ives, who was running for governor of New York, was one of several G.O.P. liberals urging postponement. Flanders, COHC, p. 13.

[100] New York Times, Sept. 25, 1954, p. 1; Sept. 26, 1954, pp. 1, 5.

energies to "exposing graft, corruption and Communists." In fact, what few groups still had commitments from the senator to speak were now trying to back out of them as delicately as possible.[101]

The Republicans, led by Nixon, continued to accuse the Democrats of "bending to the Red wind," but even this cry seemed to have lost its militant appeal. Almost all the liberal Democratic incumbents won reelection. In Montana, James E. Murray won a fourth term despite the distribution of 160,000 booklets featuring an ominous red spiderweb across the senator's picture. Paul Douglas turned back a challenge by a strong McCarthy supporter who had been endorsed by Eisenhower. In Wyoming, Joseph C. O'Mahoney made a comeback despite a campaign which turned heavily on the fact that O'Mahoney had served as attorney for Owen Lattimore. Republican Clifford P. Case won election in New Jersey despite a vicious smear campaign initiated by Mc-Carthy supporters, and in Oregon Richard L. Neuberger unseated Guy Cordon. In Tennessee, Estes Kefauver handily defeated a primary opponent who accused him of Communist sympathies, and then went on to win an overwhelming majority in the general election. In the House of Representatives, three of McCarthy's most vociferous supporters were defeated, and several others came perilously near the same fate. The Democrats won control of both the House of Representatives and the Senate. The meaning of the election was not entirely clear—the lessons of few elections are—but 1954 did seem to signal the end of the political dynamic which had supported McCarthy and the Communist issue.[102]

[101] Ibid., Sept. 17, 1954, p. 6; Sept. 19, 1954, sec. 4, p. 7.

[102] Ibid., Nov. 7, 1954, sec. 4, p. 1; Frederick Kuh, *Chicago Sun-Times*, Nov. 8, 1954; *Congressional Report* 3 (Nov. 19, 1954). On Nixon and the Republican campaign see Earl Mazo, *Richard Nixon: A Political and Personal Portrait*, rev. ed. (New York, 1959), pp. 139–40. For Murray's campaign see Herbert Lehman to James Murray, Oct. 16, 1954, in Special File, Lehman Papers; and Murray to Edward A. Hollander, Oct. 25, 1954, Political File, box 7, ADA Papers. On the Illinois election see Joseph T. Meek to Eisenhower, June 17, 1954; Eisenhower to Meek, July 17, 1954, both in OF 138-A-4, Eisenhower Papers; and C. M. Burgess to Robert McCarthy, Oct. 26, 1954, in box 113, Bricker Papers. On Clifford Case's campaign see Case to Robert R. Nathan, July 9, 1954, Political File, box 3, ADA Papers. On the Oregon election see Richard L. Neuberger to Estes Kefauver, Nov. 27, 1954, Subject File, Elections, Kefauver Papers. On Kefauver's campaign see Speech to Congressional Secretaries Club, April 18, 1955, in ibid. Guy Gillette, the only Democratic incumbent to fail reelection, was attacked by McCarthy during the closing days of the election. His defeat was probably due more to falling

CENSURE

In November 1954 the United States Senate turned slowly and reluctantly toward the confrontation it had so long avoided. The leadership against McCarthy had now passed into the hands of conservatives such as Arthur Watkins and John Stennis, and the implications of this turn were felt on both sides of the aisle. For the Republicans it signaled an end to that period during which the non-McCarthy conservatives could tolerate the senator because he helped their cause. Now they had to choose for or against McCarthy. Some would follow Chairman Watkins, others Majority Leader Knowland. In either case, the Republican center—on this issue—ceased to exist. For the Democrats it meant an end to the "curse of partisanship." Lyndon Johnson would continue to insist that censure was a personal issue, a matter for conscience, but not one Democratic voice was raised in McCarthy's defense, nor was a single Democratic vote cast in his favor.

McCarthy remained defiant and unbowed. He had always moved by jumps and spurts; long periods of intense physical activity were followed by short interludes of near-total collapse. By the autumn of 1954 the periods of exertion were becoming shorter and the collapses more frequent. For the first time in five years, newspaper reporters began to find him inaccessible.[103] His first reaction to the Watkins report was so mild as to attract notice in itself. He replied through his lawyer. But by the end of October he had caught scent of the approaching battle and begun to return to the tactics which had given his name currency throughout the nation. He called the coming session a "lynch bee" and freely predicted his own censure, something he attributed to a Moscow-directed conspiracy. When the Senate convened for the final debate, each senator found on his desk a pink rectangle bearing the masthead of the *Daily Worker* and filled with nineteen pages of anti-McCarthy editorials.[104]

Arthur Watkins opened the debate by introducing the commit-

---

farm prices and a traditionally Republican constituency than to any influence McCarthy may have had. John Sherman Cooper also failed to win reelection, but again this was the result of Alben Barkley's great popularity in Kentucky and not of Cooper's opposition to McCarthy.

[103] *New York Times*, Sept. 19, 1954, sec. 4, p. 7; Oct. 3, 1954, sec. 4, p. 7.
[104] Ibid., Nov. 5, 1954, p. 6; Nov. 9, 1954, p. 1.

tee's recommendations for censure. The proceedings were painful for the sixty-eight-year-old Republican. On occasion his hand jerked instinctively toward his abdomen where a spastic muscle contorted his stomach, but he grimly stood his ground against bitter attacks by McCarthy, Welker, and Jenner. "I'm not going to be pushed around or bulldozed by anybody," he declared. McCarthy lashed back with a speech denouncing the Watkins Committee for having "imitated Communist methods" and charged that the committee had made itself the "unwitting handmaiden" and "involuntary agent" of the Communist conspiracy. Once again he was aiming for the headlines. The speech, which included phrases such as "Now my fellow Americans," was released in advance of delivery. Indeed, it was never delivered at all. McCarthy waited until late in the first day of debate and then inserted it in the *Congressional Record*.[105]

The members of the Select Committee, with the single exception of the thick, colorless Francis Case, only hardened in the face of McCarthy's vituperation. One by one they came forward to call for his condemnation. John Stennis accused McCarthy of pouring "slush and slime" upon the Senate and declared that if censure failed "something big and fine will have gone out of this chamber." Sam Ervin urged the Senate to take one step further and expel McCarthy.[106] On November 16 Watkins denounced McCarthy's speech as an attack on the Senate itself and demanded a show of confidence. "Do we have the manhood in the Senate to stand up to a challenge of that kind?" he angrily demanded. Senators themselves joined in applause, and two hours later Watkins's fellow Utah Republican Wallace F. Bennett served notice on the floor that he would add to the pending resolution an amendment condemning McCarthy for contempt of the Senate because of his actions toward the Select Committee. I, too, am now "a protagonist," declared the conservative former president of the National Association of Manufacturers.[107]

[105] *Congressional Record*, 83d Cong., 2d sess., Nov. 10, 1954, pp. 15922–32, 15954; *New York Times*, Nov. 11, 1954, p. 1.

[106] *Congressional Record*, 83d Cong., 2d sess., Nov. 12, 1954, pp. 15986–89, 16007; Nov. 15, 1954, pp. 16018–22. *New York Times*, Nov. 13, 1954, p. 1; Nov. 14, 1954, sec. 4, p. 1; Nov. 16, 1954, p. 1.

[107] *Congressional Record*, 83d Cong., 2d sess., Nov. 16, 1954, pp. 16052–61, 16071; *New York Times*, Nov. 17, 1954, p. 1; Nov. 19, 1954, p. 1. Author's interview with Arthur V. Watkins, June 12, 1968.

Senate liberals were prepared, and in some cases even anxious, to challenge McCarthy all up and down the line, but they were restrained by the Democratic minority leader. "Lyndon Johnson and others are literally demanding that we refrain from rocking the boat," wrote one liberal worker. "I hate to see the entire issue decided on as narrow base as the Watkins report establishes, but I am pretty well convinced that the size of the vote is more important than the arguments that are made."[108]

Johnson's strategy was simple but delicate. He was determined to deliver the Democratic vote solidly, yet at the same time avoid any overt sign of partisanship which might frighten moderate Republicans into opposition. On the very first day of debate, after New Mexico Democrat Dennis Chavez had jumped to his feet and announced that he was prepared to vote right away, Johnson hurried over and whispered urgently in his ear. Chavez promptly sat down, thus ending the minority's contribution to the first day of debate. Two days later, however, Johnson did intervene to block a parliamentary diversion by Knowland which would have opened the Select Committee's recommendation to endless amendment.[109]

As the debate wore on, McCarthy's partisans worked hard to evade or dilute the resolution of censure. Francis Case opened the way for compromise on November 11, when he proposed that McCarthy step forward and apologize for his conduct and thus escape censure. Two days later he expressed his doubts about the language of the resolution, which he now found "sterile and negative" and "unjudicial." The following day, amid bitter charges that he had broken faith with his fellow committee members, he announced that he would not vote censure on the second of the committee's two counts, that involving McCarthy's abuse of General Zwicker.[110] Then on November 17 McCarthy, who had only a few days earlier accused Watkins of taking refuge in his illness, entered the Naval Medical Center for treatment of an elbow injury. Case quickly announced that this raised questions about

[108] Julius Edelstein to Arthur Schlesinger, Jr., Nov. 11, 1954, box 5, Benton Papers.
[109] Congressional Record, 83d Cong., 2d sess., Nov. 10, 1954, p. 15944; New York Times, Nov. 9, 1954, p. 1; Nov. 11, 1954, p. 1.
[110] Congressional Record, 83d Cong., 2d sess., Nov. 11, 1954, pp. 15959–79; Nov. 15, 1954, pp. 16038–40; New York Times, Nov. 12, 1954, p. 1; Nov. 14, 1954, p. 1; Nov. 16, 1954, p. 1.

"the Senate's courtesy and attitude toward a fellow Senator," and the following day the Senate voted to adjourn for ten days, pending McCarthy's "recovery."[111]

The delay raised hopes among those still trying to weaken or defeat the resolution. According to a strategy attributed to Styles Bridges, the McCarthy partisans hoped to begin with the ten to fifteen "bitter-enders" and then reach out for eight to ten other Republicans (such as Case) with whatever arguments could be marshaled. Then Bridges or Dirksen could go to the other Republicans and say: "Look, the party is divided and only the Democrats can profit, let's work for a common ground." Moderates such as Homer Ferguson, Irving Ives, and H. Alexander Smith might be susceptible to this approach. And once there was sufficient Republican support, Bridges could then go to Lyndon Johnson and say: "You don't want this to become a party issue. Let's find some way to compromise."[112] But Bridges and Dirksen were trying to reconstruct a political balance which the Flanders resolution and the Watkins Report had destroyed, and their efforts were unsuccessful. Even McCarthy refused to go along with a proposed substitute resolution drafted by Dirksen which "deplored" the Wisconsin senator's actions but stopped short of censure.[113]

Final debate began when the Senate reconvened on November 29. McCarthy himself introduced a unanimous consent motion to limit debate and immediately plunged the Senate into an angry argument. The agreement was worded so as to open up the possibility of new and additional censure resolutions aimed at Flanders, Fulbright, and other McCarthy foes. The Wisconsin senator had earlier declared that he would introduce ten, fifteen, or twenty-five of such resolutions in the form of amendments. Under the terms of the unanimous consent agreement, any senator

---

[111] *Congressional Record*, 83d Cong., 2d sess., Nov. 18, 1954, pp. 16143–44; *New York Times*, Nov. 18, 1954, p. 1; Nov. 19, 1954, p. 1.

[112] Maurice Rosenblatt to Marshall Field, Nov. 19, 1954, NCEC files; John Howe to William Benton, Nov. 24, 1954, box 4, Benton Papers.

[113] Edward Bennett Williams has argued that if McCarthy had been willing to accept the Dirksen resolution, a compromise might have been arranged. Williams, *One Man's Freedom*, p. 67. McCarthy's rejection of compromise was typical ("he raises on the poor hands, and always comes out the winner"), but it is difficult to believe that such a compromise was still possible at this late date. Dirksen's amendment was defeated, 66–21, on the next-to-last day of debate. For attempts at compromise by Vice President Nixon and H. Alexander Smith, see Smith Reminiscences, COHC, p. 370.

so brought up for censure would have but thirty minutes to defend himself. The terms of the agreement were immediately challenged from the floor. Spessard L. Holland of Florida demanded a ruling on whether or not amendments proposing the censure of other senators were germane and pertinent to the pending resolution. After a long consultation with the Senate parliamentarian, Styles Bridges, the president pro tempore of the Senate, ruled that such amendments would not be germane. McCarthy quickly countered by demanding that his motion be amended to provide that "any amendment relating to the censure of another Senator shall be in order." Then John McClellan took the floor. In August he had fought to ensure McCarthy his day in court, snapped the angry Arkansas Democrat. He had no intention of now allowing McCarthy to deny the same right to other senators. After a prolonged argument McCarthy finally backed down and the Senate reached an agreement to limit debate.[114]

The last days of debate were harsh and vindictive. Jenner attacked Ralph Flanders, shouting across the Senate until the presiding officer gaveled him down. Welker walked back and forth across the floor muttering obscenities. On the next to last day Arthur Watkins took the floor again and once more, now in a strained, indignant voice, demanded that the Senate invoke censure upon McCarthy. Then William Knowland spoke against the resolution, completing his long-delayed rendezvous with the Republican right. In 1953 Knowland's selection as majority leader had been opposed by a small group of Republican ultraconservatives who preferred as their own candidate Everett Dirksen.[115] Now, little more than a year later, Knowland was forced to choose between this group and the pro-Eisenhower Republican moderates. His decision was partially influenced by the comparative strength of the two factions. The moderates were disorganized and leaderless. They were also less vindictive. In time they would forget his apostasy; the McCarthyites would not. Knowland's decision was also conditioned, however, by his determination to maintain a position of strength in the foreign policy debate then raging between the Eisenhower administration and its conservative Re-

---

[114] *Congressional Record,* 83d Cong., 2d sess., Nov. 29, 1954, pp. 16149–78; *New York Times,* Nov. 30, 1954, p. 1.

[115] The group, which was led by Styles Bridges, included McCarthy, William Jenner, John Bricker, Herman Welker, George Malone, and Homer Capehart. *New York Times,* Aug. 4, 1953, p. 1; Aug. 5, 1953, p. 1.

VOTE ON A RESOLUTION TO CENSURE
SENATOR JOSEPH R. McCARTHY

| DEMOCRATS | | REPUBLICANS | |
YES	NO	YES	NO
Northeast			
Lehman *(N. Y.)*		Bush *(Conn.)*	Purtell *(Conn.)*
Green *(R. I.)*		Payne *(Me.)*	Bridges *(N. H.)*
Pastore *(R. I.)*		Smith *(Me.)*	Martin *(Pa.)*
		Saltonstall *(Mass.)*	
		Cotton *(N. H.)*	
		Hendrickson *(N. J.)*	
		Smith *(N. J.)*	
Unrecorded —		Ives *(N. Y.)*	
Kennedy *(Mass.)*		Duff *(Pa.)*	
		Aiken *(Vt.)*	
		Flanders *(Vt.)*	
(3)	(0)	(11)	(3)
Border States			
Frear *(Del.)*		Williams *(Del.)*	Butler *(Md.)*
Clements *(Ky.)*		Cooper *(Ky.)*	
Hennings *(Mo.)*		Beall *(Md.)*	
Symington *(Mo.)*			
Kerr *(Okla.)*			
Monroney *(Okla.)*			
Kilgore *(W. Va.)*			
Neely *(W. Va.)*			
(8)	(0)	(3)	(1)
South			
Hill *(Ala.)*			
Sparkman *(Ala.)*			
Fulbright *(Ark.)*			
McClellan *(Ark.)*			
Holland *(Fla.)*			
Smathers *(Fla.)* Paired.			
George *(Ga.)*			
Russell *(Ga.)*			
Ellender *(La.)*			
Long *(La.)*			
Eastland *(Miss.)*			
Stennis *(Miss.)*			
Ervin *(N. C.)*			
Scott *(N. C.)*			
Johnston *(S. C.)*			

DEMOCRATS		REPUBLICANS	
YES	NO	YES	NO

Daniels (S. C.)			
Gore (Tenn.) Paired.			
Kefauver (Tenn.)			
Daniel (Tex.)			
Johnson (Tex.)			
Byrd (Va.)			
Robertson (Va.)			
(22)	(0)	(0)	(0)

Middle West

Douglas (Ill.)		Carlson (Kan.)	Dirksen (Ill.)
Gillette (Ia.)		Ferguson (Mich.)	Capehart (Ind.)
Humphrey (Minn.)		Potter (Mich.)	Paired
Burke (Ohio)		Thye (Minn.)	Jenner (Ind.)
		Abel (Neb.)	Hickenlooper (a.)
		Case (S. D.)	Schoeppel (Kan.)
			Hruska (Neb.)
			Langer (N. D.)
			Young (N. D.)
			Bricker (Ohio)
			Paired.
			Mundt (S. D.)
		Unrecorded —	
		McCarthy (Wis.)	
		Wiley (Wis.)	
(4)	(0)	(6)	(10)

Rocky Mountain and Pacific West

Hayden (Ariz.)		Watkins (Utah)	Goldwater (Ariz.)
Johnson (Col.)		Bennett (Utah)	Knowland (Cal.)
Mansfield (Mont.)			Kuchel (Cal.)
Murray (Mont.)			Millikin (Col.)
Anderson (N. M.)			Dworshak (Idaho)
Chavez (N. M.)			Welker (Idaho)
Jackson (Wash.)			Malone (Nev.)
Magnuson (Wash.)			Brown (Nev.)
O'Mahoney (Wyo.)			Cordon (Ore.)
			Barrett (Wyo.)
Morse (Ind., Ore.)			
(10)	(0)	(2)	(10)

Totals (including pairs) 47   0   22   24
Final vote (excluding pairs): 67-22

publican critics. He needed power in the Senate in order to continue his campaign for a militant and aggressive Far Eastern policy. Thus the mutually reinforcing pressures of party factionalism, institutional jealousy and ideology prompted Knowland and other party conservatives to join the bitter-enders.[116] After the majority leader had taken his seat Lyndon Johnson broke his long silence to call for censure. "In my mind, there is only one issue here—morality and conduct," declared the minority leader. "Each of us must decide whether we approve or disapprove of certain actions as standards of Senatorial integrity. I have made my decision." McCarthy's language toward his colleagues, declared Johnson, did not even belong in the *Congressional Record*. It would be "more fittingly inscribed on the wall of a men's room."[117]

On December 1 the Senate finally began to vote, rejecting amendments by Dirksen, Mundt, and Bridges. The following day they voted to condemn McCarthy on two counts—for contempt and abuse of the Subcommittee on Privileges and Elections in 1952, and for contempt and abuse of the Senate and its Select Committee in 1954. The vote was overwhelming. Every Democrat present (forty-four in all) and the Senate's lone independent (Wayne Morse) voted to condemn McCarthy. The Republicans were evenly divided between the old Taft partisans who were most numerous in the West, and the more moderate Eisenhower Republicans who were heavily concentrated along the Eastern seaboard. Only three senators, McCarthy, John Kennedy, and Alexander Wiley, were unrecorded.[118]

116 In a speech attacking the Eisenhower administration in November 1954, Knowland denounced the idea of coexistence as a "trojan horse" which would lead to national destruction. *New York Times*, Nov. 16, 1954, p. 1. For an analysis of Knowland's position on the censure see William S. White in ibid., Dec. 2, 1954, p. 1; and Arthur Krock in ibid., Dec. 3, 1954, p. 26.

117 *Congressional Record*, 83d Cong., 2d sess., Nov. 30, 1954, p. 16186; Dec. 1, 1954, pp. 16279–82, 16291–93; *New York Times*, Dec. 2, 1954, p. 1.

118 The censure count relating to General Zwicker disappeared into a parliamentary mousetrap. A motion by Bridges to table this part of the resolution was defeated, 55-33. A motion to substitute for it Senator Bennett's amendment censuring McCarthy for his attacks on the Select Committee carried 64-23, and the amendment itself carried 64-24. There was no direct vote on the original count itself. According to Senator Watkins, Lyndon Johnson went to him on the floor and demanded that this count be dropped because there were at least fifteen Democrats unwilling to vote for it. *Congressional Record*, 83d Cong., 2d sess., Dec. 1, 1954, pp. 16329, 16335–36, 16340; Dec. 2, 1954, pp. 16370, 16380–81, 16392; *New York Times*, Dec. 3, 1954, p. 1. Watkins, *Enough Rope* (Englewood Cliffs, N. J., 1969), p. 149. Author's interview with Arthur Watkins, June 12, 1968.

The final resolution carried amid bitter and sullen laughter from McCarthy's partisans. As soon as the tally had been completed Bridges demanded of Nixon, then presiding, whether the word censure appeared in the resolution. Nixon replied that it did not. "Then it is not a censure resolution," declared Bridges, while Jenner, Welker, and Malone all broke into loud laughter. The vice president, while not admitting Bridges's point, exercised his prerogative as presiding officer to change the title of a resolution to conform with its text. He struck the word censure from the title, changing it to "Resolution relating to the conduct of the Senator from Wisconsin, Mr. McCarthy."[119]

This was, of course, a piece of semantic and parliamentary nonsense. The word condemn had been used in the last Senate censure, that of Hiram Bingham in 1929. And if there remained any doubt as to the relative meaning of the two words, Senator William Fulbright quickly erased it by reading to the Senate the dictionary definition of both. Even McCarthy could concede the underlying humor of this tomfoolery. For a moment the amiable Irishman peeked out from behind the facade of the crusader. "Well," he told reporters, "it wasn't exactly a vote of confidence." And then once more he drew behind the image he had created of himself. "I'm happy to have this circus ended so I can get back to the real work of digging out communism, crime and corruption."[120]

EPILOGUE

The political forces which ended McCarthy's career were broad and complex. They undoubtedly included the army-McCarthy hearings and the increasing difficulty with which Republicans in both the White House and the Senate were able to suffer McCarthy's divisive tactics. There were shifts, though rather slight, in public opinion, an ever-increasing opposition within the press, and perhaps most importantly, a rejection of McCarthy by America's national leaders themselves. It was in the Senate, however, that the McCarthy drama began, and it was there that the final scenes were played out.

The censure proceedings were accompanied by an intensification

[119] *New York Times*, Dec. 3, 1954, p. 1; Dec. 4, 1954, p. 8.
[120] *Congressional Record*, 83d Cong., 2d sess., Dec. 2, 1954, pp. 16392–94; *New York Times*, Dec. 3, 1954, p. 1.

of McCarthy's own self-destructive impulses. "Joe is going over the precipice and dragging everything with him," declared one Republican senator.[121] On July 30 McCarthy himself called up the Flanders resolution. He brushed aside gambits by Francis Case and Karl Mundt which would have allowed him to apologize and perhaps escape censure. He refused to accept a compromise resolution urged upon him by Dirksen, Goldwater, and Edward Bennett Williams. He even introduced himself the unanimous consent agreement which foreclosed the possibility of a long delaying action. And if, after the final tally was taken, there remained any unresolved doubts, he quickly removed them on December 7 by a harsh attack on President Eisenhower. "They're shooting at me from the other end of the Avenue," he told Karl Mundt, who tried to stop him. "I've got to say something." He accused the president of "a shrinking show of weakness" toward Red China and declared that he had been "mistaken" in believing that Eisenhower would fight Communists vigorously. He "apologized" to the American people for having urged the general's election in 1952.[122] The horrified reaction among even his most stalwart supporters showed that McCarthy had indeed gone "over the precipice."

The censure also marked the collapse of the "McCarthy balance." For five years the Republican party had allowed McCarthy a privileged sanctuary because of the issues he symbolized and their role in the Republican drive for power. Now twenty-two Republicans declared that his conduct had brought the Senate into disrepute and was to be condemned. Even most of the twenty-two who voted against censure recoiled from McCarthy's harsh attack on the president. Knowland, Millikin, Mundt, Purtell, Butler, and Goldwater all hastened to disassociate themselves from Joe's last outburst.[123] In the end McCarthy was left to the embrace of Welker, Jenner, and Malone.

Some observers saw in the censure a vindication of the Senate "establishment." "It was the Institution," wrote William S. White, with reverential capitalization, "that finally brought him to book." For sixty-seven senators McCarthy was now *persona non grata*.

[121] *New York Times,* Nov. 14, 1954, sec. 4, p. 5.
[122] Ibid., Dec. 8, 1954, pp. 1, 18, 19; Dec. 10, 1954, p. 1; Dec. 12, 1954, sec. 4, pp. 1, 8.
[123] William S. White, ibid., Dec. 5, 1954, sec. 4, p. 3; White *Citadel,* pp. 126–33.

Henceforth he would receive "the silent treatment." The members of the newly elected Eighty-fourth Congress would not debate him, they would simply ignore him.[124] "The man who more than any other caused the final condemnation," again according to White, was Lyndon Baines Johnson. It was his achievement, White has argued, "to an almost incredible degree."[125] The minority leader had entered the struggle in August 1954. He helped create the Watkins Committee and saw to it that its report would be filed before the Eighty-third Congress adjourned. He was also responsible for keeping debate on the narrow and nonideological ground of Senate custom and tradition. He restrained Democratic liberals, encouraged reluctant conservatives, and through manipulation of parliamentary procedure helped insure a final showdown.

All this was predicated on the assumption that the Senate had to deal with McCarthy, however; and in the early summer of 1954 this was not at all as certain as it appears in retrospect. The Republican leadership desperately hoped to avoid a confrontation over McCarthy, and the Democrats were scarcely more enthusiastic. But Flanders and his supporters forced the McCarthy question upon the Senate in a manner which it could not evade. Flanders and Watkins lifted "the curse of partisanship" which had paralyzed all previous attempts to restrain McCarthy. Theirs was at best a hard and lonely struggle. "The Institution" wanted nothing more than to avoid the issue altogether. Both Flanders and Watkins were practically ostracized during this period by their Republican colleagues. Yet these two men, the whimsical New Englander and the narrow, ascetic Mormon, demanded no less of the United States Senate than that it come to terms with Joe McCarthy.

[124] *New York Times,* Dec. 8, 1954, pp. 18, 19; Dec. 10, 1954, p. 1; Dec. 12, 1954, sec. 4, p. 8.
[125] William S. White, ibid., Dec. 5, 1954, sec. 4, p. 3; White *The Professional: Lyndon B. Johnson* (Boston, 1954), pp. 49–50.

CONCLUSION

HATEVER OTHER MEANING the events of that turbulent autumn of 1954 may have contained, they marked the end of Joe McCarthy and of an era. During the Democratic Eighty-fourth Congress he was conspicuously ignored. His speeches—he continued to deliver harsh and extreme attacks—were greeted by unusual displays of disorder and inattention. The Republican leadership offered him a seat on the Committee on Committees, but even this gesture could not halt his downward plunge. He continued to send insulting letters and telegrams to the White House; these went unanswered. When he sought to embarrass the president on the eve of the Geneva conference, the resolution which he had introduced was rejected by a vote of 77-4.[1] The press, long the unwilling instrument of McCarthy's campaigns, now entered into a tacit compact to ignore him. At the annual Gridiron banquet of the Washington press corps, the heroes were Eisenhower and Watkins; the only mention of McCarthy was a passing reference to a "loud mouthed kid" who had "elbowed his way to obscurity."[2] In a few months the slick magazines were already asking, "Whatever happened to Joe Mc-Carthy?" His fellow senators, at least those who cared to comment, were of one mind. "McCarthyism?" said Republican Henry Dworshak. "Haven't heard anything about that lately. I thought we had done with that at the last session." "McCarthyism is no longer an issue," agreed Democrat Henry Jackson. "I don't even think about it." Perhaps the final word was that of Arthur Watkins. "There is more peace on the Hill."[3]

As for McCarthy, perhaps, as Richard Rovere has argued in his compassionate essay on McCarthy's "last days," the senator suffered an internal collapse which destroyed not only his will to power but even his will to live. Or perhaps he simply realized that the game he knew and feared must someday end was now concluded. Even at the height of his notoriety he had understood only imperfectly the forces that had propelled him into the roaring political storms of the 1950s. How unnerving the silence that followed his censure must have been. There was time now for a private life; but toward the end even this was interrupted by illness and finally, on May 2, 1957, by death.

Behind the rise of Joe McCarthy to national power lay at least five interrelated and interreacting lines of causation: a fear of radicalism which sometimes bordered on the pathological; the course of America's cold war with the Soviet Union and its not-so-cold war with North Korea and China; the singular character and abilities of Joseph McCarthy; the structure of power both within the Senate and between the Senate and the Executive; and the routine operation of American party politics.

The first of these, what has been called the anti-Communist persuasion, has been a persistent theme of American history in this century. While it dictated the slogans and style used by McCarthy in his sudden rise to power, it was not in turn diminished by his equally sudden demise. The cold war furnished the concrete staples of party debate, and it was of some significance that McCarthy's rise coincided with the outbreak of hostilities in Korea while his decline came not long after the armistice.

Of greater importance was McCarthy himself. He was not

---

[1] McCarthy to Eisenhower, March 3, May 18, 1955, in OF 154-H, Eisenhower Papers; William Benton to John Howe, Jan. 11, 1955, box 4, Benton Papers; Doris Fleeson, *New York Post*, June 22, 1955; William S. White, *Citadel: The Story of the U. S. Senate* (New York, 1956), p. 133; Richard H. Rovere, *Senator Joe McCarthy* (New York, 1959), pp. 237–38.

[2] *New York Times*, Dec. 13, 1954, p. 18; Rovere, *Senator Joe McCarthy*, pp. 238–39; author's interview with Arthur Watkins, June 12, 1968; author's interview with Willard Edwards, May 26, 1966.

[3] "Whatever Happened to Joe McCarthy?" *Picture Week* 1 (July 16, 1955): 4–9.

the most gifted demagogue this country has ever known, but his talents in this direction were considerable. His stubborn unwillingness to underplay his hand or to back down from a battle was his great strength and in the end his undoing. He also understood the cumbersome, decentralized, and individualistic nature of the Senate's internal processes, and he was a skillful manipulator of that body's institutional jealousy of the Executive.

But McCarthy's power and influence rested on more than this. His triumph was the consequence of Republican partisanship and, after 1950, of Democratic acquiescence. To many Republicans he symbolized the issues generated by more than a decade of attacks against the Democratic administrations of Franklin Roosevelt and Harry Truman. Most Democrats feared him as a threat to personal and party fortunes. As a result, neither party acted to check McCarthy or to restrain his excessive behavior. In this sense both McCarthy and McCarthyism can be understood as products of the normal operation of American political parties.[4]

In the end McCarthy was brought down by the Senate, although this would have never been possible had McCarthy not finally become an embarrassment to his own party and had not the Senate been forced against its will to confront him. Even then the Senate circumspectly avoided the very issues which were central to the entire McCarthy controversy. For the practical politicians who governed within the Senate this was sufficient—the McCarthy interregnum was ended. For those more critical of the American party system there were two further observations—that if instrumental politics were responsible for McCarthy's defeat, they were also responsible for his rise and for the prolongation of his power, and that between 1950 and 1954 the politics of the possible were also the politics of fear.

[4] On this point see especially Michael Rogin's penetrating and insightful analysis in *The Intellectuals and McCarthy: The Radical Specter* (Cambridge, Mass., 1967), pp. 216–60.

BIBLIOGRAPHICAL ESSAY

MANUSCRIPTS

The McCarthy period is still so close as to limit access to important manuscript collections. Some of the leading figures of those years remain active in public life today, and even among the families of those now retired or deceased there is an understandable reluctance to release private papers. The McCarthy Papers themselves are deposited at Marquette University but are closed and likely to remain so for quite some time [Mrs. Jean Kerr Minetti to author, October 7, 1966]. Nevertheless, a number of manuscript collections have been of particular value in the preparation of this study.

The most important single source was the Washington files of the National Committee for an Effective Congress. Beginning in 1953 the NCEC Clearing House collected an enormous amount of material on McCarthy's Senate career. This included the notes collected by Jack Anderson and Ronald May for their biography of McCarthy, the files of Gerhard P. Van Arkel relative to McCarthy's libel suit against William Benton, and the files of Warren Woods, Drew Pearson's attorney in the columnist's suit against McCarthy. The Clearing House researcher also collected voluminous press clippings, magazine articles, and congressional documents, now rather chaotically scattered through ten large filing cabinets. The files contain a large amount of correspondence relative to the Clearing House's various "operations" against McCarthy and especially the censure movement. Although these files must necessarily be used with care, they do present a uniquely "inside" picture of how the Senate functioned with regard to McCarthy.

The William Benton Papers (Manuscripts Division, State Historical Society of Wisconsin) were also extremely valuable. The collection is small (five boxes) but consists entirely of material relating to McCarthy. Senator Benton and his chief aide, John Howe, were extraordinarily busy memoranda writers, and the collection provides a running commentary on McCarthy's five years in the spotlight.

The papers of Senator Ralph E. Flanders appear in three locations. The bulk of the senator's wide-ranging correspondence (164 boxes) is deposited at the Syracuse University Library. This finely indexed collection includes also press releases, radio broadcasts, and other valuable materials. Thirteen boxes of the senator's papers are in the Manuscripts Division of the State Historical Society of Wisconsin. Most of this is constituent mail originating after Flanders made his first attack on McCarthy, but there is some correspondence by the senator himself. Most of the material which went through Flanders's office during the censure movement may be found scattered through the files of the National Committee for an Effective Congress. This includes both political correspondence to and from Senator Flanders and an additional 10–15,000 letters (mostly abusive) from the public.

The Thomas C. Hennings Papers (Western Historical Manuscripts Collection, University of Missouri) were of considerable help, although they still remain unprocessed. I am especially indebted to Donald J. Kemper, who helped guide me through this large collection. The Robert C. Hendrickson Papers (Syracuse University) were also of some help. The Hendrickson Papers contain one of the eight original copies of the important "Preliminary Report" filed by the staff of the Subcommittee on Privileges and Elections in 1952.

The Herbert H. Lehman Papers, Columbia University, were especially helpful, as were the Estes Kefauver Papers, University of Tennessee; the Theodore F. Green Papers, Library of Congress; the Alexander Wiley Papers, State Historical Society of Wisconsin; and the Americans for Democratic Action Papers, also at the State Historical Society of Wisconsin. The following collections were also of some value: Millard E. Tydings Papers, University of Maryland; Tom Connally Papers, Library of Congress; Kenneth S. Wherry Papers, University of Nebraska; Hugh A. Butler Papers, State Historical Society of Nebraska; Blair Moody Papers, Michigan Historical Collections, University of Michigan; Arthur Vandenberg Papers, W. L. Clements Library, University of Michigan; Arthur V. Watkins Papers, Brigham Young University; Alben Barkley

Papers, University of Kentucky; and the John W. Bricker Papers, Ohio Historical Society.

The mammoth collections housed by the Harry S. Truman Library, Independence, Missouri, and the Dwight D. Eisenhower Library, Abilene, Kansas, were both very helpful, though their value is somewhat limited by the fact that both men restricted large files of their personal correspondence. In contrast to what I had been led to expect, I found relatively more material on McCarthy by Eisenhower and his presidential staff than by Truman and his top advisers. The papers of presidential aide Stephen J. Spingarn (in the Truman Library) were especially valuable in the field of internal security and civil liberties.

CONGRESSIONAL DOCUMENTS

The first source through which to study Congress remains the speeches and debates of the *Congressional Record*. Congressional debate, however, as Donald Matthews has observed in *U. S. Senators and Their World*, is often not debate at all. Most votes are determined well before the speech-making begins, and few are changed. What senators present in lieu of debate are long and often eloquent rationalizations for supporting or opposing a particular measure. Individual senators, moreover, approach any given debate so as to fulfill many functions and in response to many pressures. Some senators will speak simply to their constituents, however defined. Others will speak directly to the Senate itself, invoking the customs and traditions and camaraderie of the Upper Chamber. Some will deliver narrow, legalistic "briefs," as befits a body of lawyers. Still others speak to the headlines, to provide the ideological and emotional appeal to rally the faithful. Some senators, often the most important, seldom speak at all.

It is not enough for a senator simply to speak on the floor. It remains for the members of the press to carry the essence of the "debate" to the newspapers. More often than not, a senator's aides will alert the Senate press gallery for a "major" speech and will furnish the newsmen with mimeographed press releases. With McCarthy this process became a fine art. Before his famous attack on General Marshall, for example, McCarthy called a press conference to announce that on the following day he would attack the secretary of defense. Few correspondents read the speech. Most of it was never even delivered but simply inserted into the record. They picked from it, as McCarthy intended they should, a few of his more inflated accusations and wrote their stories on this basis. Once written, these stories were in turn immortalized in countless newsroom morgues, where they served as the basis for quick coverage still to come.

The voluminous hearings conducted by congressional committees were an even more important source for this study. Congressional hearings, however, must of necessity be approached with a great deal of caution. To begin with, the complete transcript of committee proceedings is seldom if ever published. When the committee holds public sessions for the explicit purpose of taking testimony, the transcript is usually, though not always, printed. Even at this stage, however, the record is often subjected to congressional censorship. As recently as 1967, Secretary of Defense Robert S. McNamara, in an appearance before a committee, sharply criticized the Congress for its inattention to the needs of Washington schoolchildren. Although his remarks were carried by national television, they were deleted from the printed record of his testimony. McCarthy made use of this *sub rosa* practice in 1947, when he chaired a series of hearings into housing conditions, and again in 1953, when he became chairman of the Government Operations Committee and its Permanent Subcommittee on Investigations.

Congressional committees also proceed in executive or closed session. When testimony is given during these closed sessions, the transcript may or may not be printed, according to the committee's discretion. McCarthy frequently abused this circumstance by conducting hearings in executive session and then going to reporters himself to deliver fanciful and inflated versions of what had occurred. Only occasionally are the records of a committee's procedural deliberations included in the transcript, and even here the senators frequently go "off the record" when the discussion becomes too heated or the procedural problems too tangled. Minutes are kept of all committee meetings, but these are not generally available to researchers.

The nature of congressional hearings themselves, moreover, invites misinterpretation. A congressional "investigation" is not really an investigation at all, but rather a means of certifying and publicizing the information already gathered by investigation. The witnesses are almost invariably coached, either by some politically interested party or in some cases by the witness's own legal counsel. Committee proceedings, moreover, are only technically nonadversary. When important political issues are at stake, the committee members almost always assume at least some of the functions of prosecutor and defense counsel. Thus, like the *Congressional Record*, such hearings must be used only within the context of additional evidence and commentary.

Although McCarthy's name has become almost synonymous with congressional investigations, he was more investigated than investigating. In fact he thrived on the drama and public notice which such hearings brought him. The Tydings Committee hearings (U. S., Congress, Senate, 81st Cong., 2d sess., Committee on Foreign Relations, *State Department Loyalty Investigation* [Washington, D. C., 1950]) were called to investigate McCarthy's first charges against the State Department. Although his accusations were indeed "a fraud and a hoax," as the Democrats on the committee declared, the committee majority overreached itself in attempting to crush McCarthy and instead helped make him a symbol of Republican partisanship. The Tydings Committee report (U. S. Congress, Senate, 81st Cong., 2d sess., Committee on Foreign Relations, *State Department Loyalty Investigation,* Senate Report 2108 [Washington, D. C., 1950]) was accepted by the Senate along strictly partisan lines.

The hearings on the 1950 Maryland election campaign (U. S., Congress, Senate, 82d Cong., 1st sess., Committee on Rules and Administration, Subcommittee on Privileges and Elections, *Maryland Senatorial Election of 1950* [Washington, D. C., 1951]) were conducted by a "hearings subcommittee" under the chairmanship of Mike Monroney. The presence of two Republicans, Margaret Chase Smith and Robert Hendrickson, added a bipartisan flavor to the subcommittee's report (U. S., Congress, Senate, 82d Cong., 1st sess., Committee on Rules and Administration, Subcommittee on Privileges and Elections, *Maryland Senatorial Election of 1950,* Senate Report 647 [Washington, D. C., 1950]). The report condemned the "back street" campaign waged in Maryland and sharply criticized McCarthy's role in it. The report was received by the Rules Committee on a 9-3 vote, with Smith and Hendrickson joining the Democratic majority.

The Subcommittee on Privileges and Elections also conducted the faltering investigation of McCarthy instigated by William Benton in 1951 (U. S., Congress, Senate, 82d Cong., 1st and 2d sess., Committee on Rules and Administration, Subcommittee on Privileges and Elections, *Investigation of Joseph R. McCarthy* [Washington, D. C., 1952]). The final report of this subcommittee was signed by Senators Hennings, Hayden, and Hendrickson and eventually became the basis for McCarthy's condemnation in 1954 (U. S., Congress, Senate, 82d Cong., 2d sess., *Investigations of Senators Joseph R. McCarthy and William Benton,* Committee Print [Washington, D. C., 1952]).

Neither the army-McCarthy hearings (U. S., Congress, Senate, 83d Cong., 2d sess., Committee on Government Operations, Permanent Subcommittee on Investigations, *Charges and Countercharges Involving Secretary of the Army Robert T. Stevens, John G. Adams, H. Struve Hensel and Senator Joe McCarthy, Roy M. Cohn and Francis P. Carr* [Washington, D. C., 1954]) nor the Watkins Committee hearings (U. S., Congress, Senate, 83d Cong., 2d sess., Select Committee to Study Censure Charges, *Hearings on S. Res. 301* [Washington, D. C., 1954]) need detailed explanation. The majority report on the army-McCarthy affair was generally mild (U. S., Congress, Senate, 83d Cong., 2d sess., Committee on Government Operations, Permanent Subcommittee on

Investigations, *Charges and Countercharges* . . . , Senate Report 2507 [Washington, D. C., 1954]). Senator Potter issued supplementary views declaring that he was "convinced the principal accusation of each side . . . was borne out." The Democrats were sharply critical of both McCarthy and Secretary Stevens. The Watkins report (U. S., Congress, Senate, 83d Cong., 2d sess., Select Committee to Study Censure Charges, *Report on Resolution to Censure*, Senate Report 2508 [Washington, D. C., 1954]) was, of course, the basis of McCarthy's final condemnation.

McCarthy was also involved, either directly or indirectly, in a host of other congressional investigations. Two of these predate his speech at Wheeling. During the Republican Eightieth Congress he chaired several sessions of the Joint Committee on Housing, the vice-chairmanship of which he had plucked from beneath the indignant nose of Charles Tobey (U. S., Congress, House, 80th Cong., 1st and 2d sess., Joint Committee on Housing, *Study and Investigation of Housing* [Washington, D. C., 1947–1948]). In 1949 he became involved in the controversial investigation of the "Malmedy Massacre" (U. S., Congress, Senate, 81st Cong., 1st sess., Committee on Armed Services, *Malmedy Massacre Investigation* [Washington, D. C., 1949]). McCarthy himself came under investigation by a subcommittee of the Senate Banking and Currency Committee which first called attention to his $10,000 literary deal with the Lustron Corporation (U. S., Congress, Senate, 81st Cong., 2d sess., Committee on Banking and Currency, Subcommittee on Reconstruction Finance Corporation, *Study of Reconstruction Finance Corporation—Lustron Corporation* [Washington, D. C., 1950]).

In late 1950 McCarthy and his aides became involved in the disreputable campaign to discredit Assistant Secretary of Defense Anna M. Rosenberg. An investigation of Mrs. Rosenberg's nomination by a subcommittee of the Armed Services Committee sent McCarthy and several Hearst employees ducking for cover (U. S., Congress, Senate, 81st Cong., 2d sess., Committee on Armed Services, *Nomination of Anna M. Rosenberg To Be Assistant Secretary of Defense* [Washington, D. C., 1951]). McCarthy himself was a prime "witness" at the hearings by a subcommittee of the Senate Foreign Relations Committee into the nomination of Ambassador Philip C. Jessup as a delegate to the United Nations (U. S., Congress, Senate, 82d Cong., 1st sess., Committee on Foreign Relations, *Nomination of Philip Jessup To Be United States Representative to the Sixth General Assembly of the United Nations* [Washington, D. C., 1951]). Finally, the investigation of the Institute of Pacific Relations by the McCarran Internal Security Subcommittee (U. S., Congress, Senate, 82d Cong., 1st and 2d sess., Committee on the Judiciary, Subcommittee on Internal Security, *Institute*

of Pacific Relations [Washington, D. C., 1951–1952]) was initiated as
a result of McCarthy's charges and conducted so as to provide a veneer
of credibility for his accusations.

McCarthy's own investigating was almost entirely limited to 1953,
when he chaired the Permanent Investigations Subcommittee of the
Senate Committee on Government Operations. His prime objective was
publicity. The information elicited during the hearings he conducted
was well known to the FBI and other security agencies and usually to
other congressional investigators. The House Committee on Un-American Activities, for example, had taken a close look at the Fort Monmouth
material before passing it by as unpromising.

According to its own count McCarthy's investigations subcommittee
initiated 445 "preliminary investigations" and 157 "investigations"—
whatever this may have meant. The subcommittee conducted seventeen
public or semipublic hearings, most of them chaired by McCarthy himself. His main target was the State Department—its filing system, its
information program, its teacher exchange program, and East-West
trade (U. S., Congress, Senate, 83d Cong., 1st sess., Committee on
Government Operations, Permanent Subcommittee on Investigations,
*State Department—File Survey; State Department Information Program
—Voice of America; State Department Information Program—Information Centers; State Department—Student-Teacher Exchange Program;
Control of Trade with Soviet Bloc* [Washington, D. C., 1953]).

During the summer of 1953 the senator sought new targets. His
most sustained effort was a brief investigation of the Government Printing Office (U. S., Congress, Senate, 83d Cong., 1st sess., Committee
on Government Operations, Permanent Subcommittee on Investigations, *Government Printing Office* [Washington, D. C., 1953]). Then
in the autumn he began his final series of investigations into the
defense industry, the Army Signal Corps laboratories at Fort Monmouth,
and the army itself (U. S., Congress, Senate, 83d Cong., 1st sess.,
Committee on Government Operations, Permanent Subcommittee on
Investigations, *Subversion and Espionage in Defense Establishments
and Industry; Army Signal Corps—Subversion and Espionage;* and
Communist Infiltration in the Army [Washington, D. C., 1953–1954]).
Much of the record of these last hearings remains incomplete because
many of the sessions were conducted in private and the testimony was
not always printed.

I have cited within the text a number of other miscellaneous investigations into "communism and subversion." It would serve no
good purpose to repeat these citations, but the interested reader may
consult U. S., Congress, Senate, 84th Cong., 1st sess., *Internal Security
Manual,* rev. ed. (Washington, D. C., 1955) for a summary of these
investigations. Only one further point should be made. The investiga-

tions into communism and subversion are a handy index to the rise and fall of the Communist issue in American politics. During the Seventy-ninth Congress (1945–1947) there were only four such hearings, comprising a total of ten days of testimony and all conducted by the House Committee on Un-American Activities. During the Republican Eightieth Congress (1947–1949), the number of investigations leaped to twenty-two, conducted by six different committees. There were twenty-four investigations of "communism and subversion" during the Eighty-first Congress, and the number climbed to thirty-four in the Eighty-second. During the Republican Eighty-third Congress, the "investigating Congress," the number of investigations rose to an all-time high of fifty-one. By 1955, however, the number had dropped back well below 1947 levels. The Communist issue had been championed by the Republicans in their drive for office. The Democrats at first resisted and then gave in to this pressure. By 1955 the issue had lost much of its appeal, the Republicans were divided, and the Democrats were in control of the Congress.

THE PRESS

To a considerable degree "Joe McCarthy" was the creation of our communications system. Like most instruments through which the past is mediated the press was an active and not a passive agent. The very questions it asked determined the answers it reported. And these answers in turn shaped the total political context. Nor were these actions always conscious, consistent, or premeditated. The nation's prestige press was overwhelmingly opposed to McCarthy, yet by the very intensity of its coverage it helped assure his permanence as a symbol of Republican partisanship.

The most important news source for the preparation of this study, as the notes surely attest, was the *New York Times*. The *Times* is the closest thing this country has to a national newspaper, and its coverage is the most complete. As befits a national paper, its viewpoint is not monolithic. The editorial page during this period was moderate—moderately conservative and moderately liberal. It was conservative enough to support Eisenhower in 1952, but liberal enough to fret and worry over the general's passivity during 1953 and 1954. *Times* editorials, many of them written by John B. Oakes, were sharply critical of McCarthy. The paper's columnists and reporters presented a broad spectrum of views. Arthur Krock usually could be depended upon to write apologetics for the Eisenhower administration. James Reston was wise, witty, and quite often indignant at the continued tolerance shown McCarthy by both the administration and the Senate. William S. White had privileged entree to the inner councils of the Senate leadership, and though his observations were heavily colored by his proximity to these powerful men, he remained one of the shrewdest and surest interpreters of senatorial politics.

In addition to the *New York Times* I found useful supplementary material in a wide variety of other newspapers. The *Washington Post* was especially valuable for capital politics, while the (Madison) *Capital Times* and the *Milwaukee Journal* paid close and continuing attention to the antics of their state's junior senator. The *Chicago Tribune* was useful as a guide to McCarthy's right-wing support. The *Washington Times-Herald,* before its merger with the *Post,* was a poor man's *Chicago Tribune.* The *Wisconsin State Journal* and the *Appleton Post-Crescent* were among McCarthy's strongest advocates in his home state. Finally, I made sparing use of a dozen or so other newspapers, the citations of which appear among the notes.

McCarthy exploded into the periodical press as well, though I have relied less on this source than on the day-to-day coverage by newspapers. The so-called news magazines were especially worthless. *Harper's, Atlantic, Saturday Review, Commentary,* and other quality periodicals offered insightful articles on McCarthy, although none surpassed the newly established *Reporter* on this particular subject. The *Nation* and the *New Republic* are more useful to the student of American liberalism than to the student of McCarthy himself. The *Progressive* was more valuable, although here again the purpose was candidly polemical. *Plain Talk,* the *Freeman,* and the *American Mercury* were convenient guides to the response of the far right.

SECONDARY LITERATURE

The McCarthy controversy generated an enormous amount of writing, both scholarly and popular, and though much of this literature is not directly relevant to the more narrow issues of this study, it does serve to place McCarthy and McCarthyism in a broad perspective.

McCarthyism   Much of this secondary literature falls into categories shaped by the individual author's definition of McCarthyism. These categories are anything but exclusive, yet of necessity they determine a given writer's approach to this complex phenomenon.

Many Americans, for example, saw McCarthyism primarily in terms of its implications for traditional libertarian values. In no decade in American history have civil liberties been scrutinized so carefully or defended so eloquently. Many studies have been concerned with the broad problems of loyalty and dissent, with freedom of speech, freedom of association, and due process. See John W. Caughey, *In Clear and Present Danger: The Crucial State of Our Freedoms* (Chicago, 1958); Henry S. Commager, *Freedom, Loyalty and Dissent* (New York, 1954);

and Robert E. Cushman, *Civil Liberties in the United States* (Ithaca, N. Y., 1956). Other studies have focused more narrowly upon the problems posed for traditional liberties by the governmental process itself. See John Lord O'Brian, *National Security and Individual Freedom* (Cambridge, Mass., 1955); Eleanor Bontecou, *The Federal Loyalty-Security Program* (Ithaca, N. Y., 1953); and Ralph S. Brown, *Loyalty and Security Employment Tests in the United States* (New Haven, Conn., 1958). Alan D. Harper, *The Politics of Loyalty: The White House and the Communist Issue, 1946–1952* (New York, 1969), is a solid monograph but appeared too late to be of help in the preparation of this volume. Also see the excellent study by Thomas C. Reeves, *Freedom and the Foundation: The Fund for the Republic in the Era of McCarthyism* (New York, 1969).

The civil libertarians by and large have been concerned with the consequences of what has been broadly called McCarthyism, but others have been preoccupied with the question of what produced this climate of intolerance. Most general historians have attributed McCarthyism to the frustration and internal stress produced by the cold war in general and by the conviction of Alger Hiss and the fall of Nationalist China in particular. See, for example, Eric F. Goldman, *The Crucial Decade— And After: America, 1945–1960* (New York, 1961), and Herbert Agar, *The Price of Power: America since 1945* (Chicago, 1957).

But if the cold war explained the objective circumstances from which McCarthyism erupted, it did not explain his style, rhetoric, or mass appeal. Under the leadership of Richard Hofstadter, Seymour Martin Lipset, and Daniel Bell, a number of historians and social scientists have turned to the concept of status anxiety in an attempt to explain mid-twentieth-century American politics. McCarthy's support, they have argued, came from groups rising or falling in status who vented their accumulated discontents on their betters. This accounts for the anti-intellectual and anti-establishmentarian mood of McCarthyism, the scorn for "egg-sucking liberals," "dilettante diplomats," and "the bright young men who are born with silver spoons in their mouths." The best introduction to this argument may be found in Daniel Bell, ed., *The New American Right* (New York, 1955), and its revised edition, *The Radical Right* (New York, 1963). The interested student should also consult the individual works of the various contributors, as well as the growing body of literature cited in the notes of the revised edition.

But if theories about status politics help to explain the peculiar style and rhetoric of McCarthyism, they leave quite as many questions still unanswered. To begin with, there are certain methodological questions. The polls on which many of these arguments depend show a relatively high incidence of pro-McCarthyism among groups experiencing status change. They do not show, however, whether those responding favorably to the senator actually perceived this change as such. Most of the data, moreover, applied to the relatively small group of ardent McCarthy supporters. What needs explanation is the larger segment of the population which did not support McCarthy so much as tolerate him. And beyond this, assuming the widespread presence of status grievances, why did these resentments become especially powerful and politically operational during the late 1940s and the early 1950s?

A partial answer to these questions involves a political definition of McCarthyism. McCarthyism was not just a response to status anxieties or to the cold war, but was generated also by the political system. This interpretation is scarcely original; it seemed self-evident to reporters who covered Washington during the McCarthy years. In 1960 Nelson Polsby reemphasized the political aspects of McCarthyism in a provocative article, "Toward an Explanation of McCarthyism," in *Political Studies* 8 (Oct. 1960): 250–71. More recently Earl Latham has developed at great length a somewhat similar argument in *The Communist Controversy in Washington: From the New Deal to McCarthy* (Cambridge, Mass., 1966). For Latham McCarthyism was the function of a conservative drive for power which, frustrated by the reelection of Harry S. Truman in 1948, asserted itself through the legislative branch. The best of the recent studies in this area is Michael Paul Rogin, *The Intellectuals and McCarthy: The Radical Specter* (Cambridge, Mass., 1967). Rogin challenges the work of "pluralist" scholars like Hofstadter, Lipset, and Bell who have interpreted McCarthyism in terms of mass politics, populist appeals, and the "radicalism" of the right, and in a brilliant closing chapter insists instead upon the role of political elites in creating and sustaining McCarthyism.

The rise of the Communist issue in America may be traced in part through the history of the Dies Committee and its successor, the House Committee on Un-American Activities. See August R. Ogden, *The Dies Committee* (Washington, D. C., 1945); Robert K. Carr, *The House Committee on Un-American Activities, 1945–1950* (Ithaca, N. Y., 1952); and most recently, Walter Goodman, *The Committee* (New York, 1968). Alistair Cooke's *A Generation on Trial* (New York, 1950) is a reporter's impressions of the Alger Hiss case. Whittaker Chamber's *Witness* (New York, 1952), has become a minor classic in the literature of ex-communism, but it should be read with great discretion and against the background of the enormous controversy involving both Hiss and Chambers. Earl Latham's *The Communist Controversy in Washington* is the fullest discussion of the rising Communist issue, but even this volume is inadequate.

The growing stress of partisan politics may also be traced through the breakup of postwar bipartisanship and the rise of the "China issue." See especially Bradford H. Westerfield, *Foreign Policy and Party Politics*

(New Haven, Conn., 1955), and Norman Graebner, *The New Isolationism: A Study in Politics and Foreign Policy since 1950* (New York, 1956). The "New Isolationism" (the phrase was originally Arthur Schlesinger, Jr.'s) was neither entirely new nor isolationist. It included many of the underlying elements which had determined the postwar policy of containment and won for it bipartisan support. On the Korean War and the dismissal of General MacArthur see John W. Spanier, *The Truman-MacArthur Controversy and the Korean War* (New York, 1965); Richard H. Rovere and Arthur Schlesinger, Jr., *The MacArthur Controversy and American Foreign Policy*, rev. ed. (New York, 1965); and especially Ronald J. Caridi, *The Korean War and American Politics: The Republican Party as a Case Study* (Philadelphia, 1968). Both the "China issue" and the MacArthur controversy were but other faces of the Republican drive for power which generated McCarthyism as well.

Senator Joe McCarthy   There has been no adequate biography of McCarthy himself, and most of what has been written about him runs toward the polemical. One of the earliest of such efforts was Oliver Pilat and William V. Shannon, "Smear, Inc.: The One-Man Job of Joe McCarthy," *New York Post*, Sept. 4-23, 1951. Jack Anderson and Ronald May added to this a large amount of new and borrowed material for their muckraking *McCarthy: The Man, the Senator, the "ISM"* (Boston, 1952). Morris Rubin and the Wisconsin Citizen's Committee on McCarthy's record contributed to this body of partisan literature *The McCarthy Record* (Madison, Wis., 1952), and Rubin returned to the lists in 1954 with "McCarthy: A Documented Record," *Progressive* 18 (April 1954).

McCarthy's own contribution to the partisan debate is *McCarthyism: The Fight for America* (New York, 1952), a typical example of the extravagant tommyrot for which he was so famous. William F. Buckley, Jr., and L. Brent Bozell, *McCarthy and His Enemies: The Record and its Meaning* (Chicago, 1954) is a thick but meanly argued *apologia* for McCarthy, largely aimed at defending the senator against charges leveled against him during the Tydings Committee hearings. Also see Roy Cohn, *McCarthy* (New York, 1968), a friendly if none too reliable memoir by the senator's protégé.

Of all that has been written on McCarthy personally, the only lasting contribution is that of Richard H. Rovere, *Senator Joe McCarthy* (New York, 1959). Rovere has assimilated the best insights of many contemporary observers, added to them his own sharp perceptions, and set them down with a remarkably graceful and facile style. McCarthy may not have been what Rovere has called him, America's "most gifted" demagogue, but he was surely a character of extraordinary proportion.

Among unpublished studies of McCarthy and McCarthyism are the following: John P. Steinke, "The Rise of McCarthyism" (M.A. thesis,

University of Wisconsin, 1960); Karl Ernest Meyer, "The Politics of Loyalty: From La Follette to McCarthy in Wisconsin, 1918–1952" (Ph.d. diss., Princeton University, 1955); Frank J. Kendrick, "McCarthy and the Senate" (Ph.D. diss., University of Chicago, 1962).

Owen Lattimore's *Ordeal by Slander* (Boston, 1950) describes the professor's experiences in the wake of McCarthy's charge that he was the "top Russian espionage agent" in America. One of his lawyers, Thurmond Arnold, carried the story on through the McCarran Committee hearings in *Fair Fights and Foul: A Dissenting Lawyer's Life* (New York, 1965). Stanley Kelley, Jr., *Professional Public Relations and Political Power* (Baltimore, Md., 1956) contains an informative chapter on the role of public relations man Jon Jonkel in the 1950 Maryland election. Arnold Forster and Benjamin R. Epstein, *The Troublemakers* (New York, 1952) describes the campaign to block the confirmation of Anna M. Rosenberg as assistant secretary of defense.

Herbert L. Packer, *Ex-Communist Witnesses: Four Studies in Fact Finding* (Stanford, Calif., 1962) contains a critical evaluation of Louis Budenz, one of McCarthy's principal mainstays, and Harvey Matusow's *False Witness* (New York, 1955) describes the experiences of a McCarthy informant and witness who apparently played practically every end against the middle. Telford Taylor, *Grand Inquest: The Story of Congressional Investigations* (New York, 1955), and Alan Barth, *Government by Investigation* (New York, 1955), are both highly critical of the use and abuse of Congress's investigatory powers. James A. Wechsler, *The Age of Suspicion* (New York, 1953) is the autobiographical account of a liberal newspaper editor's personal experience before McCarthy's committee. Louis Bean, *Influences in the Mid-Term Election* (Washington, D. C., 1954) is an assessment of the impact of McCarthy in the 1952 senatorial elections. For reasons which appear in the text it would seem that it is not entirely a work of disinterested scholarship and should be evaluated accordingly.

Martin Merson, *The Private Diary of a Public Servant* (New York, 1955), describes the impact of McCarthy's investigations on the State Department information program. The book is not a diary, however, and should be used with some discretion. It grew out of an article originally prepared for *Saturday Evening Post* under the signature of Robert L. Johnson, Merson's friend and superior who headed the International Information Agency. Johnson withdrew the article, however, and when portions of it later appeared under Merson's name he privately disavowed it. [See John Howe to William Benton, Dec. 14, 1953, box 4, Benton Papers; Robert L. Johnson to Eisenhower, Oct. 18, 1954, OF 8-D, Eisenhower Papers.] For an evaluation of McCarthy's "investigation" of the Fort Monmouth radar laboratories, see Scientists Committee on Loyalty and Security, Federation of American Scientists,

Fort Monmouth: The Scientists Examine the Investigation (New Haven, Conn., 1954), and "Fort Monmouth One Year Later," *Bulletin of the Atomic Scientists* 11 (April 1955).

Michael Straight's lively and perceptive *Trial by Television* (Boston, 1954) remains the best account of the army-McCarthy hearings. G .D. Wiebe, in "The Army-McCarthy Hearings and the Public Conscience," *Public Opinion Quarterly* (Winter 1958–1959): 490-502, argues that the hearings had only a negligible impact on McCarthy's public support, but also see John Fenton, *In Your Opinion* (Boston, 1960). David P. and Esther S. Thelen, "Joe Must Go: The Movement to Recall Senator Joseph R. McCarthy," *Wisconsin Magazine of History* 49 (Spring 1966), is a thorough and intelligent study of the attempt to unseat McCarthy during the spring of 1954. Edward Bennett Williams's *One Man's Freedom* (New York, 1962) presents the recollections of McCarthy's attorney.

Congress and the President   The definitive study of the postwar Senate is Donald Matthews, *U. S. Senators and Their World* (Chapel Hill, N. C., 1960), but see also David B. Truman's excellent work, *The Congressional Party: A Case Study* (New York, 1959). Harry M. Scoble, *Ideology and Electoral Action: A Comparative Study of the National Committee for an Effective Congress* (San Francisco, 1967) is a detailed study of the small organization which helped defeat McCarthy in the Senate. William S. White, *Citadel: The Story of the U. S. Senate* (New York, 1956) is an effusive collective biography of what White calls "the institution." *The Taft Story* (New York, 1954) and *The Professional: Lyndon B. Johnson* (Boston, 1964), both by White, are admiring and uncritical appraisals of these two powerful Senate leaders. A better journalistic appraisal of Johnson's career is Rowland Evans and Robert Novak, *Lyndon B. Johnson: The Exercise of Power* (New York, 1966). Arthur V. Watkins, *Enough Rope* (Englewood Cliffs, N. J., 1969), is a memoir by the senator who chaired the select committee on censure.

Few senators during this period have received good biographical treatment. An exception is Donald J. Kemper's workmanlike *Decade of Fear: Senator Hennings and Civil Liberties* (Columbia, Mo., 1965). Also see Allan Nevins, *Herbert H. Lehman and His Era* (New York, 1963), and Winthrop Griffith, *Humphrey: A Candid Biography* (New York, 1965). Arthur Schlesinger, Jr., *A Thousand Days: John F. Kennedy in the White House* (Boston, 1965), and Theodore Sorenson, *Kennedy* (New York, 1965), both devote considerable space to the late president's relations with McCarthy. Both authors attempt to place the Massachusetts senator in the best possible light.

There is still no satisfactory general history of the Truman administration, though the recent growth of scholarship in this period appears encouraging. The most recent account is Cabell Phillips, *The Truman Presidency: The History of a Triumphant Succession* (New York, 1966). Phillips is a fine newspaperman, but his discussion of Truman and internal security is in error both in matters of fact and interpretation. Truman's memoirs, *Year of Decisions* and *Years of Trial and Hope, 1946–1952* (Garden City, N. Y., 1955–1956), are quite inadequate and graceless.

The Eisenhower administration produced a few more firsthand accounts, but these too must be approached with discretion. Eisenhower's *The White House Years: Mandate for Change, 1953–1956* (New York, 1963) is only slightly more valuable to the historian than are Truman's recollections. Sherman Adams's *Firsthand Report: The Story of the Eisenhower Administration* (New York, 1961) is useful but glides over far too many important questions. Emmet John Hughes, *The Ordeal of Power: A Political Memoir of the Eisenhower Years* (New York, 1963) is the most incisive volume but is limited at points by the brevity of the author's service. Robert Cutler's sprightly *No Time for Rest* (Boston, 1966) contains the recollections of another of Eisenhower's advisers. Earl Mazo's friendly biography of Vice President Nixon, *Richard Nixon: A Political and Personal Portrait* (New York, 1959), contains much valuable information on the Eisenhower years. The best single volume on the early Eisenhower administration remains Robert J. Donovan, *Eisenhower: The Inside Story* (New York, 1956).

INDEX